Fiction

Refracts

Science

Fiction Refracts Science

Modernist Writers from Proust to Borges

Allen Thiher

University of Missouri Press
Columbia and London

Copyright © 2005 by
The Curators of the University of Missouri
University of Missouri Press, Columbia, Missouri 65201
Printed and bound in the United States of America
5   4   3   2   1   09   08   07   06   05

Library of Congress Cataloging-in-Publication Data

Thiher, Allen, 1941–
    Fiction refracts science : modernist writers from Proust to Borges / Allen Thiher.
        p.   cm.
    Summary: "Examines the relationship between science and the fiction developed by
modernists, including Musil, Proust, Kafka, and Joyce. Looks at Pascalian and Newtonian
cosmology, Darwinism, epistemology, relativity theory, quantum mechanics, the development
of modernist and postmodern fiction, positivism, and finally works by Woolf, Faulkner, and
Borges"—Provided by publisher.
    Includes bibliographical references and index.
    ISBN 0-8262-1580-7 (alk. paper)
    1. Literature and science.   2. Science in literature.   3. Fiction—20th century—History
and criticism.   I. Title.
    PN3352.S34T55   2005
    809'.9336—dc22   2004029232

☺™ This paper meets the requirements of the
American National Standard for Permanence of Paper
for Printed Library Materials, Z39.48, 1984.

Designer: Stephanie Foley
Typesetter: Phoenix Type, Inc.
Printer and binder: Thomson-Shore, Inc.
Typeface: Granjon

For Irma

Contents

Acknowledgments

This book began to take shape in courses taught at the University of Missouri-Columbia and in research undertaken for a preceding volume about literature and science. It took on its precise form during a year spent as a visiting fellow at Clare Hall at Cambridge University. I give hearty thanks to the Research Council at the University of Missouri for the research leave that allowed me to take advantage of the stimulating environment and the research facilities at Cambridge, and to Clare Hall and its fellows for their generous reception and especially for the many discussions that stimulated my work and ideas. I would also like to express my gratitude to the students and faculty in the Department of History and Philosophy of Science at Cambridge who organized reading groups from which I profited, as well as to Cambridge's Isaac Newton Institute for Mathematical Sciences, whose open doors granted a neophyte cosmologist entry into colloquia on some of the most exciting research taking place today. Specific debts of gratitude must also be expressed to those who read part or all of this work in manuscript, such as Sandy Camargo, Audrey Glauert, Noah Heringman, David Hayman, and Timothy Materer. And of course special thanks to Irma Dimitrova for readings and much more.

A Brief Overview

This book is something of a sequel to my *Fiction Rivals Science,* a study of French fiction in the nineteenth century, culminating in Proust. Here I envisage European modernism from a comparitist viewpoint, beginning with considerations of the sciences that the first modernists encountered when they began to write. After my prefatory comments and a first chapter on the science modernists knew, in subsequent chapters my goal is to show what the first generation of modernist fiction writers took from science as well as what they criticized in it. After chapters dealing with the epistemology that informs the novels of Musil and Proust, I consider the two most influential modernists, Kafka and Joyce, to examine how they understood science as law, and law as knowledge, and how this understanding is central to their work. In the penultimate chapter I examine the way in which the next generation of modernists—represented by Woolf, Faulkner, and Borges—turned the preceding modernists' work to good account in their development of fictions that are essentially thought experiments. The conclusion is a coda surveying some aspects of postmodernity's ongoing encounter with science.

I have no pretentions to offer an exhaustive account of what science meant for fiction in the twentieth century. However, I do believe that my focus here should illuminate the central underpinnings of much of what modernist writers sought to achieve, and this with a precision not yet available in the critical literature on modernism. Clearly, modernist writers knew that a critical encounter with science was central to their creative projects. Science is thus inscribed in the novels themselves as part of their representation of a world. To illustrate these projects I have drawn upon physics, cosmology, chemistry, the philosophy of mathematics and logic, medicine, and biology and found that each of these disciplines sheds new light on often interpreted novels, when appropriately brought into play.

Some may think that my treatment of medicine is inadequate, given its omnipresence in modern life. I would answer that critique by noting that the disciplines mentioned along with medicine are already too rich in insights to be encompassed exhaustively in one book. Medicine, genetics, and, indeed, eugenics demand in fact a separate study for their relation to modern fiction, one which I hope to complete in fact in the near future.

Finally, hovering over this study is the shadow of Pascal, for it was he who schooled the modernists in their cosmology—the big picture about humanity's place in the universe. The anguish with which Pascal endowed the study of science still plays a role when one contemplates the cosmological framework within which one situates all other disciplines and the interpretations of human existence they imply. I hope that his shadow is not overly intrusive, but Pascal's presence loomed ever larger as I wrote this study—in fact, my working title was "Pascal's Grandchildren." It is perhaps the main perduring strand, connecting the beginnings of modernity, born of the scientific revolution, with the late twentieth century. This is not to say that Pascal was more important for the development of modern science than, say, Galileo, Descartes, or Newton; but it is to say that Pascal is the interpreter of that science who has had the greatest existential resonance for moderns trying to figure out how they got here, to this place we call modernity, or postmodernity, that condition in which the mind is suspended in the void that Pascal was perhaps first to find a not very comfortable place.

Fiction

Refracts

Science

Introduction

Prefatory Thoughts on
Two or More Cultures

My purpose in this book is to study the way modernist literature has dealt with modern science. Neither "modernist" nor "modern" is meant in a polemical way. I am using these terms in the sense they have in most histories of literature or science. If there is a controversial side to this book, it may lie in my presupposition that science and literature share a cultural matrix setting forth presuppositions, axioms, and constraints for all endeavors to make sense of the world. This is not a structuralist or poststructuralist assumption, for I do not identify culture with language, nor do I assume that "reality" is determined by language. From my point of view, reality is usually a metaphysical notion, often used as a premise for dubious arguments. The idea of a cultural matrix is, instead, an empirical notion, for we encounter it whenever we draw upon the overlapping groups of assumptions that members of a given community use to understand the world. However, the fact that these assumptions can be articulated in various languages does not logically entail that they must be identical to language or that they are in some sense logically dependent upon any given language, be it verbal, mathematical, iconic, or whatever semiotic form one can think of.

Any given cultural matrix has developed in time and in this restricted sense is historical in origin. More interesting perhaps, at least in the West, each cultural matrix is also subject to constant modification. These modifications are the subject matter of intellectual and cultural history. To understand this history is to understand the process through which a community has come to believe what it believes today, or to know what it takes to be knowledge. Intellectual history is thus in part a self-reflexive enterprise, fraught with all the logical difficulties attendant upon any self-reflexive mode of thought.

1

A cultural matrix offers axioms for understanding when one reads literary texts and when one seeks meaning in the world. Sometimes these axioms overlap, especially concerning logical principles and deductive procedures. There is nothing mysterious about this process for understanding understanding. Nobody understands anything in a vacuum. A wealth of past assumptions is always the starting point for finding meaning in the present or construing it from the past. There are no revolutions in thought, if by "revolution" one means a total break with the cultural axioms that guide understanding. However much modern readers may question the assumptions they have inherited, they are nonetheless thrown back on some of these assumptions, if only to have a position from which to question other received assumptions. That questioning in itself is a valuable activity is of course the modern assumption par excellence, and primary among the institutions and practices that promote questioning as a cultural activity are science and literature.

Science and literature thus share common features. They are underwritten by a cultural matrix that promotes the questioning of that cultural matrix, though not simply in view of creating paradoxes. By preserving the assumption that questioning is meaningful, our culture at once demands the questioning of the assumptions that underwrite our culture and shows that conservation and change are valued simultaneously. Promoting change or questioning are not inevitable roles for science or literature: historically, both institutions have been as much engaged in affirming and defending the cultural matrix as in changing it.

It would be difficult today, though apparently not impossible, to doubt that science is an extremely important part of the modern cultural matrix—I say this thinking of those cultural critics who challenge scientists for their lack of self-understanding and for their supposed imperialism. It is less difficult to challenge the idea that literature is also one of the most important interpreters of the cultural matrix. Literature's lack of demonstrable power undoubtedly keeps it from being criticized in the way science is. Lack of power notwithstanding, literature is nonetheless an extremely important institution for questioning culture and its assumptions. For example, it is important for dealing with science as part of culture. Or, more precisely, insofar as literature deals with the most important assumptions of modern culture, it is in fact obliged to confront science. And this is a fortiori the case when literature deals with knowledge, the special cultural province for which science makes its imperial claims. This relation of literature and science has a history, and one may date the beginning of it roughly with the "scientific revolution" in the seventeenth century. For an understanding of modernism, I will thus presently begin with the seventeenth-century mathematician and philosopher Blaise Pascal, who combined literature and science in perhaps the most anguished critique of science that our culture has seen.

It may be objected that this view of science and literature holds that their relation is asymmetrical. To a large extent this is true, for literature interprets science, but the converse does not seem to hold, unless one believes that there is a science of literature. Historically, "modern" could be taken in fact to describe a state of affairs in which literature assumes an interpretative relation to science, but science no longer has a relation to literature. From this perspective again, modernity begins to emerge in the seventeenth century.

One, but not the only, way to consider this state of asymmetry is to observe that literature is in fact a broader activity than science in the sense that literature can encompass, through its symbolic representation, all knowing activities. In principle, it can interpret all levels of knowledge that are in some sense less complex than the act of representation that literature undertakes. The formalisms for arriving at the quantum numbers describing an electron are complex, but the states of an electron described by this procedure are simple compared to the number of features necessary to describe a synapse or, higher up on the scale of complexity, the motivation of a human being "using" these synapses. Rigorous science, as Pascal knew, seems always to involve delimiting a domain and then describing it with the smallest number of principles possible. In this sense science seeks the opposite of the complexity literature revels in, especially when science seeks to find an algorithm for principles. I say this knowing well that complexity theory and chaos theory have come to complement analytical models for describing phenomena. Chaos theory attempts to understand, in nonlinear terms, how simple initial conditions can eventuate in extremely complex phenomena, whereas complexity theory strives to determine if complex problems are subject to computational models. In a sense, then, both theories are extensions of what Pascal saw as science's desire to come up with basic principles.

It seems that only in premodern times do we find literature and science conflated such that literature is science, or that science derives its insights from literature. Modern physics has no Lucretius—unless it be the French polymath Raymond Queneau—for the development of science since Copernicus has relegated the poet to a position exterior to scientific discourse. In our modern cultural matrix, literary insight rarely plays a role in the actual elaboration of science. Scientists often refer to the aesthetic qualities of their theories and draw analogies between art and science, and some even evoke examples of how literary texts have inspired them, but that is a rather different matter from the actual contribution of literature to science; or conversely, from the way science offers theme and insight to literature. This study seeks to demonstrate that science has played a role in modernist literature and its genesis in almost every regard: form, themes, and values.

Many humanists, and their contemporary antithesis, the antihumanist postmoderns, probably do not share this view. They intuitively feel that science and literature cannot be conjoined in any meaningful way. This view is widely held. Therefore, in this introduction I will discuss a major source of such a view, one constantly, if perhaps regrettably, evoked in both literary and scientific essays. I refer to C. P. Snow's famous description of "two cultures" in his *The Two Cultures and the Scientific Revolution* (1959). Snow claimed that scientists and literati live in different worlds, and in making this claim, some fifty years ago, Snow did more than set off a noisy tempest in a teapot that has somehow remained a necessary point of reference. He rejuvenated a cultural assumption whose history, I will later show, extends well back beyond the scientific revolution. Pitting knowledge against poetry, Snow's assumption has its roots in Plato, but it has taken on its most recent avatar in the postmodern polemic generated by scientists who find that literary postmodernism is largely drivel, and by postmodern theorists who reduce science to politically motivated social constructs or to gratuitous metaphors.

In the context of this animosity, the challenge to an interdisciplinarian study respectful of both science and literature is to justify the assertion that there is any commonality between the two domains. My assertion of a cultural matrix that is larger than either science or literature already contains a partial response to the objection that writer and scientist live in two distinct cultures. In addition, I would argue that the notion of two cultures is an inadequate way of describing our epistemological quandaries. On the one hand, we often dream of living in a unified monistic or holistic culture while, on the other hand, we find our world fragmented not just into two epistemic realms, but into multiple realms that seem to have little in common. One, two, or multiple epistemologies, these are all possibilities contained by the contemporary cultural matrix in which competing epistemologies are at work.

Snow, a Cambridge fellow educated in physics who also wrote novels, coined the expression "two cultures" to describe the fact that humanists are denizens of a nonmathematical realm of discourse that has nothing in common with the discourse that modern science unceasingly creates with ever-renewed theoretical formalisms. Or, conversely, scientists live in a world of models and formalisms that cannot be translated into terms accessible to nonscientists. Therefore, scientists and humanists live apparently in two different universes because they have two different modes of knowing the world. Since Snow, this thesis has undoubtedly received indirect support from the views of theorists of science like Michel Foucault and Thomas Kuhn, thinkers who postulated that modern scientists live in different worlds from their forebears because modern scientists live on the other side of an "epistemic rupture" and view the world through new "paradigms." Theories proposing breaks in history inevitably endorse the idea that epistemology determines the world one lives in. This is a pervasive idea, implying not only that scientists and humanists live on different planets, but that scientists themselves are incapable of communicating with each other if they do not work with the same axioms.

Snow was hardly original with his thesis about two cultures. It takes little reflection to realize that the idea originated in Plato. Of course Plato did not content himself with wittily chastising poets for their deficiency in science, as Snow did. Plato wanted to ban them from the ideal Republic for their failure to know true reality. After Plato, and in spite of Aristotle, the recurrent history of competing epistemologies in our culture endows Snow's thesis in *The Two Cultures* with a certain plausibility. Moreover, as is inevitable in Anglo-Saxon countries, Snow's thesis builds upon a confusion of culture and education. It is undoubtedly true that education in England, as well as in most European countries, has been usually characterized by early choices: the typical student is either educated from a young age in science and mathematics (or in a technological field deriving from basic science), or the student opts for humanistic disciplines. Education in the United States is less specialized: students often learn little at the earlier secondary level so that they must be given a modicum of general education at the university. Whatever the final configuration, however, modern education demands some specialization.

In recognizing that schools and universities aim ultimately at specialization, one should not, however, confuse the structure of education with what people actually know. The history of education offers many examples in which institutionalized education had little role in promoting knowledge. During the Renaissance and the continental Enlightenment, the propagation of knowledge had little to do with universities. Today, often little in the education that writers and scientists receive can suggest the commonality of interests that actually characterizes many writers and scientists. Most important writers in the twentieth century, and earlier for that matter, have been vitally interested in scientific questions. This assertion can be borne out by examining writers' works, their critical statements, and their biographies. Modern writers from Proust, Musil, and Woolf through Beckett, Sarraute, and Pynchon have often known science with competence and technical specificity, whether they received a scientific or a literary education. (I add without undue irony that it is also true that writers are usually far more diverse in their interests and capacities than the professors who study them, especially those professors who take refuge in the presumed incommensurability of the two cultures to justify their often aridly narrow academic specialization.)

Educational issues are central to Snow's essay, and one reason it made such an impact is that it decries the deficiencies of Western educators in a critical ideological context. In 1959 the Western powers perceived themselves at a critical historical turning point in their competition with the Soviet Union. Snow's depiction of a failure of education, at this moment in the Cold War, struck a resonant chord. After Soviet scientists put Sputnik in orbit, many believed that defects in Anglo-American scientific education had somehow created deficiencies, if not actually allowing Russian superiority, in areas that could endanger the security of the West. In this ideological context, with perhaps not the most cogent reasoning, one could deplore that the separation, in education, of science from humanistic aims also compromised the security of the West. Educators could lament that a lack of attention to liberal values, and the educational resources that could promote them, might ensure the triumph of totalitarian communism in much of the world—especially among peasants who, unduly impressed by Russian scientific superiority, did not have the capacity to understand liberal values.

At least that was one reading of Snow's message. Literary critic Lionel Trilling saw it somewhat differently, however. In an acerbic critique, he interpreted Snow's essay to say that if Russia and the United States simply let the beneficent technocratic scientists run things, then the world would be a better place, or as Trilling insisted, "the real message of *The Two Cultures* is that an understanding between the West and the Soviet Union could be achieved by a culture of scientists." Trilling's reading is shrill, but it does explain why Snow became a widely read author behind the Iron Curtain.[1]

The negative reaction to Snow came largely from literary intellectuals like Trilling. They felt insulted for being called arrogant and denigrated for their putative incapacity to grasp the scientific understanding of the world. The separation of the arts and the science faculties, Snow maintained, had resulted in the formation of a literary elite that had only the foggiest notions about what the scientific description of the universe entails. Though Snow also characterized scientists as often having only a superficial knowledge of humanist culture, the brunt of Snow's critique is directed against the humanists' failure to produce a better world (which also provoked Trilling into an angry defense of the social achievements of his Victorian heroes). Snow gave an example of humanists' ignorance with the following anecdote. When he asked once, at a cocktail party for literary scholars, if anyone could state the second law of thermodynamics, the request received only dumbfounded negative responses. This question was, according to Snow, the equivalent of asking if anyone had ever read a play by Shakespeare—and getting a negative answer.[2] With some jocularity, he charged the literary elite with being Luddites; and he directed the charge not only against Cambridge fellows, but also against modern writers and critics among the then current heroes of modernity. From Snow's liberal perspective, to be a Luddite was an ethical crime in a world in which humanists and scientists must count upon scientifically directed technology to meet the problems of an expanding, often hungry population that confronts devastating health problems, often because it simply does not have enough to eat.

Anger about Snow's mistreatment of literary intellectuals has undoubtedly obscured the fact that he was as much concerned with the ethical necessity of technology, in a world given over to injustice and hunger, as with the difficulties of conversing about science at Cambridge cocktail parties. His essay is ethical in intent and, as such, demonstrates that Snow was also a part of that literary tradition of which the Victorian Matthew Arnold is perhaps the most noteworthy exemplar: a very English tradition that conceives of literature as a form of moral education. And Cambridge is not an indifferent location for this skirmish. An outsider to this tradition, the German scholar Lothar Fietz argues,

1. Trilling's essay first appeared in *Commentary* 33 (1962) and is quoted here from his *Beyond Culture,* 141. For an overview of two cultures and today's science wars, see David Cordle's *Postmodern Postures: Literature, Science, and the Two Cultures Debate.*

2. Snow, *The Two Cultures: And a Second Look,* 14.

for example, that Snow and his most vociferous critic, fellow Cambridge scholar F. R. Leavis, shared complementary versions of this Anglo-Saxon commitment to Arnold's ideal for which Cambridge has been a center. In fact Fietz would have it that Cambridge University, at least since the time of Francis Bacon, has been a battleground for the two cultures.[3] Perhaps it requires a foreigner to note that English intellectuals, as exemplified by Cambridge scholars, usually share common ethical assumptions about literature, even when they may violently disagree about their consequences. These shared assumptions may explain in particular why the English turn more often to Arnold than to, say, a far greater poet like Baudelaire for their literary theory. Baudelaire thought, with some contempt, that ethics had little to do with poetics.

In his response to Snow, Cambridge's best-known literary critic, F. R. Leavis, was certainly concerned with values. Leavis was the type of critic who, to quote literary scholar Robert Boyers, showed "that a belief in value may be interesting even to those who are anxious to deny value judgment as a legitimate mode of criticism, and that criticism is itself a response to life more than a specialist response to accredited texts."[4] Refusing to separate knowledge and ethics, Leavis believed in the proposition, succinctly formulated earlier by Matthew Arnold, that literature, as knowledge, is a criticism of life. This was an idea that Arnold's Darwinist friend, Thomas Huxley, was willing to endorse in his debate with Arnold, though he demanded recognition that natural science is also necessary for criticism of life, for life is a subject about which biology has something to say. It is noteworthy that in the nineteenth century Arnold and Huxley, unlike Snow and Leavis, had been able to remain on friendly terms while discussing whether science should replace literature as the basis for education.[5] Such was not the case in Snow and Leavis's near repetition of the debate on education first held by Arnold and Huxley. According to Leavis, Snow denigrated, in his description of two cultures, Leavis's values by suggesting that anything less than quantified clarity does not fully qualify as knowledge, to which Leavis

---

3. Fietz, "Cambridge und die Diskussion um das Verhältnis von Literatur und Naturwissenschaft," in Gerhard Müller-Schwefe and Konrad Tuzinski, eds., *Literatur-Kultur-Gesellschaft in England und Amerika: Aspeckte und Forschungsbeiträge. Friedrich Schubel zum 60. Geburtstag*, 113–27.

4. Boyers, *F. R. Leavis*, 68.

5. See Arnold's "Literature and Science," first given as a Rede Lecture in the Senate House at Cambridge University, then many times on American tour, available in *Discourses in America* and in Lionel Trilling's *The Portable Matthew Arnold*. Huxley's side is found in "Science and Education," in his *Collected Essays*, vol. 2.

responded with outraged hostility, in a vitriolic attack showing that Snow had hit upon a sensitive nerve.

Snow had characterized as Luddites many of the flame-bearers whom Leavis was promoting for the modern literary canon, such as the antimodern modernist D. H. Lawrence. However, whether Luddite beliefs are to be ascribed to modernists was not the only issue on which Leavis and Snow were opposed. Beneath the invective, the core issue is epistemological and concerns the question of the commensurability between types of knowledge. It was on this question that Leavis attacked Snow, especially for his comparison of understanding thermodynamics with reading Shakespeare:

> It simply hasn't occurred to him [Snow] that to call the master scientific mind (say Rutherford) a Shakespeare is nothing but a cheap journalistic infelicity. He enforces his intention by telling us, after reporting the failure of his literary friends to describe the second law of thermodynamics: "yet I was asking something which is about the equivalent of Have you read a work of Shakespeare's?" There is no scientific equivalent of that question; equations between orders so disparate are meaningless.[6]

For all his dislike of philosophy, Leavis brings up a philosophical question about a basic epistemological dilemma: do our different orders of knowledge have some kind of shared criteria that allow us to relate them in some unifying way? The answer is apparently negative.

Moreover, Leavis appears to accept Snow's idea that scientific knowledge is always quantified knowledge. This position allows him to maintain that one is not a Luddite simply because one can obviously see that there are problems of knowledge that do not lend themselves to quantification. I would add that there is also scientific knowledge that does not involve quantification, but Leavis is not interested in this point. He is willing to accept Snow's truncating view of scientific knowledge in order to press forward his own argument—in brief, to deny that he, or his favored writers, are Luddites because of their belief that there is knowledge other than the quantified knowledge proposed by science:

> The advance of science and technology means a human future of change so rapid and of such kinds, of tests and challenges so unprecedented, of decisions and possible non-decisions so momentous and insidious in their consequences, that mankind—this is surely clear—will need to be in full

6. Leavis, *Two Cultures? The Significance of C. P. Snow,* 27.

intelligent possession of its full humanity (and "possession" here means, not confident ownership of that which belongs to us—our property, but a basic living deference towards that to which, opening as it does into the unknown and itself unmeasurable, we know we belong).[7]

Poised somewhere between Arnold and Heidegger, this remarkable sentence points up, by its very stylistic complexity, the evaluating twists and turns of a nonscientific mind working to find language that can qualitatively correspond to the world's complexity. In this proposition Leavis wants to demonstrate the necessity of nonquantitative standards of evaluation—of which this sentence itself is an example—that stand opposed to the calculating mind for whom mathematical description is the ultimate certification of knowledge. Therewith, Leavis wants to show that he is fully aware of the complexity of dealing with an unknown future about which Snow, in his optimism, seems unaware. But with this, he also affirms that there are indeed two cultures, though it is apparently not scientific culture that will be able to face the future.

Leavis's complexity stands in sharp contrast with Snow's confident straightforward assertion of the potentially quantifiable facts with which he describes social reality as well as the ignorance of Cambridge dons. The contrast could not be more pointed between Leavis's qualifications of qualifications and Snow's pointed, but unambiguous, statement that most literary intellectuals act "as though the scientific edifice of the physical world was not, in its intellectual depth, complexity and articulations, the most beautiful and wonderful collective work of the mind of man."[8] Snow asserts the epistemic complexity of scientific achievements, but he does so in a way that affirms the clarity of scientific procedures because of their necessary transparency. One is hardly obliged to accept Snow's circular optimism—is science really that transparent? Nor need one wring one's hands with Leavis—will lamenting tragic complexity achieve anything? In any case one can take leave of Snow and Leavis by noting that Leavis made an impressive rejoinder to Snow while implicitly agreeing with much that was dubious in Snow's argument concerning two opposing modes of knowledge. Epistemological dualism remains intact. Their opposition has henceforth come to symbolize the epistemological positions that often automatically come to mind when turning to the question of science's relation to litera-

7. Ibid., 26.
8. Snow, *Two Cultures,* 14.

ture. However, this debate is hardly the last word on the matter, even if it often is the first.

With regard to the relation of epistemology and ontology it is also indisputable that we have an equally long tradition arguing for the unity of knowledge and hence for the unity of culture, and ultimately of the world. This tradition maintains that, underlying the manifest forms of being, and knowledge thereof, is epistemological unity, reflecting perhaps some unified reality or holistic substance. In fact, the very belief that there is "reality" would often seem to depend upon the acceptance of some epistemic monism. Thus "reality" would be the principle that, in a single epistemological grasp, unites all aspects of being. The origins of the belief in one culture and one epistemology are also to be found in Greek thought, among the pre-Socratics whose quest for a unified principle of knowledge characterizes thinkers as various as Thales, Anaximander, and Heraclitus. In many important respects, in fact, monism is the more venerable tradition in Western philosophical thought.

The belief in unity has manifested itself in more recent centuries in various monisms, in Spinoza and Hegel, as well as twentieth-century physical theory that would ultimately derive all knowledge from one principle reflecting the underlying structure of the world. After Newton a scientific version of this kind of epistemological monism first evolved rapidly in the eighteenth century, for the reign of classical dynamics almost persuaded European intellectuals that all knowledge must take the form of mechanical causation reflecting the rule of rational determinism in every corner of "reality"—and reality was in effect defined as what is encompassed by mechanical causation. From Newton and Locke through Laplace and Kant, and beyond, variants of this belief that knowledge finds its ultimate criterion in one rational principle have recurred, sometimes dominating our intellectual culture to such an extent that the difference between a sonnet and a theorem could be construed as simply the difference in the domains to which reason can be applied. Today's desire to find a "final theory" may also reflect a thirst for monism. In brief, a dream of epistemological unity remains an ideal for much of the scientific and philosophical world, perhaps much like a normative ideal that allows continued belief in "reality."

A leitmotif of modern criticism of science has concerned the loss of unity that, according to this critique, modern science brought about when it destroyed a unified cosmology. Historians and philosophers of science from E. A. Burtt in the 1920s to more recent moderns like Alexander Koyré or Stephen Toulmin have asserted, and usually deplored in sotto voce lamentation, that a putative cosmic unity went asunder when Galileo, Descartes, and Newton undertook the objectifying of nature by reducing it to abstract, quantified relations.[9] The modern critique—in effect a critique of itself—turns on conflating the epistemological and the ontological: new and varied means of knowing are taken to signify a loss of belief in the unity of what is known. So that scientists as well as interpreters of science have often experienced the increase in modes and types of knowledge as a loss as well as a gain, a loss of unity and a gain of precision—or the trade-off of precision and soul that Musil was at pains to evaluate in his modernist exploration of science, *The Man without Qualities.*

Against this view of the loss of unity modern thinkers have erected the argument that the proliferation of types of knowledge does not destroy a belief in one universe, though it shows that the universe is ordered in terms of levels of knowledge. Holism demands hierarchy. Contemporary complexity theorists have promoted this theory with their vision of epistemological unity based upon emergent levels of organization. Of course, the notion of hierarchies of knowledge also goes back to the Greeks, as does its dialectical opposite that all is one. For example, Plotinus bequeathed a modified Platonism to the early Christian church with his vision of the overflowing levels of being, which is a locus classicus describing how knowledge and being are organized hierarchically. In short, the dialectic between monism and pluralism, with many variants, has been a constant feature of the epistemological life of Europe from the Greeks through Hegel and Heisenberg—with monism receiving its most powerful recent expression in the theories of contemporary physicists who, to paraphrase the title of Steven Weinberg's *The Dream of a Final Theory* (1994), dream of uniting all forces uncovered by particle physics a unified "final" theory of matter.

Monism and dualism are hardly the only modern epistemological options, and a third viewpoint may seem more essentially in accord with modernity. This is the belief that there is no unity to knowledge, and hence little unity to culture, because all knowledge is fragmented. The mind that accepts this view

---

9. I refer here to Burtt, *Metaphysical Foundations of Modern Physical Science;* Koyré, *From the Closed World to the Infinite Universe;* and Toulmin, *The Return to Cosmology: Postmodern Science and the Theology of Nature,* and *Cosmopolis: The Hidden Agenda of Modernity.* For a more recent overview, see Peter D. Smith, *Metaphor and Materiality: German Literature and the World-View of Science, 1780–1955.*

argues, conflating epistemology and ontology, that if there is no unity to knowledge, perhaps then there are multiple worlds, each one arising through the procedures for knowledge that we use when we put different questions to reality. "Reality" loses much of its meaning in this context, to be sure. One can tie all this together perhaps by taking the viewpoint that the essential description of modernity is that, at different times and in different places, many moderns wistfully want to subscribe to the view that there is only one culture based on reason and only one cosmos unified by hierarchies of knowledge; but that these same moderns are also willing to entertain the view that there are two cultures based on the opposition of the objectivity of scientific procedures and of the humanists' pursuit of values. When pressed on the issue, most moderns finally find no unity to knowledge at all. The latter view then entails the recognition that culture is a fragmented notion at best, and that knowledge today involves multiple levels of sui generis inquiry that can be related at most only by ordering different levels of description. This idea can be found, notably, in the physicist Heisenberg, who argued that noncontradiction among levels of description is the only principle of the unity of knowledge when knowledge no longer has any unity. Heisenberg is a representative thinker of a third type of scientific modernity: a scientist with a broad literary and philosophical culture, he did not accept anything like a belief in two cultures, while his own theorizing about quantum mechanics destroyed any belief in monism.

"Pluralistic" is an appropriately neutral way to describe the accommodation that pragmatically dominates the type of epistemological thought developed by Heisenberg after he and Bohr had established the foundations of quantum mechanics in the 1920s. In elaborating his epistemological thought, Heisenberg often defended with eloquence, in essays written for a broad public, the doctrine of uncertainty that he formulated for quantum mechanics. He also formulated more general epistemological views, the influence of which have been considerable, especially in the literary community. In these philosophical writings Heisenberg taught that knowledge is a composite affair, involving many "regions of reality" that come into existence because of the type of knowledge that illuminates them. Heisenberg argued that, in seeking to order knowledge, scientists and philosophers can delineate levels of knowledge, each with different objects, but in no way hope to reduce knowledge to a single sphere, or two spheres, since knowledge is always limited in its scope, deriving from closed systems or procedures that at best can only illuminate limited *Erfahrungs-bereiche* —areas of experience, or regions of reality.

In describing science as a discrete series of areas that can offer knowledge only about separate regions of reality, Heisenberg recognized that knowledge is larger than science in any narrow sense. Knowledge encompasses a good many regions, from chemistry, classical physics, and quantum mechanics to symbolic representations such as art and poetry. In his philosophical thought Heisenberg did not thus simply develop the epistemological implications of quantum mechanics, most notably of the "uncertainty principle" of which he was a primary theoretician.

For example, in a manuscript Heisenberg circulated during the war years, now entitled *Ordnung der Wirklichkeit* [Order of Reality] for its 1989 publication, Heisenberg argues that today no single science can dominate knowledge by imposing a unified epistemological model, as was the case during the heyday of classical Newtonian dynamics. For example, the emergence of biology as a natural science has brought with it new connections or *Zusammenhänge* that, though described by concepts not in contradiction with those of physics or chemistry, are not reducible to the laws of physics or chemistry.[10] The task of modern epistemology is thus to find the relational order that best organizes the regions of reality disclosed by the inquiring mind. The philosopher should not undertake this task, Heisenberg argued, with a sense that he or she is undertaking something revolutionary, since the epistemologist is participating in an ongoing historical task, one complicated, but not changed, by the fact that relativity theory and quantum mechanics have opened up new domains of experience. Organizing the relation of areas of knowledge was a task of understanding begun by the pre-Socratics. Heisenberg's sense of the historical nature of the cultural matrix in which he worked was, to say the least, highly developed.

In 1942 Heisenberg gave a lecture in Zurich in which he expounded his vision of multiple realities. In this lecture he also overtly refused any ultimate epistemological grounding to science. In describing these domains of reality Heisenberg appeared to anticipate much that is found in contemporary complexity theory. He speculated that the ordering of the various domains should be conceived as levels, or *Schichten,* whose relative position to each other depends on levels of complexity.[11] There is no facile positivist rationalism in Heisenberg's thought elaborated during the war, for, with a sense of existential bleakness, he described in his lecture that all domains of knowledge emerge in

10. Heisenberg, *Ordnung der Wirklichkeit,* 97–118.
11. Heisenberg, *Deutsche und judische Physik,* 119.

different ways from "groundless depths" on which we seek to build our forms of knowledge: "There will never be a final foundation for knowledge, never a solid system of concepts that are valid for all domains of knowledge, and about which we can say without reservation that it is 'true.'" [es wird nie eine endgültige Grundlage der Erkenntnis geben, nie ein festes System von Begriffen, das für alle Bereiche der Erkenntnis genügt, von dem wir also ohne jeden Vorbehalt sagen können, dass es "wahr" sei.][12] Heisenberg's negative thoughts about the possibility of rationally grounding our fragmented knowledge are the converse side of a thought that recognizes in multiple forms of knowledge the crowning achievement of humanity.

In later essays after the war Heisenberg refined these notions that have clearly exerted a strong influence on the postmodern belief in the ungrounded nature of knowledge. He insisted in works like *Physics and Philosophy* (1962) that science involves a knowing mind that, in seeking knowledge, does not divide the world into "different groups of objects but into different groups of connections."[13] Multiple groups of connections can be represented by a "closed and coherent set of concepts, axioms, definitions, and laws" that may in turn be represented by a mathematical scheme, or may not. As this description points up, underdeterminism characterizes "reality," for multiple sets of concepts can be used to characterize the multitudinous regions we feel obliged to call reality.[14] Heisenberg called the creation of a closed set of concepts, applied to a given region, an "idealization"; and with this term he went on to compare science and art, especially art and mathematics, as analogous in their formal properties that allow an idealization based on axioms and recurring properties. Art is always an idealization, and therefore the two processes, that of science and that of art, share common properties.[15] There is perhaps an implicit Platonizing here, but one that results in quite different conclusions from those of Plato, whose dualism, I am arguing, underlies the doctrine of two cultures.

Heisenberg also recalls the earlier physicist Mach, the positivist for whom mind was an illusion, but who nonetheless saw in science a process of idealization based on the mind's power of abstraction. Notwithstanding Mach's influence on his thought, Heisenberg does not go as far as his positivist precursor in transforming science into a creative affair. For Heisenberg, art and literature, like

12. Ibid., 120.
13. Heisenberg, *Physics and Philosophy: The Revolution in Modern Science,* 107.
14. Ibid., 108.
15. Ibid., 108–9.

science, are important levels of idealization for which there is no substitute, since neither art nor science is the equivalent of the other, although they share analogous traits. By contrast, Mach, in his more extreme views, seems to have believed at times that science is largely an affair of parsimonious, and hence felicitous, fictions.

Heisenberg's meditations on multiple connections describe modern science and thought with breadth and cogency. His fragmented pluralism seems more contemporary than Snow's two cultures. However, against both Heisenberg and Snow remains a belief in monism whose power is not to be underestimated. The dream of a monism uniting known and knower has an aesthetic appeal that resonates in modern science and literature and undoubtedly will continue to do so. I offer a recent example. Consider, with appropriate critical distance, that with the description of several genomes, including our own, we may in fact be witnessing the emergence of a new biological monism. With the completion, more or less, of the description of the human genome, concerned scientists have issued a call for unifying the approaches to knowledge of human existence. Some scientists want genomics to be a discipline that will orient all others in discovering the unified knowledge of what it is to be human; or, as the noted specialist in human evolution Svante Pääbo wrote in the historic issue of *Science* unveiling the genome:

> It is a delusion to think that genomics in isolation will ever tell us what it
> means to be human. To work toward that lofty goal, we need an approach
> that includes the cognitive sciences, primatology, the social sciences, and
> the humanities. But with the availability of the complete human genome
> sequence now in hand, genetics is in a prime position to play a prominent
> part in this endeavor.[16]

Many domains of experience are involved in garnering knowledge of humanity, but it appears that genomics will be the master science unifying a holistic view of the human world. This desire may already be foundering on the recognition that genes are simply a pathway to describing the production of proteins, and that the relation of proteins to living behavior opens up a realm of incredible complexity.

Pääbo appears to waver a bit in his vision of the emerging unity of knowledge about humanity. However, such wavering does not characterize the new

16. Pääbo, "The Human Genome and Our View of Ourselves," 1220.

type of physicists in their affirmation of the unity of all. The string theorists, those who will one day have a "unified theory of everything," exude a sprightly confidence in the unity that has eluded the scientific world since the demise of classical dynamics. Or as Brian Greene puts it in his prize-winning *The Elegant Universe,* Einstein was, in his dreams of a unified epistemology grounding all of physics, simply ahead of his time:

> More than half a century later, his dream of a unified theory has become the Holy Grail of modern physics. And a sizeable part of the physics and mathematics community is becoming increasingly convinced that string theory may provide the answer. From one principle—that everything at its most microscopic level consists of combinations of vibrating strands—string theory provides a single explanatory framework capable of encompassing all forces and all matter.[17]

No one can doubt that the Holy Grail, whether it exists or not, has powerfully influenced the human imagination; and so has the dream of monistic cogency, of a unified vision of known and knowing, that stands as a rebuff of our paltry efforts to know a bit of this and that. Is Greene's Holy Grail more interesting than a world known by an indefinite number of modes of knowledge? There is no ready answer, except perhaps to note again that the dialectic of one and many is a permanent feature of our cultural matrix. (Greene's string theory demonstrates this dialectic with a vengeance in that his unified physics may fragment the cosmos into an infinite number of alternative universes.) With this historical viewpoint in mind, and no longer in thrall to a close-minded belief in two cultures, let us turn now to some of the questions brought up when we ask if modern fiction and science know the one, or the many, or have any shared views about much of anything, especially about that omnipresent ghostly being, inhabiting every nook and cranny of the universe, called "reality."

17. Greene *The Elegant Universe,* 15.

Chapter One

What the Modernists Knew about the History of Science from Pascal to Heisenberg

In the wake of the Enlightenment, in the wake of Newton as codified by Kant, modernists had to ponder the idea that science had imposed a worldview that made of science the adjudicator of the epistemic limits of the world. This worldview is based on a powerful, and perhaps circular, idea: epistemology and cosmology are implicitly wedded in the viewpoint that what is known, is what is. Hegel looms large in shaping this worldview, but so does positivism; and it was positivism that shaped most scientists' thinking at the end of the nineteenth century. The rich historical scholarship of the nineteenth century had made modernists also aware that there is another historical perspective complementing the view that epistemic modernity begins with Galileo, Descartes, Leibnitz, and Newton. Modernists knew that the epistemological grounds for the very concept of worldview, including the scientific worldview, lie in Greek philosophy beginning with the pre-Socratics. The education Proust, Joyce, Musil, and most other modernists received meant that they were well grounded in classical thought, and that they knew that what foreshadows the modern scientific worldview can be found, most pointedly, in Plato. They were aware that Plato and Book Ten of *The Republic* are the grounds for a belief in two cultures, one mathematical, the other not. Plato is not the ultimate source of this belief, however, since behind Plato stands the mystical Pythagorean cult of mathematics and the mathematical mysticism existing from the dawn of history, which culminated in Plato's idea that the source of true knowledge is mathematics and its ideal structures. Knowledge of these structures constitutive of logos describes or, better, *is* the structure of the world. Knowledge and cosmology are one, at least theoretically, as Plato's *Timaeus* illustrated, or, in a different monist register, the *Parmenides*.

Modernists could see that epistemological modernity is the culmination of several historical strands, which find beginnings in the cosmological thinking of the pre-Socratics, the mathematical idealizing of Plato, the empirical rationalism of Aristotle, and later Christian metaphysics deriving in its turn from the Greeks, especially neo-Platonism. Specifically for the formation of the rationalist scientific worldview, the most important strand coming from the Greeks lies in Plato's evaluation of mathematics as the supreme form of knowledge. One cannot overestimate the importance of the Platonic model for inspiring modernists with a respect for the idea of epistemic transcendence. This respect is clear in spite of the fact that Plato's proclamation that mathematics is the only road leading to knowledge was accompanied by a radical devaluation of Greek literary culture. For one had to consider the ethical dimension to Plato's evaluation of the superiority of mathematics, as when he asserts in *The Republic* that what relies on measurement and calculation will be the best element of the mind (603). The Platonic paean to quantification springs from a vision of a universe ruled by logos, that Greek concept that united language, reason, proportion, and mathematics in one term. Logos is accessible only to those trained in the mysteries of quantification that generate Plato's cosmos in the first place.

There is a logical circularity presiding over this worldview, and it is powerful in its evaluation of mathematics as the only true form of knowledge. Plato's relevance for the present is great, and not only because the model of metaphysics found in much modernist work takes Plato as a model. Modern science, when not in the thrall of antimetaphysical positivism, also argues that the necessary logical circularity of Platonic mathematical reasoning guarantees what the Nobel Prize–laureate Eugene Paul Wigner called "The Unreasonable Effectiveness of Mathematics in the Natural Sciences"—to use the revealing title of his famous essay pondering why mathematics works at all to describe the world.[1] Plato remains modern precisely because his work first codified Greek number mysticism to propose a cosmos consisting of invariant processes described, and generated, by mathematical relations. Platonism remains a dominant doctrine among philosophers of mathematics and mathematically minded theorists of

1. This classic paper is found in Wigner, *The Collected Works of Eugene Paul Wigner*, vol. 6, and it is also available on the Web at the Eugene Paul Wigner site.

physics. Thus, it is not surprising that Platonic metaphysics resurfaced as an important undercurrent of both modernist aesthetics—as found in symbolists like Mallarmé or his young disciple James Joyce—as well as modern mathematical physics.

Modernists were also well aware that in the Middle Ages Aristotle became the dominant authority for all important scientific questions. Not rejecting, however, the neo-Platonism of the Augustinian tradition, the later Middle Ages flirted with two epistemologies, or three, if one includes theology and its doctrine of revelation. The medieval mind could use the mathematics of the Platonic Ptolomeic description of the cosmos at the same time it used the teleological Aristotelian description. (They practiced complementarity well before modern physics came up with the principle.) When modernists contemplated medieval thought, there was much to inspire them in its Aristotelian indifference to mathematics.

Consider in this regard Dante's cosmology: complete within itself, it needs no mathematical underpinnings to impose itself upon the questing mind, as a total epistemic vision, with a unified structure. True, Dante calls himself a geometer at the end of the *Comedy,* but he does so only in the final simile to recognize that geometry is incommensurate with the world. The geometer cannot square the circle—*misurar lo cerchio*—and mathematics is inadequate to describe the revelation he seeks. In Dante the encyclopedia of the real is given in one self-enclosed book, which, with appropriate adjustment, is a succinct description of the modernist project from Proust and Joyce through Musil and Mann, not to mention the parodist versions thereof later found in Borges and Queneau. The epistemic model Dante proposed for a totalizing seizure of the world is probably as great an influence on the modernists as any subsequent work.

However, when looking at the Greeks and the medieval development of Greek thought, modernists confronted the fact that the revival of Platonism in the early Italian Renaissance made it impossible not to take seriously Plato's mathematical mysticism. After Kepler and Galileo's work, it appears that mathematics may well be the language of nature. Galileo's success in demonstrating the truth of this proposition heralded the arrival, in a recognizably modern form, of arguments about the nature of knowledge that derive from views about the nature of nature. As in the case of Plato, scientific epistemology imposed an ontology. However, modern epistemology concerns not only ontology—it also asks about the nature of the knowing mind. This is not a question that Greeks asked—though Dante did—but after the scientific revolution it became a central question. For the modernists, in the wake of Pascal, Descartes, and Kant, the question arose whether mind is to be considered part of nature, and thus perhaps a kind of computer that knows essentially by using formalisms or algorithms that describe both nature and the mind knowing nature. Or, alternately, is mind somehow different from the nature that it studies? An affirmative answer to the latter question seems almost inevitably to suggest that mind then imposes upon nature some kind of epistemological grid that is a projection of mind's nature, when not the mind's own creation. Or, in the idealist version, that mind really only knows itself.

The modern scientist may accept that the only legitimate or reliable form of knowledge is knowledge that can be expressed as an algorithm, but that does not answer the question as to where lies the locus of this mathematical formalism. The positivist physicist Mach posited the mind itself as the locus for all formalisms describing relations attributed to nature. In this regard Mach's thought was the culmination of a development that began when Descartes said that mind was separate from nature. Another alternative to Descartes was the viewpoint of his own followers, the materialist Cartesians, who by and large saw mind as one part of the great machine of nature that Descartes had defined as extended matter. Cartesians, unlike Descartes, were often rigorously monistic, especially Enlightenment doctors and *philosophes*.

Modernist thinking about knowledge turned on the debate about mind. Modernist writers were obliged to take quite seriously an epistemological dichotomy between, on the one hand, the view that the knowing mind is a measurer of quantitative facts and, on the other hand, the belief that the mind is a locus for the elaboration of kinds of knowledge that cannot be measured. These viewpoints remain powerful, today, for the debate about the nature of mind has hardly reached any consensus. At the turn of the century most modernists formulated their first, and often final, views on epistemology by drawing upon the formulations this debate had taken in Pascal's *Pensées*. Most succinctly, Pascal provided the modernist generation with an education in epistemological options, and there is not a major writer of the first generation of modernists who does not reflect on him.

Blaise Pascal, the French physicist, mathematician, and apologist for Christianity, is not a postmodern hero, so it is fitting to offer a brief introduction to the creator of the sharpest early modern formulation of scientific epistemological dualism. In Pascal, the literary and the scientific mind were unhappily joined in a kind of brilliant struggle to which modernists were extremely sensitive.

For in Pascal's work is found the first modernist sense that there are at least two ways of knowing even if there is only one known cosmology given by the unified scientific worldview. The formulation of two ways of knowing took shape when Pascal staged a self-accusatory debate with himself. This debate is enacted in his unfinished defense of Christianity, *Les Pensées,* as well as in a number of his less-known works. In all these writings Pascal advances probably the first modern critique of the scientific worldview by a modern scientific mind. In defending religion against scientifically literate nonbelievers, Pascal does not directly argue against scientific method on religious grounds, nor does he invoke revelation, Aristotelian causality, or scholastic logic. Arguing as a scientist, Pascal proposes that purely mathematical thought is inadequate to deal with the complexities of decision making. The reduction of knowledge to an algorithm cannot account for the complexity of experience. Experience shows, according to Pascal, that there are two dominant modes of knowledge that he ascribes to two different operations of mind. Opposed in Pascal's thought stand the axiomatic mind versed in the procedures of geometry and the intuitive mind gifted in dealing with the modes of knowledge permitting more nuanced activities, such as survival in society.

In effect, this staged confrontation of the mathematical scientist Pascal with Pascal the epistemologist dramatizes the first intellectually interesting critique of the new scientific worldview. Accompanying this hostile critique is, moreover, an interpretation of the first recognizably modern, which is to say, angst-filled, cosmology. But Pascal's bleak existentialist vision, for all its modernity, should not cause one to overlook the modern scientific epistemologist in Pascal. With scientific rigor, Pascal wants to show that mathematics is inadequate for most knowledge, especially the knowledge he wants. To make this demonstration Pascal describes a cosmology that is at once totally derived from mathematical thought and invested with the terrors of a mind that cannot find, in mathematics or elsewhere, the knowledge it needs to assuage its anguish. The path from Pascal's seventeenth-century cosmology to Kafka's search for the law is not long.

Pascal's cosmological vision is determined by mathematics. Seventeenth-century cosmological knowledge is based on geometry, produced by what Pascal calls the *esprit de géometrie,* or, essentially, the scientific mind. Mathematical and scientific thought are rather one and the same for Pascal, as for Newton, since the nature of space is identified with Euclidean geometry. However, according to Pascal, geometrical thinking, or doing physics based on logically related propositions, has nothing in common with the intuitive thinking that produces his second mode of knowledge, knowledge produced by the *esprit de finesse,* or nonaxiomatic knowing that deals with indefinite numbers of principles. *Finesse* stands opposed to *géometrie* in a dialectical relation, for, in setting up this basis for two types of thinking, Pascal is also, before Hegel, the first modern practitioner of dialectics.

Much of the impetus behind Pascal's decision to separate mathematics from other forms of knowledge stems from his desire to overcome nature, that fallen realm of contradiction impervious to any knowledge other than that offered by dialectics. Mathematics offers certain knowledge, but, alas, the certainties of mathematical reasoning are too limited to be of interest to a man thirsting for a certain knowledge of God. In this vein Pascal could write to fellow mathematician Fermat that mathematics is useless since the certainties of geometry are too limited even for the ordinary conduct of human affairs, so most knowledge must be based on grounds other than the mathematical.[2] For most knowledge we must rely upon procedures that are too complicated and diffuse ever to offer certainty. Proust will rely as much on this argument as any other for his epistemology separating artistic knowledge from science.

Uncertain knowledge is produced by illumination and insight, by the *finesse* characterizing the gentleman whom Pascal wants to convince, along with himself, of the truth of Christian dogma. From our historical perspective, the concept of the *esprit de finesse* is not so time-bound as simply to reflect the historical conditions in which Pascal wrote for enlightened libertines. Pascal's argument with himself inaugurates a modern debate about the nature of knowledge and certainty, starting with his description of mathematics:

> The principles are palpable, but removed from common usage; so that people are not accustomed, for lack of practice, to look in that way; but if one looks only slightly, one can see the principles in their entirety; and it would be necessary to have a defective mind in order to reason badly from principles so obvious that it is almost impossible that they not be grasped.
>
> But in the *esprit de finesse* the principles are of common usage and present before everyone's eyes. You only have to look around, without any violent exertion; it is simply a matter of being endowed with good sight, but one must have very good sight: for the principles are so disconnected and

---

2. I refer to Pascal's letter to Fermat of August 10, 1660, quoted in Hans Loeffel, *Blaise Pascal,* 27.

in such great number that it is almost impossible to grasp them all. So, the omission of one principle leads to error; and thus one must have very clear vision in order to see all the principles at stake, and then an accurate mind in order not to reason falsely from recognized principles.[3]

The philosopher Brunschvicg put this passage at the beginning of his edition of *Les Pensées,* and there is a strong argument in favor of taking it to be the logical starting point for Pascal's thought. The opposition of two types of mental operations is based on two epistemologies that, from Pascal's perspective, lead to incommensurate forms of knowledge. In opposing neo-Platonism, mathematician Pascal is also making larger epistemic claims (or smaller, as one chooses) in that he is asserting that there are many domains for which knowledge cannot be conceived axiomatically, or for which there is no conceivable algorithm. Contrary to what today's adepts of artificial intelligence claim, Pascal, one inventor of the computer, maintains that many mental operations are not computable.

In making his argument against quantitative reasoning, Pascal is a mathematician who finds deficiencies in axiomatic reasoning that tries to deal with the normal complexity of the world. "Principles" abound to explain everything. However, one cannot normally find the connections that would tie them together and make them amenable to expression by an algorithm. The very number of principles one can adduce submerge any possible computation in a sea of incommensurables. I interpret Pascal's reasoning accordingly in a strong mathematical sense: the number of principles one can usually adduce is incommensurate because there is no recursive procedure that allows them to be reduced to an algorithm. His thought could thus be formally called an "anti-axiom theorem," and using this theorem Pascal gave grounds for maintaining that there are at least two fundamental modes of knowing.

Pascal's argument thus has consequences much like Gödel's theorem. Gödel showed the impossibility of formalizing the proof of a self-contained system. For Pascal, the idea that most areas of inquiry can be modeled like a self-contained system is in itself an illusion, so it is impossible to systematize most knowledge through geometric deductive procedures. With his view of complexity Pascal excluded most domains of knowledge from mathematical description. In fact, in his description of the complexity dealt with by *finesse,* Pascal anticipates Gödel and his argument against the possibility of the logical closure

---

3. Pascal, *Les Pensées,* 1–2. Translation modified. This is a translation of the Brunschvicg edition. Hereafter cited parenthetically in the text.

of any formal system, or as Gödel says: "It can be proved rigorously that in *every* consistent formal system that contains a certain amount of finitary number theory there exist undecidable arithmetic propositions and that, moreover, the consistency of any such system cannot be proved in the system."[4] Here Gödel is talking about axiomatic systems, and his argument can be taken to imply that no axiomatic system can be grounded in certainty, since any attempt to ground a formal system in itself must result in infinite complexity through the infinite regress that self-referential statements entail. Pascal's description of the infinite complexity of most phenomena undermines knowledge in an analogous way by refusing the closure that certainty demands. In refusing omnipotence to scientific formalisms Pascal opens up an epistemic space in which writers from Dostoyevsky through Kafka and Woolf will work. They will work with a blind faith in that space in which, as Pascal put it most pointedly, the heart has reasons that reason doesn't understand.

Pascal's dualistic epistemology is consonant with the cosmology he bequeathed the modernists. This cosmology reflects Pascal's belief that, as literary scholar Hugh Davidson has described it, nature itself is contradictory. This contradiction is demonstrated by a mathematical argument. Nature encompasses at once the infinitely small and the infinitely large and thus harbors within itself contradictory oppositions.[5] Nature is contradictory because the infinite lurks there, waiting to undermine the scientist's attempt to find a final ground for it. Comparably, if Pascal argues against the possibility of applying axiomatic thinking outside of the narrow realm of geometry and physics, it is also because an infinite number of causes can be adduced for any effect. The potential presence of the actual infinite throughout the cosmos sabotages any attempt at limiting the innumerable principles that the intuitive mind or *finesse* must deal with. The multiplication of infinities has no end and, therefore, no possibility of a final reckoning.

It is worth stressing that from the time of Descartes and the scientific revolution to Richard Feynman and contemporary particle physics, fleeing the infinite has been a leitmotif of modern science. Pascal's contemporary Descartes showed that one could avoid, by decision or by fiat, the contradictions brought up by infinity by simply avoiding it. In the *Meditations,* for example, Descartes wants

4. Kurt Gödel, "On Formally Undecidable Propositions," trans. Jean van Heigenoort, in S. G. Shanker, ed., *Gödel's Theorem in Focus,* 41.

5. Davidson, "Le pluralisme méthodologique chez Pascal," in Jean Mesnard, et al., eds., *Méthodes chez Pascal,* Actes du Colloque tenu à Clermont-Ferrand, 10–13 juin 1976, 22.

to discuss the nature of man, but he refuses to define the nature of man because any call for a definition means, in order to define one's terms, setting out on a trip along an infinite chain of definitions for which there will be no end. Or in examining the infinitely small in his treatise on *The World,* Descartes refuses to allow the infinite to sabotage cosmological considerations. Dealing with hardness and liquidity in that work, Descartes writes, "The difference between hard bodies and those that are liquids is the first thing I would like you to note. To that end, consider that every body can be divided into extremely small parts. I do not wish to determine whether their number is infinite or not; at least it is certain that, with respect to our knowledge, it is indefinite and that we can suppose that there are several millions in the smallest grain of sand our eyes can perceive."[6] The classical scholar will no doubt rejoin that Descartes's strategy is not unlike Aristotle's cleverness, with which the Greek scientist pointed out that the infinitely small is a potentiality, but not an actuality of substance. The infinite has been a bother for quite some time.

Facing perpetual contradiction Pascal has recourse to dialectics, for only dialectical play with contraries mimes, as it were, the contradictions of existence and nature itself. Dialectical argumentation in *Les Pensées* aims ultimately to convince the skeptical reader that only Christian dogma can account for the contradictions that the scientific mind generates. This is framed as a probabilistic argument, which is not surprising since Pascal was the inventor of probability theory. Seeking the most probable knowledge of human fate in an infinite universe, the gambler in Pascal pits contraries against each other to show that only dialectical reasoning can describe humanity's lot in the cosmos described by science. Dialectics offers an account of humanity's fallen position in the world, as well as the limits of knowledge, because probabilistic knowledge of human fate has to be derived from first principles, the probable truth value of which is no greater than their opposite. A and -A have equal plausibility, so that concepts like misery and grandeur, for example, can with equal justification, which is to say with the same probability, describe humanity's miserable lot:

> Wretchedness being deduced from greatness, and greatness from wretchedness, some have inferred man's wretchedness all the more because they have taken his greatness as a proof of it, and others have inferred his greatness

---

6. Descartes, *Le Monde, ou Traité de la lumière,* 17. For Richard Feynman and his mathematical tricks for getting rid of infinite quantities that creep into quantum electrodynamics, see his *QED: The Strange Theory of Light and Matter.*

with all the more force, because they have inferred it from his very wretchedness. All that one party has been able to say in proof of his greatness has
only served as an argument of his wretchedness to the others, because the
greater our fall, the more wretched we are, and *vice versa*. The one party is
brought back to the other in an endless circle, it being certain that in proportion as men possess light they discover both the greatness and the
wretchedness of man. In a word, man knows that he is wretched. He is
therefore wretched, because he is so; but he is really great because he
knows it. (Pensée 416, p. 110)

The contemporary reader may find a strong postmodern resonance to this dialectic, with its play of antitheses suggesting the ungrounded nature of any assertion. Pascal's work is plainly at the origins of the dialectical thought of Hegel,
Derrida, and countless later thinkers.[7] Pascal describes a decentered universe
in which oppositions undermine each other. This is the cosmos the modernist
writers by and large accepted. Non-Euclidean geometries, then general relativity, and finally the cosmological models describing the Big Bang have all undoubtedly complicated Pascal's picture of a cosmos invested by the physical
infinite, but, I note, to complicate is not necessarily to supersede.

Pascal transformed medieval dialectics into a modern epistemological procedure. In effect Pascal draws upon science to force us to visualize a universe
that, after Galileo, appears to be characterized by an actual, physical infinity.
When Pascal describes this universe, he wants his reader to attempt to entertain an image of the contradictory nature of humanity's lot in a universe whose
space, now expanded by astronomy, goes beyond what either the imagination
or the intellect can grasp. The earth has been reduced to a speck circling a sun
in the midst of other stars:

> Let man then contemplate the whole of nature in her full and grand
> majesty, and turn his vision from the low objects which surround him.
> Let him gaze on that brilliant light, set like an eternal lamp to illumine the
> universe; let the earth appear to him a point in comparison with the vast
> circle described by this heavenly body; and let him be astonished by the

---

7. In the *Encyclopedia* Hegel defines dialectics: "The abstract or rational form, which
says what something is; the dialectical negation, which says what something is not; the
speculative-concrete comprehension: A is also that which it is not, A is non-A." Which
leads to the following dubious affirmation: "Every Concept is rational, is abstractly opposed
to another, and is united in comprehension together with its opposites." From Dagobert D.
Runes, ed., *Classics in Logic,* 360.

fact that this vast circle is itself but a very fine point in comparison with that described by the stars in their revolution round the firmament. (Pensée 72, p. 16)

Every spatial comparison baffles the mind, imposing the conclusion that, in this cosmos from which God appears absent, infinite space can only be contemplated as a contradiction that defies imaginative vision or geometrical comprehension.

The historically minded modernist knew that the infinite space of a decentered universe has antecedents in such medieval philosophers as Boethius and Nicholas de Cusa.[8] But Pascal's description of an infinite cosmos, with no differentiating traits that would allow localization in space, transforms the medieval matrix for describing this infinity. Pascal describes a modern universe, anticipating the contemporary cosmological principle which, postulating the symmetry of space, asserts that the universe presents the same aspect from every viewpoint.[9] Pascal's description of the universe is based on a principle of non-differentiation that allows no meaningful comparisons: "We only produce atoms in comparison with the reality of things. It is an infinite sphere, the centre of which is everywhere, the circumference nowhere" (Pensée 72, p. 16) This spatially isotropic and homogenous universe is the universe of modernity, the modernity of Proust, Joyce, Kafka, and Musil; Pascal gives its inaugural image in presenting the cosmos that humanity inhabits as a cosmos without differentiation, resembling a geometric desert.

In taking his distance from classical thought physicist Stephen Hawking has observed that for classical cosmology this homogeneity was imposed by the nature of the infinite: "In an infinite universe, every point can be regarded as the center because every point has an infinite number of stars on each side of it."[10] However, Hawking also notes that contemporary Friedmann models of the universe assume that the universe looks identical in whichever direction we look—which is compatible with the view that the universe is expanding.[11]

8. Boethius makes the following comparison: "Thou has learnt from astronomical proofs that the whole earth compared with the universe is not greater than a point, that is, compared with the sphere of the heavens, it may be thought of as having no size at all." From *De Consolatione Philosophiae,* quoted in A. C. Crombie, *The History of Science from Augustine to Galileo,* 1:31.

9. See Max Jammer, *Concepts of Space: The History of Theories of Space in Physics,* 3d ed., 83.

10. Hawking, *The Cambridge Lectures,* 9.

11. Ibid., 26.

Friedmann used Einstein's general theory of relativity to describe a cosmos that has curved space and is expanding according to its density. (Some of his work describes a hyperspherical universe that has no boundaries but is of finite volume.) In contrast to Pascal's universe, it is technically a closed universe.[12] I bring up this point for those who would argue that Pascal's science lost relevance at some point in the twentieth century, after Einstein, Friedmann, or perhaps Hubble. From the purely existential point of view of a human observer contemplating the cosmos, I stress that it would appear to make little difference if the universe is modeled by Friedmann and varies according to density, or by Pascal and has actual infinite extension. In either case, we are at the center of a universe without a center, though, in Friedmann's version, the cosmos may collapse one day. Of course the great difference between Pascal's cosmos and the one endorsed by most contemporary scientists, since 1922 or so, is that our contemporary cosmos is expanding. This has not resolved the problem of the infinite, however, and the debate about it goes on. As I write, for example, I read that the M theory of infinite branes of Neil Turok and his collaborators at Cambridge holds that "time is infinite, space is infinite, and they have always been there."[13] Perhaps Pascal was right.

Pascal says, in one of his most revealing moments, that the silences of these infinite spaces are terrifying. So, turning his back on this anguish-provoking spectacle, he invites the readers of *Les Pensées* to come back to the earth and their "little dungeon." Pascal's strategy is to show that the infinite, and its contradictions, inhabit the smallest corner of the smallest space. Turning to the microscopic world Pascal's mathematical reasoning illuminates how the infinitely small in its smallness equals the infinitely large, and he proposes the following thought experiment with a hypothetical scientist looking at the microscopic world:

> Let a mite be given him, with its minute body and parts incomparably more minute, limbs with their joints, veins in the limbs, blood in the veins, humours in the blood, drops in the humours, vapours in the drops. Dividing these last things again, let him exhaust his powers of conception, and let the last object at which he can arrive be now that of our discourse. Perhaps he will think that here is the smallest point in nature. (Pensée 72, p. 17)

---

12. See the *McGraw-Hill Encyclopedia of Physics,* 2d ed., 1202.
13. Charles Seife, "Eternal-Universe Idea Comes Full Circle."

By identifying space with the geometry that describes it, Pascal can deduce that an infinite number of infinite worlds will be found within the smallest insect:

> I will let him see therein a new abyss. I will paint for him not only the visible universe, but all that he can conceive of nature's immensity in the womb of this abridged atom. Let him see therein an infinity of universes, each of which has its firmament, its planets, its earth, in the same proportion as in the visible world; in each earth animals, and in the last mites, in which he will find again all that the first had, finding still in these others the same thing without end and without cessation. Let him lose himself in wonders as amazing in their littleness as the others in their vastness. (Pensée 72, p. 17)

The mathematical possibility of infinite divisibility leads to the conclusion that one can never conceive an end to the smallness that exists in nature. The dialectic of the great and the small demonstrates that the infinite is ready to sabotage any attempt by the human mind to grasp the nature of the cosmos, a point repeated by modernists from Kafka through Borges.

Caught between two infinities, mind is always to be found in the middle of its own creation, trapped between the extensions of its own imagination. Mind is, so to speak, a situated condition, localized by its very nature as part of its environment. Accordingly, Pascal's conclusion about humanity's place in the universe is that it, geometrically speaking, must be stuck in the middle, in such a way that a human being resembles a nothingness when compared with the infinitely great, a whole when compared with the infinitely small. It is largely because of the nature of mind that humanity can represent itself as existing in a middle point between all and nothing, in the center between infinities. This is an image that modernity has made its own, for it is only a short step to conclude, with Kant, or later with Mach, that the mind lies at the center of all knowledge; or, dialectically, with Kafka, Beckett, and Borges, that the mind, with its thirst for knowledge, is an impossible condition generated by infinite contradiction.

I conclude these considerations of Pascal with the following observation that Pascal's universe does not survive only in the literary imagination. Consider a contemporary mathematical physicist like the overtly Platonist Roger Penrose, who also situates humanity in terms of the unimaginable mathematical scales that describe our universe. Though based on finite time and spatial frames, the dimensions Penrose uses to describe the universe are so great and so small that the mind is boggled much in the same way that it is overwhelmed when entertaining Pascal's mathematical infinities. Penrose's cosmology embraces spatial scales going from the size of the known universe to the Plank length—the latter being something smaller than 10^{-35} meters. Practically speaking, as Penrose assures his reader in *The Large, the Small, and the Human Mind*, the physicist need only confront spatial dimensions ranging from 10^{27} meters, the present visible size of our universe, to 10^{-15} meters, or the characteristic size of sub-atomic particles. In terms of time the contemporary cosmologist must think about a scale ranging from the 10^{-23} of a second for short-lived particles (though the "chronon" of Plank time-scale is shorter) to 10^{20} seconds for the lifetime of the currently expanding universe that apparently began with that singularity known as the Big Bang perhaps some fourteen billion years ago. With these dimensions in mind, the mathematical physicist draws, for our literary imagination, quite Pascalian conclusions from his diagrams of temporal and spatial scales:

> It is intriguing to note where *we* are in the diagram, namely the human scale. With regard to spatial dimensions,...we are more or less in the middle of the diagram. We are enormous compared with the Plank length; even compared with the size of particles, we are very large. Yet, compared with the distance scale of the observable Universe, we are very tiny. Indeed, we are much smaller compared with it than we are compared with particles.[14]

And on the "logarithmic scale" it appears we live almost as long as the universe—compared with the life expectancy of particles: "As far as spatial sizes are concerned, we are very much in the middle—we directly experience neither the physics of the very large nor the very small." Penrose puts a buffer zone between the modern reader and the infinite by inserting the human mind in a middle territory in which it cannot directly confront the cosmos's micro- and macro-cosmic dimensions. But the infinitely great and the infinitely small clearly live on to threaten the imagination with the incommensurable.[15]

Except for his pivotal role in the development of modern mathematics, Pascal was not very influential historically before the modernists read him. If it is clear that the existential sense of what it means to be an inhabitant of a small

14. Penrose, *The Large, the Small, and the Human Mind*, 6–7.
15. Ibid.

planet in a big cosmos began to emerge in the seventeenth century, it must be said that the European attitude toward the cosmos, during the next two centuries after Pascal, was noticeably less anguished than his. Enlightenment thinkers were considerably less attentive to contradiction. In the Enlightenment world thinkers took pride in being subject to Newton's laws; Descartes's dualism was accepted with a certain equanimity; and *philosophes* often reduced Descartes's and Newton's thought to a monistic materialism, since the mechanistic side of their natural philosophy could be interpreted to mean that the entire universe was a physical domain in which mechanistic philosophers felt at home. After the triumph of Newton's natural philosophy, in fact, most scientists were little interested in contradiction, alternative epistemologies, two or more cultures, or the existential problems of the infinite.

Eighteenth-century astronomy and mechanics were characterized by a hubris that led physicists to believe in the theoretical possibility of a totalizing determinism that would allow the knowledge of everything. By the latter part of the nineteenth century, however—not to mention today—Pascal seemed much more a contemporary than those eighteenth-century scribblers for whom the Newtonian codification of celestial mechanics buttressed the belief that humanity is destined, by some beneficent providence, to live in the best of all possible infinite worlds. The pessimistic jibe of Pascal's complexity theorem, embodied in his description of the *esprit de finesse,* suggests why Pascal was not well received by the Enlightenment and why he only became a major intellectual presence for modernists. Against the Enlightenment, Pascal had already argued in effect against the possibility of the total quantification of knowledge that later eighteenth-century Enlightenment thinkers, with their assurance of convinced Newtonians, thought possible, thanks to their belief that all could be known by using the equations describing mechanics. The late Enlightenment mathematical physicist Laplace openly flaunted his belief in the possibility of total determinism—though a lack of divine knowledge on his part obliged this atheist to content himself with elaborating Pascal's probability theory to fill in for regrettable ignorance.

It is true that an exemplary Newtonian like Voltaire ended up rather pessimistic about a world that, in *Candide,* he could liken to a sailing ship full of rats. Nonetheless, in *Micromégas,* he dismissed Pascal as a bad metaphysician. For Voltaire, and for many Enlightenment thinkers, conflicting epistemologies was not a theoretical issue. They lived in the uniform epistemic culture of rationality, founded upon universal reason, of which Voltaire's theater was one exemplar and geometry another. There are, as Voltaire quipped, no sects among geometers; and perhaps no essential difference between a physicist revealing eternal reason and a poet celebrating reason in poetic forms revealed by the same reason.

Pascal appealed to a modernist generation that, rightly or wrongly, believed that the Enlightenment culture based upon classical physics and the power of reason had destroyed some earlier cosmological wholeness. In the wake of the romantics, modernists knew that the medieval geocentric cosmos, first elaborated by the Alexandrians, had little in common with the cosmology that was described with increasing mathematical rigor from Copernicus through Enlightenment physicists like Lagrange and Laplace. The modernists also grew up at a time when the conditions of possibility for the Enlightenment's unified cultural matrix were strained by new epistemological developments. On the one hand they witnessed the creation of new geometries, a subject to which I will return. On the other hand, the nineteenth century, in rejecting the classical belief in fixed rhetorical forms, also saw the transformation of poetical rhetoric, as it became a rhetoric with a sense of its place in history. This change in rhetoric corresponded to new epistemological developments that made temporality an intrinsic part of what is known. Historical becoming was recognized in literature, as well as in archaeology and historiography, as an essential dimension of knowledge. The poets and historians, in harmony with Hegel and Darwin, also declared history and narration to be adequate and necessary forms of knowledge when knowledge must take the form of a description of temporal processes.

One could plausibly argue that a dualistic belief in two epistemologies resurfaces then with a new twist, since the historical sense relies upon something like the *esprit de finesse* that Pascal saw as the mode of knowledge that would have to deal with infinite complexity. This is not, however, an argument I want to make. Historical epistemology may deal with complexity, but it also deals with empirical conditions that allow for the validation of hypotheses with various degrees of probability. (Pascal's direct influence on the development of probabilistic thinking is of course obvious.) Sciences such as history and archaeology, or biology and paleontology, are linked in this regard, and it is more useful to look upon the emergence of probabilistic historical epistemology in the nineteenth century as a new development in Western thought. And with this there arose what can be called the realist sense in literature that, from Balzac through Zola and beyond, explicitly represents events as synechdoches for historical probabilities.

One can characterize the new forms of knowledge developing in the nineteenth century in the following way. That narration and history are forms of knowledge, both in the humanities and in the sciences, demanded the recognition that some disciplines must deal with temporal dynamics to order the infinite complexity that accounts for, say, the existence of a culture or the evolution of a species. It is important to see that the development of historical epistemology does *not* represent another separation of humanistic thought and science, since, in both science and the humanities, historical epistemology stood, and stands, in sharp contrast with the epistemology of rational mechanics or other forms of axiomatic thinking for which time is not an essential dimension. "Two cultures" is not the most felicitous way to describe these new sciences, for the development of historical thinking opened up new domains of experience, going beyond any dualism. Heisenberg can be understood in this light: science deals with multiple regions of reality subject to multiple epistemologies.

The necessity to separate out knowledge involving time and knowledge for which temporality is not essential was a new issue for scientific epistemology in the nineteenth century. It is not an issue, for example, in Newton's theory, because gravitational attraction takes place instantly, so that time has no role in the law of mutual attraction. Indeed, the processes described by Newton's three laws are theoretically reversible in time. The Enlightenment's enshrinement of rational mechanics as a possible model for all knowledge, from astronomy to medicine, was challenged as non-Newtonian models showed themselves necessary for areas for which rational mechanics was simply inadequate. Integrating temporality into knowledge was fundamental to the founding of geology and biology, as well as to new theories in physics, such as when, in the nineteenth century, scientists began to elaborate concepts like energy and entropy, the keys to thermodynamics. In other words, geology and biology, as well as certain key theories in physics, began to take on a modern appearance about the same time that historicism was first elaborated, this in the wake of the development of empirical history during the Enlightenment. Emblematic in this regard is the fact that the best model for emulation that the geologist Lyell found, after Newton, was the historian B. G. Niebuhr. History could be a model for physical science because of a new epistemological axiom decreeing that phenomena carry within them a historical dimension as an essential part of knowledge. Historical sciences are based on this axiom, and so are geology and evolutionary biology. Not too surprisingly, even today there is no consensus about

the role and meaning of temporality in many areas of science, such as thermo-
dynamic systems—including that system called the universe.

Thermodynamics allows physicists to narrate a history, when not histories,
of the universe. For the bearing this theory has on the future, rather more than
for what it says about the past, thermodynamics singularly contributed to a
modernist sense of existential malaise—adding another dimension to the cosmic alienation inherited from Pascal. Thermodynamics says that humanity
lives in a cosmos whose most probable final destiny is an increase of the disorder that already may seem insufferable. Thermodynamics radically undoes
any sense that the cosmos might have a telos, and in this regard it has probably
had greater impact on literature and philosophy than any analogous influence
that one could later assign to, say, relativity theory or quantum mechanics.
Only evolutionary theory has upset a far greater number of people, since the
abstract calculations demonstrating entropy are comprehensible only to the scientifically literate. Thermodynamics and its concept of entropy predict that the
cosmos will have a story with an end, if not a telos, for the universe will one
day run down and grow silent.

Thermodynamics was formulated before the major modernists were born.
The theory began to take shape when the concept of energy received its modern formulation, allowing the formulation of the second law of thermodynamics of which C. P. Snow was fond. After Carnot's brilliant anticipatory theorizing in the early nineteenth century, the concept of energy was clearly formulated
in 1847 in Helmholtz's paper on the conservation of energy ("Uber die Erhal-
tung der Kraft"). In 1859 Clausius then offered the dominant formulation of
the first and second principles of thermodynamics by showing that the energy
of a closed system (including the universe) remains constant while its entropy
strives toward a maximum. Entropy was Clausius's term in 1865 for the measure of heat lost or gained by a system relative to its total temperature. For an
ideally reversible system energy would remain constant, as would entropy.
Clausius thought that disorder was the real meaning of the second principle.
Then, in 1877, Boltzmann interpreted the second principle as a statement of
probabilities, not as a causal statement, which means that the growth in entropy
is the most probable state of affairs of any system. For all macrosystems, irreversible disorder is the most likely state of affairs, and time is an irreversible
measure of the disorder that increases as energy is dissipated. When time came
to be defined as the measure of irreversible growth of disorder, the stability of

the Newtonian cosmos seemed to have disappeared forever. This was the new physics in which the first modernists were educated—at the same time they were educated in Pascal and Newton.

Complementing physics, geology was an equally important source of intellectual debate during much of the nineteenth and early twentieth century. Geology contested the mythic constructions of the cosmos that envisaged the earth as a home in which humanity had been destined to live. The extension of geological time into the past defied the imagination so that a physicist like Lord Kelvin had trouble believing how immensely old the earth might be. The development of the geologic time scale, beginning with Hutton in the eighteenth century and then Lyell's classic exposition in his *Principles of Geology,* continued the expansion of cosmic time begun in the seventeenth century. Pascal's anguished description of the infinite reaches of space was nearly matched by the geologists' portrayal of the countless eons through which the earth had undergone the transformations of which fossils were an enigmatic record. Or as Lyell wrote, in misquoting his predecessor Hutton, "In the economy of the world . . . I can find no traces of a beginning, no prospect of an end."[16] And to this description of the potentially infinite extension of time he added, with clearly Pascalian overtones, remarks on the "slow agency" of natural process:

> The imagination was first fatigued and overpowered by endeavoring to conceive the immensity of time required for the annihilation of whole continents by so insensible a process. Yet when the thoughts had wandered through these interminable periods, no resting place was assigned in the remotest distance. . . . Such views of the immensity of past time, like those unfolded by the Newtonian philosophy in regard to space, were too vast to awaken ideas of sublimity unmixed with a painful sense of our incapacity to conceive a plan of such infinite extent.[17]

With this new quasi-infinity of time, the stage was set for the development of evolutionary theory—which needed the presupposition of an enormous period of geological time to account for the uninterrupted evolution of life from simple to increasingly complex forms. Geology offered a dual history, one describing an earth upon which humanity appears to be transient, and another presenting an earth which itself is transient in the history of the cosmos. For the pathos of its temporality, and for its nearly sublime vision of unceasing change

16. Lyell, *Principles of Geology,* ed. James A. Secord, 16.
17. Ibid.

through boundless time, geological theory became an integral part of the modernist worldview.

Science began to tell a history of a world from which humanity had been absent. This narrative became the foundation for a new science, detached from natural history, and named biology, most famously by Lamarck. Biology existed from the moment it acquired a basic explanatory model, the history of the development of life forms. Many early nineteenth-century scientists, including Lyell and the paleontologist Cuvier, could not accept Lamarck's theory of evolution, for they feared the atheistic implications of the reduction of humanity to the status of one animal species among others. In fact, it was with great chagrin that Lyell saw that his geological theory of constant slow change was a model for the more successful evolutionary theory that his friend Darwin proposed after Lamarck. Darwin's doctrine of selective adaptation gave biology the means to construct a cogent narrative explaining the appearance and disappearance of those extravagant, if evanescent, life forms that geology and paleontology unceasingly disinterred. With the development of criteria for paleontological dating, this narrative history of the appearance and elaboration of life forms became ever richer, starting with such attested beings as Ordovician echinodermata or such hypothetical creatures as Precambrian protists—characters in a narrative in which humanity has had only a brief role late in the story. In fine, every modernist writer had to come to grips with the great historical hypothesis called evolution, now biology's fundamental theory, and hence the fundamental theory of how humanity came to exist in a cosmos which did not seem overly concerned about whether humanity was there or not.

Biology impinges directly upon the way humanity imagines its place in the world. Perhaps less obvious in its importance, but equally as important for the modernist imagination, was the transformation of the Western cultural matrix brought about by the development of non-Euclidean geometries. These geometries revised beliefs about the foundations of mathematics and, most notably, freed the scientific mind from the belief that Euclidean geometry was an intrinsic property of space. The Kantian epistemology that dominated scientific minds throughout much of the nineteenth century and beyond, was put in question by this development in mathematics, for Kant, as well as Pascal and Newton, had accepted that Euclidean geometry was a metric, or function, intrinsic to space. The demonstration in the nineteenth century that Euclidean geometry is not necessarily intrinsic to space opened a realm of epistemological possibilities that the philosophical and literary mind slowly assimilated.

The new geometries shook the foundations of knowledge at least as radically as geology or biology. Such is the viewpoint of the doyen of the history of mathematics, Morris Kline, who stresses that the two concepts that have "most profoundly revolutionized our intellectual landscape since the nineteenth century are the theory of evolution and non-Euclidean geometry."[18] The impact of evolutionary theory is evident in the anguish it still causes school boards in Kansas; however, the geometries developed by Gauss, Lobachevsky, Bolyai, and Riemann had equal impact for transforming the scientific worldview. Before any application of these geometries was discovered, the impact of non-Euclidean geometry was first to alter the view that science held about its relation to the world. When Euclidean geometry lost its status as the absolute determinant of physical reality, the mathematical models proposed by science ceased to appear intrinsic to the nature of the phenomena described. As mathematical physicists like Poincaré quickly recognized, the scientist could choose the metric best suited to the problem to be solved. Models and laws could therefore be viewed as matters of choice, of construction, or as fortuitous inventions used according to pragmatic criteria.

This moment when models cease to be regarded as intrinsic to the phenomena is perhaps the moment when modernity in science and, concomitantly, in literature begins. The term "modernity" is relatively unimportant, for I am not promoting the idea that a "paradigm shift" occurred. What is important is that, within a relatively short period of time—the time it took for thinkers to accept that mathematics could be viewed as a creative matter freed from any intrinsic attachment to the world—scientists and artists could conceive the idea that there are unlimited possibilities for the construction of epistemic models. In this context Pascal's views about the limits of mathematics take on a new sense, for it appears that mathematics indeed resembles a game. When limits are conceived as ludic rules, of course, constraints become springboards to expansion, and an unceasingly expanding world is precisely what modern mathematics has become. Moreover, the idea that formal modeling is a ludic activity contains within it much that explains modernist experimentation in fiction.

The new geometries suggested that mathematics can be as creative as art, and that scientific models using mathematics are also comparable to artistic inventions. The first modernist generation, that of Proust and Joyce, grew up during the time when physicists like Duhem, Mach, and Poincaré were pursuing

18. Kline, *Mathematics for the Nonmathematician,* 452.

the theoretical implications of this idea for scientific modeling; these scientists theorized that there are an indefinite number of explanations or models that can generalize a fact—to paraphrase what Poincaré published in 1902 in *La Science et l'hypothèse.*[19] This undeterminism does not exult in the arbitrary, for Poincaré stressed that one type of mathematical model often works better than another when it comes to describing processes in the universe. Epistemologists have been working ever since to discover what ties mathematical explanation to the processes observed in nature. Perhaps at best one can say, as Poincaré observed, that the ties are there, and there are many of them.

The transformation of thinking about the foundations of mathematics ushered in a new epistemological freedom whose consequences were simply enormous. It held sway over the greatest scientific minds, not least of which was Einstein. For example, after publishing his paper on special relativity in 1905, and after Minkowski had worked out a description of space-time as a continuum in four dimensions, Einstein found that non-Euclidean geometry could replace the Euclidean model to describe the four-dimensional space-time manifold that he then used in the theory of general relativity to describe the curvature of space and to explain gravity—to paraphrase Morris Kline.[20] Non-Euclidean geometry can describe a curved space-time that, as many cosmologists have subsequently speculated, may be consonant with a bounded, though perhaps infinite, universe. The important lesson was not so much that Newton was wrong—in most cases he wasn't—but that in addition to Newton there are other ways of describing the cosmos involving other epistemological assumptions and different mathematical models.

And with regard to literature, the transformation of the cultural matrix by mathematics suggested to more than one writer that literature could be as creative as the new geometry in proposing new models to account for the daily grind usually described with arithmetic or realist fiction.

Science at the Turn of the Century

The preceding remarks on nineteenth-century science point out that the foundations for much of what is modern in modern science was largely

19. Poincaré, *La Science et l'hypothèse,* 171.
20. Kline, *Mathematics for the Nonmathematician,* 452.

elaborated before World War I: geology, evolutionary biology, thermodynamics, field theory, Mendelian genetics, non-Euclidean geometry, the first work on
atomic theory, and the special theory of relativity. There is of course no date at
which one can say modernity suddenly or finally existed, and it is obvious that,
for an understanding of modernist literature and science, one must follow important developments that continued uninterruptedly, after the war's outbreak
and beyond, as the foundations of modernity took shape. Einstein's general
theory of relativity was published during the war, in late 1915; Eddington's
measure of light bent by gravity, as predicted by general relativity, then confirmed Einstein's prediction about the effect of gravity—and made him a famous figure—after the war, in 1919. After the Great War, major moments in
the development of modernity before World War II include the development
of quantum mechanics in the 1920s, Hubble's discovery of the red-shift effect
in 1929 suggesting cosmic expansion, Gödel's theorem in 1931, Dobzhansky's
major synthesis in 1937 linking evolution and genetics, and the recognition
that atomic physics had the power to develop weapons never dreamed of before. Thus, for an accurate historical assessment of what modernists knew, it is
important to recognize that, by and large, those modernist writers educated on
the cusp of two centuries confronted much of what one takes to be modern science as a well-developed body of theory already existing at the beginning of the
twentieth century. (Recall: Proust was born in 1871, Mann in 1875, Musil in
1880, Woolf and Joyce in 1882, Kafka in 1883.) This is the moment when one
can begin to consider the interface of modern science and modernist fiction.
One should keep in mind, moreover, that neither relativity theory nor quantum mechanics could be part of an educated person's cultural assumptions before World War I, and that their import had thus to be absorbed by modernist
writers at the same time that they were being assimilated by the scientific community. The epistemological implications of these important developments in
physics only gradually entered modernist consciousness. However, they were
preceded by the development of new geometries whose implications were at
least as radical as anything later developed in physics.

The intellectual climate in which writers like Musil, Proust, Kafka, and
Joyce were educated can be illuminated by looking at the philosophy of science
that these writers absorbed when they began to meditate on the epistemic role
literature can play. By the early twentieth century, after Poincaré's demonstration that geometries were a matter of choice, after Planck had introduced dis-

continuity into the measurement of energy, after Einstein had described the relativity of temporal relationships—to suggest what was happening by 1905— philosophers of science could look upon the proliferation of disciplines, theories, and models and find it plausible that "reality" is underdetermined. Any given phenomenon could, it seemed, be described by an indefinite number of models, so that a generation before Heisenberg endorsed the idea, epistemological pluralism was the philosophical lesson given by scientist-philosophers like Poincaré, Duhem, and Mach. Pluralism suggested that creativity is as important for framing a scientific model as the putative intrinsic nature of the domain that the model represents. Literature learned from this transformation of epistemology that pluralism in effect confers autonomy upon any discourse that can define its own foundations. In this regard philosophers of science in Europe—who in the main were practicing scientists—made the question of the foundations of science a central issue. Rigorous grounding meant that every discourse from physics to biology conferred upon itself autonomy in the very recognition that it might be something other than what it was. And if the very pluralism of discourses suggested that no discourse was entirely constrained by the world, then epistemology itself became an important self-reflexive enterprise called upon to justify itself. The philosophy of science became a thriving business in this context.

Modernist writers were educated in an environment in which three dominant trends characterized the philosophy of science. Perhaps most important were the dominant reductionist tendencies, neopositivist in orientation. This neopositivism is represented by a physicist like Mach, who saw science as satisfying our psychological need for regularity by promulgating "laws" based on sensations that more or less overlapped some objective state of affairs. *Ubereinstemmung* is Mach's term to describe the relation of laws to experimental data, as he puts it in *Erkenntnis und Irrtum*. Mach thought this relation was always an approximate affair since there is never *Exaktheit* in nature.[21] Mach concluded that laws are simply subjective hypotheses that establish relations between sensations. Physics and psychology are two sides of the same coin from Mach's perspective, so that it might appear that scientific laws are descriptions essentially of what goes on in a scientist's mind. Mach also endorsed Hume's view that causality is a metaphysical myth. The young Einstein and the Copenhagen

21. Mach, *Erkenntnis und Irrtum,* 2d ed., 456.

theorists of quantum mechanics were directly influenced by Mach. In fact, when it came to a rigorous critique of the use of concepts, virtually nobody interested in science escaped Mach's influence.

Opposing Mach was a distinct second tendency in the philosophy of science, represented by physicist and epistemologist Ludwig Boltzmann, who took over Mach's chair in Vienna in 1903. One of the great physicists of the nineteenth century, Boltzmann was obliged to defend his own work on physical systems against positivists like Mach, who scoffed at what they saw as Boltzmann's metaphysics. Boltzmann was an anti-idealist who taught that science proposes hypotheses, undergirded necessarily by metaphysics, which lead researchers to further discoveries. In his own work on entropy, for instance, Boltzmann had described how in kinetics entropy increases in function of increasing molecular randomness. For this theory, he had been attacked by positivists for his commitment to atomism as a realist hypothesis. Boltzmann's views represented the future of science insofar as his defense of idealization pointed up the role hypotheses play, as well as the statistical and probabilistic nature of the models of systems that describe many phenomena. (His realism was continued by Einstein and his defense of idealization by Heisenberg.) One might well wonder why, given Mach's benighted refusal of atomism, Mach's positivist philosophy seems to have largely triumphed over Boltzmann, at least in the first part of the twentieth century, especially among the logical positivists. Mach's attack on causality and on the realist interpretation of models was repeated later in the Copenhagen interpretation of quantum mechanics: Heisenberg refused any realist interpretation of the formal description of perceived relations in quantum mechanics, and Bohr rejected causality as a concept for describing particles.

Finally, a third trend in the philosophy of science, represented by Poincaré, contended that science is indeed a matter of "conventions" adopted on the basis of simplicity and economy. Though influenced by Mach, Poincaré did not think that the adaptation of conventions is in any sense a subjective matter. Objective phenomena are separate from mind, as Poincaré said in *The Value of Science,* refuting the view that laws are the "artificial work" of scientists. He held that facts are facts, and if it happens that they satisfy a prediction, this is not an effect of a scientist's volition.[22] But, in agreement with Mach, Poincaré

---

22. Poincaré, *The Value of Science,* trans. George Bruce Halsted, 122.

did hold that reality is underdetermined and that an indefinite number of models might explain the same phenomena, in the same way that we might use different geometries to describe space. Mathematics and science are granted a great deal of autonomy by Poincaré, who saw that both consisted in inventive, inductive acts, though Poincaré allowed that, in framing hypotheses, science is more constrained by facts than is pure mathematical induction. Poincaré was a very influential epistemologist, for he was a gifted writer whose works on epistemology were read by Einstein and Bertrand Russell, as well as the general reader—if Proust and Joyce may be called "general readers" in this context.

These competing epistemological positions lent themselves to wide debates among intellectuals, artists, and writers, as well as scientists, arguing for or against analogies between literature and science, or art and mathematics. And questions about the autonomy of representation, in the creation of scientific and mathematical models, paralleled discussion of the relative autonomy of literature and art, for the epistemological issues were common to all. The modernist concern with the autonomy of art was not, therefore, simply a continuation of romantic aesthetics, however much writers like Musil and Proust meditated upon certain aspects of romantic theory. A poet like Valéry offers a pointed example of how the antiromantic modernist drew upon the philosophy of science when meditating on the nature of his discourse. In meditating upon Mallarmé's quest to find certainty in literature, the young Valéry drew directly upon Poincaré for his *Introduction à la méthode de Léonard da Vinci* (1894) to find grounds for describing the autonomous "rigor" of literary creation. Valéry took up Poincaré's view of the recursive nature of intellection while pondering Mallarmé's desire to eliminate the aleatory from the knowledge—or revelation—that literature should offer. Citing Poincaré's recent description of "reasoning through recurrence," Valéry proposed that this type of reasoning also gives rise to artistic creation as a form of pure intellection.[23] Like mathematics and science, literature is a matter of procedure, a form of epistemic bootstrapping resembling what Poincaré called "induction" in his description of recursive procedures in mathematics. Valéry adopted this point of view to demonstrate that literature is as autonomous as the mind itself and, like mathematics, can ground itself in its own operations.

23. Valéry, *Oeuvres,* 1:1163.

What the Modernists Had to Learn

Let us now turn to those years after 1905 and later developments in physics. Discussions of literature and science usually lean on these developments, especially on relativity theory with its new models of space and time, and on quantum mechanics with its formalisms for describing the ever-growing world of subatomic particles. A first caveat in this discussion is that one must be attentive to historical context in order not to project onto modernist writers concerns with scientific theories with which they became acquainted only late in life, if at all. Proust and Kafka probably knew little about these developments; Musil, Mann, and Joyce came to know them well; but nobody born into the generation of Proust, Musil, Woolf, and Joyce could have been educated in relativity theory or quantum mechanics in their youth. A second caveat is that scientists, no less than writers, had to reconcile the new theories of Planck, Einstein, and Heisenberg with the worldview of classical cosmology that many were slow to relinquish. They wanted to hold onto the classical science that, after more than two centuries of existence, had become the basis for common sense. It is often argued that the new physics eroded the foundations of classical science, though this metaphor, with its emphasis on structure and stability, is not quite appropriate. It is equally appropriate to say that the new theories in physics opened up new domains, as Heisenberg put it, that were simply not amenable to description by classical models. The fact that assumptions that worked in one domain did not work in another was unsettling. Pluralism and indeterminacy seemed unavoidable necessities that brought with them a troubling fragmentation of knowledge.

One can conveniently date the beginning of this process of transforming basic science at 1900, the year during which the physicist Max Planck formulated the theory of quanta. To explain incoherences in the classical theory of heat radiation from a black box, Planck postulated that heat energy or light "can be emitted and absorbed only in the form of certain discrete energy packages," as the ebullient physicist George Gamow explained in his influential *Thirty Years That Shook Physics: The Story of Quantum Mechanics*.[24] This development occurred at the historical moment when some physicists thought, as physicist Alastair Rae puts it, "that the basic fundamental principles govern-

---

24. Gamow, *Thirty Years that Shook Physics: The Story of Quantum Mechanics*, 6.

ing the behavior of the physical universe were known," because "everything appeared to be subject to Newton's mechanics and Maxwell's electromagnetism."[25] This belief in the final unity was questionable even at the time, since Maxwell's equations were not reconcilable with Newton's principles. But additional doubt about the end of theory came when Planck's formulation introduced discontinuity into the explanation of physical phenomena. Planck's concept of the quantum of energy introduced a fault-line into classical physics' view of the universe as a continuum. The fault-line grew larger when Einstein used Planck's concept in 1905 in formulating the photon effect. He accepted that Planck's law imposed a restriction on the energy of any resonator: energy existed only as zero or as an integral multiple of an energy quantum. But, as historians as diverse as Thomas Kuhn and Mary Joe Nye have insisted, nobody really wanted to accept this radical idea at first; notably, Planck himself resisted the implications of his own theory.[26]

Discontinuity has implications for more than physics. The very idea of discontinuity suggests that "reality" is not a seamless plenum found behind every manifestation of knowledge. This includes the knowledge proposed by literature and art, as well as philosophy and science. Historically speaking, one can argue that discontinuity produced a fault-line between Newton and modernity, a fault-line that had first emerged as epistemology began to discredit classical determinism. Emblematic of modernity is the loss of belief in the universal determinism that Laplace, universalizing the Newtonian worldview, had promulgated. Perhaps the most important scientific work in this regard was Poincaré's attempt to solve the three-body problem, a problem that since the eighteenth century had stumped physicists trying to find equations that could describe the mutual attraction of, say, the sun, the moon, and the earth. In 1890 Poincaré showed that the problem is not integrable, which is to say, that it has no generally valid analytical solutions.[27] Poincaré's work on three bodies suggested that classical determinism was thus severely limited by complexity. Moreover, this realization was accompanied by recognition that Maxwell's

25. Rae, *Quantum Mechanics: Illusion or Reality?* 2.

26. See Kuhn, *Black-body Theory and the Quantum Discontinuity, 1894–1912,* and Nye, *From Chemical Philosophy to Theoretical Chemistry: Dynamics of Matter and Dynamics of Disciplines, 1800–1950.*

27. See the essay "Three Body Problem: Gravitational," in the *McGraw-Hill Encyclopedia of Physics,* 1280.

development of the concept of "field" to explain electromagnetism was not really consonant with classical mechanics.[28] Conjoined with the epistemological writings of Poincaré and Mach, the growing doubt that mechanics could explain more than the simplest phenomena opened the way for an acceptance of indeterminacy.

Indeterminacy was not quickly accepted by early twentieth-century physicists, even after Bohr and Heisenberg had made indeterminacy central to quantum mechanics in the twenties. Einstein was the most famous case, and followers of Einstein have sought various ways of introducing causality into quantum physics. This is not surprising, since the Western cultural matrix contains opposing axioms about determinism and stochastic processes, such that it is as counterintuitive to discount causality as it is impossible to find it at work in all physical domains.

Literary history offers an analogy with the history of science in this regard. The concept of indeterminacy is central to understanding the difference between many nineteenth-century realist fictions and modernist works written after the turn of the century. The modernist novelist no longer believed it was necessary, or even possible, to depict a world in which every effect could be explained by an antecedent cause. After Mach, the universality of causality itself was placed in question, when not rejected, and, with this questioning, various subsidiary beliefs: the loss of determinacy placed in question the necessity, for knowledge, of linear order or logical hierarchies based on causal relations. The loss of a belief in strict causality disposed the literary mind, from Proust to Faulkner, to look favorably on types of experimentation that a belief in strict causality did not encourage.

Planck's quantum theory did not lead immediately to quantum mechanics, and historical accuracy demands the recognition that Einstein's formulation of relativity theory preceded the development of quantum theory. Moreover, these theories are separate intellectual achievements. Modernist writers encountered Einstein's special theory of relativity, published in 1905, and his general theory presented in 1915, well before they could have heard of quantum mechanics. However, relativistic thinking was a feature of contemporary science before Einstein, since relativity theory was "in the air," as the always enlightening Martin Gardner points out in *The Relativity Explosion*. Physicists like Lorentz and Poincaré were both very close to formulating something like it. In 1904

28. This point is made by Feynman, *QED,* 51–52.

Poincaré gave a lecture in which he predicted "that there would arise an 'entirely new mechanics' in which no velocity can exceed that of light, just as no temperature can fall below absolute zero."[29] Also in 1904, to explain the failure of the famous experiment by Michelson and Morley to detect any changes in the speed of light that might be due to the effect of a putative ether, Lorentz (along with Fitzgerald) hypothesized that a body moving uniformly in a straight line would undergo a contraction in the direction of the movement.[30] However, as Gardner points out, neither Poincaré nor Lorentz had grasped the implications that relativity has for time: there can be no absolute notion of simultaneity in time if the speed of light is a constant.

Both scientists continued to think, like Newton, that one absolute time permeated the universe, and indeed that the hypothetical ether could provide a universal framework of reference. After Einstein's 1905 paper on relativity, the ether has no meaning, as the physicist Arthur Stanley Eddington said in 1920 in his widely read *Space, Time, and Gravitation,* a Galileo-like dialogue in which a "relativist" explains geometry to a physicist.[31] Eliminating recourse to the ether as the necessary substance for the propagation of light waves was one of Einstein's most unsettling ideas, for the ether's disappearance seemingly deprived the cosmos of any binding substance and hence structure. The notion of relativity itself was at once familiar and quite new. Classical physics recognizes the relativity of spatial frameworks—something we experience in a train when we are not sure if it is the train or the station that is moving. But nothing in the classical worldview allowed the relativity of simultaneity. Temporal relativity is a simple, but counter-intuitive idea which ultimately means that there are only local times. Einstein demonstrated that temporal relativity ensues logically from two axioms: that the laws of nature are the same for all observers in uniform relative motion and that the speed of light is constant regardless of the motion of the source or the detector of light. Therefore, measurements of space and time must vary between frames of reference to maintain the absolute value for the speed of light.[32] And from the formalisms provided by the Lorentz

29. Gardner, *The Relativity Explosion,* now reprinted as *Relativity Simply Explained.* My references are to the latter, p. 39, for Lorentz and Poincaré, and p. 64, for the quote from Poincaré's speech.

30. This is well explained by Stamatia Mavrides, *La Relativité,* 5.

31. Eddington, *Space, Time, and Gravitation,* 15.

32. This point is made by G. D. Coughlan and J. E. Dodd, *The Ideas of Particle Physics: An Introduction for Scientists,* 2d ed., 10.

transformations used by Einstein to relate frameworks of reference, it follows that dimensions of solid objects are indeed changed by velocity. In brief, as newspapers and philosophers tried to explain to the public after World War I, at speeds approaching that of light, rods grow shorter in the direction of their speed, and clocks slow down. For a public trying to understand Stravinsky and Freud, perhaps these ideas did not seem so outlandish, not if they had already digested Poincaré's earlier claim that we could learn to perceive in more than three dimensions. Picasso and Braque might seem to be giving lessons to that effect.

Einstein's influence was so pervasive that it is important to dwell on his work, both for what writers like Musil, Joyce, and Faulkner did with it, and to understand how one can accurately compare Proust with Einstein. By imagining an observer on a moving train, and another outside the train, Einstein showed that they would have different temporal frameworks. To make his point he asks that one visualize the following example. Two bolts of lightning hit points x and y behind and in front of the traveler in the train, but equidistant from the exterior viewer. To the exterior viewer, situated midpoint between x and y, these events appear simultaneous, whereas to the traveler, traveling toward point x, x must appear to occur before the event at point y—since the light from x would reach him before the light from y. These images are imaginable images, from the phenomenal world, a world now bereft of absolute temporality—just as it was bereft of an absolute metric framework after the earlier work of the mathematicians.

It took a mathematician to formalize these pictures, and Hilbert's protégé Hermann Minkowski enthusiastically filled the role. Using notions developed by Poincaré, Minkowski showed that the space of events, or the entire world in space and time, can bear similarities to the Euclidean space of points, with an inertial system playing a role analogous to a set of three orthogonal Cartesian axes in Euclidean space.[33] He made time another variable in the definition of objects on the "four-space" of events, using coordinates that behave as special vectors or "tensors." The upshot of this formalization was that Minkowski proclaimed that time and space are no longer independent realities, or, in one of the most quoted lines in modern science, "henceforth space in itself and time in itself sink to mere shadows, and only a kind of union of the two preserves an

---

33. I paraphrase here Wolfgang Rinderler, *Introduction to Special Relativity,* 2d ed., 50.

independent existence," to cite Eddington's approving quotation in *Space, Time and Gravitation*.[34]

Einstein himself noted that Minkowski's world could be regarded "in a formal manner as a four-dimensional Euclidean space..." through the use of Lorentz transformations that correspond to a "'rotation' of the co-ordinate system in the four-dimensional 'world.'"[35] This Euclidean formulation was satisfactory for the special theory's field of application, that of inertial systems in uniform motion. To enlarge the scope of his theory, Einstein turned then to non-Euclidean geometry. In the theory of general relativity that he formulated in the years between 1905 and 1915, Einstein "generalized" the theory for all motion, including accelerated motion. In particular Einstein had to explain the operation of gravity. In Newton's universe gravity is a form of instantaneous action. Einstein had to account for the apparently instantaneous effects of gravity in a relativistic world in which the speed of light is the limiting speed for the transmission of information. Gravity, as described by Newton, violates the special theory of relativity, because if the gravitational field of a body is instantaneous throughout space, gravity would be propagated with the equivalent of infinite velocity.

In a move that changed the way scientists think about space, Einstein postulated the equivalence of acceleration and gravity. As the example of a falling elevator shows, on a local scale all physical effects of a gravitation field are indistinguishable from the physical effects of an accelerated coordinate system. However, according to cosmologist Robert M. Wald in his *General Relativity,* Einstein's boldest stroke was then to hypothesize that the metric of space-time is not flat, but that the worldlines of freely falling bodies in a gravity field are the geodesics of curved space-time. Gravity is thus part of the structure of space-time.[36] Space-time is curved and is amenable to description by a non-Euclidean geometry. To this end Einstein adapted a four-dimensional Riemannian geometry. Martin Gardner points out the generalized role now played by time in the general theory: "Instead of a fourth space dimension, however, Einstein made *time* his fourth dimension. There is nothing mysterious or occult about this concept. It merely means that every event that takes place in the universe is an

34. Eddington, *Space, Time, and Gravitation,* 30.
35. Einstein, *Relativity: Special and General Theory,* trans. Robert W. Lawson, 122.
36. Wald, *General Relativity,* 67. A comparable point is made in the entry "Relativity" in the *McGraw-Hill Encyclopedia of Physics,* 1198.

event occurring in a four-dimensional world of spacetime."[37] It is perhaps difficult to see how this picture can enter the literary imagination—though one can picture a geodesic and its non-Euclidean representation of space. Yet, the import of relativity theory for rethinking temporality has been pervasive, for time is now a part of ontology in a way never conceived before.

The cosmological implications of general relativity has an existential import which rather reinforces the Pascalian doubts that modernists already had about being at home in this universe. General relativity allows the infinite expansion of the universe, a fact that greatly bothered Einstein. However, the astronomer Hubble announced in 1929 that his measurement of the redshift hardly allows any other conclusion than that the galaxies are accelerating away from us. Einstein's equations for describing the relation between mass and gravity then became the instruments for trying to determine whether the universe will expand indefinitely or if it might at some point collapse. There is of course a difference between the unlimited physical infinity Pascal attributed to space and the space of possibly infinite expansion that relativity allows. Moreover, relativity theory also permits one to conceive the universe as bounded. One might say that the transition from classical cosmology to the cosmos of modernity is marked by a preference for an infinitely expanding Riemannian curved space-time over Pascal's unbounded Euclidean openness. However, it is not clear if more existential solace is to be found in the idea of a bounded universe undergoing infinite expansion than in a universe characterized already by an actual infinite—all the more so in that if the universe does not infinitely expand, then it will be subject one day to collapse.

Actually, since the advent of relativity theory the cosmological debate has included several options, including the steady-state cosmos that the indomitable Fred Hoyle defended until his death in 2002. Some scientists preferred closure to openness, or to quote another work by cosmologist Robert Wald, "The idea of a closed universe—finite yet without boundary—is very aesthetically appealing. On these aesthetic grounds and philosophical grounds most theorists have tended to believe that the spatial geometry of the universe is that of the three-dimensional sphere." In spite of his aesthetic preferences, in his *Space, Time, and Gravity* of 1977 Wald thought that the best observational evidence favored an open universe with hyperboloid geometry.[38] More recent research, measur-

---

37. Gardner, *Relativity Simply Explained,* 80.
38. Wald, *Space, Time, and Gravity,* 45.

ing the density fluctuations of the cosmic microwave background, suggests that humans now live in a flat universe, one of the three possible models allowed by general relativity.[39] According to the "new cosmology" of the new millennium, it appears that we may be condemned to live with Pascal's infinite space, or a version thereof, for some of the latest research bets that the universe is probably not going to collapse. Evaluating research measuring the mass of the universe, involving hundreds of thousands of galaxies, Marc David writes that cosmologists are close to "converging on a reliable estimate of the mean mass density of the Universe. All indications point towards an infinite Universe that will expand forever."[40] Is Pascal again vindicated?

The early modernists stood initially on much the same small earth ball as Pascal, though, after World War I, they found themselves looking at the infinitely expanding Friedmann universe without a center, at a space looming around a planet whose age defied the imagination and upon which the presence of life appeared to be a cosmic accident. When the modernist looked at the micro-side of the cosmic scale, things did appear somewhat different for someone with Pascal in mind—and all modernists, at one time or another, had Pascal in mind.

The Modernist Version of the Infinitely Small

After the work of nineteenth-century science, one no longer needed the paradoxes of classical geometry to be baffled by the incredibly small. The microscope had opened up a microcosm for the first modernists, and then the incredibly small became even smaller with the development of atomic theory, starting, say, with Thomson's work on electrons at the end of the nineteenth century, Rutherford's explanation of radioactivity in 1903, and Bohr's theory of the hydrogen atom in 1913. However, Pascal's imagining of infinitely small worlds lodged within ever smaller worlds has remained remarkably apt for an imaginative appropriation of a world of rocks and animals, infested with microbiological beasts made up of smaller organs, cells, and organelles, these systems in turn made up of molecules, composed of atoms, and now today harboring leptons and hadrons, these latter made up of quarks that may admit yet of ever

39. I refer to several articles in *Nature* of April 27, 2000, and especially to Wayne Hu, "Ringing in the New Cosmology."
40. David, "Weighing the Universe."

more so-called elementary particles, or perhaps even strings enfolded in eleven dimensions, so that the final building blocks of matter seem to fade away elusively, infinitely smaller and smaller, with each increase of a cyclotron's power, or with the new twists given to vibrating strings produced by the poetry of the contemporary mathematical imagination.

But let us dwell on the first decades of the twentieth century. After Planck's formulation of the quantal nature of energy in 1900 and Einstein's description of the photon in 1905, the Danish physicist Bohr applied the idea of quanta to describe atomic structure. In 1913 he described the absorption and emission of the spectra of the hydrogen atom by combining Planck's description of quantum discontinuity with Rutherford's model of the atom as a nucleus surrounded by electrons in orbit. With this description Bohr created as many problems as he solved, and another fifteen years or so were required, with the work of other physicists, to elaborate a model that would offer a coherent, albeit perhaps paradoxical, theory of the world of atoms and particles. This model is quantum mechanics, and, with relativity theory, it has perhaps had the greatest influence on the literary imagination of all strictly twentieth-century developments in science.

A fundamental problem for Bohr was to make a coherent description of particles, such as electrons and photons, that could account for the fact that they can behave either as particles or as waves. As the American physicist Richard Feynman often pointed out, one can grasp what is involved in this dilemma when one understands the problems posed by the two-slit experiment, an experiment first performed in the early nineteenth century. In the modern version, photons or electrons are shot at a barrier with either one or two slits open, and the patterns are then detected on a detecting plate or film behind the barrier. If the scientist sends a stream of photons through a single slit, the pattern on the detector will be a spot. If they are sent through two holes at the same time, the result is an interference pattern as if a wave were going through the two slits. But if the observer tries to detect through which slit the photon is passing, the interference pattern is no longer formed, so that, as physicist Alastair Rae observes, "it seems that light passes through one slit or the other in the form of photons if we set up an experiment to detect through which slit the photon passes, but passes through both slits in the form of a wave if we perform an interference experiment."[41] This apparent capacity of

---

41. Rae, *Quantum Mechanics,* 8.

photons or electrons to "read" in advance the nature of the experiment leads Rae to speak of the "dependence of the properties of a quantum system on the nature of the observation being made on it."[42] This type of formulation prompts many to conclude that the observer creates the observed.

This dependence of the observed upon observation can be stated somewhat differently. For example, Feynman frequently declared, with some satisfaction, that nobody understands the basis for quantum mechanics: "I will summarize, then, by saying that electrons arrive in lumps, like particles, but the probability of arrival of these lumps is determined as the intensity of waves would be. It is in this sense that the electron behaves sometimes like a particle and sometimes like a wave. It behaves in two different ways at the same time."[43] Feynman's description may give little succor to those who want a world of noncontradictory invariant processes that obey the law of the excluded middle. These minds are not a minority, and it must be said that contemporary thought in physics is in fact no longer in the thrall of paradox. Typical in this regard is work, coming after Feynman, like Philip R. Wallace's *Paradox Lost* (1996). Wallace restricts considerably the range of speculation permitted by quantum mechanics. With regard to the two split experiment in which photons or electrons act as waves or particles, he argues that, if one takes de Broglie's wave hypothesis at face value, one sees that the particle is a wave and must go through both slits. Then the detection of a point particle can be interpreted as a quantum transition localized by the detector, which means, he concludes, that "there is not an iota of evidence that humans have any special role in physical phenomena."[44]

Feynman's playful presentation of quantum enigmas differs from Heisenberg's discussion of uncertainty, but Heisenberg has been the scientist to whom humanists have usually turned for their ideas about quantum mechanics and epistemological paradox. Heisenberg was far more willing than Feynman to entertain ideas that imply that the results of particle experiments are dependent upon the observer. In contrasting the classical scientific worldview with the view promoted by quantum mechanics, Heisenberg often declared that the behavior of particles cannot be discussed apart from the process of observation

42. Ibid., 9.
43. Feynman, *The Character of Physical Law*, 138. This work contains lectures from 1962.
44. Wallace, *Paradox Lost: Images of the Quantum*, 29. In this vein I note former literary theorist, now philosopher of science, Christopher Norris's defense of Einstein and a realist interpretation of physical theory in his *Quantum Theory and the Flight from Realism: Philosophical Responses to Quantum Mechanics*.

(Beobachtungsvorgang). Consequently, the laws one formulates about particles are not about the particles in themselves—(or particles *"an sich,"* a formulation that suggests the "thing in itself" of Kantian metaphysics, or something hidden in the realm of noumena). Rather, as Heisenberg said in a late essay, in quantum theory the representation of the objective reality of particles has "evaporated" by being dissolved into the "transparent clarity of a mathematics that presents, not the behavior of elementary particles, but *our knowledge* of this behavior."[45] With the idea of dissolution, Heisenberg thought that he had described the workings of the formalisms of quantum mechanics. The tautological nature of this notion shows that, from a certain logical perspective, Heisenberg had to be right, for one can hardly speak of the behavior of particles without speaking of the knowledge one has of that behavior. (It is seemingly contradictory to know something without knowing it.) From another perspective, Heisenberg's interpretation shows the influence of Mach's notion that the psyche is the ultimate locus of physical law. The Copenhagen interpretation of quantum physics is permeated by Mach's positivism.

Heisenberg argued that the epistemological transformations brought about by quantum theory did not apply to all of science, or even all of physics, but only to a closed system of concepts and laws that fit determined regions of experience *(Erfahrungsbereiche)* (124). This is basically the argument I outlined in the Introduction. At times, however, Heisenberg enlarged the scope of his argument:

> If one can speak of an image of nature in the natural sciences of our time, it is really a matter no longer of an image of nature, but rather of an image of our relation to nature. The old division of the world into an objective unfolding [*Ablauf*] in space and time on one side, and the mind in which this unfolding is mirrored—the Cartesian distinction of "thinking matter" and "extended matter"—is no longer appropriate as the starting point for an understanding of modern natural science. (125)

This thinking leads to the idea that scientific method can influence the object of its investigation, that method in effect seizes the object of investigation and reshapes it so that "the method can no longer be distanced from its object" [dass . . . der Zugriff der Methode ihren Gegenstand verändert und umgestaltet, dass sich die Methode also nicht mehr vom Gegenstand distanzieren kann] (126).

---

45. Heisenberg, "Das Naturbild der heutigen Physik," in *Schritte über Grenzen,* 2d ed., 115. Hereafter cited parenthetically in the text.

Heisenberg's emphasis on the role of observation and "method" in quantum mechanics has been seized upon by many who want to derive idealistic or even mystical interpretations from it. This is an almost automatic interpretation if, overlooking the restrictive positivist sense of what Heisenberg says, one takes Heisenberg to mean that the "real cause" of the behavior that characterizes particles is not found in the particles, but in the mind of the physicists. New Age interpreters can then claim that quantum mechanics is the science of paradox because it describes things that move without following a law of mechanical motion, that it thus overthrows objectivity, and that it recognizes that what we think may physically influence what we observe—to paraphrase one thinker's view of quantum mechanics' revolutionary potential.[46] However, one may wonder if, in 1927, when Heisenberg published the paper proving that it is impossible to determine simultaneously both the position and the momentum of a particle, he realized that he was a revolutionary transforming epistemology, not to mention philosophy in general. In this seminal paper interpreting matrix mechanics, "Uber den anschaulichen Inhalt der quantentheoretischen Kinematik und Mechanik," Heisenberg expounded the uncertainty principle to bring about a coherent way of dealing with the wave-particle duality as well as the impossibility of treating particles with the coordinates of classical dynamics. In this paper Heisenberg is the rigorous positivist, clearly in the tradition of Mach, who refuses to indulge in speculation about "ultimate reality." The positivist in Heisenberg says that it is useless to suggest that there might be a real world hidden behind the observed universe of statistical regularities described by quantum theory.[47] The rejection of depths hidden behind observable behavior—or the rejection of hidden variables—entails that the scientist must be content with describing the momentum of a particle, but not its position, or vice versa, for certainty about one variable entails uncertainty about the other. But this positivist speculation refusing speculation allows one to entertain the idea that, if nothing lies behind the mind's perception of statistical behavior, then nothing exists except the mind's perception. For this reason Einstein, adopting an increasingly realist epistemology, could not accept Bohr and Heisenberg's interpretation of quantum mechanics.

Perhaps the most radical of Heisenberg's later speculation was developed in the wake of fellow physicist and philosopher C. F. von Weizsäcker. This

46. Fred Alan Wolf, *Taking the Quantum Leap: The New Physics for Nonscientists*, 3–5.
47. Quoted in Max Jammer, *The Conceptual Development of Quantum Mechanics*, 330.

speculation is found in the idea that the probabilistic nature of quantum laws means that classical logic needed to be revised, because the probabilistic reading of quantum states imposes a revision of the law of the excluded middle. The P or ~P of logic must be modified to allow for statements expressing probabilities situated between total affirmation and total negation, or quite simply, as Heisenberg put it, "In quantum theory this law 'tertium no datur' is to be modified.[48] Heisenberg speculated that quantum logic might allow for a scale of possibilities of which classical logic, with its either/or, would be a "limiting case." In this new logic the excluded middle would cover the full range of probabilities between null and one. With the exclusion of the law of the excluded middle, paradox seems to be given a scientific imprimatur. Writers from Borges to Robbe-Grillet have not ignored the experimental possibilities suggested thereby, nor have the many scientists now looking for a way of doing quantum computing.

Quantum theory imposed a number of themes that rather quickly became part of modern epistemic discourse: the dissolution of the laws of identity, the possible transformation of logic and the abolition of causality, or the belief that one can think a-logically. These themes hover over modernist undertakings even when they are not fully worked out in a formal thought experiment. They in turn generated counter-themes, such as the quest for founded identity, the grounding of knowledge in the law, or the search for a rigorous thought transcending historical determinants. These themes characterize science as much as literature, say, in Einstein's defense of realism against the indeterminacy of quantum theory, in Musil's critique of Mach's rejection of causality, or in Proust's defense of the certainty of subjective identity. The modernist writer dreams of grounded knowledge as well as stochastic models. Perhaps most emblematic of this dream was Einstein who, against Bohr, declared that God doesn't roll dice, which meant that he, Einstein, refused to accept stochastic processes as the ultimate explanation of the bedrock reality of the universe. The unceasing flow of articles on quantum indeterminacy appearing in scientific journals today, especially on non-locality, suggests, however, that God may rather enjoy gaming. The argument continues.

The reader who wants to understand science at least as well as Musil, Mann, and Joyce must recognize that in relativity theory and quantum mechanics, modern physics includes two approaches (and more) to the basic knowledge of

48. Werner Heisenberg, *Physics and Philosophy: The Revolution in Modern Science*, 181.

nature, depending on whether the scientist is dealing with its macroscopic or microscopic aspects. This means that, as every modern physical theorist from John Bell to Roger Penrose has pointed out, physics describes nature in what seem to be two incompatible ways. On the one hand, the methods used for the "classical" level of macroscopic reality are Einstein's relativity theory, Maxwell's equations for electromagnetic phenomena, or classical Newtonian mechanics; on the other hand, physics at the quantum level relies upon Heisenberg's matrix mechanics, Schrödinger's wave equation, Feynman's quantum electrodynamics, and other formalisms to describe the world of particles. Einstein's realism posits that a cosmic causal order transcendent of mind awaits discovery. By contrast, Bohr's quantum mechanics proposes that order is a function of the formalism constructed by the scientific mind. Einstein's relativity theory is thoroughly causal, whereas Bohr and Heisenberg's quantum mechanics allows seemingly paradoxical indeterminacy. Thus the classical level obeys theoretically deterministic systems that rely upon continuities described, for instance, by the calculus. The quantum level is not deterministic and is described by appropriate formalisms that can account for its discontinuity. Most notably, as astronomer Colin A. Ronan puts it in his lovely *A Natural History of the Universe,* gravity is important at the macroscopic, but not at the microscopic, level. Einstein's gravitational theory, as proposed by general relativity, is valid for a space in which things are continuously divisible, whereas quantum theory is not.[49] In quantum theory one must suppose that in certain circumstances electrons move in discrete jumps from one part of space directly to another, thus providing a pointed example of how the microcosm of the atom differs markedly from the macroscopic world—though one may muse, as Thomas Mann did on several occasions, that the macroscopic universe having an expanse of 10^{20} meters hardly seems a more human world than the stochastic world of capricious electrons.

These ideas find reflection in modernist fiction because nearly every modernist novelist believed that literature is a form of knowledge addressing humanity's place in the universe. Quite simply, fiction proposes knowledge about history, self, society, and nature. Since the nature of knowledge is a central question in fiction's interrogation of science, I will first focus on questions of epistemology drawn from the world of science. In this regard Musil and Proust are exemplary in the way that they self-consciously use fiction to meditate upon fiction as a mode of knowledge. Conscious of the epistemological dilemmas

49. Ronan, *A Natural History of the Universe,* 21.

that science, after Poincaré and Mach, had created for itself, Musil and Proust confronted science and measured off what it could know. With this delimitation of science, their fiction could then define its own epistemic domain vis-à-vis science. In this self-delimitation, literature necessarily took into account what science claimed to offer as knowledge. By pointing out the limits of science, as in Proust, literature could stake out knowledge that properly belonged to literary representation. Or, alternatively as in Musil, literature could seek a domain where science and literature, finding some common axioms, might reveal knowledge beyond the fragmented understanding available when modern science and literature are taken as two separate domains.

To be sure, in their treatment of science within their works, Musil and Proust offer striking contrasts: Proust accepts science within the limits of its own domain, whereas Musil dreams of a new form of knowledge, embodied in literature, that might transcend science. But both set forth bravura examples, in their meditations on epistemology, seeking to justify the claims to knowledge that literature can make against the claims of imperial science to be the final adjudicator of knowledge. Musil wanted to overcome the positivism that turned the world into the mind's representation. He was a fiction writer who did not believe that the object of knowledge is a fiction. By contrast, Proust created a great fiction that celebrates both knowledge of the world and the power of the mind to appropriate the world through self-knowledge. Perhaps this is why many consider Proust the greatest novelist of the twentieth century. He portrayed a historical world deriving from harsh *physos*—the objective nature that the pragmatic mind usually believes to exist—while allowing the narrative mind contemplating itself to gratify its fantasies and desires to create an order transcending nature. Knowledge overcomes knowledge in the creation of a self knowing itself with certainty.

Chapter Two

Robert Musil and the Dilemma of Modernist Epistemology

Like many Viennese intellectuals, Robert Musil distrusted the idea that natural science or mathematically oriented social sciences could offer knowledge that fully satisfied human needs and desires. Moreover, Musil dreamed of a discourse that would rise above regional discourses that fragmented knowledge into so many domains of experience. Facing the various domains of knowledge, be it of literature or science, he was suspicious of the very idea of their autonomy. He wanted to unite the rational precision of exact theory and the ethical feeling found in poetic discourse in one unified whole. The nineteenth-century astronomer and statistician Quetélet had invented the statistical concept of the "average man," an abstract being delineated with all the precision of statistical reality, but, Musil asked, did statistical knowledge accurately describe every or, indeed, any real individual? Could scientific knowledge be applied to the individual case? Musil asked if there were not some epistemological unity that could or should be respected by both writer and scientist if either were going to offer authentic knowledge that engaged the individual subject. Examples of this knowledge are not easy to find, and, in the end, Musil could not resolve the conflict between unity and multiplicity in some satisfactory synthesis. He died without finishing his great project, *Der Mann ohne Eigenschaften,* or *The Man without Qualities.*

In asking basic questions about what authentic or relevant knowledge fiction could offer, Musil self-consciously aspired to find the basis for the unity of knowledge. This aspiration was never free of doubt. The brash assurance that, for example, the young Valéry showed about finding the unity of mind in the procedures by which mind seizes its own operations represents an optimism that was hardly shared by all writers, or scientists for that matter, and least of all by Musil. But unity represents a temptation in whose thrall Musil—engineer, psychologist, and writer—stood throughout his life. As much indebted to mathematics as to poetry for his epistemological beliefs, Musil meditated early on Valéry's belief that mathematics and literature shared common origins. The Holy Grail of the unity of knowledge was never out of Musil's mind, but his doubts about the possibility of epistemic unity also lasted a lifetime. A dialectic of desire and doubt undergirds Musil's fictional work, work that, as much because of its exemplary failure as in spite of it, has been recognized as among the most important written in the first part of the twentieth century. As much as any modernist writer, in his struggle with questions of knowledge Musil believed that literature must come to grips with science, and his expertise in both makes him a natural springboard for inquiry into the modernist attempt to reconcile the epistemologies Musil saw separating the two.

Musil received a scientific education in engineering and in psychology. Taking up the study of philosophy, he then wrote a doctoral thesis criticizing the positivist epistemology of Ernst Mach. Musil's thesis, "Beitrag zur Beurteilung der Lehren Machs" (literally, "Contribution to an Evaluation of Mach's Doctrines"), published in 1908, shows the intensity with which Musil lived a commitment to science and literature, for his thesis is a lively defense of realist epistemology against Mach's positivism. Though Musil could not accept Mach's epistemology, he admired the power of Mach's thought. In fact, Musil, like many others, never freed himself from Mach's influence. He wrote his critique of Mach's positivist rationalism, moreover, at roughly the same time that he wrote his first novel, *Die Verwirrungen des Zöglings Törless* (1906), a work that established him as perhaps the most insightful chronicler of psychopathologies ready to explode in German and Austrian modernist culture. The novel is known in translation as *Young Törless,* though it could be translated "The Confused Sufferings of Student Törless," since the title recalls the psychopathology presented in Goethe's *The Sufferings of Young Werther.* What is remarkable, then, is not only that Musil was writing a novel at roughly the same time that he was engaging in a scientific disputation, but also that his desire to define literary epistemology is as important for the scientific thesis as his use of science is for a novel written to convey psychological understanding.

Musil's thesis on Mach is clearly the starting point for understanding his concern with epistemology. If one, inevitably, reads the thesis with an eye on *The Man without Qualities,* one must keep in mind that the novel evolved over the many years of Musil's ongoing inner debate with Mach's philosophy of science. In the thesis it is clear that young Musil first wanted to exorcise Mach's influence by showing the weaknesses of Mach's positivism. In criticizing Mach, Musil knew he was taking on the most influential philosopher of science at the time. At the very moment Musil was writing his thesis, Einstein was respecting Mach's strictures on how the unexamined use of physical concepts such as mass, time, and space can import metaphysical notions into science—though it was probably only after Musil had finished his thesis that he learned that Mach's influence is directly present in the definitions Einstein used in the special theory of relativity published in 1905. In any case, Musil wanted to take on a scientific thinker pivotally involved in the dominant trends in contemporary science.

The epistemological restrictions used in formulating relativity theory and later in the interpretation of quantum mechanics impressed young Musil as restrictions that limited access to knowledge of human concerns. Musil saw no place for human concerns in the kind of empiricism that Mach had defined and imposed as the reigning physical theory. Therefore, Musil wanted to find the weak points in an epistemology that declared that physical theories were simply so many representations that could be replaced by other representations as functional descriptions. Musil was loath to accept Mach's view that reality is underdetermined and that theories are fictions simply having a demonstrated usefulness. He was hungry for something like what metaphysicians call "reality." From Musil's realist perspective, Mach's views denied any real knowledge about a unified world—the knowledge needed to unify accurate knowledge with action. Finally, as Hannah Hickman stresses in her *Robert Musil and the Culture of Vienna,* Musil reacted especially strongly to Mach's view that science, though it describes facts as minutely as possible, does not offer an explanation of the world containing those facts. Musil wanted knowledge that explained the world in itself.[1]

For starters, the realist Musil was not prepared to accept Mach's view that the law of causality is something of a fiction, a conclusion imposed by the reductive view that laws are merely functional descriptions. Realism, and the world it wants, finds little support in the view that the equations establishing relations between variables are an interesting, but non-necessary attribute of the perceiving mind. According to Mach, functional relations are simply relationships perceived between sensations; some are part of physics, some of psychology. This is not a dualism; it is a question of observational perspective. Much

---

1. Hickman, *Robert Musil and the Culture of Vienna,* 150–63.

like his physicist contemporary Pierre Duhem, Mach believed that models are simply heuristic devices and have no logical necessity. In adopting Hume's critique of causality, Mach said that science portrays a world of arbitrary relations.

Musil scoffed at the idea that one can live without causality. In the thesis, translated as *On Mach's Theories,* Musil stresses the points he has demonstrated in order to show the difficulties involved in living without causality as a basic principle:

> The course of our argument began with the requirement of a demonstration that experience can be grasped in a scientifically satisfactory way yet without going beyond what is perceivable. And it took us from there to the interpretation of functional connexion as a matter of economy and calculation, from this to a denial of natural necessity. And from there in two different directions: on the one hand, to the role of idealization and of the process of abstraction, which, we said ... could only misleadingly be held to be the foundation of idealization; and, on the other hand, to the view of science as a mere economical inventory and collection of instruments, a view which follows from the denial of natural necessity.[2]

Musil refuses the idea that idealization is simply a matter of abstracting from sense data according to the arbitrary connections that a scientist may arbitrarily perceive. He implies that the connections are not arbitrary, since representation is constrained by natural necessity. In his defense of epistemological realism, Musil agrees with the later Einstein, who also argued that necessity constrains what an observer can offer as an idealization. In his portrayal of Mach's viewpoint on causality, Musil in fact takes delight in finding a large number of quotations in which Mach contradicted himself on the principle of causality, since, when dealing with the world of events that actually impinges upon consciousness, Mach, like most ordinary mortals, did act as if there were objective regularities imposed, with causal force, by nature itself.

---

2. Musil, *On Mach's Theories,* 75. Herafter cited parenthetically in the text. In *Robert Musil: An Introduction to His Work,* Burton Pike sees an affinity of attitudes between Musil and Mach in four areas: Mach's concepts of the complete relativism of physical and psychological phenomena; life as a dynamic process of becoming in a Darwinian sense; knowledge based on experiment; and the need for a new synthesis of the natural sciences and philosophy, which corresponds roughly to the ideal expressed by Ulrich in his quest for a fusion of "exactitude and soul" (35–36).

The thought of Mach, Einstein, and Musil outlines a central debate about scientific epistemology in the early twentieth century. Einstein took to heart Mach's rejection of metaphysics when he framed definitions for his theory of relativity. Yet, in his philosophical thought Einstein never accepted Mach's positivist limitations of science. Mach's limiting knowledge to immediate sense data led him, in all good logic, to reject any belief in the substantial "reality" of the invisible atoms of atomic theory. Consequently, Mach had little taste for the rigid definitions of Einstein's relativity theory. Resembling the Einstein he did not yet know, the young engineer and novelist Musil was motivated, in his critical reaction to Mach, by a realism that accepts causal constraints. Musil was also motivated by hostility toward relativity, though in this case, against Mach and his version of relativity theory.

Mach was a relativist who refused to recognize absolute time and space precisely because "reality" is known simply in the form of bundles of sense data that cannot be absolutely constrained by any framework. For Musil, as for a scientist like Planck, Mach's kind of relativity and his psychology dissolved the world into arbitrary sensations. In an insightful study of the power of Mach's thought, Guillaume Garreta stresses this side of Mach's work according to which what one takes to be a "thing" is in fact a symbol in thought representing a complex of sensations having only a "relative stability." Writes Garreta, Mach held that

> there is no permanent nucleus hiding behind phenomena, the world of the thing in itself and of the transcendental is an imaginary world. Showing this, Mach took the counter-viewpoint of traditional realism, even the refined form given realism by Helmholtz, according to which sensations are not the faithful reproduction of things, but rather their symbol. For Mach, the thing is an abstraction, and its "elements" are what is real.[3]

What one perceives—a thing's "elements"—are the basis for all knowledge, and since all elements are of the same type, Mach's epistemology can be characterized as a reductive monism.

The psychologist in Musil was quick to show that the very nature of sense data and perception is problematic. In defending the view that epistemic representation aims at an invariant necessity, known by a knowing self, Musil

---

3. Garreta, "Ernst Mach," in Pierre Wagner, ed., *Les philosophes et la science,* 634.

thought he had attacked the Achilles' heel of positivism. Sense data, as Musil pointed out in his thesis, is central to Mach's epistemology, but the concept itself is accepted a priori and has no conceptual rigor: "What is a bundle or complex of sensations? What is a law-governed connexion between sensations? Before ideas [*Vorstellungen*] such as these can be considered they must be made scientifically precise" (73). According to Musil, Mach offers no rigorous definition of sense data. He has defined knowledge as sense data with no real concrete example of what constitutes sense data, and, in short, can be accused of making an a priori definition function to cover up what needs to be explained.

With equal a priori assurance, according to Musil, Mach dissolves the knowing self by declaring it to be one more idealization. Mach's dismissal of the self has had wide resonance and pronouncements like the following, which are widely quoted: the self is just an "ideelle denkökonomische, keine reelle Einheit" (an ideal unity demanded by the economy of thought).[4] The self is an epistemological necessity, since representation demands that something be represented to something else. The need for mimesis produces belief in a self. But such a self, viewed as a product of epistemological necessity, is also something of an illusion, as Freud, another follower of Mach, later said, and which a generation of poststructuralists have since untiringly repeated. What is a self when it only exists to serve the necessities of representation within a relativist framework? This is a central question that Musil wrestled with over the next four decades after the thesis. At a later date the question took the following shape: can a self in itself have any properties that are really its own? Musil's Ulrich, the man without properties, was created, in part, to ponder precisely this question.

Young Musil wants to oblige the reader of his thesis to recognize that, if Mach has no precise definition of sense data, then one must doubt that science offers anything more than so many arbitrary images of relations, images painted on the observing retina like so many "pictures" of the facts. Musil points out that the positivist becomes in fact a metaphysician by finding images where it is dubious that they exist. Moreover, he asks, what are these images for which there is only an illusory self to entertain them? Or perhaps nobody sees them. That is actually a suggested response in the answer that another Viennese writer, Ludwig Wittgenstein, gave in elaborating on Mach's ideas.

---

4. Mach, from *Breiträge zur Analyse der Empfindungen* (1886), quoted by Franz Kuna in Malcolm Bradbury and James McFarlane, eds., *Modernism, 1890–1930*, 122.

Wittgenstein's first theory of language in the *Tractatus,* elaborated at Cambridge in the years after Musil published his thesis, describes language itself as a "picture of facts" that are supposedly visualized in language in the form of *Sachverhalten.* These facts visualized in language are the substance, but also the limits, of what language can say. Wittgenstein's example suggests that positivism often accompanies mysticism, for Wittgenstein's nearly mystical belief in silence seems to spring from the impossibility of describing the pictures that he attributed to language. Or, alternatively, Wittgenstein's belief that essential matters escape language may spring from his belief that what language might picture isn't really essential in any case. I bring up Wittgenstein here because he and Musil shared the same cultural matrix, that of the world of Viennese modernism, and both reacted strongly to Mach. Wittgenstein developed his later philosophy in direct reaction against the metaphysics of the visual, for he realized that nobody ever saw a picture in language. It is noteworthy that both Wittgenstein and Musil reacted to the limits of positivism with mystical flights. Musil never ceased looking for the language that might be adequate to these flights, and Wittgenstein never stopped looking for an adequate way of describing language.[5]

The subsequent history of positivism was largely determined by the way Mach interpreted scientific discourse as a mathematically organized picturing of relations from which metaphysics must be banned. In the conclusion to this study I will argue that this history has had an important influence on what we call our postmodernity. At this point suffice it to say that Mach's positivism insists that the mathematical relations called scientific laws are not causal relations, but "mimetic reproduction of facts in thought," to cite a later widespread interpretation of Mach.[6] And so laws are supposedly reports on sensations, and nothing more, and the self that sees them is an unfortunate, if seemingly necessary, presupposition—a fact that Musil pointed out with no little irony. Musil's defense of the integrity of the self in perception in his early career is motivated by a desire to defend a realist view of the self. It derives in part from his

---

5. Surprisingly, there is no reference to Wittgenstein in Musil's *Tagebücher,* though in *Band* 2, rev. ed., editor Adolf Frisé notes the overlap between the *Tractatus* and Musil's later thought on aesthetics and ethics: in the *Tractatus,* 6.421, Wittgenstein declares ethics and aesthetics are transcendental and one, whereas Musil says that he has always thought that aesthetics and ethics are the same. Musil, *Tagebücher,* rev. ed., ed. Adolf Frisé, 2:562.

6. From "Ernst Mach," in *Encyclopedia of Philosophy,* 6:291.

exposure to Köhler and the developing theories of Gestalt psychology. It parallels Heidegger's later defensive phenomenological description of the integrity of perception in *Being and Time* (which, I add, also seems to be largely motivated by an attempt to defuse Mach's epistemology by, without naming it, reducing it to the errors of the Cartesian worldview). The young Musil was attracted by those theorists of knowledge who believe that the individual act of perception only makes sense when conceived as existing as part of a whole. One should not suppose that this is, strictly speaking, a scientific question, for the desire for unity is as much aesthetic or ethical as epistemic in origin. Musil's desire for unity later motivates his attempt to embody the knowing and the known self in a novel offering an epistemic seizure of some totality, a grounded totality revealed by epistemic unity.

In a comparable vein, young Musil's distaste for relativity also springs from his defense of the realism that Mach's rejection of absolute epistemic frameworks threatened. Musil believed that it makes sense to speak about absolute frameworks when dealing with everyday appearances. His objection to Mach's relativity aims at preserving the possibility of knowing things, specifically the identity of things in time, within some constant framework that thus preserves a world possessing epistemic solidity—though Musil's character Ulrich later entertains some Machean doubts as to whether that solidity exists. Knowledge and temporality, for young Musil, are interrelated, and not simply in relativistic terms, or as he says in the thesis:

> It is precisely the fact that one can speak of the same spatial or temporal behavior even though one is making comparisons with different bodies (by which is meant that judgements about, for example, the time, could be made by reference to a clock, the earth's angle of rotation, a fall in temperature) which is evidence for the claim that such a behavior is independent of the bodies we resort to for purposes of comparison. (42)

Musil is arguing that "something independent" must resist being dissolved into relations that have no existence other than in relative descriptions. In brief, Musil conceives of relativity as inimical to realism, since relativity, as the young Musil conceives it, dissolves all properties into a question of frameworks, which eliminates the possibility of defining qualities as things in themselves. This question remained of crucial importance for the novelist who, as he matured, resisted while recognizing the strong attraction exercised by the idea, shared by no less than Mach and Poincaré, that knowledge can only be of relations between things, not of things or qualities in themselves. It became the ironic subject of his great novel.

Musil's reaction to Mach, in his novel and in his thesis, presents a role reversal one might expect from writer and scientist: the writer defends the reality of reality against the scientific epistemologist for whom the knowledge of laws or functions is essentially a fiction created by autonomous scientists. A Machean scientist ends up looking like a novelist, or so Musil suggests in the thesis: "Necessity, concludes Mach, is only to be found in the relations of mutual dependence between our concepts, in the ideas we have of law and so on; but since these are gained by idealizations, necessity can only be read into nature in a fictitious fashion" (69). Musil implies that the modern fiction writer wants more from science than fictions. By arguing that Mach must agree in the end that rationality always decrees that some theories fall out of competition, and that others win, Musil wanted science to be responsible to the world in which humanity lives. Hypotheses must agree with facts, and not just on the basis of economy, as Musil says, but by "normal epistemological criteria" (44), which is to say, by conforming to some invariant objectivity. Musil wanted to show that only in its theorizing, but not in its practice, does science remove the world from our grasp.

In fine, Mach was a representative, for young Musil, of how science had unsettled the confidence one could have in the knowledge science offered about the world. Musil's angst about science's demolishing its own certainty lies at the heart of *Young Törless,* his portrayal of the artist as a young scientist. The need for epistemic certainty expressed in this novel could hardly be reconciled with Mach's dismissing causality, with his presentation of space and time as relative notions with no absolute dimension, nor with his reduction of laws to functional notations or pictures of sense data. With great theoretical elegance, Mach had dissolved knowledge into a series of operations whose only logical requirement is economy and consistent fidelity to experience—whatever that might mean. It is precisely the question of fidelity to experience that, in the novel, Musil brings to the fore in his depiction of the boy Törless, especially in the portrayal of the boy's education in science, and of Törless's needs, needs notably not fulfilled by that education.

In *Young Törless,* much as in the thesis, Musil wants to show that Mach and much of modern scientific epistemology is contradictory in dismissing the idea that there is some bedrock nature to which scientific knowledge conforms in its representations—not least of all because this bedrock is existentially as well as epistemologically necessary if there is to be a world whose invariant solidity can give the lie to our irrational fantasies. Musil set out to do more than simply deplore the loss of the unity of knower and known or the belief in a substantial reality to which science gives access with reasonable certainty. As *Young Törless* amply demonstrates, he also wanted to examine the dangers of antiscientific currents that were emerging at the turn of the century. These currents declared such things as the transcendental ego, the unconscious self, and ethnic or racial identity to be the basis for privileged knowledge, opening the doors to irrational cults as varied as theosophy, mystical nationalism, and finally fascism. Critical of positivism, and fearful of its opposite, Musil was concerned in his first novel with the relations of epistemology, ethics, and politics.

Young Törless is a novel portraying doubt and anguish about science while depicting grotesque alternatives to that doubt, alternatives springing directly from the uncertainties created by modern science. These alternatives to the anguish of uncertainty are notably the sadism practiced by Törless's fellow students and their perverted pursuit of a will to power. In portraying these students, Musil depicts the modernist need for certainty by contrasting young Törless's Pascalian anguish about the cosmos with the irrational beliefs and practices his fellow students use to overcome a lack of certainty. This description should make it clear that it would be a mistake to see in *Young Törless* simply a prelude to *The Man without Qualities,* for the novel is an extraordinarily original portrayal of the roots of the nihilism that Nietzsche had also seen about to be unleashed upon Europe. Reflecting upon Nietzsche in *Young Törless,* though hardly endorsing Nietzsche's own nihilist vision of the will to power, Musil meditates upon science's incapacity to offer knowledge that meets human needs—or the failure of science to offer knowledge as an alternative to the irrational promises of redemption in which Musil saw the outgrowth of nihilism.

Young Törless is an introduction to the psychic distortions of modernity, and, as such, it commands the same interest as Joyce's *Portrait of the Artist* or Gide's moral parables, or perhaps even greater interest insofar as the distortions Musil portrays are the roots of National Socialism. These distortions are found specifically in the beliefs and values of four schoolboys being educated in an Austrian private secondary school. Despite the school's provincial setting, the boys are inheritors of Austria's imperial tradition as well as participants in

Viennese modernism. Much as in Flaubert's work—the scientifically objective Flaubert who gave modernism much of the rhetoric of its fiction—the events narrated in the novel are indirectly filtered through the consciousness of the central character, Törless, the youth whose initiation into the world is traced through critical episodes in his life as a boarding student. Törless is a sincere boy, wanting genuinely to understand the world, who is disconcerted to discover within himself possibilities for homoeroticism and sadism.

Two older students enact perversions opposing Törless's intuitive notions of decency: Reiting, an admirer of Napoleon, worships power in order to dominate others, whereas the more intellectual Beineberg rejects rationalism in the name of superior, supernatural values. Beineberg's beliefs are summed up in his exaltation of *die Seele,* or the world spirit that offers escape from the limits of bourgeois rationality. Both Reiting and Beineberg represent nascent Nietzschean explorers of the irrational. Musil also shows that their irrationalism is grounded in sexual impulses, for the young men practice sadistic eroticism in exploiting the novel's fourth major character, the helpless and androgynously attractive Basini, to whom Törless is also drawn. Reiting and especially Beineberg exploit Basini sexually while using grotesque forms of torture to dominate him in affirmation of their aggressive will to power.

Beineberg is an especially interesting demonstration of achieving transcendence with a whip, since, as Musil himself later discovered in helplessly watching the Nazis' success, a future SS man was ready to step forward in Beineberg, an adolescent adept of Indian philosophy. The ties between asceticism and power are patent in this youthful devotee of esoteric thought. Beineberg's father is a military officer from whom Beineberg has inherited an attitude that leads him to live in world-denying fantasy. As Nietzsche claimed, self-denial is a ploy for the attainment of superior knowledge, which is to say, power. Musil's description of the quest for revelation undertaken by Beineberg's father underscores that he and his son pursue a modern gnosis that wants to abolish all limitations on knowledge—which in context appears to be an affirmation of a desire for unlimited power. In practice, a requisite for success in their quest for knowledge is that these adepts refuse all debate about alternatives:

> When he [the father] read, he did not want to reflect on opinions and controversies, but, from the very instant of opening the book, to enter as through a secret portal into the midst of some very exclusive knowledge.

Books that he read had to be such that the mere possession of them was as it were a secret sign of initiation and a pledge of more than earthly revelations. And this he found only in books of Indian philosophy, which to him seemed to be not merely books, but revelations, something real—keys such as were the alchemical and magical books of the Middle Ages.[7]

This passage is a concise summary of the antithetical stances toward the world that Musil saw in modernity as he was working on his doctoral studies and thinking about Mach and Nietzsche. On the one hand, Musil, himself educated in science, was accustomed to evaluating probable opinions and constantly changing theories, and hence he saw the necessity of dealing with "opinions and controversies." On the other hand, in Vienna and Berlin, he frequently encountered the type of mind that wanted sudden revelations, without question, of "something real." In these demands Musil might ironically see a caricature of his own desire for certainty and mystical unity—but later he also knew that he had seen the prefiguration of the Nazi affirmation of truth without debate. In any case, the young Musil understood well that the will to power embodied in these demands for certainty must reject the epistemological practices of science—what Nietzsche had called the illusions of science because of its belief in truth. In practice Musil saw that the rejection of rational procedures for knowledge led in turn to nihilistic demands for revelation, as in *Young Törless,* or to insanity, as in the case of the Nietzschean Clarissa in *The Man without Qualities.*

Revelation was, moreover, the fundamental goal not just of Indian philosophy, theosophy, and other, often quirky doctrines of 1900 that promised transcendental truth, but also of many modernist literary texts. Any consideration of modernism must ponder the epistemic role of revelation. Though Musil was intuitively skeptical about revelation, *Young Törless,* by dramatizing the perceptions of its protagonist, counts revelation among its most important rhetorical strategies. This is not surprising. In the works of most modernist writers, revelation, in the many, varied senses of the term, is a constant strategy, if not a temptation. In particular, by dramatizing privileged moments of perception, the writer can lay claim to privileged knowledge. The range of uses and abuses of the rhetoric of revelation is broad. It encompasses Joyce's early doctrine of epiphanies, which he later largely abandoned, as well as the notion of essence

7. Musil, *Robert Musil: Selected Writings,* ed. Burton Pike, trans. Eithne Wilkins and Ernst Kaiser, 17–18. Hereafter cited parenthetically in the text.

Proust's narrator formulated. Proust's example shows that revelation can be both an epistemic strategy and a rhetorical ploy. Musil's contemporary, the poet Rilke, was, and perhaps remains, the master of the rhetoric of revelation that offers, in language, epiphanies forever remaining beyond the power of language. This example was not lost on Musil, who, with his own ambiguity, yearned for a revelation of totality springing from a unified epistemology while distrusting any belief that truth might lie beyond the domain of rational inquiry.

In the creation of a younger alter ego who confronts proto-fascist irrational-ists like Reiting and Beineberger, Musil's distrust is shown in the way he illus-trates the epistemic enchantment worked by irrational revelation. Törless is also fascinated by revelation as though by the power of magic, for the other characters offer him various revelations, such as the seeming magic of gratu-itous evil or the discovery of desires he had never known. Törless is fascinated by Reiting and Beineberger's practice of sadism, by the certainty with which they find grotesque solutions to doubts about certainty. Their exercise of power over Basini seems to confirm the power of their knowledge. Raw cruelty thus briefly illuminates the darkness that surrounds Törless, a darkness emblematic of his fall into uncertainty. Törless's fall is Musil's central theme: Törless undergoes the revelation that the cosmos, humanity's house, has become dark with the advent of modern cosmology. In the course of the novel he learns that the illuminations and revelations promised by sadism or esoteric posturing are only sham attempts to bring light to the darkness pervading the world. Ironi-cally complicating his desire for light is the fact that science, the embodiment of the light of knowledge, has in fact largely been responsible for bringing darkness to the world.

Darkness is a leitmotif in many modernist works portraying a fall from knowledge into unbearable uncertainty. It stands behind the anguish one finds, for example, in the poetry of Musil's contemporary Trakl, a master of dark revelation. Trakl concludes his hymn to the night "Gesang zur Nacht" with a revelation that concisely describes Törless's experience:

Du bist in tiefer Mitternacht
Ein Unempfangner in süssem Schoss,
Und nie gewesen, wesenlos! (ll. 119–21)

[You in deep midnight
An unreceived/unconceived one in the sweet bosom
And never have been, are beingless!]

This outcry against the void parallels Törless's intuitive experience of darkness. Being refused reception in one's home—"being beingless"—is a modernist description of alienation when the light of knowledge fails to provide essential illumination. In this state the quester for light experiences the loss of all footing as night invades the world and the cosmos recedes. For Trakl, this experience was *Umnachtung,* the loss of the light of reason in the night of madness. Suicide was his response.

This same cosmic night impinges upon Törless's consciousness, and his experience recalls Trakl's in the way that Törless skirts insanity. Törless flees the world of adults, only to find isolation, his *Einsamkeit.* In isolation he undergoes a negative revelation that discloses a world plunged into darkness:

> This darkness was a world apart. It had descended upon the earth like a horde of black enemies, slaughtering or banishing human beings, or, whatever it did, blotting out all trace of them.... The world seemed to him like a sombre, empty house, and in his breast there was a sense of awe and horror, as though he must now search room after room ... until in one room the doors would suddenly slam behind him and before him and he would stand confronting the mistress of the black hordes herself. (24)

This negative epiphany does not take place in the confines of romantic darkness that Novalis described and which fascinated Musil. Törless's nightmare unfolds in the harsh light of day, when the brilliance of the sun impresses upon Törless the endlessness of dark space. The objective power of light, the rationalist symbol of knowledge, pursues Törless into a darkness in which he recognizes the cosmos as an abode harboring madness. Musil shows this revelation to be strongly correlated with Törless's need for science. Törless has a strong interest in mathematics and Kantian philosophy. He is a potential scientist who suddenly senses, under the sun, his cosmic exile.

Törless intuits that mathematical representation might offer some structure bringing order to the void. He tries to imagine the world described by mathematics. He desires a world of rational certainty, but mathematics is also a source of anguish when he is overpowered by the infinite's invading his world. Lying in the grass, Törless looks at the sky and sees it to be a blue, ineffably deep hole between the clouds. This hole has no end; it appears simply to be a movement moving always away, an unending movement toward the infinite—a previously empty concept whose capacity to engender anguish Törless suddenly discovers some three centuries after Pascal. The sky is a menace for the boy who desperately needs a closed world in which there are certainties, moral rules, and a means for knowing the inner world of others—in short, a bedrock certainty that allows one to negotiate the world with some security of judgment based on knowledge. Törless's perception could lead to insanity, for in the moment of his revelation Törless knows a "sort of madness that made him experience things, processes, people, all as something equivocal" (73). Turning his eyes toward the sky, the boy feels the sky's empty silence confronting his deep solitude: "Der Himmel schwieg"[8] [The heavens were silent], and, in this negative perception, Pascal's anguish is renewed in Törless's perception of the silence of the infinite. The silence of Pascal's empty spaces reverberates in its endless emptiness, and Törless knows that under the unmoved, silent arch of the sky he is alone, like a little living dot under this giant, transparent dead body, in a timeless, unspeaking world—"in einer zeitlosen schweigenden Welt" (67). He feels himself to be nothing more than a geometric point in the unfolding infinite.

Perhaps as much as any later modernist writer, Queneau or Borges included, Musil conceived the epistemic possibilities of literature with the sensibility of a mathematician. This sensibility is found in Törless's intuitive grasp of the infinite, with which Musil has updated Pascal by dramatizing that the modern schoolboy's perturbation is brought about by the very thought of the infinite. He portrays convincingly that a modern schoolboy, who has in effect mastered roughly the level of mathematics Pascal had developed, could react to his scientific education in existential terms. Musil gives Törless a mathematician's intuitive understanding of the infinite, for, to paraphrase Shaughan Lavine's argument in *Understanding the Infinite,* the intuitive grasp of the indefinitely large can serve as the basis for the idealization that leads to the concept of the infinite.[9] In Pascal's case, this intuition of the infinite led to a desperate need to combat mathematics with religion. However, Törless does not embrace religion. Momentarily, he finds a surrogate for religion in the temptations of a sadistic will to power. He allows himself to be cajoled by Reiting and Beineberg into joining in their torture of the hapless Basini. Quite directly, then, the experience of groundlessness, of what Trakl called his "unbeing," leads Törless to try the perverse surrogates for belief that the schoolboys invent.

His mind nearly unhinged by the illumination of infinite darkness, Törless

8. Musil, *Sämtliche Erzählungen,* 67.
9. Lavine, *Understanding the Infinite,* 7.

seeks advice from an adult. Most pointedly, he does not go to the school's priest for help, but rather to the mathematics teacher. He wants an explanation of the foundations of mathematics and, therewith, perhaps some idea about what he can know with certainty. His demand for an explanation is part of a quest for principles with which the boy can build a picture of the world. His desire for a picture suggests that Musil has in mind Mach's doctrine about the mimetic nature of propositions. Mach's notions are implicitly called into question in Musil's presentation of Törless's unsuccessful attempt to picture things with mathematical propositions. Törless wants these propositions to give him images of the world. Imaginary numbers, however, make Törless dizzy. He cannot picture how the calculation of things that do not exist in the real world—imaginary numbers—allow the description of things that do exist. For Törless, using imaginary numbers to picture the world is like using a bridge "where the piles are there only at the beginning and at the end, with none in the middle, and yet one crosses it just as surely and safely as if the whole of it were there" (85). Confronting his teacher with his demand for coherence, Törless summarily learns that mathematics is a world unto itself. He is shunted aside by the teacher with the feeble explanation that one must live in this world for a long time in order to feel what is necessary in it (90). The teacher tells the boy that he must, for the moment at least, believe in the *Denknotwendigkeiten,* the "necessities of thought," that the teacher offers him. As Beineberg later gloatingly points out to Törless, the teacher's response, essentially a demand that the boy believe on faith, is not much different from what the priest would have told him.

Törless's anguish reflects Musil's doubts as to whether science offers any understanding of the world and its moral complexities, those complexities that Pascal left to the *esprit de finesse.* But the doubts that Musil expresses about science are not intended to promote some superior wisdom, since the alternatives to science, in *Törless* and Musil's other works, are superstition, the ludicrous striving for knowledge beyond reason, and, finally, ideological aberrations. Science may be destructive of the light, but Musil leaves no doubt that contempt for scientific rationality is ultimately part of a nihilist mentality that, in promoting the irrational, ends up embracing absurdities at best and perversions at worst.

In *Törless* Musil dramatizes the irrationalist mentality most pointedly in Beineberg, whose contemptuous rejection of natural science seems almost naturally to accompany his enjoyment in physically torturing Basini, most notably when Beineberg wants to force Basini to overcome the laws of nature. Beineberg tries to hypnotize Basini and, aiming a loaded revolver at him, orders him to demonstrate the power of mind over matter. Beineberg feels no remorse in literally undertaking an "experiment" on the boy, since he sees in Basini an inferior being who has no significance in comparison with the great world soul that, embodied in Beineberg, justifies Beineberg's existence. Beineberg coldly expresses his contempt for this inferior being in declaring that, when a hiker encounters such a creature as Basini on the road, the hiker perforce must consider him to be as insignificant as a worm or a rock, and then decide with indifference whether to step over him or to crush him under foot. (Cruelty was never better portrayed than in the contempt expressed by Beineberg in the original German: "irgend etwas muss ja auch der bedeuten, aber sicher nur etwas so Unbestimmtes wie irgendein Wurm oder ein Stein am Wege, von dem wir nicht wissen, ob wir an ihm vorübergehen oder ihn zertreten sollen," 57.) Beineberg's language is, thirty years in advance, the language of the SS troops and the concentration camps, here linked to Beineberg's belief that one's superiority is as much a matter of gnosis as blood (and the Italian-sounding "Basini" perhaps implies a racial contrast between the two). To be sure, when placed in the context of the early twentieth century, Beineberg's attempt to use hypnosis to force Basini to defy the laws of nature is satirical, though the savage beating that Beineberg administers to Basini, when the body inevitably fails, cuts short the satire of modernist irrationality. The beating points out squarely that violence is readily sanctioned by irrational belief, especially when this belief encounters limits to its will to power.

Törless finally turns away in disgust from Reiting and Beineberg, those embodiments of a culture that would reject science in the name of irrational revelation and power. However, there is no triumph in this rejection. In his portrayal of Törless, Musil seems to endorse the Pascalian verdict that mathematical science, once the science of certainty, can do nothing to assuage the anguish of growing up in an infinite universe that seems to have lost its foundations. Unlike Pascal, however, and in spite of his malaise about the foundations of mathematics and of scientific propositions, Musil did not renounce his allegiance to mathematics as a model for thought. He saw no alternative to the rationalism that the scientific mind proposed as a goal. (One can argue that Pascal, having recourse to probability theory for his famous wager in favor of faith, found no alternative either.) Musil's allegiance meant that his attitude was constantly evolving. The rapidly evolving world of science, with its unceasing production of new theories, obliged the scientist in him to stay alert with unceasing questioning. That Musil was honing the ideas he expressed in his thesis is evident, a few years later, in his 1913 essay with the Pascalian title, "Der mathematischer Mensch" [The mathematical man].

In this essay published in the same year in which the first volume of Proust's *A la recherche du temps perdu* appeared, Musil writes that if it is clear that the foundations of mathematics are no longer a source of certainty, it is also clear that, in a world now given over to technology, the machines designed with the use of the calculus run quite well—whatever be the status of their foundations. Hence, according to Musil, the mathematically minded are burdened with an intellectual scandal: modern scientists live in a well-constructed house that has no foundations; they live in what Musil called an intellectual house standing in midair. By 1913, a year before the outbreak of World War I, Musil considered that this lack of foundations was no more a scandal than the fact that mathematical physicists in recent years had seemingly denied the existence of space and time—and for reasons that rose up as "palpably as an automobile, and became quite credible."[10] From these remarks one infers that by 1913 Musil found himself inclined to accept Einstein's 1905 theory of special relativity and the description of space-time that Minkowski derived from it in 1907—for reasons "quite credible."

Living with the relativity of temporal and spatial frameworks the mathematical *Mensch* was thus learning to live with paradoxes of reason derived from mathematical thinking. Or, as Musil went on to say in his essay, acceptance of modern science requires a certain rationalist courage: "After the enlightenment the rest of us lost courage. A minor failure was enough to turn us away from reason, and we allowed every barren enthusiast to inveigh against the intentions of a d'Alembert or a Diderot as mere rationalism. We beat the drums for feeling against intellect and forget that without intellect . . . feeling is as dense as a blockhead [dick wie ein Mops]."[11] From Musil's perspective, mathematicians offer an example of ethical courage in the face of postromantic irrationalism. This essay pinpoints a moment when the dilemmas, in which Musil remained caught up for the next thirty years, were taking definite shape in his mind. It shows a moment when Musil's thought crystallized around the problem of relating scientific precision, for which mathematics is the model, to the messy world that literature represents in all its fallen glory—a world that in

10. Musil, *Precision and Soul: Essays and Addresses,* 42.
11. Ibid., 42–43.

less glorious moments was soon to give Musil a first world war and then fascistic nationalisms to worry about. In brief, the central themes of *The Man without Qualities* were emerging as Musil meditated on the epistemological foundations of science.

The Man without Qualities

With the genesis of Musil's *The Man without Qualities* in mind, one can also see that Musil's perspective on epistemology remained Machean in spite of himself, and perhaps more so later in life than earlier. One diary entry in particular shows the ongoing nature of his inner debate with Mach whenever he thought about scientific problems. Shortly before publishing the first part of *Man without Qualities*, Musil read an essay published in 1929 by the founder of wave mechanics, the Austrian physicist Erwin Schrödinger. In this essay, entitled "Das Gesetz der Zufälle" [The law of chances, in the sense of probabilities], Schrödinger, an early critic of the Copenhagen interpretation of quantum mechanics, gave a statistical analysis of quantum phenomena. Reflecting on Schrödinger's interpretation of stochastic processes, Musil first writes in his diary that, in his interpretation of chance, Schrödinger was perhaps too "oriented" by the statistical nature of entropy.[12] Musil's reaction shows that his first impulse on reading a work on statistical laws was to react against statistical reasoning that presupposes the substantial reality of microevents underlying the processes it discerns. His instinct was to favor Mach against Boltzmann, whose work on the statistical nature of entropy first set out a model for Schrödinger's use of statistical reasoning.

However, the diary entry shows that Musil was also attracted to the physicist's idea that there are laws of chance underlying particle behavior. Musil finally recognizes that there are statistical laws describing invariant macrophenomena that derive, as it were, from totally aleatory microevents. A system in its totality will obey statistical laws even if there is no causal law describing the behavior of any individual component or particle in the system. In effect Musil was drawn to Boltzmann's way of describing the order of disorder in spite of Mach's hostility toward the reality one might ascribe to the microworld. Mach never accepted that one had the right to believe in the substantial

12. Musil, "Das Gesetz der Zufälle," in *Tagebücher*, rev. ed., ed. Frisé, 1:524.

"reality" of the invisible particles described by the atomic hypothesis. Boltzmann's work theorizes that what we take to be the necessary regularity of the
phenomenal world and its invariant processes are composed of individual
events and happenings for which no individual prediction is possible. This
concern with the laws of chance is reflected in Ulrich's musing on the relation
of microevents and statistical laws and regularities that characterize social and
historical processes. So if we may assume that, when he read Schrödinger, Musil
had already written the first chapters of *The Man without Qualities,* then the
diary entry points up that Musil had never stopped being concerned with the
way mathematics may describe invariant, though probabilistic processes that in
themselves are composed of chance events.

These concerns occupied Musil throughout the time he was writing *The
Man without Qualities,* which is to say, until the end of his harried life. In late
diary entries from around 1940, for example, Musil was still trying to reconcile
particle physics with Mach's distrust of the metaphysics that he found in invisible entities. In Notebook 30, Musil tries to puzzle out what one can mean by
"atom" in contemporary physics: "*Re: atom physics.* 'Atomon,' the indivisible, as
a conception belongs in the category of the 'thing' but, of its basic nature, contradicts it."[13] The atom as a thing has produced a contradiction, since its behavior as described by the formalisms does not coincide with what is usually
meant by the word. Musil also found a contradiction in applying the concept of
"thing" to particles like electrons, which can be described both as waves and as
particles by quantum theory. But Musil thought that Machean epistemology itself allows one to escape the paradox he saw in this dual description or in the
falsely unifying concept of "thing":

> It is not contradiction if, according to Mach, one does not demand any-
> thing more than some kind of unambiguous linkage. Of course, it will
> then only be with some reservation that one may talk of "projectiles" and
> such like. The difficulties emerge from the search (whether justified or
> not) for a model based on "things." Grasping, in conceptual terms, the
> smallest particles as "divisible" and "indivisible."[14]

Finding that pseudoproblems arise from the misuse of terms, Musil saw that
the idea of "thing" is problematic when used outside of the domain of the term's

13. Musil, *Tagebücher,* rev. ed., ed. Frisé, 1:788.
14. Ibid.

application. Thus a philosophical problem arises through using concepts without examining their implications. Analysis of concepts shows that one creates problems by misusing language, such as what happens when one applies the idea of a concrete particle, like a marble, to an electron, whose behavior can be alternatively described as a wave or a particle. Musil saw that the new quantum mechanics entails the description not of things understood as absolute solids, but of "a new relation of appearances"—"eine andere Bindung der Erscheinungen." His description is couched as a purely Machean formulation of how science functions in its alternative descriptions.

Musil's thought here is another example that Mach's lesson, for realists like Einstein and positivists like Heisenberg, was that abuse of concepts can mislead thought. Musil was part of a company of thinkers who found that the analysis of concepts was the beginning of epistemology. I stress this point because the Machean idea that knowledge describes a relation of appearances also describes the literary epistemology that, for more than ten years before this diary entry, Musil had begun developing in *The Man without Qualities*. For it seems that the older Musil was less certain that knowledge could, in fact, ever be more than an ordering of appearances. Mach remained a dominant influence on Musil's understanding of epistemology—even if, as Musil knew, Boltzmann was the victor in the actual practice of science.

The writer who wrote the essay on mathematical *Mensch* did not by accident, in *Der Mann ohne Eigenschaften,* create a hero, Ulrich, the man without qualities, who is a mathematician. Admittedly, he is a mathematician who solves few equations during the course of the novel. Musil's mathematician has taken a year's vacation from life, leaving his mathematical work on the periphery of the novel. Ulrich may solve few equations, but rarely in fiction, with the exception of Proust, does one encounter such finely developed meditations on epistemology, on the possibility of knowledge, and on the various regional sciences proposing less general knowledge than mathematics. Ulrich's meditations on epistemology endow the novel with a self-reflexive dimension in which the work indirectly takes itself for its own subject matter, which is to say, the novel itself is the project of unifying knowledge in one seamless grasp of ethics, sensibility, and science. The stakes are not small.

At the novel's beginning Ulrich has withdrawn from professional life. He creates at first a symbolic, ascetic emptiness around himself. This emptiness creates a space for meditation on epistemic issues as well as on social and psychological questions. Social issues dominate the first part of the novel when

Ulrich is receptive to all that goes on around him as he frequents the social spheres in which idle aristocrats and socialites look for some political or charitable action, such as the "Parallel Action," that will offer them the illusion of meaningful activity. Volume 2 of the novel, as translated, takes on an even more self-reflexive tone after Ulrich meets a "forgotten sister" with whom he shares his meditation on knowledge and on what knowledge might mean for his relation to the world and to her. The genres of the essay and of fictional narration often merge into what one might call the fictional dramatization of the work of the mind in meditation. The Swiss poet and Musil's translator into French, Philippe Jaccottet, describes this embodiment of mind in fiction admirably well:

> Ulrich and Agathe retire to their house, far from the world. . . . They have only one marvelous and dangerous concern: access to the "other state," that second species of reality about which Ulrich explains to his sister that one's premonition of it is anterior to every religion, that its light shines in all that's best about human life. . . . It is not only from the puppets of the Parallel Action that the brother and the sister detach themselves, and not only from European idealism, from the Vienna of 1913, from a sclerotic morality, a dying art, it is, progressively, from space and time. . . .[15]

Leaving space and time, Ulrich would, if he could, enter the realm of myth.

Ulrich does not reach this realm, and not simply because Musil's novel is not finished. Musil probably could not complete it because he could not create, for Ulrich, a definitive discourse uniting science and ethics, rationality and creativity, or knowledge and mystical belief. The model for a discourse incorporating all of these spheres, described at times in the novel itself, suggests that the work should ideally arrive at a point beyond science and ethics and re-create the unity of culture that Musil postulated as the only foundation for a discourse that could meet human needs. Such a mythic discourse would be scientific and ethical; in fine, it would be an epistemic *Gesamtkunstwerk* offering knowledge of a renewed culture and knowledge of how to achieve that knowledge. It would transcend the limitations of literature and science to create the embodied myth of total culture. Ulrich, and Musil with him, dreamed of a literary utopia.

Of course, Musil's failure to finish the novel is also because he died, after periods of poor health, in exile after the Nazis' triumph in Austria forced him to

---

15. Philippe Jaccottet, *Eléments d'un songe,* 24–25.

take refuge in Switzerland. The history of the novel's genesis and its publication also suggests that, as the political situation became impossible for him, Musil came, in a sense, to live the novel as he wrote it, which may mean that he did not want to make a final decision about where to go with it, or to conclude with something less than a utopian ending, any more than he wanted to make decisions that would limit the possibilities of life—both in and out of the novel, assuming he made such a distinction at the end. Life imposes its limits, of course, but as long as he was alive, Musil could and did experiment with imagined alternatives to the novel that became an alternative life in a barbarous world given over to the madness whose roots he had laid bare in his first novel, *Young Törless.*

Understanding the novel's publishing history helps make sense of the book the reader encounters today. Musil published Book One of the novel, containing Part One and Part Two, in 1930. Most recently translated as "A Sort of Introduction" and "Pseudoreality Prevails," they form a continuous sequence of 123 chapters. Musil followed these sections in 1933, the year Hitler took power, with the first 38 chapters of Book Two, or in the translation Part Three, "Into the Millennium (The Criminals)." Under pressure from his publisher, Musil was about to publish another 20 chapters in 1938, but, according to one version, he withdrew the galleys at the last moment to continue to work on them. Hitler's annexation of Austria that same year then meant that Musil had to continue to work on the novel with little hope of publication. Free from publishing pressure—and without any regular livelihood—he was also free to imagine various endings for the novel. At his death in 1942 he left manuscripts in various stages of completion, testifying at once to the grandiose schema he had in mind and to the very fact that his ongoing imaginative experimentation probably did not let him finish the novel.[16]

The sections of the novel that Musil himself published are sufficient to make of him one of the premier modernists, especially for the way that he deals with the role science plays in determining one's experience of the world. However, Musil's failure to find a conclusion to his novel also powerfully demonstrates

16. Adolf Frisé has offered a large selection of these manuscripts in his edition of *Der Mann ohne Eigenschaften* in the *Gesammelte Werke,* and Burton Pike has translated a selection "From the Posthumous Papers" in conclusion to Sophie Wilkins's admirable translation of the first parts of *The Man without Qualities.* References to Frisé's edition are hereafter cited parenthetically in the text as "MoE." References to Wilkins's translation are hereafter cited parenthetically in the text with volume numbers.

the limits of the modernist project of saving culture through literary discourse. In Musil's case this meant saving culture through the creation of a myth reconciling literature and science in a totalizing vision. The failure the novel illustrates is the failure to create a mythic discourse. Needless to say, this is a very modernist failure. Had Musil succeeded, he would have created a discourse overcoming the binary oppositions he saw undergirding modernity. Within the novel itself Ulrich reflects upon the various forms these oppositions take and attempts to elaborate an epistemological position that transcends the two Pascalian epistemologies that he finds at work in most thinking. Or, if one prefers, Ulrich wants to undo the oppositions and conflicting tensions underlying the belief in two cultures.

Ulrich's constant recourse to irony underscores the difficulty of the task. The rhetorical stance created by the play of irony in the work is complex, for at times one feels that Ulrich and the narrator are one in their viewpoint. At other times one feels that Ulrich, the ironist, exists at some distance from the narrator and, by implication, from Musil. The reader is constantly obliged to evaluate the stance of the speaking voice, of the indirect narration, and of the implied author. Unifying this rhetorical play is the presence of a mathematical thinker who never ceased living, as an alienation, the polarities imposed by such oppositions as the geometric mind and the intuitive soul. The fictional mathematician, Ulrich, the man without qualities, comes undoubtedly closer than his ironist creator to transforming his life into lived myth. But how much closer is an interpretive question.

In the briefest synopsis of the now more than seventeen hundred pages available in translation, one can say that the novel narrates, after Ulrich's retirement from the life of science in August 1913, his sexual imbroglios, his involvement in absurd civic activity, and finally his meditations on transforming epistemology. He becomes part of the Parallel Action, a movement looking to justify its existence by doing something for Austria. Its participants finally propose to celebrate, in 1918, the forthcoming seventieth jubilee of the Austrian Kaiser. They do this in part to outdo the German Kaiser's proposed celebration of the thirtieth year of his reign during the same year, that fated 1918 that, in retrospect, was to offer neither Kaiser anything to celebrate. After Musil's ironic and often satirical depiction of a society unknowingly, but tenaciously, heading for its own demise, the novel then focuses on Ulrich's relation to his sister, through which, in some unfinished versions of the work, they appear to have achieved a mystical unity. In some completed texts and in various drafts, Musil suggests that Ulrich's relation to Agathe, his other half, his Siamese twin as it were, might result in a union not unlike that of Isis with Osiris. These drafts suggest that Ulrich would have found a love to overcome his dismemberment—his alienation by modern culture. To achieve this impossible union he needs to flee to a world beyond conventional morality and knowledge (MoE, 905). And there, like the androgyne, Ulrich might find his double and be restored with his other half, such as Plato, our first mathematician metaphysician, once described with the myth of reunion (MoE, 963).

In the introduction to his translation of the posthumous parts of the novel, Burton Pike says that Ulrich and Agathe would have somehow rejoined the world after the failure of their attempt to achieve *unio mystica*.[17] It is not clear why Pike thinks that they would have failed, at least in Musil's imagination, though the question must remain open. In any case their return to the world would be a necessity if their mythic union were to propose an example of unity to the world of alienation against which the mythic union should stand out in triumph. Musil himself seems to have been uncertain about what he wanted to achieve by playing with incest. It is noteworthy that after having published part of the novel, Musil looked for an interpretive framework to justify to himself his imaginative flights. He wrote in his diary the following lines comparing the novel to a poem he had written:

> Reminded of the Isis-Osiris poem. It contains the novel in 'nucleo.' A charge of perversity has been leveled against the novel. Counter this as follows: the archaic and the schizophrenic find convergent expression in art, yet, in spite of this, are totally different from one another. In just the same way, the feelings of brother and sister for each other may be perverse, or may be myth.[18]

Like Joyce, who explicitly used the Greek myth of Ulysses, much like Proust, who used the myth of the Fall and redemption in time, much like dozens of modernists, in fact, Musil shows here that he had become caught up by the siren song of myth as a possible way of achieving his dream of a unified discourse. But Musil, who had studied psychology, knew that he was also attracted by psychopathology, which, in its modernist forms, uses literature as models for hermeneutics. He was attracted by the type of psychological discourse that can

17. Musil, *The Man without Qualities,* ed. Pike, trans. Sophie Wilkins. Pike's commentary is from p. xii, found in the middle of vol. 2 of the translation.

18. Musil, *Diaries, 1899–1941,* entry from years 1930 to 1938, 423.

find in overt psychopathology the mythic foundations of everyday behavior. Freud and Jung are obvious examples in this regard, and Freud's universalizing of the child's desire for incest sets out an obvious parallel. Musil's alluding in the diary to the psychoanalytic theory that schizophrenia is a regression to a primitive or archaic stage in human development—to a putative mythic stage— is an ingenuous way to transform incest into a foundational myth. But it is not very convincing, and one may doubt, as Musil's failure to finish the novel shows, that he was very convinced himself that incest could represent more than a defiance of conventional morality.

The first two books of *The Man without Qualities* demonstrate that Musil initially had a more definite idea about what he wanted to accomplish. Clearly, he wanted to respond to the epistemological challenge of Nietzsche and Mach, as well as to the triumph of the new physics that Musil had puzzled over in his essay "The Mathematical Man." He wanted to do this by relating scientific epistemology to the historical world of relentless processes that may or may not have an explanation. The novel begins by emphasizing its historical context, since the man without qualities picks a not indifferent date for his year's vacation from life: a day in August 1913. With great irony the novel begins with a scientific description of that day: a weather report. Musil points up that science allows a precise description of a most typical of days. However, this typical day is one that is moving ever closer to the fated August day in the following year when all of Europe would blow up and a world war would ensue that would put an end to the Austrian empire. The novel thus begins with a demonstration of science's purchase on everyday life and with an interrogation of that science. It asks, What does the accumulation of mathematical descriptions about a day's ordinary processes show about that day in the course of human events? With this question, in effect with this ironic demonstration of the questions at the heart of knowledge, the counting of days implicitly begins. However, this infinitely expandable novel moves like an asymptote toward that fated summer day in 1914. Coming ever closer, the novel never reaches the murderous day about which thousands of thinkers and ordinary mortals have later asked, What was its cause? Rather, the novel demonstrates that time is filled with innumerable events that might be linked in the causal chain or chains that, in the novel, center upon Ulrich's finding an occupation, *in vacuo,* working to plan the jubilee of the Emperor who would have no empire in 1918.

Time seems to expand with the novel's progression. Ulrich begins to ruminate upon love and epistemology and, as Jaccottet observed, to remove himself from time. However, whatever the mythic dimension that starts to take shape in the novel, the reader is aware that reversed historical perspectives coexist throughout the book. Ulrich looks to a future that will not exist, toward 1918 and its celebrating Kaisers, whereas the novel's implied author and the reader look back on a past unfolding toward catastrophes, including the destruction of that empire that Musil ridicules even as he recognizes its quaint attraction. Musil and his narrator entertain the proposition that the laws of social evolution are at work in 1913, even if nobody can know them—until history reveals them as those inevitable developments that, in 1913, were produced by trillions of free choices. The double perspective produces an epistemological cramp. Historical events are there, not to be denied, but the causal chains that lead to them are as elusive as the meaning of the weather.

Intellectual issues like these are filtered through Ulrich's consciousness. The narrator reports on Ulrich's consciousness, but he leaves it to the reader to ask what this character represents. Ulrich is rich enough not to work. He has been a successful mathematician and, earlier in his life, had dabbled in poetry. From the outset the reader suspects that some basic binary oppositions are lurking in this character. Yet, Ulrich himself maintains that he is a man without qualities. To understand what the poet-mathematician means by "quality," I suggest that Musil's definition of the term in his thesis offers insight. In the thesis qualities—or those *Eigenschaften* that Ulrich does not have—are precisely those properties that would accrue to a centered concept that defines a thing in itself. Musil argues that things have qualities in the sense of nonrelativistic properties. Thus against Mach, the young Musil maintains that real properties are *not* relative notions defined by the measurements of functions:

> It is clear that the reaction that one grasps under the designation "having the mass X" is more closely connected with a body in which it is constantly found than with the comparative bodies that are present in an arbitrary way, but not in an individual example, so that there is found in experience, to which Mach appeals, at least the beginning for the formation of a concept of property [*Eigenschafts-begriff*].[19]

A property or quality—an *Eigenschaft*—in Musil's sense is an invariant trait, part of a recurrent constellation, that can be defined in itself as a positive trait that needs no other contrasting trait for definition. Mach's relativism is undercut

19. Musil, *Beitrag zur Beurteilung der Lehren Machs,* 64. My translation.

if Musil can demonstrate that qualities exist that are not necessarily defined in relation to something else. A recurrent property in this sense would offer access to the invariance that Musil wants to be the ultimate criterion or arbiter of knowledge.

However, this kind of *Eigenschaft* is precisely what Ulrich says he lacks: he can find in himself no invariant trait, definable in itself, that would vouchsafe him the reality of a self that is confident about what it knows. In this sense Ulrich is a grown-up Törless who knows that his demand for something knowable in itself with certainty is contrary to the received epistemic notions of his era. He is well aware that he lives at a time when, for example, fellow mathematician Poincaré said that one can only know the relations between things, not things in themselves. In spite of himself, but living with his time, Ulrich seems obliged to be a Machean positivist, for his reason does not allow him to reject the dominant epistemic conventions of his cultural matrix. Herein lies the importance of irony. Through irony he can disengage himself from these conventions. With a self-awareness born of critical irony, Ulrich allows himself to play various roles: a neo-Machean epistemologist, a mystical quester, and, at times, a rather Nietzschean immoralist. To have no qualities means that Ulrich can try out many properties. In Ulrich, Musil has created an intellectual who wants to test the logical consistency of the basic epistemic axioms undergirding his cultural matrix—especially received polarities such as feeling and reason, precision and intuition, and the other antinomies that seem to block thinking when one starts to think like a mathematician arguing against a poet, or vice versa. In his role as mathematician and critic, Ulrich finally calls to mind, quite intentionally, a modernist Pascal: he does this through his dialectical dialogues with himself, but also in sotto voce anguish about his doubts, when he is drawn to one pole and then to another, embodying the perpetual crisis produced by the need for precision and feeling, the basis for the two epistemologies Ulrich examines.

There is great intellectual pleasure found in Ulrich's and the narrator's constant irony, satire, and wit alternately questioning and affirming the premises of post-Enlightenment culture. On the one hand, Musil's constant satire of deviance from rationalist axioms underscores the intellectual demands that someone—the narrator or Ulrich—places upon the reader and upon himself. On the other hand, the rationalist in the novel—alternatively the narrator or Ulrich—is engaged in a stringent critique of the limits of reason. This critique results in a dynamic struggle between what Musil often called *ratio* and *Mystik,* or the reason and mysticism at the center of Ulrich's life. (And which

Musil saw at the center of his own life: he notably begins his diaries with the statement, "Rationality and mysticism, these are the poles of the times.")[20] Especially in Book One of the novel Musil satirically points out the lack of commensurability between precise thinking and thinking that deals with values and judgments—which restates for modernity the conflict that Pascal saw between the *esprit de géométrie* and the *esprit de finesse*.

Perhaps the most pointed example is the case of the criminal Moosbrugger, a socially marginal character who has senselessly murdered a prostitute. This borderline psychopath captures the attention of Ulrich's friend Clarissa, who wants to make a cause célèbre of the case because, if the legal authorities find the man sane, they will also execute him. In her own growing madness Clarissa sees a Nietzschean adventurer in this inarticulate man whose probable insanity makes him an object of scientific investigation and legal interpretation. Scientific thinking and legal thinking clash as doctors and lawyers argue about Moosbrugger's putative insanity. The medical doctors think he is insane. However, "their reluctance as scientists to make exaggerated claims on the basis of the available evidence prevented them from challenging the verdict of the lawyers" (1:149). On the basis of legal rhetoric rather than any scientific criteria, the woman-hating Moosbrugger is declared responsible for his actions and thus guilty of murder: "The trial led Ulrich to reflect that the division between psychiatrists and lawyers could be seen as merely one instance of the widespread division in daily life between, on the one hand, scientists and other workers whose activities were based on facts and empirical evidence, and on the other, philosophers, lawyers and writers, whose professional sphere was that of values" (1:149). In the case of the petty criminal momentarily turned psychopath, the scientists abdicate to the authority of lawyers, a group that regards values as its professional domain (1:149). This abdication can be construed as a failure of knowledge, or science, that Ulrich finds emblematic of society's failure to attempt to base action on knowledge. Ulrich's critical mind can only puzzle about what creates or justifies the schism between knowing, judging, and finally acting.

Musil's questioning critique permeates the novel, since nearly every character is involved in questions relating knowledge and action. The fact that Ulrich's

---

20. For this aspect of Musil's work I have found useful Wolfdietrich Rasch, "Der Mann ohn Eigenschaften," in Renate von Heydebrand, ed., *Robert Musil;* also, Elisabeth Albertsen, *Ratio und "Mystique" im Werk Robert Musils,* and Frederick G. Peters, *Robert Musil, Master of the Hovering Life.*

father has been a legal scholar allows an acerbic portrayal of what makes up a career in the domain of judging. His father has made a judicial career of defining responsibility in harsh terms, mainly in endless arguments against other legal scholars, much of which seems to have little to do with knowledge of what responsibility is. The endless ratiocinations that go into legal disputes contrast with the simple necessity of bearing the responsibility for making judgments. Ulrich must make judgments, for example, about the Nietzschean Clarissa, who, in her madness (and disappointment with her nongenius husband), not only wants to save Moosbrugger, but to produce an *Ubermensch* by having a superman baby by Ulrich. Decision-making is the stuff of daily life, but the knowledge needed for decisions often is simply lacking or derived from irrelevant sources. In Moosbrugger's case, most pointedly, Ulrich wonders how anyone can find scientific knowledge that allows one to decide that somebody, even a marginal being like Moosbrugger, should be legally murdered.

Decision-making taken in the aggregate goes to make up history. Ulrich intuitively feels that all events are interrelated in some sense, in the infinite complications of individual acts and judgments that meld into social wholes that, in their temporal unfolding, are called history. In his debates with himself, and then with his sister, about how one might have knowledge of these infinite complications, Ulrich considers a series of epistemological polarities. For example, a key polarity, which underlies the crisis that vacationer Ulrich lives in the spring of 1914, is the fundamental problem of knowing the dichotomy created when one looks at society either as a historical totality or as a series of discrete individual facts, such as automobile accidents, muggings, and adulterous love affairs, which taken together make up the whole. The totality might be envisaged as that Hegelian realm of unfolding history and society that stands opposed to the individual *Tatsache,* or the elementary unit of scientific discourse called the empirical fact. Or, alternatively, the social whole can be considered as the realm of statistical necessity in which one can know with near certainty the laws of the total collectivity—how many traffic deaths, robberies, and adulteries will occur in Austria each year—and not know at all what will befall the individual Austrian on an given day:

> Thus there are really two kinds of outlook, which not only conflict with each other but, which is worse, usually coexist side by side in total non-communication except to assure each other that they are both needed, each in its place. The one is satisfied to be precise and stick to the facts, while

the other is not, but always looks at the whole picture and derives its insights from so-called great and eternal truths. The first achieves success, the other scope and prestige. (1:268)

The narrator—or is it Ulrich?—seems to oppose Hegelian historicism to Machean empiricism in his attempt to decide how one might have knowledge of society. Ulrich sees that prestige accrues to the man of action who can manipulate people with an eye on the totality—such as the industrialist-cum-intellectual Arnheim, whom Ulrich must deal with at the Parallel Action. By contrast, success can be defined as the pragmatic success of the scientist dealing with the precise mathematical relations—the Einstein or Planck who defines the coordinates describing physical reality. Prestige notwithstanding, Musil shows that the businessman, pretending to know the totality in its eternal truth, is letting Europe drift toward World War I.

In his study of Musil and probability theory, the philosopher Jacques Bouveresse asserts that Musil opposed Hegel and "his successors" in almost every respect.[21] This is true, but should be nuanced. However much the novel condemns the delusions of those who believe they understand the social totality, Musil also suggests that one must attempt to have some view of the developing totality if one is to make informed judgments about social goals. One must attempt to understand the laws that might be shaping the direction of history. As Bouveresse points out in his rich study of Musil's "l'homme probable," the rational thinker, the "man of probability," must attempt to understand the totality in scientific terms, if it is to be understood at all. In this sense, Ulrich muses on mathematical models when he wonders, for example, if one can reconcile knowledge of the iron laws of statistics with the aleatory activities of the billion individuals whose caprices in the aggregate can be shown to obey those laws. Ulrich wonders if the problem is not unlike the problem of prediction in kinetics or particle physics. For instance, one can predict with near certainty the rate of decay of an element brought about by radioactivity, without knowing which specific atom will give up a particle; analogously, statistical laws allow the prediction of how many people will be run over on the streets of Vienna each year—and the novel duly documents a traffic accident—but these laws are incapable of predicting who is the unfortunate burgher whose life will be expended in confirmation of the laws' power. Meditating on law, society,

21. Bouveresse, *L'Homme probable*, 256.

and history in the first part of the novel, Ulrich is, then, a mathematician who wonders if there could be any application of Boltzmann's statistical physics to social processes—and he is perplexed by the fact that the invariant statistical laws of social processes have no immediate import for any individual.

Finding himself sharing the common ignorance of social development, but aware of his lack of knowledge, Ulrich dreams of overcoming ignorance in a utopia of exactitude where science and action are joined. This conjoining would allow him to reinvent morality, since morality demands the difficult knowledge of what is possible as well as what should be. This utopian melding, presupposing a single epistemology, would require that Ulrich know precise facts that somehow add up to a meaningful unity or totality; but the chaos of daily experience makes him distrust the idea that a totality has any meaning. As the novel unfolds, Ulrich reflects increasingly upon his utopian conjoining of knowledge and action in a meditation on the opposition between the need to understand the totality and the exigencies of precision or exactitude. (And the historical context in which Musil found himself facing fascism made this need for knowledge of the direction of history at once all the more imperative and seemingly impossible.) Ulrich narrates in an attempt to know the *Ganzheit,* the putative totality, which presupposes a consciousness capacious enough to grasp the totality necessary for judgment. This yearning to seize the imbrication of all events finally means that any event or idea that can pass the muster of plausibility can go into the novel: Ulrich's meditations, sexual affairs, conversations, writings on psychology, as well as his "essays" about the epistemological split between exactitude and totality. The novel ceases to be a narrative to become something like an encyclopedia or a series of essays. Musil conceived of the essay in fact as a genre offering an epistemological blending of science and poetry, and the novel comes at times to resemble a renarrated essay. But Ulrich's project demands that, even within the essay form, there must be narrated events that can represent, as so many synecdoches, the totality, since limited human perception dictates that the totality can only be grasped as an unfolding of disparate, single events. Lacking the totality, necessarily as it were, the anti-Hegelian narrator can only theorize that, from these musings may emerge the desired total picture, though the Machean epistemologist lurking in Musil's narrator, as well as in Ulrich, suspects that all the little mimetic pictures in the world will never add up to any totality. Totality may be one more myth, given a patina of plausibility by the success of scientific method in making statistical predications; but it is a myth used by various ideologues in, and out of, the novel to bolster their private ambitions and obsessions. As such, it is a myth to be reckoned with.

Hyper-conscious of the epistemological polarities—or antimonies, if one prefers—that undermine his attempt to know what history, morality, or simply good judgment might be, Ulrich is obliged to think self-reflexively about the means for representation that he, the mathematician-poet, has at his disposition. If there is to be a commonality allowing a unified knowledge, one uniting judging and knowing, the whole and the pictured part, the commonality must spring from an understanding of the common quest for representation that seemingly underlies all cultural activity. Ulrich is again rather Machean in his anthropology of knowledge, for he says, with a Machean turn of phrase, that knowledge is based on modeling or representation, as one can variously translate *Darstellung*. The split between scientific and literary modes of knowing derives from the polarity between the type of propositions that the mind uses in modeling, or, as Ulrich puts it, from the type of language used for *Darstellung*. In a moment of insight about language and representation, Ulrich reflects on what he calls "The Two Trees of Life and a Proposal to Establish a General Secretariat for Precision and Soul" (in Part Two, chapter 116). Such a secretariat would, Ulrich imagines, overcome the opposition of science and values by reconciling propositions that represent two opposing modes of representation. These modes are, on the one hand, the representation achieved by figurative language and, on the other hand, the representation offered by unequivocal language, or that of *Eindeutigkeit*. In this description of art and science, then, the language of univocal science and precise truth is set against *das Gleichnis,* fictive representations and their figural truths.

In imagining his secretariat to reconcile these opposing modes of representation, Ulrich finds that his own life has taken the shape of two opposing trees representing the two basic life impulses that animate these modes of knowledge. Ulrich perceives, before meeting his sister, that in the opposition of these fundamental impulses lie the grounds for his failure to find a unity to his own life:

> Now, as he realized that this failure to achieve integration had lately been apparent to him in what he called the strained relationship between literature and reality, metaphor and truth, it flashed on Ulrich how much more all this signified than any random insight that turned up in one of those meandering conversations.... These two basic strategies, the figurative and the unequivocal, have been distinguishable ever since the beginnings

of humanity. Single-mindedness is the law of all waking thought and action, as much present in a compelling logical conclusion as in the mind of
the blackmailer who enforces his will on his victim.... Metaphor, by contrast, is like the image that fused several meanings in a dream; it is the
gliding logic of the soul, corresponding to the way things relate to each
other in the intuitions of art and religion. (1:647)

Ulrich is committed to each way of representation, though he is highly critical
of the abuses of each. Both the pedantic scientist and the misty-eyed mystic are
objects of his scorn; indeed, the narrator attributes to Ulrich contempt for those
who are less than rigorous: "He despised those who could not follow Nietzsche's dictum to 'let the soul starve for the truth's sake,' those who turn back,
the fainthearted, the softheaded who comfort their souls with spiritual nonsense and feed it—because reason allegedly gives it stones instead of bread—
on religious, metaphysical and fictitious pap, like rolls soaked in milk" (1:43).
And the novel duly satirizes several characters needing metaphysical and fictitious pap, those who cannot live with the Spartan demands for truth made by
Mach, not to mention Nietzsche.

    However, Ulrich is hardly offered as a contrasting model of rectitude. In
spite of his passionate convictions in Parts One and Two the man without qualities often seems to be little more than a passive observer who rather helplessly
finds that his life "demonstrated the presence of the two fundamental spheres
of human existence in their separateness and in their way of working against
each other" (1:648). Undermined from within, a center without properties,
Ulrich gives himself over later in the novel to a thought experiment about a
mystical union with his sister. Thought experiments are frequent in later modernist fiction, and Ulrich's may seem like a prototype: in his case contemplating
incest is like combining, in the imagination, unknown chemicals and seeing
what might ensue. To be sure, his thought experiment also underscores Ulrich's
yearning for a culture wherein his nascent mysticism would find a unity lacking in modern culture. Through his character's thought experiment, Musil himself seems to have wanted to test the basic axioms of Western culture. The experiment, had Musil ever worked it out to a single coherent conclusion, might
have obliged the reader to entertain some rather radical results: to wit, does it
follow axiomatically that the restoration of the unity of culture entails undoing
such basic conventions as the prohibition of incest? Musil goes beyond his contemporaries, the French surrealists, in this imaginative experimentation; and,
as I suggested earlier, Musil's Viennese dreams of unity also resemble a positive

version of Freud's negative mythical vision of everyman's quest for unity through incest. Alas, Freud decreed no return to unity and bequeathed universal alienation with the Oedipal complex. Unlike Freud and more like the utopian surrealists, Musil was apparently drawn to the idea that transcendence might involve rewriting eros. This is not an unfamiliar leitmotif in the modernist utopian imagination, from Rimbaud and Breton through Marcuse and Laing.

Ulrich's wistful dreams of conjoining science and mystical experience is illuminated by Musil's reaction to Mach's description of the limits that science imposes upon representation. Mach laid down strict limits as to what one can say with authority, limits even more severe than those imposed by the Kantian empiricism that romanticism contested with its exaltation of feeling, dream, and madness. (Musil was very interested in romantics like Novalis for this reason.) But by imposing reductive epistemological limits, Mach implicitly suggested, like Kant before him, that much of great human interest lay beyond these limits. Fellow Viennese philosopher Wittgenstein also arrived at this conclusion in meditating on the limits of the sayable, for Wittgenstein came to believe that, if the logical positivists were in some sense right, then ethics and transcendental questions were better addressed by, say, a Tolstoy, whose fictional work could show these realms even if it is not possible to formulate epistemic propositions about them. In this sense Wittgenstein's positivism leads to mysticism. Ulrich's case is again analogous to Wittgenstein's. Musil's novel transformed itself, as he lived it, into the dream of demonstrating mythically an a-theistic mysticism, with the emphasis placed on "showing" this mysticism in ways that get beyond the limits of the empirical proposition. This is not to say that Ulrich ever overcomes the constraints of reason; one cannot even say that Ulrich wants to overcome them. Reason constrains knowledge in a positive sense, and Ulrich is as much an opponent of skepticism and irrationality as he is a sometime partisan of mysticism. Moreover, one cannot even imagine that Ulrich could ever, like Pascal, use probability theory to suggest that the irrational might be a good bet. Ulrich wants to bet on a mystical union that could be shown, could be experienced, and could be communicated. This is not a wager one is likely to win.

Some of the richest development of Ulrich's thought unfolds in the later chapters, in "From the Posthumous Papers" of *Man without Qualities*. In Ulrich's meditations and his conversations with his sister Agathe, Musil develops some of his most pertinent ideas for literary epistemology. In the chapter "Genialität als Frage" [Genius as a problem] Ulrich recognizes the underdetermination of all phenomena, but he must also entertain Musil's unflagging belief that it must be possible in some sense to know an immanent reality in phenomena. Mach remains the unnamed interlocutor when Ulrich, meditating on Hume's skepticism, considers Hume's favored example for dismissing causality: "For it was not reluctantly that one reproached empiricism, which was all too simpleminded and confined to its rules, that according to it the sun rises in the east and sets in the west for no other reason than that up till now it always has. And were he to betray this to his sister and ask her what she thought of it, she would probably answer ... that the sun might one day do it differently" (2:1352) Agathe repeats Hume without knowing who he is, and so Ulrich smiles in recognition that skeptical empiricism is a natural inclination of youth, desirous of discovering all on its own. But he is less cheerful when he recognizes the ethical dangers that skepticism can bring: "But from the assertion that awaiting the rising of the sun in the east every day merely has the security of a habit, it is only a step to asserting that all human knowledge is felt only subjectively and at a particular time, or is indeed the presumption of a class or race, all of which has gradually become evident in European intellectual history" (2:1352). These lines anticipate postmodern relativism. Of course, Musil was writing them after Hitler had taken power, with a double perspective deriving at once from his critique of positivism and his experience of the Nazi science that had replaced rationalism with "knowledge" born of its racist biology and nationalist myths. Ulrich's remarks reflect a recognition that relativist skepticism seems to corroborate Nazi science. In the context it is clear that Ulrich's remarks reflect Musil's own wonder about what criteria for truth might allow relativism to say something against fascist science. Musil had directly seen that, unlike the more genteel relativists, the Nazis, having defined truth by its belonging to "a class or race," were willing to prove their superior knowledge with a bullet.

Within the context of the novel, Ulrich is meditating on European culture from a point that is constantly nearing the catastrophe of August 1914. He is also reflecting on the empiricist thinker that modern liberal culture has produced. This thinker is the type of successful pragmatist—or opportunist—that Ulrich cannot abide:

> This is the type of the empirical man ... who has become such a familiar open question, the person who knows how to make from a hundred of his own experiences a thousand new ones, which, however, always remain

within the same circle of experience, and who has by this means created the gigantic, profitable-in-appearance monotony of the technical age. Empiricism as a philosophy might be taken as the philosophical children's disease of this type of person. (2:1352)

Ulrich intends to indict Europe's technologically proficient exploitation of the science that is incapable of creating a new culture. The Marxist will undoubtedly see in Ulrich's indictment a description of the closed logic of capitalism and its use of science in the creation of need. The Heideggarian would recognize the conditions in which science as part of metaphysics has imposed its domination upon the globe. These judgments may find a complement in the idea that, with his description of the closed system of the technological age, Ulrich also suggests, in the metaphor of a child's disease, the need for growth, for maturity, and for a richer culture than one founded simply on the unending renewal of needs and their elementary satisfaction through ever-larger doses of technology. Empiricism is not so much condemned here as is its application by a type of entrepreneur, the empirical man, the dominant type of the liberal era in which the closed logic of capitalist expansion is virtually unquestioned, even by socialist and fascist regimes.

In these later chapters the image of a closed circle describes society, but it also describes the dilemma of Ulrich's attempt to break out of the epistemic limits that circumscribe him. Ulrich and the narrator turn in an epistemological circle, alternately affirming and doubting. Most of the time they are unable to overcome their ironic doubts about whether it is possible to affirm anything beyond the most limited empirical affirmations—the dilemma of positivism—though at other times they seem committed to at least the possibility that one can rationally describe the world, its development in history, and perhaps a preferable alternative. Ulrich's commitment to this project is accompanied by a belief that adequate representation has to be found to bridge the gap between two epistemologies, which is to say, a kind of projective faith undergirds his belief in alternatives. Perhaps the best example of Ulrich's intellectual acrobatics is found in the posthumously published chapter "Das Sternbild der Geschwister Oder die Ungetrennten und Nichvereinten"—a paradox translated as "The constellation of brother and sister; or, the unseparated and not united." In this chapter Ulrich discusses love with his sister Agathe, and, in so doing, he tries to define the nature of the symbolic representation that he envisages as the basis for knowledge of the totality. Ulrich is in an unusually affirmative mood with his sister when he stresses the commonality of mathematics and poetry, of novels and physics, in this chapter whose title underscores his thirst for unity in difference, or the unseparated and not united. Agathe herself offers an example of unity in difference, for love of the sister is love of self, which is to say, of the double that is different and the same. So love resembles, from this perspective, a type of representation—as Ulrich suggests in narrating to Agathe a tale like that of Martin Guerre, in which a man falsely represents himself to a woman as her husband returning from years at war. The man is accepted by the wife as the authentic husband, and he is at once the same—a husband—and differ-ent. According to Ulrich, this is the nature of every sign or symbol: it "is" what it represents while remaining different from what it signifies. Thus conceived, representation is a utopian act that erases differences while maintaining them, whether in love's artifices or in the calculations of a mathematician.

The epistemologist may cavil at this view of symbols, but Ulrich uses this view of identity within difference to assert that, by the very nature of represen-tation, all representation is underdetermined, though not arbitrary. Ulrich ex-plains this idea to Agathe in the following way:

> Do you recall what I said about the intellectual portrayal of nature, of its being an image without similarity? There are many quite different ways in which anything can be apprehended as the exact image of something else, but everything that occurs in this image, or results from it, must in just this one specific view always be a depiction of what investigating the original image demonstrates. (2:1402)

The possible multiplicity of representations derives logically from the episte-mological axiom that phenomena are underdetermined: the only epistemic de-mand one can make of a representation is that, in the "quite different ways" that things are apprehended, one must be able to demonstrate the commonality of an "original image." Invariance is found in an original image, which may allow the claim that, thus defined, reality exists and can be known. But knowl-edge is mimetic, thus always privileging a specific view or representation. Somewhat as in Mach and young Wittgenstein, vision is privileged in Ulrich's later meditations, though in what Ulrich calls an "unsensory notion of image-ability" (2:1402). Personally, I am slow to cavil at this point, however much I distrust any epistemological position privileging the visual. Ulrich has a powerful argument. His view allows for the commonsense recognition that art and literature may provide as many representations as there are artists and writers; at the same time this view recognizes an underlying invariance of what is represented through the agent of representation, be it through mathematics, poetry, or painting. With this Ulrich hopes that underdetermination and a near mystical belief in the real are about to be reconciled.

With this view of sameness in multiplicity Ulrich goes on to suggest how to overcome the opposition between modes of knowledge. He adumbrates a theory of panrepresentation:

> In this sense a mathematical formula can be the image of a natural process, just as much as a portrayal established by external sensory similarity. A theory can in its consequences accord with reality, and the effects of reality with theory. The cylinder in a music box is the portrayal of a way of singing, and an action [*Handlung*, "action" or "plot"] portrays a fluctuating feeling. In mathematics, where for the unsullied progression of thought one would most like to trust only what can be counted off on one's fingers, one usually speaks only of the precision of coordinates, which has to be possible point for point. But fundamentally, everything can also be regarded as a portrayal that is called correspondence, representability for some purpose, equal value and exchangeability, or equality in respect to something, or undifferentiability, or mutual appropriateness according to some kind of standard. (2:1402–3)

The undifferentiability that representation differentiates is the name Ulrich would give to his own mythic creation of love. In this naming lies the center of Ulrich's final temptation, vision, dream, or whatever one may call his desire to make all representations finally meld in unity. It is not easy to pin one label on his attempt to abolish or sublimate through myth the two Pascalian epistemologies.

From Ulrich's description of the multiple forms of representation it would be plausible to infer that two epistemologies are a myth: knowledge is multiple, obeying no fixed typologies, and accountable only to that which it represents. Ulrich's theory of representation also implies that modernity trades on the idea that anything can represent anything else. Joyce perhaps better than Musil knew how to organize this possibility, specifically in *Ulysses'* catalog of everything in Dublin as so many moments in universal myth, not to mention the revels of panrepresentation of *Finnegans Wake*. However, unlike Joyce, Musil distrusted this impulse to allow anything to represent everything else, and Ulrich's opening tirades about pop culture in the novel show that he is irritated by the idea that a race horse or a boxer can symbolize anything other than themselves. Ulrich comes only late in the novel to his theory of panrepresentation, and, throughout much of the novel, Musil's distrust of the heterogeneity of modeling allowed by underdeterminism reveals itself in an expressed dislike of the idea that representation is such a fluctuating, when not fickle, instrument. This distrust comes out pointedly in the portrayal of the capitalist intellectual Arnheim, who knows that, in economics, exchange values turn on representations that allow for all types of metamorphoses. If late in the novel Ulrich himself recognizes that "equal value and exchangeability" are forms of representation, it is also true that at the novel's outset Ulrich does not want to participate in a society in which athletes can be represented as geniuses. Ulrich evolves and has perhaps contradictory ideas, but it is clear that he consistently dislikes a manipulator of representations like Arnheim.

In conclusion, I underscore that Musil was obliged to work in a historical context that, from 1914 on, was relentlessly catastrophic. This is the context for understanding that he could devote his life to seeking a myth that could propose a literary epistemology reconciling poetry with the axiomatic precision of mathematics and an objective respect of empirical fact. In this context it is more than understandable that he might be tempted to become his own epistemological hero, or to create that hero in his mathematician alter ego, Ulrich. But Musil lived out his life in a time during which heroism ceased by and large to be possible in literature.

I turn now to Marcel Proust, Musil's contemporary, whose vision was not centered on the new era of mass movements and homicidal utopias. Perhaps this allowed Proust to create an epistemological explorer to whom literature offered a venue for an aesthetic heroism in his search for the plenitude of time past. Heroism is not a term usually associated with Proust, but, in melding his life with his fiction, Proust found in writing an extension of life that allowed him to transcend the asthma that usually confined him to his room in the later years of his life. This epic in transcendence can, I think, be called heroic, as can his fictional narrator's determination to overcome death by writing a novel. One could even say that Proust's narrator achieved something like the mode of representation that Ulrich dreamed of. For Proust worked out, in the novel, his own theory to account for the multiplicity of representations allowed by both art and science. Proust offered, in response to science, probably the most elaborated epistemology to be found in any literary work after Dante, both in its textual embodiment in the novel and in the theory the novel proposes about its own existence. So with Dante's encyclopedic knowledge of the Fall and Resurrection as an antecedent, we may approach Proust's literary epistemology, along with Musil's marvelous failure, as highpoints of the modernist attempt to shape knowledge as art.

Chapter Three

Proust, Poincaré, and Contingency

In both his life and his work, Marcel Proust offers many points of comparison with his contemporary Musil, most notably because both writers are central to an understanding of the epistemological dilemmas of modernism. A significant difference is, of course, that Proust's eudonistic literary vision is mainly centered upon a Europe that had not yet embraced war as its major form of economic activity. But their lives were comparable in that, like Musil, Proust seems to have melded his life with his fiction. From another perspective, however, these writers' lives offer reverse symmetry. Proust elaborated his literary epistemology following an itinerary that was the opposite of Musil's. Musil began life with an education in science and positivist philosophy and ended exploring a labyrinth of mythological possibilities. By contrast, Proust began his career under the influence of symbolist poets and their quest to endow the immanent moment with something like transcendence, but he finished his life working out, in *A la recherche du temps perdu,* a rigorous epistemology that differentiates literature from science. Proust worked out in the novel his own theory to account for the multiplicity of representations allowed by both art and science.

Before dealing with Proust's concept of knowledge, the reader may find it useful to review a few facts situating Proust's work. Proust is known primarily for one novel, *A la recherche du temps perdu.* The novel's title was later translated by Scott Montcrieff, borrowing from Shakespeare's thirtieth sonnet, as *In Search of Things Past,* though "In search of time past" is the title's literal sense. Proust published the first volume in 1913, and the final volume saw light, posthumously, in 1927, some five years after Proust's death. Thus, it was published after Musil published *Young Törless,* but before *The Man without Qualities,* and approximately at the same time as Joyce's *Ulysses* and several of Kafka's later tales such as those in *A Country Doctor* or *A Hunger Artist.*

Like Musil, Proust did not live to oversee the publication of the full novel. However, unlike Musil, Proust left the novel essentially complete, though with some parts still in need of final revision. Successive editions have made greater and greater refinements of the text. Points of contention remain about what should be the proper editing of some sections, but, as the novel now exists in two successive Pléiade editions, and with alternative texts available for the section called *La Fugitive* or *Albertine disparue,* it seems safe to say the novel is finally finished. By and large, it should be stressed, the architecture of Proust's novel was complete upon his death, even if the first edition of it was something of a shambles.

After an initial period of search for, and hesitation about, the novel's subject, Proust seems to have constantly had in mind the overall structure of his work. He envisaged it as an extended bildungsroman encompassing a life span beginning with childhood memories and ending with the final revelation that his protagonist should finally fulfill his vocation as a writer. Between these two points, the novel was indefinitely expandable, and Proust probably would have poured even more experience into it, had he lived longer. Like Musil and Joyce, Proust endorsed the modernist idea that there are no limits as to what can go into a novel. With Dante and the Bible as antecedents, he believed that the encyclopedia of life demands all forms of knowledge for its representation. Or, from the viewpoint of the novelistic project of narrating a recovery of paradise, the fall from paradise demands the narrator know everything if paradise is ever to be found again at all.

Proust's novel presents an extraordinary counterpoint of fictional realism and the modernist search for transcendence. In pursuing both realism and transcendence, it refuses the direct emulation of science that French writers, from Balzac through Zola, had often seen as their goal. This is not to say that Proust in any sense rejects science. He acknowledges the rule of science in the world of objectivity and draws widely upon science to describe that world. But in so doing Proust grants literature its own object of knowledge: the subjective world of the individual subject. From this perspective, *A la recherche du temps perdu* can be viewed as a far-reaching attempt to reconcile the scientific worldview with the possibility of vouchsafing poetic value to the individual life. In his novel Proust wanted to find a space in which poetic salvation can be achieved in spite of science's relentless reduction of the world to phenomena that can be described, if not explained, by mathematical equations and mechanical laws. Drawing directly upon scientific epistemology, Proust demonstrates that literature has access to realms that science cannot describe, and with the demonstration of the epistemic power of literature, Proust's novel restates Pascal's two epistemologies so as to define the space of literary knowledge.

The novel's rhetorical structure is of fundamental importance for this demonstration of knowledge through literature. The novel is cast in the form of a fictional autobiography in which, from some undefined point in time, a first-person narrator, presumably named Marcel, recalls his life from its earliest moments. He narrates its unfolding until, late in his life, he finally accepts the task to be a writer. The novel's first-person narrator is thus at once the hero participating in the events recalled and an older narrator looking back upon a younger version of himself in time past. In the novel's first volume, *Du côté de chez Swann (Swann's Way),* the narrator recalls his childhood, often spent with his parents at his grandparents' home in the village of Combray. In addition, the first volume contains a unique act of third-person narration, *Un Amour de Swann,* in which the narrator tells of the unhappy love of the intellectual bourgeois Swann for the cocotte Odette, a love affair that took place before the narrator was born. This novel within the novel prefigures, in the deceptions experienced by Swann, what the narrator later experiences in life. The young narrator dreams of love, but he does not really find it realized in his first love for Gilberte, Swann and Odette's daughter.

The second volume is entitled *A l'ombre des jeunes filles en fleurs (Within a Budding Grove,* or, more recently, *In the Shadow of Young Girls in Flower).* It turns on the narrator's encounters with young women, such as the enigmatic Albertine at Balbec, the seaside resort where he also meets Elstir, the painter who initiates him into art. Initiation into society takes place in the central sections of the novel, in the volumes called *Le côté de Guermantes* and *Sodome et Gomorrhe (The Guermantes Way* and *Sodom and Gomorrah).* They introduce the narrator, often with irony or satire, to the comic futilities of Parisian aristocratic mores and to the wiles of perversion spread throughout every level of society. The grandly homosexual Baron de Charlus is a major figure in this portrayal of the vices and glories of French society. Then, in the following two volumes, *La Prisonnière* and *La Fugitive* (the latter also called *Albertine disparue;* or *The Prisoner* and *The Fugitive*), he narrates his hopeless love for Albertine, his jealousy, her flight from him, and her death. As the Russian critic Serguei Botcharov puts it, Proust's narrator obsessively relives this love so that, by dint of remembering it, he can exhaust it.[1] Time is recovered in the work's final volume, *Le Temps retrouvé (Time Regained),* and the narrator concludes his autobiography after the Great War and his long stay in a clinic. This volume relates his return to society and his final discovery of what art is and, with this, the meaning of a writer's vocation. In effect Proust concludes the novel with the discovery that the narrator has within himself, in the accumulated years of his life, the material for a novel—perhaps the very novel that the reader has just read.

Proust's accomplishment in writing *A la recherche du temps perdu* is, in many respects, the culmination of symbolist poetry's desire to reconstitute the uniqueness of lived experience. That desire, in counterpoint to the scientific desire to find invariant generalities, provides a significant context for understanding Proust's epistemological thought and practice. Much modernist fiction inherited from symbolist poetry, in France and elsewhere, a desire to get around the imperial claims of science to decide what constitutes knowledge. Poets gave to novelists the desire to surpass science by achieving transcendence—transcendence understood as the revelation of the unique truth of experience conveyed in figurative language. To justify their claims to transcendence, symbolist poets proclaimed poetry to be an autonomous realm whose autonomy was defined by its poetic language, a language superior in some sense to ordinary discourse. Thus understood, poetry can be seen as making a counterclaim against science in that poetic language proposed access to superior epistemic spaces—epiphanic spaces of revelation—not accessible to science.

Proust took up the task of finding a transcendental form, but, in contrast to poets like Baudelaire and Mallarmé, he never entertained the idea of excluding science from literature. It is almost an understatement to say that Proust was extremely interested in science. It is clear that by the time he began writing, he was critically aware of the major questions that science was dealing with at the beginning of the twentieth century—and that he had a sense of the epistemological stakes that few writers, or scientists for that matter, have ever shown. Proust wanted to deal with science on its own ground and in its own terms. He did not do so to limit the epistemic issues that a novel can embody. On the contrary, he wanted to discern what he called the laws of time or the laws of objective experience. He wanted to embody objective laws in the realistic component of his novel that takes the form of a social chronicle; and, with regard to the

---

1. From Serguei Botcharov's introduction to Marcel Proust, *Du côté de chez Swann,* 4.

individual, he wanted to find and describe the laws dictating the processes that condemn the body to destruction in time. In writing a novel Proust intended to show that fiction offers knowledge that at once uses what science proposes and then goes beyond science to offer knowledge of a transcendental realm inaccessible to it. In short, Proust combines Poincaré and Baudelaire.

Proust encountered in France, as Musil did in Austria and Germany, the influence of thinkers like Mach, Duhem, and Poincaré, which promoted a more active interest in epistemological questions than was the case in England. In the London and Cambridge of the late nineteenth century, in fact, many scientists viewed science as a soon-to-be-completed task, especially as far as the basic laws of nature—or the laws of physics—were concerned. There was a widespread belief that, with Maxwell's work on electromagnetism, physics had practically arrived at, to use a more recent expression, the final theory. This smugness was accompanied in some quarters by a belief that epistemological questions had largely been resolved. By contrast to England, in the France of philosophers like Boutroux and Bergson the idea that positivist science had fairly well settled most epistemic problems set off a revolt against this self-satisfied imperial attitude. (One might compare this revolt with the critique Musil undertook of Mach, though the idea of a final theory would be largely meaningless from Mach's viewpoint: the belief in indeterminacy means nothing is final.)

It is also true that, among the more thoughtful scientists on both sides of the Channel, a feeling of disquiet was growing that there were too many unsolved problems in the details of the worldview proposed by Newtonian celestial mechanics and dynamics. Classical physics had not really dealt with problems created, for example, by the interpretation of thermodynamics and electromagnetism and their relation to Newtonian mechanics. It was, however, largely on the continent that new developments took place. In Germany one thinks immediately of Planck and Einstein, with Planck's formulation of the quantum of energy in 1900 and Einstein's papers on photons and on special relativity in 1905. In the France of *la belle époque,* Boutroux and Bergson's critique of classical determinism and positivism was also carried out by Poincaré in his mathematical scientific work. In working on the three body problem, or in formalizing the probability of statistical mechanics, Poincaré saw that the end of basic science was hardly in sight. After all, Poincaré's theorem that formalizes statistical probability allows the possible, if not the probable, happening in the course of time of almost any configuration of events: molecules rushing out of the bottle have a slight probability at some time in eternity of rushing back in again. Boltzmann's entropy was the most probable state of affairs for the universe, but Poincaré's incipient chaos theory theoretically allowed for the possibility that energy just might organize itself in ways not predicted by the usual random running down.

Like Valéry, who drew upon Poincaré, Proust was respectful of the science that included by the time he was writing such ascendant paradigms as Darwinian biology, the medical revolution based on microbiology, the nearly completed systematic classification of modern chemistry, Maxwell's field equations, and Poincaré's early formulations of relativity. By the early twentieth century, which is to say, when Proust began to formulate his narrative project, the epistemic space carved out by science had become far larger, in a relatively short time, than the world described by Newton and Laplace, those emblematic mechanical thinkers who had given the Enlightenment a deterministic worldview. Proust's science included Newton and Laplace, but as rethought by epistemologists like Boutroux, criticized by Bergson, and redefined by Poincaré in work on such problems as indeterminacy. Poincaré's thought was disseminated not only through many papers in scientific journals, but also in quite accessible essays in literary and philosophical journals and then in books on epistemology that were something like best-sellers. Poincaré had a central position in debates on science in France, and, for this reason, I am now going to argue that Poincaré's conventionalism is a crucial starting point for understanding the epistemology Proust elaborated in *A la recherche du temps perdu*.

In discussions of Proust and science, Proust has been frequently compared to Einstein. However, it was Poincaré, not Einstein, who dominated epistemological thinking in France in the years before the publication of *Du côté de chez Swann.* At a later date, shortly before his death, Proust was intrigued by comparisons made between his work and Einstein's thought. But the fact is that Proust probably had no knowledge of Einstein's relativity theory before the last years of his life. Einstein's thought was little known in France, outside of the realm of physicists, before the end of World War I. Einstein was not quickly accepted by most French physicists, and even Poincaré showed himself a bit ungenerous in his later failure to recognize that Einstein had indeed gone well beyond him in theorizing relativity.

In the context of French intellectual history Poincaré's work is a reasonable and, I argue on the basis of the novel itself, necessary starting point for understanding how Proust viewed science. Let us briefly consider that work. It is extremely diverse. As noted earlier, Poincaré proposed a version of a theory of relativity shortly before Einstein published his 1905 paper. In working on the difficulty of calculating the mutual attraction of three centers of gravitation—the so-called three body problem—Poincaré developed some of the early work upon which chaos theory is based. The fact that young Valéry borrows his procedure for defining mind from Poincaré underscores that Poincaré had become in France the public model of the scientist as thinker, especially for his role in debates concerning non-Euclidean geometry and the implications it had for the foundation of mathematics and for the nature of scientific models. What we have seen of Poincaré's role in Valéry's development confirms what Linda Henderson, in her *The Fourth Dimension and Non-Euclidean Geometry in Modern Art,* has shown about Poincaré's widespread role in French intellectual life during the 1880s and 1890s. Henderson stresses that Poincaré's writings were at the center of debates in France about the foundations of mathematics, which inevitably led to discussions about the nature of knowledge and certainty. Argued in widely read journals in France and elsewhere, the arguments pitted Kantians, who defended a belief in the a priori necessity of Euclidean geometry, against positivists and empiricists, who rejected the metaphysical idealism underlying the Kantian position. Henderson has persuasively documented Poincaré's importance in bringing this debate about the epistemology of mathematics to a wide public:

> The importance of the French debate was twofold. It gave non-Euclidean geometry currency in Paris among intellectuals, and out of this debate emerged the definitive statements on this subject by Henri Poincaré, the mathematician-scientist and writer who, more than any other individual, was responsible for the popularization of non-Euclidean geometry in Paris. . . .
>
> In 1887 Poincaré first published his theory that the axioms of geometry are neither synthetic a priori nor empirical, but are conventions, a view now generally accepted as the solution to the controversy. . . .[2]

Poincaré's conventionalism rejected both the experimental nature of geometry as well as its status as an a priori construct: the first because non-Euclidean geometry shows that Euclidean metrics are not intrinsic to space, and the second because the belief in the a priori nature of mathematics argued against the

2. Henderson, *The Fourth Dimension and Non-Euclidean Geometry in Modern Art,* 15. The relation to Poincaré is also suggested in Nicola Luckhurst, *Science and Structure in Proust's "A la recherche."*

possibility of establishing new geometric systems. It was now clearly the case that the mind was capable of creating new geometries. These arguments were all spelled out in Poincaré's lucid prose in works such as *La Science et l'hypothèse* (1902), a widely read treatise on the nature of science and mathematics that has remained a popular work to the present day.

Poincaré's conventionalism entails freedom of choice. The scientist is free to chose the geometry that seems most convenient, for neither Euclid's nor Lobachevsky's geometry is true or false. Poincaré made this conventionalism into a coherent epistemological doctrine that many artists and writers took to heart, for Poincaré made mathematics seem more like art. In Poincaré's thinking, mathematical formalisms were viewed as a product of the human mind to be used according to one's needs. Yet a loss accompanied the viewpoint, the loss of a priori experimental truth value, and with this it appeared that certain truth no longer characterized mathematics.

Certainty was no longer part of the ontology of mathematics and, by implication, of physical systems constructed through mathematical deductions. The "conventional" nature of mathematics entailed the conclusion that truth was a matter of use, not of ontology; and with this conclusion one could no longer point to mathematics as an example of a body of certain truths about the world. Thus, certainty no longer seemed to belong to a world that science could describe in any number of different ways. Musil's work presents one reaction to this viewpoint, and Proust's another. Like Musil, Proust meditated on the nature of certainty when he set out to define the kind of knowledge art can offer. Proust's discovery of certainty in individual experience may well be the unique feature of his novel, though this discovery in no way challenges Poincaré's conventionalism as a description of knowledge that one can have of the objective world.

Poincaré underscored the underdetermined nature of reality in arguing that conventionalism in mathematics carries over to physics and other sciences dealing with empirical laws:

> If a phenomenon carries with it a complete mechanical explanation, it will carry with it an infinity of other explanations that will equally as well account for all the particularities revealed by experiment.
>
> And that is confirmed by the history of every part of physics; in optics, for example, Fresnel believed in vibration that was perpendicular to the plane of polarization. Newmann thought it was parallel to this plane. Scientists looked for a long time for a "experimentum crucis" that would give

grounds for deciding between these two theories and one could not be found.[3]

The choice of a theory is guided, as Poincaré puts it, by considerations where "the personal contribution" is very great, though considerations like elegance and simplicity are also common. What is essential is that this conventionalism, arguing for the epistemological underdetermination of reality, undermines the belief in certainty as a form of a priori necessity. Kant's epistemology founders here, as do the Newtonian underpinnings of the realism of two preceding centuries of realist writers from Defoe to Zola. But contained within this viewpoint is the invitation to redefine what might be the locus of certainty in a world that, like the world of Musil's young Törless, was suddenly in need of certainty.

The conventionalist epistemology elaborated by Poincaré finds strong resonance in the aesthetic modernism of a writer like Proust, who readily accepts that absolute certain truth cannot be given by science, because science's generalized laws, in their contingency, have probability, but no certainty. Certainty must be granted by some necessity that science does not or cannot deal with. Epistemic necessity does not characterize the objective world, even if, as Proust's novel demonstrates at length, the objective processes occurring in that world often appear to have a probability approaching certainty. But these processes do not characterize the subjective world. Taking his cue from Poincaré's epistemology—or from epistemological notions exactly resembling Poincaré's—Proust's narrator develops the idea that if certainty does not exist in the objective world described by science, then it may be found in the subjective world of unique experience. For, at the very least, Poincaré and Proust shared a common cultural matrix whose basic axioms imposed the recognition of the loss of certainty in knowledge. One can say that this loss was overdetermined in that it was largely a consequence of several developments: the discovery of the multiple geometries one can use to construct epistemic models, the subsequent epistemological underdeterminism, the formalizing of stochastic processes, as well as the discovery of the nature of complexity. In fine, empirical reality allows only contingent propositions. Accepting this loss of certainty, and perhaps to compensate for it, Proust endowed his novel with an epistemological framework that allows his narrator to lay claim, for the truths of his individual experience, to the type of certainty that mathematical science once offered.

3. Poincaré, *La Science et l'hypothèse,* 248.

Proust's narrator affirms that certainty and necessity characterize the knowledge granted by the narrator's unique experience. This certainty derives from
the nature of what is unique: it can only be what it is. What is unique is certain
because it can be no other way—in marked contrast to science's knowledge
that is represented through general models that can be replaced by other general and thus contingent models. In this regard Proust seems to have taken a
cue from Mallarmé, for Proust's narrator argues, implicitly, that fiction, by its
autonomy, can create a realm whose ontology guarantees whatever it affirms:
the unique can exist in fiction because it can be imagined to exist. Therefore it
has a curiously certain existence, since nothing contingent can be imagined to
replace it. Perhaps this certainty accrues to every past event, because from the
perspective of the present moment anything that belongs to the irreversible
realm of time past can only be what it was. Projecting his search onto the past,
Proust's novel is a quest for certain knowledge that stakes out an epistemic
space outside of those realms occupied by science: Proust's narrator can find
certain knowledge if he can gain access to that subjective realm that is *not* subject to the underdeterminism that Poincaré, among others, ascribes to the
objective world known by the various sciences. The past fixes the unique with
total certainty, and it is up to the writer to bring this past to representation, and
hence to make it known.

It cannot be said that Proust or his narrator flaunts any relation to Poincaré.
In fact, Proust makes only one reference to Poincaré in the course of *A la
recherche du temps perdu*. This reference occurs when a friend of the narrator,
the aristocratic Saint-Loup, says in a conversation that Poincaré has shown that
mathematics isn't all "that certain." One may doubt whether Saint-Loup has
been a diligent reader of Poincaré, but his comment mirrors public reaction to
the debates on scientific epistemology that had been widespread in circles beyond those frequented by scientists. Saint-Loup's comment on Poincaré points
up that certainty and uncertainty were public issues in France, and that something as esoteric as concern about the foundations of mathematics, brought
about by the puzzles proposed by non-Euclidean geometry, could occupy the
usually frivolous aristocracy of Faubourg Saint-Germain. Or, at least we see
that epistemological and scientific questions were being asked, though perhaps
not answered, in those salons frequented by Proust's narrator.

The philosopher Vincent Descombes, in his very engaging *Proust et la philoso-
phie du roman* (1987), has argued that, in a philosophical sense, no "thought"
takes place in Proust's novel. I cite a thinker as eminent as Descombes for the

pleasure of disagreement, since his is a paradoxical way to read a novel in which not only is the narrator clearly a theorist, but the novel itself is a demonstration of its own epistemology. Descombes's attitude toward literature is one that I hope to undo: Proust's novel demonstrates that novelists as well as mathematicians can think about apodictic structures or procedures that grant certain knowledge, and a novel may do so in intellectually satisfying ways. Proust's novel recognizes that the criteria by which certainty is characterized vary from one type of discourse to another, as does the meaning of certainty itself. The possibility of a multitude of types of epistemic criteria hovers on the background in Proust, as in Musil, though for Musil this is as much a cause for worry as for a feeling of being freed from epistemic limitations. Proust does not allow, as Musil does, the multiplicity of possible models for knowledge to distract him from his quest for artistic certainty. Proust's demonstration of certainty is rigorously singleminded, beginning in the "Combray" section of *Du côté de chez Swann* and culminating in *Le Temps retrouvé*.

Proust divides his world, following basically a dualist epistemological perspective, into the subjective and the objective in such a way that each side reinforces the other, their mutual relation creating a unity of knower and known in which the knower is ultimately the realm in which the known is found. These two realms divide up the epistemological territory. As long as there are only two realms—the certain and the contingent—the narrator can shore up his subjective quest for certainty against the laws of contingency by actually affirming contingency in its own realm, which in turn all the more firmly defines the subjective realm of certainty. Proust can face the probabilistic nature of most knowledge, as defined by thinkers like Poincaré, Mach, and Duhem, and frame the question of the certainty of artistic truth in dialectic response to the uncertainties of the intellect that scientific conventionalism describes. At this juncture one might expect to find a potential rivalry between literature and science, at least to the extent that a writer's claims to certain knowledge could lead to claims of superiority. In Proust this potential rivalry is defused by his evenhanded concept of artistic truth, which concedes the objective world to science and accordingly incorporates scientific truth into the novel's objective world. In fine, Proust's narrator grants scientific knowledge its domain, such as the one described by Poincaré, and, in acknowledging that domain, demonstrates that art occupies a separate epistemic realm—though the two domains exist together within the unifying framework of the novel.

Much of the way Proust frames the perception of the certainty of artistic truth seems to mirror directly the way in which Poincaré set out the terms for understanding the limits of knowledge in works like *La Science et l'hypothèse.* Consider, for example, the often quoted description of the church that stands at the center of Combray, the church that the narrator so dearly loved and continues to see: "an edifice, one might say, occupying a space with four dimensions—the fourth being that of Time—, unfolding through the centuries its nave, which, from span to span, from chapel to chapel, seemed to overcome and cross over, not merely a few meters of space, but successive periods of time from which it continually emerged victorious."[4] This reference, made by Proust's narrator, to time as the "fourth dimension" of spatial reality, is probably an allusion, not to Einstein's relativity theory, but to Poincaré's claim that, if we were to receive a different education, we could localize phenomena of the exterior world in non-Euclidean space or even in a space with four dimensions. (Or as he says in *La Science et l'hypothese,* one can represent to oneself "un monde à quatre dimensions.")[5] Proust's narrator is in a sense theorizing his own relativity theory by using what Poincaré's work outlines as a theoretical possibility. I will return to this point presently; what I want to emphasize here is that Proust is sensitive to the way in which Poincaré liberates the imagination with his non-Euclidean sense of the multiple dimensions that might go into perception if it were freed from Euclidean dimensions.

Poincaré imagines, for example, that one could visualize Lorentz transformations, which is to say, that one could perceive objects becoming smaller as they approached the speed of light. Rather literally, Poincaré apparently believed that with proper education humanity could perceive in ways other than those described, or prescribed, by the usual education confined by the three dimensions of Euclidean geometry. Poincaré was close to formulating Einstein's relativity theory. However, neither Lorentz nor Poincaré imagined the relativity of time. As Martin Gardner points out in *The Relativity Explosion,* this was the great conceptual step Einstein took, in rejecting Newton's premise that one time metric permeated the entire cosmos.[6] If one wants to compare Proust with

4. Proust, *A la recherche du temps perdu,* ed. Pierre Clarac and André Ferré, 1:161. My translations from French will be from this edition, hereafter cited parenthetically in the text.

5. Poincaré, *La Science et l'hypothèse,* 91.

6. Gardner, *The Relativity Explosion,* now reprinted as *Relativity Simply Explained,* 7.

Einstein, perhaps the best comparison would focus on the way they both drew upon work by thinkers like Poincaré to formulate their own conceptions of time, arguably in somewhat comparable ways. Proust drew upon Poincaré's type of epistemology in formulating ideas that make certainty in art relative to the artistic subject. Formulating his own version of relativity, he used the loss of certainty in mathematics and science that he found in Poincaré or in the wake of Poincaré (or that he could have found in Hume and in Mach's use of Hume, for that matter). The essential starting point is the loss of absolute certainty in science, which gives Proust grounds to argue for the certain knowledge that he finds in art.

Proust's narrator knows, of course, that the physical sciences do offer a type of truth. And readers will miss a great deal if they are not attentive to the way, in dealing with knowledge, Proust's narrator alludes frequently to scientific paradigms that dictate truth about objective phenomena, including the narrator's own body. As part of its epistemic premises, the novel accepts that medicine and physiology, as well as classical mechanics and thermodynamics, describe the objective world—by definition, that is their realm. The narrator explicitly accepts science's role in formulating knowledge of contingent reality, all of which should in fact be amenable to description by laws. Accordingly, and with some hyperbole, Proust's narrator actually extends the range of phenomena described by laws beyond what science had really accomplished in the early twentieth century (or today). He constantly evokes, for example, the "laws" that putatively dictate the development of individuals and culture in time. Proust's narrator harbors none of the doubts about collective laws, dictating individual behavior, that torment Musil's Ulrich. Admittedly, the narrator himself becomes a bit nonplussed at his use of botanical laws to describe the development and behavior of homosexuals such as the Baron de Charlus and his loves. Proust's narrator is at times, as he himself recognizes with appropriate humor, an overly enthusiastic scientific thinker.

In general, Proust's narrator accepts, for contingent, objective reality, the descriptive power of the positivist hierarchy of discourses. This hierarchy proposes that every level of epistemic analysis is subject to a superior determination by the laws of the next, more general level of discourse. For instance, Proust's narrator declares that there are specific social laws and that these are then subject to the higher and more general laws of temporality, by which one might think of thermodynamics and entropy. There are the specific laws of the body and the mind, which are then subject to determination by the more general laws of physiology and, above all, the laws of heredity invented by nineteenth-century medicine. That Proust has no more idea as to what constitutes heredity than Darwin had is of little importance. He accepts, with the a priori certainty of much nineteenth-century medicine, that there must be something like laws that dictate hereditary, which then allows him to document their effect. Like an unending research project, Proust's novel needs its three thousand pages to document how these putative laws of heredity dictate the way that society and characters develop—and in turn how the laws of physics and physiology are at work as so many examples of the most general "laws of time." Time is the space these various laws need—much time—for their realization in determining the evolution of character, and finally the collapse of the body.

This aspect of Proust's narration may seem at times to present something of a caricature of determinism, as, for example, when, after hundreds of pages, the narrator discovers that he, too, offers one more example of the way in which hereditary laws determine character development. Zola would certainly have approved of the development that leads to the discovery by Proust's aging narrator that he has come to resemble, not only his father, but above all, his Aunt Léonie, the old eccentric who refused to leave her room in Combray—the room that was the center of the child's paradise recalled and re-created in the "Combray" section at the novel's beginning. As a young man, the narrator thought that he was, in every important respect, the opposite of the aunt who found reading to be a waste of time. As a mature man, he discovers that his aunt's character has come to rivet him, too, to his bed, where he endlessly meditates in jealousy upon his lover, Albertine:

> Now, even though each day I found a cause for it in a particular discomfort, what made me remain so often in bed was a being—not Albertine, not a being that I loved—but a being having more power over me than a loved being, one who had transmigrated into me and was despotic enough to quiet my jealous suspicions, or at least to stop me from going to see if they were grounded or not, and that being was my Aunt Leonie. (3:78–79)

Transmigration is here Proust's mythic equivalent of inheritance; it is his translation of the laws of the transmission of character traits, which dominate the development of characters in *A la recherche* with a mechanical rigor in which only late-nineteenth-century medicine could believe—which is to say, theories of inheritance as they were conceived before the elaboration of the Mendelian theory of inherited traits became after 1900 the basis for modern genetics. From Saint-Loup to the Baron de Charlus, every Proustian character is ruled mechanically by laws of inheritance, laws that model one's flesh and pick one's sexual preferences, that color the eyes and determine posture and gait, and that cause tics and manias.

If the narrator constantly consults a barometer because his father did so obsessively, this suggests that Proust, like Darwin, entertained a neo-Lamarckian theory of the acquisition of traits. But this is only one of many contingent theories that can be evoked with regard to what the narrator frequently calls the laws of time, as well as the laws of the soul and the laws of the body and its development. These laws or paradigms are interlinked to create a deterministic tapestry portraying decline, mutation, and death as the inevitable result of human existence. When at the novel's outset the older narrator looks back upon his childhood to ask if his entire past is dead, he is implicitly making appeal to a number of frameworks that make sense of such a question. He knows that thermodynamics, physiology, and hereditary science all spell out death as the end product of human development. But these truths granted by science are contingent in that any number of scientific models could be used to explain them. Mach would not have disagreed.

These laws are a product of intelligence, and these products of the intellect are unable to reach the truth of the subjective world, because, as the narrator says, this world is locked up in nonintellectual sensations: "And so it is with our past. We waste our effort when we attempt to evoke it; all our intellect's efforts are useless. It is hidden outside of the realm of the intellect and its reach, in some material object (in the sensation that this material object would offer us) whose existence we do not suspect" (1:44). As Baudelaire's work had earlier demonstrated to a generation of symbolists—and which the narrator seems to accept without reservation—only sensation can get around the limits of intellect and provide the substantive plenitude that restores knowledge of our subjective world. The knowledge offered by poetic discourse is conceived as a knowledge of the fullness of things in their sensorial richness. Such a Baudelairean concept of knowledge demands perforce that in a literary work the fullness of sensation must be captured by linguistic means, by images and metaphors, and by the rhetorical structure in which these images are embedded. The writer's task, which is as much epistemic as poetic, is to find the images and the plausible rhetorical structure that can offer access, in a fiction, to a world of certainty that exists therein because of the autonomy of fictional discourse: fiction itself guarantees certainty because there is no alternative to certainty's existence if it is declared to exist.

One of the goals of Proust's novel is, then, to describe the necessity and hence certainty that Proust's narrator finds in the fullness of his own subjective truth. To this end the novel must show, convincingly, that subjectivity has a certainty that contingent truth does not have. An understanding of the novel's rhetorical structure is a key to understanding that one can meaningfully speak of the necessity of a unique experience. The work's rhetorical structure is designed to give access to the narrator's certain knowledge, and Proust's rhetorical strategies take on a clearer meaning when they are considered as part of his narrator's epistemic quest aiming at a certainty that science cannot offer. This certainty is centered on the knowing subject depicted in the novel, the first-person narrator. Proust's first-person narration is told by a limited observer who usually grants the reader access only to the world of the narrator's subjectivity (with the notable exception of the omniscient narration, about a time occurring before the narrator's birth, that he relates in *Un Amour de Swann*). The narrator knows, self-consciously, that he can deal only with what I call the narrator's own inertial system: the narrating self is the framework of reference for all that happens in the novel. This produces a type of relativity, though it is not directly related to Einstein's concept, for subjectivity is not part of Einstein's special theory—in spite of frequent misinterpretations in this regard. Proust's narrative framework, anchored in a subjectivity, determines that time and space are perceived in the work relative to the narrating self. Temporality is an absolute for Newtonian cosmology and its realm of contingent truths, and in this respect Proust's novel breaks with Newtonian objectivity in portraying the novel's subjective time and space relative to the narrator. Or, more precisely, a central function of the rhetorical structure is to disengage the narrator's subjective space from the space of objectivity. The rhetorical structure is designed to separate subjectivity from the objective realm wherein science and its contingent laws rule supreme and to create, as it were, a space within which another ontological order reigns. This is a space of unique subjective certainty. In this sense, Proust may appear more Machean than Mach in breaking with Newtonian objectivity by defining the self and its sensations as a producer of knowledge.

The first pages of the novel work to "delocalize" the narrator. He is often sleeping, or present in chambers in which he is uncertain about spatial coordinates. The boundaries separating dream, aesthetic perception, and perception of waking reality are blurred as the narrator's mind wanders. From the outset the narrator is situated so that there is no absolute narrative space that can be called the present space of narration. All dynamics in the novel, and all development therein, is recorded and measured in a space that is defined strictly by reference to the narrator's mind. His subjectivity offers the only framework for viewing the objective novelistic world, and it is never clear where he may be located, so that even time recalled exists finally in function of a self lying outside of the objective coordinates of space and time. This is the radical sense of the narrator's dictum when he says, at the novel's outset, that a man who sleeps holds in a circle about himself the thread of the hours, the order of years and of worlds (1:5). Proust is willing to grant absolute time to the world of Newtonian science and its domain, the domain of laws that destroy the body; but he reserves for his narrator's epistemic realm another version of time, the time in which the narrator functions in a space defined by the narrator's personal sensations.

Proust makes a unique use of verb tenses to create a rhetorical structure that in effect withdraws his narrator's subjectivity from the space of normal objectivity. For example, the first sentence in the novel gives us a narrator who says, rather bizarrely, that he has gone to bed early for a long time—"Longtemps, je me suis couché de bonne heure." In this opening sentence, the composed past tense functions somewhat like the English present perfect tense in that it seems to relate a past act to the present moment, or the fictional present moment during which the novel is being narrated. The past is thus situated relative to an undefined present moment that must be the present moment of the fiction's enunciation. Logically, only in the present moment can the narrator narrate his past life unfolding in the imperfect tense, the iterative tense narrating the repetition of acts carried out in the past. The imperfect tense, the French *imparfait,* is the tense that the narrator usually uses to describe the often mechanical unfolding of repetitive events, as opposed to unique events narrated in the literary past tense. However, it is also true that he uses the imperfect tense to describe and narrate events that seem logically to have been unique occurrences, but the imperfect endows these events with a sense of repetition that transforms them into repeated acts, recurring as memory repeatedly entertains them.

The novel's temporal framework is thus polarized between the nonsituated present moment of the act of narration and the imperfect tense that describes the past for a narrator who is situated outside that past. In this way Proust creates the sense that the narrating narrator, who is never situated in a precise place in the novel, is outside the temporal flow governed by the laws of time ruling over objective reality. The reader largely knows, or vaguely feels, that the narrator is narrating in a present moment because the *passé composé,* or composed past, is used by the narrator, albeit only a few times in the course of the novel. Each time this tense is used, it situates the narrator in a present moment, a moment of dreaming or awakening, outside the temporal flow of ordinary experience. This experience is narrated in the imperfect tense, though sometimes in the literary past tense, since the narrator uses these two past tenses for those contingencies than can be described by the laws of time, the laws that impose dissolution upon all material things.

Notably, the *passé composé* is the tense used at the beginning of the novel to first recall all of Combray and the narrator's childhood in their complete fullness. This recall is effected through images re-creating the sensations of the past, after the narrator finds, through the sensual associations sparked by the taste of a pastry and a sip of linden tea, that "tout Combray et ses environs, tout cela qui prend forme et solidité, est sorti, ville et jardins, de ma tasse de thé" (1:48). The translation is ambiguous: "all of Combray and its surroundings, all of that which can acquire form and solidity, the city and the gardens, has emerged/sprung from my cup of tea." Combray can be restored in all its fullness, and, therewith, the narrator can entertain the certain knowledge of his past existing as a present. However, the act of narration itself never coincides with what is narrated, just as the narrator never coincides with himself as a character who, in the novel's past experience, is subject to the laws governing the novel's unfolding. The past can explode into the present moment of the act of narration, but it never ceases being a past that has unfolded according to the laws of time.

A bit of recapitulation may be useful at this point. We have seen that the goal of Proust's narrator is to shape a work of art that respects and, indeed, makes use of the laws of time and contingent processes, the laws of physics and physiology, at the same time that he seeks the realm of certain truth. (And it is perhaps difficult to make more than what the scholastics called a distinction of reason between Proust's and his narrator's project, for the narrator's project will be what Proust's has been.) Since certain truth does not exist in the realm of contingent laws, it must exist in a realm where these laws hold no sway. It must be found in a realm other than that of the many, indifferent laws that can be invoked to describe the essentially underdetermined world of historical and physical phenomena. The writer must go beyond the aleatory world that poets like Mallarmé deplored and from which Baudelaire sought escape. Opposed to this domain is that unnamed realm inhabited by the narrator-observer who looks from his narrative framework upon the world and, in so doing, finds a perspective that is not subject to contingency—for he discovers that his perceptions cannot be inscribed in any deterministic matrix that would represent them by means of a scientific model. At this point, then, the narrator can say that contingency is transformed into necessity. The artist converts contingent impressions into a necessary realm of knowledge when the artist can embody his or her random sensations, or perception, into a work of art. The work of art is a realm of necessity because it is unique to that artist and hence to a subjective framework of reference that is different from all others. In its uniqueness it defies contingency—like the two ways leading from Combray, or the church at the center of the village, that are necessary parts of the revelation of the subject's world, which can be no other than what it is because that is what it was.

With these ideas in mind we see that Poincaré's epistemological theory coincides with the narrator's theory about the artist's unique perception in many important ways. For example, the belief that the artist's mind can escape the deterministic laws of the universe, as described by classical physics and physiology, is also suggested by Poincaré's epistemology. Poincaré played a fundamental role in relegating determinism to a restricted role in epistemic problems, and this type of restriction buttressed a concomitant belief that there are realms sheltered from the iron-hand of deterministic laws. The loss of the belief in determinism is an essential point for understanding Proust in particular and modernism in general. As suggested earlier, this loss resulted in large part from the interpretation of the kind of work in physics undertaken by Poincaré on the three body problem. Proust's narrator seems aware of the implications of the three body problem, especially in his meditation on complexity. In this regard he is typical of a large public at the time for whom the unsuccessful attempt to work out the dynamics of the attraction among three bodies was generally taken to signify the end of the theoretical possibility of prediction granted by a total determinism.[7] To be sure, Proust does not entirely reject the

7. On this point, see Morris Kline, *Mathematics: The Loss of Certainty*, 61–62.

theoretical claims for determinism, at least not for the ordinary world of objective phenomena for which his narrator offers his numerous examples of deterministic laws that rule over the body and society, including his own body. But Proust accepts that determinism has limits. He finds them in his narrator's own mind.

The type of underdeterminism Poincaré formulated provided, moreover, further justification for Proust's postulating that there is a realm in which determinism does not hold sway. Poincaré said that knowledge of objective reality is always relative to the subjective realm, and he offered justification for the conception of what I have called the inertial framework of the artist's self, or the framework created by the subjective perception of Proust's narrator-artist.[8] Representation is always relative to a subject. Moreover, the way Proust's narrator theorizes the primacy of the subjective realm in the determination of what one knows parallels Poincaré's idea that the subject has the power to opt for any of the indefinite number of models and laws with which the knower chooses to describe reality. And both Poincaré and Proust's narrator agree that what the subject cannot opt for, what the subject must accept as a necessity, is the subject's experiential world of sensation and perception. In essence, once the subject has experienced the world, that is the world experienced. The world is the ultimate determining locus of experience. Neither Poincaré nor Proust are in any sense idealists.

With his sense of relativity, Poincaré went so far as to deny that perception was determined by any geometry intrinsic to the nature of things in space. If we think the world exists in three dimensions, this is an effect of habit. This idea is not the same as the idealist claim that mind determines perception. On the contrary, mind itself is determined by habit. Analogously, Proust's narrator also theorizes at length about habit's determination of perception. The narrator's opening meditation on the world, when habit has lost its grip on perception, seems to reflect directly Poincaré's radical vision of the possible indeterminacy of perception. For example, in his essay "Space and Geometry," Poincaré affirms that there are no laws intrinsic to the nature of perception:

> [the association of ideas]...is...the result of a *habit;* this habit itself results from very numerous *experiences;* without any doubt, if the education of our senses had been accomplished in a different environment, where we should have been subjected to different impressions, contrary habits would

8. See Allen Thiher, *Fiction Rivals Science: The French Novel from Balzac to Proust,* 197.

have arisen and our muscular sensations would have been associated according to other laws.[9]

Perception is radically underdetermined by Poincaré. The plausibility of this kind of claim is also essential for Proust's affirmation that the artist's perception offers a unique truth that escapes from the rule of law, for habit is also a psychological "law" in Proust. It is the dominant law of a mind that does not reflect upon its perceptions. But habit can be broken. With proper education, to restate Poincaré's claim, we could become habituated to two dimensions, or perhaps even to those four dimensions that Proust's narrator finds in the church at Combray. Poincaré claims that we could use either Euclidean or non-Euclidean geometries to describe or to perceive the real, and Proust's narrator seems to respond by seeing a fourth dimension embodied in the church.

Devotees of science fiction probably have little difficulty with these ideas, since, to suggest another perspective on the question of perception and geometry, they probably already have in mind that in *Flatland* Edwin A. Abbott outlines a classic thought experiment about what it would be like to live in a two-dimensional universe. If Proust did not know this work, he certainly did know that of H. G. Wells, a writer Proust refers to in the novel and in his correspondence as early as 1902. Proust was undoubtedly fascinated by the way Wells used the idea that four-dimensional perception permits time travel. Of course, Proust's time travel goes in the opposite direction from the anti-utopian future toward which Wells sends his scientist in *The Time Machine*.[10] Proust's traveler goes in exploration back into the past, effecting a return to that moment when the narrator perceives the past as an embodied fourth dimension, the dimension investing things and sensations of time lost.

Hopefully, it is now clear how radically Proust translates the underdeterminism of perception with his narrative structure. His narrator finds escape from habit in his own subjective realm, where, at the novel's outset, he must be situated outside of the ordinary world of space and time. Therefore, one must literally accept the narrator's claim that, as a sleeping man, he escapes the empirical laws and patterns that habit usually accepts, because, to cite again the famous line, this time in Moncrieff's translation, the dreamer "has in a circle

9. Poincaré, *The Foundations of Science,* 69.
10. Proust mentions H. G. Wells in *Le côté de Guermantes* (2:193) with a reference to *The Invisible Man.* Earlier in his correspondence he calls Wells this "English Jules Verne" ("Lettre à Mme Léon Yeatman, March, 1902," *Correspondance,* 3:37).

round him the chain of the hours, the sequence of the years, the order of the heavenly host."[11] Sleep, sensual recall, and finally self-reflexivity can break with habit. With this break the conventional laws governing matter and perception no longer necessarily hold, no more than do the metric conventions that habit accepts for ordering the regular perception of space and time. Only then can the narrator perceive his necessary world of certain truth.

A la recherche du temps perdu embodies an elaborate epistemological dualism precisely to justify this underdeterminism. Proust's epistemic strategy is to use classical scientific models to talk about a largely deterministic world exterior to the narrator, but a relativist and conventionalist model to talk about the subjective world of the narrator's unique perception. This mix corresponds, interestingly, to Baudelaire's idea that a novel is a mixed genre, containing objective truth as well as self-sufficient poetic correspondences that, in Proust's case, translate the narrator's subjective experience. In the wake of Baudelaire, but with more epistemological rigor and considerably less irony, Proust stakes out for his narrator the self-sufficient realm in which Baudelaire found poetic autonomy—Baudelaire's realm of beauty produced by correspondences in language.

Poetic self-sufficiency in Proust derives first from the writer's impressions, for they are the unique material that forms the truth of the narrator's world and hence the certain truth of art as found in the novel. These impressions are not contingent, though they owe their existence to chance because they come about through fortuitous encounters. But once the impressions are given to the narrator, they are his necessary material for certain truths. It is a necessity in this sense that the narrator recovers the entire first section of the novel, "Combray," in a fortuitous encounter when he tastes a bit of pastry that he has dipped into a cup of linden tea. In this chance, but not at all paradoxical, encounter, the narrator overcomes the contingencies of ordinary existence, which is to say, this experience cannot be explained by those deterministic paradigms of physics and physiology that, unfortunately, condemn us to death—a contingency, it must be said, about which one can have little doubt. Moreover, the experience born of linden tea is a direct translation, from poetry to fiction, of Baudelaire's doctrine of *correspondances,* but one occurring as an epistemic experience contrasting with the knowledge characteristic of the world of laws. The narrator's

---

11. Proust, *Remembrance of Things Past,* trans. C. K. Scott Montcrieff, 1:4. References to Montcrieff's translation are hereafter cited parenthetically in the text with volume numbers.

present sensations coincide with sensations he experienced in the past, and, through the correspondence between the two, the past is resurrected in the present. All of Combray surges forth as the living paradise of the narrator's youth. In this moment "Combray" is, for the narrator, a form of necessity that escapes contingency. When converted into writing, it is a necessity for the reader, too.

Proust begins his novel with a demonstration of the certain truths of Combray that the narrator must then later recover, once he has gone through the years of experience that constitute the novel itself, with its portrayal of characters and society beginning at a time before the narrator's childhood and lasting until the period after World War I. Proust could have expanded these sections indefinitely, for they present, in all their fortuitous contingency, the development of characters and events interlinked in that empirical realm of history that has no intrinsic necessity. One may speculate that, had death not cut short Proust's life, the novel might have been even longer. But my earlier comment about the novel's architecture should now take on new meaning, since Proust had, from the beginning, an ending given by his epistemic model. Revelation of the nature of aesthetic knowledge is destined to come at the end when the narrator discovers the meaning of artistic experience in the context of the novel itself, in discoveries that take place, years later, after the episode with the linden tea and the *madeleine*. It is at the end of the novel that he can fully interpret what the earlier episode with the *madeleine* meant, in the analysis that the narrator proposes in *Le Temps retrouvé* when time is recovered.

The narrator's final analysis of his perceptions in *Le Temps retrouvé* takes place, however, after he had realized some years earlier, in his meditation on art and literature in *La Prisonnière,* that art is analogous to science in its study of relations. These earlier reflections on the nature of art are an essential complement to the narrator's later theorizing about art and what he must do to write a work of fiction. In a moment of self-reflection, when he explains the nature of art to Albertine, the narrator contemplates the example of the music of the composer Vinteuil. Trying to find a general reason for the effect that the music has upon the listener, the narrator entertains two hypotheses about art. On the one hand, Vinteuil's sonata seems to be a form of transcendence that escapes intellectual explanation. Art in some sense offers access to a reality lying beyond the limits of ordinary perception. This hypothesis might even explain, he thinks, the type of pleasure the narrator felt at the outset of the novel upon experiencing the memories of Combray recalled by the cup of linden tea. On the other hand, he reflects upon what he calls the materialist hypothesis—"celle du néant"—or the hypothesis about the nothingness to which we, as material beings, are destined by the laws of physiology and physics that govern our bodies. This hypothesis would seemingly reduce art to being the reproduction of a psychological state, having no more reality than any other such state. In this case, art has the status of a state of feeling that science has not yet analyzed. Comparing Vinteuil's musical phrase with an inner state analogous to the one the narrator had earlier experienced upon tasting the *madeleine* and the linden tea, he asks, What makes these states different from any other experiential state? He has no ready answer.

The simple fact that Vinteuil's musical phrases resist analysis does not necessarily mean that there is something more real in them than in the experience of ordinary reality, the "material" reality that the mind encounters everywhere. At this point the narrator questions whether science can, in principle, ever account for such a complex psychological phenomenon. The spirit of doubt, he says, suggests rather that the states produced by the musical phrases cannot be analyzed precisely because they place in action too many forces for which we as yet have no account: "ils mettent en jeu trop de forces dont nous ne nous sommes pas encore rendu compte" (3:381). Finally, without opting for either a transcendental or a materialist interpretation of art, by invoking an analogy with a system of complex forces, Proust's narrator suggests that the reduction of artistic states to component elements is too complex to be resolved—and this, it seems, is on the order of the three body problem. The order of complexity is too great, the narrator muses, for there to be any deterministic resolutions of the forces that would allow them to be described by some contingent law. An explanation of the effect of art cannot, in principle, be found using a deterministic model. I stress that the narrator is not indulging himself in symbolist self-defense against science. His thought takes the form of scientific reasoning that has not lost its relevance for an era that believes the mind is a computer.

Behind the narrator's meditation lies the notion that artistic states depend entirely upon the subjective realm of a subject. Proust's thought in this regard suggests that there is a relation of priority between the subjective and the objective, since it is in the subjective realm that one finds the origins of the objective modeling of experience given by art. Analogously, subjective choices in science lie behind the choice of a deterministic model for scientific knowledge. Or, as Poincaré puts it, it is the subject's choice to use the deterministic model that, through habit, grants the subject its operational power as a knowing subject—which the narrator also suggests at the novel's very beginning when he wonders if the immobility of the things around us is forced on them by the perceiving subject's conviction that things are themselves and not anything else. If the subject imposes determinism through choice, or by accepting it as a habit, then it is logical that the subject lies outside the realm of simple determinism in the sense of being prior to this realm. Poincaré's conventionalism seems evident in this conclusion because, quite simply, according to Poincaré, it is the subject that determines epistemic conventions—not vice versa.

At the end of the novel, rich with many earlier years of social experience, the narrator returns from his long absence from society after years in a sanatorium. This absence seems to facilitate his final discoveries about the nature of art by creating a temporal perspective that sets the present moment, in the past narration, in sharp contrast to the now distant past when the narrator was a young man. Going to a social engagement he experiences again revelations like the one granted to him at the novel's beginning by the linden tea and the *petite madeleine,* for, in the Guermantes' courtyard, he undergoes a series of sensations—epiphanies—that recall their exact equivalents in a preceding time past. After this renewed experience of the resurrection of a distant, but living, past, after these fortuitous encounters with his own unique reality, the narrator can continue to analyze the artist's task to escape from contingency—the task that the narrator has failed to undertake throughout the course of the novel when he has frequented the Guermantes' aristocratic society, loved Albertine and became obsessed with jealousy, and fruitlessly pondered his desire to be a writer. Up to this point he has not understood the writer's task, though he has recognized that mere recording of objective phenomena is not adequate. The narrator had already realized that he could not be a true artist if he merely registered in his work general essences, or if he were content simply to describe general laws (3:718–19). And in meditating upon the sterile joys of intellectual performances, such as those undertaken by the Goncourt brothers, the narrator offers a muted critique of naturalism with its objective truths modeled on scientific perception, as well as an indirect commentary on its strained emulation of, when not futile rivalry with, science.

After the final revelations in the courtyard in *Le temps retrouvé,* the narrator comes to the full realization that the creation of artistic experience entails the exploration of a unique reality. Though it may be embedded in a determinist world, it cannot be analyzed within the Newtonian or Kantian coordinates of space and time, the metric province of classical analysis. He discovers that his task as a novelist is to create by recalling the perceived real he carries within him. Now facing the prospect of death after a long period of illness, he sees that, for the remainder of time that he has yet to live, he must recall and explore the multiple sensations that are too complex to be reduced by analysis. Rather, these sensations must be freed from the patterns imposed by conventional perception and shown to be a realm of unique and necessary truth that lies outside the ken of science. This is an epistemic endeavor, though different from the discovery of relations that science undertakes, for it is the endeavor of a single knowing subject expressing a unique world.

The question is open as to whether the narrator will succeed, or whether in fact he has achieved his task precisely with the novel that we readers have in hand. It is tempting to say, and many have said, that the work is circular and narrates its own coming into being; but there is really nothing in the novel that says that this is exactly the case—or that it is not. Of course, the theory of art that the narrator discovers is the theory of art that Proust has embodied in the novel, but the fiction of the narrator's presence outside of time suggests in fact that the novel's narrated events never coincide with the space of narration. It stretches the reader's imagination to try to conceive that the narrator is an epistemic quester outside the realm circumscribed by conventional time and space, and thus outside the deterministic realm of conventional science. But it does appear that the novel's recall of the narrator's unique experience should be taken to be the fiction of something like a nontranscendental transcendence. It is with no taste for paradox that I suggest that this is perhaps the best way to consider the noncontingent realm that Proust's narrator finds in literature, art, and music. According to Proust's narrator, it is only in fiction, or art in general, that one can find the enactment of a unique truth that is necessary, as necessary as the narrator's subjective fiction that posits noncontingent truth in a contingent world. Transcendence is one way of considering this relation.

The nature of artistic truth, as the narrator describes it, is perplexing. Sensation in this world is the point of departure for the creation of what Proust's narrator calls extratemporal essences (3:871). But these are not Platonic ideas or universal essences located outside of temporal experience. Rather, they are the unique states that contain within them the temporality of the (fictional) moment of perception. This notion is well illustrated precisely when the narrator says, recalling his perceptions of the church at the center of Combray, that time is the church's fourth dimension. Proust's essences are therefore quite anti-Platonic if by "Platonic" one means a universal essence that is devoid of temporality.[12] These essences are also the antithesis of what the classical scientist describes when he uses some metric framework that defines the real by presupposing absolute time. The only frame of reference for Proust's essences is the artistic self that must find some appropriate language for communicating them—literary, musical, or visual. Once this language is found, once a framework is established, then the artist can "reestablish the significance of even the slightest signs by which the artist is surrounded" (2:1014). Then every aspect of the artist's unique experience can be converted into noncontingent meaning and certain truth. The narrator himself refuses to do more than speculate that artistic significance may derive from a realm of transcendence. His speculation is persuasive and, I add, his view of a possible transcendence is perhaps not as paradoxical as I may have implied, if one is willing to grant that the ontology of art in some sense transcends contingency. This feature of art explains much. It accounts for the historical fact that works of art, unlike scientific models, are not subject to historical revision. There will never be a "truer" version of *Don Quixote,* nor a more pragmatically adequate version of *Madame Bovary.* Finally, it is relevant that the narrator adopts a scientific viewpoint in the way he entertains alternative hypotheses about the nature of art, only to find that neither metaphysics nor science seems to offer entirely adequate explanatory models. Like all scientific issues, the question remains open to unending questioning and debate.

Analyzing his future task as a writer at the end in *Le Temps retrouvé,* however, the narrator does not turn again to metaphysics for ideas. Rather, he says squarely that the artist's task is symmetrical to the scientist's enterprise. This final comparison turns on the comparable constraints to which both artist and scientist are subject in their creativity. This symmetry is analogous to Poincaré's description of the model-making work undertaken by the scientific mind. I think it is also relevant that Poincaré had already compared the artist and scientist in their joint freedom to select models in their quest for truth. There is a reverse symmetry to this comparison, at least as elaborated by Proust, since artists do not begin by selecting a model. Rather, according to Proust's narrator, artists must start with the only experience they immediately possess— the reality of their subjective perception. The intervention of the artist's intelli-

---

12. Alain de Lattre makes this argument in *La Doctrine de la réalité chez Proust.*

gence can come only after he or she has found a realm of truth in subjective experience, or in Montcrieff's classic translation:

> Only the subjective impression, however inferior the material may seem to be and however improbable the outline, is a criterion of truth and for that reason it alone merits being apprehended by the mind, for it alone is able, if the mind can extract this truth, to lead the mind to a greater perfection and impart to it a pure joy. The subjective impression is for the writer what experimentation is for the scientist, but with this difference, that with the scientist the work of the intelligence precedes, and with the writer it comes afterwards. (2:1001–2)

According to the narrator, both scientist and writer are united in another regard. If the artist, like the scientist, is not constrained by any objective system of reference, nonetheless constraints for both exist by the very nature of research. Both seek to make discoveries in a world disclosed by research—*recherche*. Once the artist has chosen the area to explore, the artist, like the scientist, then discovers that the world imposes its limits.

These limits are immediately encountered when the narrator finally decides he will become the writer he has always fitfully desired to be: "Thus I had already come to the conclusion that we are not at all free in the presence of the work of art to be created, that we do not do it as we ourselves please, but that it existed prior to us and we should seek to discover it as we would a natural law because it is both necessary and hidden" (2:1002). The material for art is already waiting to be discovered within the artist before the artist turns to discovery.

This affirmation of discovery raises again the seemingly dichotomous nature of modern epistemology that Proust embodies in his novel. In a sense Proust overcame the dichotomy by embodying both sides of discovery in his novel, both unique poetic truth and the scientific laws that can describe objective phenomena. Proust could affirm the novel's totalizing power of discovery with good intellectual conscience because he knew he was exploiting the way modern epistemology itself oscillates between realism and antirealism, and both aspects are endorsed by Proust. In its antirealism modern epistemology says that phenomena are underdetermined. In its realism it declares that there are limits imposed by objective phenomena that cannot be transgressed. Antirealism allows that there can be as many laws and models, or theories and worlds, as there are scientists and artists. But realism points out that the world imposes a limit, specifically, the invariant relations that, because they are invariant, may be assumed and used by different models or types of explanation.

The epistemic power of Proust's novel is, in a sense, that it demonstrates that only by accepting what the mind finds as a limit to its freedom—what the world and its laws impose upon it—can the mind find certainty in itself. To point up perhaps the most persuasive of the analogies between Proust's model for art and Poincaré's philosophy of science, let us note the remarkable overlap here between the scientist and the novelist concerning artistic truth and mathematics. Poincaré's epistemology allows the mind to find a type of certainty in itself, one comparable to Proust's description of the artist's certainty. Poincaré recognized that scientific truth is largely a product of reasoning through recurrence. He describes both empirical statements and mathematical statements as products of induction. Empirical inductions are contingent statements— uncertain because they are about the exterior world so that "they rest upon a belief in a general order of the Universe, an order that is outside of us."[13] But mathematical induction can impose itself as a form of certitude because, faced with the infinite recurrence that characterizes mathematical propositions, the mind recognizes, in direct intuition, its own power to make such infinite extensions. Or to quote Poincaré: "Mathematical induction, which is to say, demonstration through recurrence, imposes itself... because it is simply an affirmation of a property of mind itself."[14] From this perspective, the type of certainty that mathematics offers is a property of the mind, and the fact that the world allows mathematics to describe it is a tribute to the mind.

Analogously, the Proustian narrator discovers his certain truths in creating art because they are, in Poincaré's sense, properties of mind. Both at the novel's beginning and at its end, the narrator affirms this viewpoint in reflections upon his discovery of his past in a meditation upon mind. He affirms that it is in his own mind that he discovers the past that is first resurrected by the accidental encounter with the pastry and a cup of herbal tea, in Combray, where the narrator discovered what he would only come to understand years later. The discovery is described as research turned toward the self. I first quote the French for its ambiguities:

> Je pose la tasse et me tourne vers mon esprit. C'est à lui de trouver la vérité. Mais comment? Grave incertitude, toutes les fois que l'esprit se sent dépassé

13. Poincaré, *La Science et l'hypothèse,* 30.
14. Ibid., 31.

par lui-même; quand lui, le chercheur, est tout ensemble le pays obscur
où il doit chercher et où tout son bagage ne lui sera de rien. (1:45)

[I put down my cup and turn toward my mind/spirit. It is the mind's task
to find truth. But how? Great incertitude, every time that the mind feels
itself outreached by itself; when he, the seeker, is altogether the dark country where he must undertake his search and in which all his mental bag-
gage will be of no use.]

This discovery that the mind is at once the seeker and the sought leads to what
the narrator defines as creation: the search by the mind within the mind itself
for those relations of experience that are now properties of the mind that
undertakes the search. The symmetry with science, or at least with that aspect
of modern science promulgated by Poincaré and Mach, is inverse in that the
artist's mind seeks the certainty of the particular, rather than a general law of
recursion. However, as the young Valéry stressed, in recursive reasoning the
mind produces certainty, and the production of certain knowledge in art resembles the certainty of mathematics: it comes through the mind's seizure of its
own procedures.

Finally, Proust's description of the artist's epistemic task is part of an epistemological critique that also characterizes Poincaré's work. The narrator makes
a critique of realism that is analogous to Poincaré's critique of epistemological
naïveté. Poincaré frequently stressed that science does not describe things in
themselves: all one can know are the relations between things. Young Valéry
accepted this viewpoint. Musil struggled with it all his life. Proust's narrator
seemingly joins Poincaré as well as Mach in rejecting the "sad realism" that
tries to give a "miserable account sheet" of the lines and surfaces of things in
themselves (3:885). The narrator maintains that the artist's task is analogous to
the scientist's search for relations, since artistic truth begins only when the artist
takes two objects and posits a relationship between them. The unique truth of
the artist's experience is rendered through the description of relations, and, in
Proust, it is usually the use of metaphor that produces artistic truth by describing,
from the artist's viewpoint, what Poincaré calls "les rapports entre les chooses" —
the relations between things.[15] Poetic practice and scientific research coincide
as forms of discovering relations.

The narrator's theory of metaphor and art is fully articulated at the end of

15. Ibid., 11.

the novel, but it is perhaps most consciously and powerfully demonstrated at the novel's beginning, especially in the use of images and metaphors in the creation of the narrator's childhood in the village of Combray and his recollection of his childhood's unique plenitude. "Combray" offers the fullest demonstration of the theory that the narrator elaborates at the end in *Le Temps retrouvé*. In re-creating—or recalling—the fullness of the past, Proust calls upon the lesson of symbolism, for the narrator's recall of the specific quality of this past experience is achieved by the use of metaphor and analogy. Not only can metaphor re-create the sensual qualities of the past as the child lived it, but metaphor presents the analogies that can also describe, if not create, the relations that exist among sensations that constitute the uniqueness of the past. Metaphor brings about knowledge of the unique event. In this sense, each metaphor is an epistemic event.

Proust illustrates this discovery of the past in "Combray" by offering an example of his first attempt at writing as a young man. By quoting this youthful writing in the text, the narrator gives an example of the restitution of the past through the reproduction of that past through writing. The youthful writing took place in the past, but remains enunciated in the present moment. In a sense this is a self-referential demonstration of temporal levels of enunciation within the text that purports to recall its own past.

Equally as interesting as the demonstration of the narrator's first use of metaphor to describe his experience is the text's subject matter. In this youthful writing, the narrator describes three church steeples seen in the distance one day during an excursion in a carriage. The choice of three bodies does not seem fortuitous. It seems plausible that the description of the three churches is Proust's oblique way of paying homage to Poincaré's work on the three body problem. (Proust can be as recondite in his allusions as are the narrator's great aunts when they pay cryptic compliments to Swann.) An allusion to the relativity one would associate with Poincaré seems implicit in the relativistic way Proust's narrator describes the motion of these three steeples as they change their position relative to the moving carriage in which the young narrator found himself as he began to write a description of them. Moreover, through this act of writing, at this moment when he describes his impressions of the three steeples, the narrator anticipates rather precisely his later ideas about writing. The literal quotation of this youthful writing allows the older narrator to offer a metaphorical description illustrating the discovery of the unique truth of the past that metaphor can bring about—for it is actually situated in that past.

Calling the steeples "flowers," and then "three maidens of legend," the youthful narrator describes how they change position, though of course their movement only reflects the relative spatial position of the moving observer. As the narrator's position changes, the steeples "move" metaphorically about, "timidly seeking their way, and, after some awkward, stumbling movements of their noble silhouettes, drawing close to one another, slipping one behind another, shewing nothing more, now, against the still rosy sky than a single dusky form, charming and resigned, so vanishing in the night" (1:140, of the following: "je les vis timidement chercher leur chemin et, après quelques gauches trébuchements de leurs nobles silhouettes, se serrer les uns contre les autres, glisser l'un derrière l'autre, ne plus faire sur le ciel encore rose qu'une seule forme noire, charmante et résignée, et s'effacer dans la nuit" [1:182].) With these metaphorical motions the three bodies have danced out their relations in a ballet that successfully describes the unique truth of that unique moment for a youthful narrator who is suddenly very happy—for could one not say that, with these metaphors, the boy narrator solved, artistically and with certainty, the three body problem? He has resolved it through the web of metaphors that relate three bodies in their mutual metaphorical attraction.

Concluding Thoughts on Proust and Musil

With this "solution" to the problem of knowledge in art, Proust's narrator knows that he is, or rather was, close to a demonstration of the necessity of the artist's truth. My hesitation about verb tenses here, and earlier, reflects that the end is contained in the beginning in Proust, with all the necessity that retrospection can confer. Proust's novel demands that one be able to say that the past *is*. It *is*, moreover, as it *was*, in its necessity as certain artistic truth. This was not the kind of solution to epistemological uncertainty that a realist like Musil could accept. In contrast with Musil, Proust really stands out as a rationalist who, in interpreting the dominant epistemology, could fulfill his need for knowledge within the confines of the cultural matrix, whereas the mathematical *Mensch* in Musil chaffed against those confines while dreaming of some "other condition" to be found in a myth beyond culture. What Musil sought was a myth oriented toward the future, not found in the past, since he regarded the past as a statistical locus characterized by invariant processes springing from an incomprehensible jumble of a trillion irrational decisions.

Like Joyce and Raymond Queneau, Musil found in history the science of human unhappiness.

Musil's novel foundered on his attempt at a mythic future unity, whereas Proust's *A la recherche* triumphs precisely by surreptitiously reintroducing the myth of salvation: Combray is saved, and paradise lost is paradise gained. But the terms of the Biblical myth are reversed by Proust. Knowledge does not drive one from the garden; rather, knowledge opens the garden. The myth of salvation is a strong undercurrent in Proust, and his literary epistemology aims at reconciling this myth with the bleak truth of science according to which the most probable future is nothingness—something of which Proust's narrator is relentlessly aware, and especially upon reentering society at the novel's end and seeing the ongoing work of time in the destruction of the flesh of his aging friends and acquaintances. Proust's work stands in sharp contrast with Musil's in the temporal positioning of myth. In their implicit and explicit appeal to myth, both writers represent the attempt of much modernist literature to make of myth a privileged discourse that can escape the contingencies of space and time. Musil may well have envied Proust's capacity to accept something like Mach's critique of knowledge, while creating a domain for artistic truth that was impervious to Mach's positivism. As Musil's diaries show, he did not want to be compared with Proust; and the rather enigmatic one-line entry there, "Gegen Proust"—against Proust—suggests that Musil actively rejected Proust's epistemology.[16]

Musil was perhaps more than a little sensitive to, and perhaps irritated by, the fact that Proust achieves his creation in part by restoring the basic epistemic separation described by Pascal in the opposition between *l'esprit de finesse* and *l'esprit de géométrie*. The mathematician in Musil knew that Proust was proposing a modernist version of the mind dealing with complexity and the mind functioning axiomatically: the artist's mind, knowing through direct intuition, has to deal with an indefinite number of principles, and perhaps for this reason it can easily go astray, but only in art and literature can one plausibly attempt to know such complex phenomena as human perception. Proust's narrator is quite aware that the complexity of art contrasts with the precision that scientific reasoning owes to the very narrowness of its field. Musil's Ulrich sets himself against

16. Musil, *Tagebücher,* ed. Adolf Frisé, 1:779. In this first edition of Musil's diaries, Frisé presents a letter in which Musil claims not to have read more than ten lines of Proust (2:701). This strikes me as a defensive commentary by Musil in reaction to the comparisons that were immediately made between his novel and Proust's.

Proust's narrator by wanting to introduce axiomatic precision into moral life and poetry, and presumably poetic insight and ethical sensitivity into science, thus creating a grand, unified epistemology. Proust and Musil ultimately had opposing viewpoints about the epistemological dualism with which Pascal inaugurates modern thought. Proust, in an almost serene way, frees the modernist mind from "science envy" by showing that the *esprit de finesse* is an epistemic equal to the scientific mind. Musil, by sharp contrast, makes despair about science ever serving human purposes into a leitmotif with which literature is still living—for example, it is a still a fundamental issue of Viennese postmodernity.

Proust proposes an epistemic divide in which literature and science share a certain mutual responsibility for offering different types of knowledge of the world. On the one hand, science has its varied protocols for truth, many of which turn upon quantification. On the other hand, in most of its operations the mind does not function according to some algorithm, as Pascal might have said and which recent thinkers as various as Berkeley philosopher Hubert Dreyfus and Oxford physicist Roger Penrose do say.[17] Very much our contemporary, at least in his implicit critique of the idea that all knowledge obeys some kind of algorithm, Proust argues in effect that literature as knowledge of the mind offers unique knowledge that can be garnered in no other way. In principle, and not just in practice, no quantification can offer knowledge encompassing the complexity of the unique human self. This knowledge can only be based upon the immediate seizure of the self's multiple complex facets, and for this literature is a, if not the, privileged tool.

Epistemological dualism is ultimately not adequate to describe these operations, and both Poincaré's and Proust's epistemologies point in fact to multiple types of knowledge that science and art offer about the multiple realms they entertain. Pascal's formulation of two types of knowledge goes a long way, however, in explaining the origins of the modernist view of epistemology and the types of knowledge held by scientists and artists. His dualism looks as if it opposes science and literature; yet, his *esprit de finesse* can be taken as a kind of general concept designating the multiple types of knowledge literature proposes in contrast to axiomatic thinking. Thus, Pascal's version of two epistemologies works equally well to illuminate Proust's success in reconciling science

17. For philosophical arguments against the idea that the mind is a computer, see Hubert Dreyfus, *What Computers Can't Do: The Limits of Artificial Reason,* and *What Computers Can't Do: The Limits of Artificial Intelligence.* For a scientific argument, see Roger Penrose, *The Emperor's New Mind: Concerning Computers, Minds, and the Laws of Physics.*

and literature, and to explain the origins of Musil's conceiving of epistemology as a binary opposition—and then impaling himself on a rigid dualism that he could not overcome in his grand desire to create a new unified epistemology for the novel. I now take the spotlight off Proust and Musil, but not Pascal, for the mathematical Jansenist casts a long shadow over, as well as provides continuing illumination of, our cultural history, extending to the next writers dealt with, Kafka and Joyce, and beyond to Woolf, Borges, and others who will presently occupy us.

Chapter Four

Kafka's Search for Laws

In its most general shape the type of knowledge proposed by science takes the form of laws. It is clearly the case that the most influential modernists like Kafka and Joyce were fascinated by the nature of the laws that science takes to be the goal of its inquiry. We have already seen that Proust and Musil were concerned with scientific law. Proust's separation of the subjective and the objective is in effect the denial that science's contingent laws can describe the workings of the artistic mind, whereas Musil's narrator doubted that the indifferent descriptions of statistical invariance called laws could ever offer knowledge of essential matters, or knowledge of things in themselves. However, neither of these viewpoints questions the belief that the goal of scientific knowledge is, ultimately and perhaps ideally, the laws of phenomena. Kafka and Joyce's work questions the possibility of the search for the law, though in different, complementary ways. Therefore, in the next two chapters I want to approach the question of the search for laws by considering the way that Kafka and Joyce embody laws and the search for the law in their fictions. In a very real sense the law is the stuff of knowledge of which modernist fiction proposes to be a revelation, and Kafka and Joyce can give one a very good idea as to the wide range of possibilities characterizing the modernist search for knowledge of law in literary experience.

What does it mean to say that, ideally, the essential activity of science is the discovery of laws or, at least, the revelation of hidden phenomena about which there has been previously no knowledge? In *The Character of Physical Law* (1965) Nobel laureate Richard Feynman offers an answer to this question. One of the most important thinkers in the development of the standard model of particle physics, Feynman describes the search for laws as the revelation of hidden rhythms and patterns of nature, not visible, but encoded in nature, to be revealed by analysis.[1] To characterize laws as rhythms and patterns suggests regularities and recurrence, perceived by a kind of aesthetic sensibility. This is not necessarily the description of law one might expect from a mathematical physicist. However, Feynman, unlike Poincaré, was not a mathematician who also did science. Rather, he was a physicist who, Paul Davies says in the introduction to *The Character of Physical Law,* was able to do mathematical physics without systematic mathematics. One will do well to keep Feynman's distrust of formalisms in mind when one turns to that elusive stuff called the laws, or the regularities and the universals that are the object of knowledge. The formalism describing the law is not necessarily identical to the law.

Moreover, if we leave aside the mathematical formalisms used to describe these rhythms and patterns, then Feynman's description of discovery makes science sound very much like an activity close to literature, and especially fiction in novels. The very word "novel," used in English to designate narrative fictions, suggests that the genre aims at discovering something new, new relations, and sometimes new patterns characterizing existence. What is novel is new, and news, we hope, will bring some information about how things are. This emphasis on the new also characterizes science's essential function as the search for new laws. In reading Kafka and Joyce one finds that this assumption of the need for the new hovers on the hermeneutic horizon, for both writers query why humanity demands, in its Faustian desire, ever new discoveries that supersede old knowledge. Both interrogate why it is contradictory to imagine, in the Western world at least, a meaningful search for knowledge whose goal would be the affirmation of what is already known. Both recall that the affirmation of the already known was the chief epistemological function of much traditional literature and science, and both ironically confront the novel fact that it is another mark of what we mean by modernity that we expect, as a matter of course, constant innovation and discovery in both literature and science.

In other words, modernism in literature sometimes undertook a critique of the drive toward modernity in science. This critique eventuated in turn in self-questioning about what one can discover through literature. In this respect both Kafka and Joyce contested the idea of perpetual discovery by, rather paradoxically, inventing radically new literary forms: they discovered new forms of revelation in a contestation of the idea that literature, like science, is a discovery of knowledge—and that by implication scientific law can meaningfully

---

1. Feynman, *The Character of Physical Law,* 13.

enter into public discourses. Kafka and Joyce contrast with each other, however, and mark out opposing positions. Kafka quite paradoxically discovers that one can ultimately discover nothing, whereas Joyce revels in showing that one can know much, perhaps everything, through literature. The net effect of their discoveries is much the same. Discovering everything is much the same as discovering nothing, and readers who want to find out what is in the distant castle Kafka presents in *Das Schloss,* in order to discover the law underlying its operations, may find themselves just as frustrated by Kafka's epistemic quest as are those readers who get lost in the dramatization of the total encyclopedia of human knowledge enacted for, or by, Joyce's sometimes dead Irishman, Finnegan, universal quester and seer of all things. Kafka inscribes an absent law, in virtually all senses of the word "law," at the center of his works; whereas in *Ulysses* and *Finnegans Wake* Joyce affirms that all laws, or any other form of knowledge, can be revealed in the literary text, in the consciousness it embodies, which is to say, in the universal consciousness that language shapes. However, Joyce's hyperbolic panlogism seems hardly any more affirmative of knowledge than is Kafka's paradoxical proposition that the final law of knowledge is that we will never recognize the final law—even if by accident we were to discover it.

Nearly every novel or story by Kafka at least implies some attempt to know the nature of the law, or *das Gesetz,* that all desire to know. Kafka's work lays bare the ambivalent senses that attach to the concept of the law. He obliges the reader to be attentive to the enticingly ambiguous relationships obtaining between law and literature, and between literature and science. Most pointedly, Kafka's parables represent the law as that which should prescribe and, at the same time, as that which should describe the regularities and invariances that might explain any given series of events that take place in the world. In this regard Kafka obliges the reader to consider the literary possibilities of physics, for literature appears as a form of search or research, analogous to the most basic science of nature: both undertake the search for a law that is never transparent. Thus hidden, encoded, but presumably manifest in all phenomena—since the phenomena are clearly there demanding an explanation—the law scintillates invisibly visible in the phenomena for which it should prescribe regularity and obedience. The law is at once what describes, but is hidden, and prescribes, but isn't known.

The history of the very notion of law is bound up with these ambiguities about prescription and description, or transparency and darkness. Natural laws, as lawyers and chemists both know, are those regularities that have been inscribed in nature and perhaps in the human heart. They are descriptions of what must be as well as what ought to be, and in some utopian world of transcendental faith these descriptive and prescriptive laws would be one and the same. It is this vision of the law that is found, for example, in Sophocles' *Oedipus the King,* in which divine laws are at once moral prescriptions and the iron laws of necessity that one cannot transgress without destroying oneself—and incurring the moral wrath of the gods. The belief that scientific laws are also part of a moral structure underlies the unity of Plato's realm of mathematics, Dante's paradise, and Kepler's world vision.

This recurrent conflation of law as prescription and description does not disappear with modern thought. One can find it, for example, in the latter part of the nineteenth century in the thoughts of the bishop-hating prophet of science, the Darwinian Thomas Huxley. Huxley preached, for reformist Victorians, the unity of scientific law and moral law as the basis for education:

> Let us consider what a child thus "educated" [traditionally] knows, and what it does not know. Begin with the most important topic of all—morality, as the guide of conduct. The child knows well enough that some acts meet with approbation and some with disapprobation. But it has never heard that there lies in the nature of things a reason for every moral law, as cogent and as well defined as that which underlies every physical law; that stealing and lying are just as certain to be followed by evil consequences, as putting your hand in the fire, or jumping out of a garret window.[2]

Huxley appears here to draw upon Kant for his formulation, the Kant who rationalized the Newtonian revolution to make the world safe for theology. Whatever the sources of his thought, the fact that the same Huxley who invented the idea of agnosticism here equates moral and scientific law suggests that the theological roots of our concept of law, in all its senses, run deep.

Theological roots probably underlie a recurrent thirst for finding the unity of science, a dream of a final vision when being would be revealed as subject to transparent laws, and the messy realms of being and doing would stand united in the mind of man. Then mind would resemble the mind of God at the end of Hegel's vision of history, and, pace Steven Weinberg, one would possess the "final theory" discussed by contemporary physicists. Perhaps one could even

2. Huxley, "A Liberal Education," in *Lay Sermons, Essays, and Reviews,* 36.

understand Feynman's curious belief that, once physics is completed, there may be no need for mathematics.[3] The dreams of the unity of knowledge have a long history, and one wonders if the contemporary belief that today one has separated the descriptive and prescriptive realms of thought is a passing moment in history. Certainly the modern dreams about the unity of mind keep alive the conflation of these two realms, though such dreams are undoubtedly the reverse side of the equally modern doubts that the law can be revealed through language, at least human language. These fleeting dreams and anguished doubts are the interpretation of the law to which Kafka has given the most powerful modern expression.

Huxley's joining of natural and moral law provides one historical context for approaching Kafka's work. Another is offered by the fact that, though trained in jurisprudence, Kafka also had some knowledge of chemistry and physics. It is of more than little interest that the young Kafka received early grounding in the basic natural sciences as well as in the law. As a young man he took the natural sciences quite seriously, to the point of imagining that he might join a friend in being a chemistry student at the university. For a brief time he even attended chemistry lectures before becoming a student of the law. Briefly, in some chemistry lectures, as well as in his secondary school studies of psychology and physics, Kafka studied scientific laws as exemplars of the law— law often conceived as the postulated transcendental unity that is the ultimate basis of knowledge. In his studies in natural science it is probable that Kafka's teachers defined the nature of physical law in the way that the chemist Louis Kahlenberg defined it for students in Wisconsin in the early twentieth century, where Kahlenberg taught after he had completed his doctoral studies with the Nobel laureate chemist Ostwald in Leipzig in 1894–95. One should consider how a German chemist like Kahlenberg, a representative of the era's most prominent and successful science, concisely defined the law much like a lawyer. He wrote in 1909, "A law, as the word is used in science, is a general statement summarizing what has actually been found to be true in a large number of individual cases that have been carefully investigated."[4] In contrast with the physicist Feynman's image of the law as pattern, it is striking that this early-twentieth-century definition of law by a chemist stresses at once the idea of statistical

3. Feynman, *Character of Physical Law*, 58.
4. I have quoted the 1916 edition of Louis Kahlenberg, *Outlines of Chemistry*, vol. 4, first published in 1909. For Kahlenberg's relations with Germany and German chemistry, see William Brock, *The Norton History of Chemistry*, 379 and 389.

invariance—based on mensuration—and a view of law that also sounds like a definition of legal procedures deriving their legitimacy from the actual cases into which an investigating judge has made an inquiry. In other words, an early-twentieth-century chemist suggests, for the seeker of the law, the allegorical conflation of knowledge as measurement and as justice. The law is at once, for the chemist, quantified description and individual prescription, which sounds remarkably like what the questers in Kafka's fiction are constantly seeking. In Kahlenberg's definition of the law, however, Huxley's sense of easy certainty is lost, for the seeker of the law must look for that "general statement" that rationally encodes the knowledge of the real by "summarizing what has actually been found to be true in a large number of individual cases." As Kafka amply demonstrates, it is with the disjuncture between specific individual cases and the general statement, inferred from the series of cases, that things begin to go astray in one's investigations.

We shall presently see that in many of his stories Kafka questions the permanence of the invariance that one grants to language. In effect he questions the power of language to name the law of the series. With that he wonders if anything formulated in language can grant knowledge of the world. In other stories, he takes a different tack and parodies the mensuration that scientific seekers of the law use as definitions of the real. These two types of tales are related in that mensuration shows invariance just as naming confers it. In Kafka both are dubious procedures. Most critics of Kafka are sensitive to the problems of language in his works, but they are perhaps less attentive to the epistemological dilemmas that Kafka bequeathed to a later generation in his parodistic allegories of measuring and quantifying. These parodies point up that measurement often constitutes an arbitrary definition, one actually used in place of knowledge of a law. Moreover, Kafka's texts insinuate that measurement is an infinite process that the seeker for the law only arbitrarily brings to an end. Kafka's texts show that measurement is a slippery two-sided process. On the one hand, once one measures a process or a series, one may feel triumphantly that, in quantification, something has been discovered. But, on the other hand, as Kafka often shows, once one measures something, one then possesses a self-contained definition of a series that often seems to be merely a tautology.

This view of quantification and definition intrigued Kafka's contemporary Wittgenstein, who asked what was the nature of the "fact" that water boils at 100 degrees centigrade. Comparisons between Kafka and Wittgenstein, born six years apart in Musil's Austro-Hungarian empire, are often revealing, and scientific realists may find that Wittgenstein often resembles a philosophical Kafka. Wittgenstein analyzed the fact that the proposition about water's boiling point looks as if it were an empirical statement that can be called a law. But, once discovered, that proposition also functions as a definition, in an almost prescriptive way, and, Wittgenstein mused, would not be very helpful if we were to encounter a colorless liquid that boiled at ninety-eight degrees. Something like such a deviant liquid is not infrequent in Kafka's work, taking the form of singing dogs, giant moles, or dutiful sons who, through no fault of their own, don't quite respect the law of their condition. Kafka's work, like Wittgenstein's questions, asks, What does it mean to encounter a specific case that deviates from the law of the series, especially when we need the definition of the series, based on the singular case, to define the singular case that deviates from it? Both chemistry and jurisprudence must confront the fact that the law that emerges from the series is problematic, for it often seems that the law exists primarily to mask the fact that most of what we encounter in our quest for the law is better defined by the way it deviates from its presumed invariance.

Nobody would maintain that Kafka's encounter with chemistry was a turning point in his life. Yet, however brief his scientific studies, his works show that Kafka constantly had in mind the modern chemical paradigm as a model of mensuration, knowledge, and rationality—for Kafka acquired his science before the impact of relativity theory or the elaboration of quantum theory in physics. What seems especially important is the way chemistry stressed the idea that scientific knowledge aims at revealing the hidden law of a given series, not at knowledge of some hidden *Ding an sich*. This was especially clear in Mendeleyev and Meyer's development of the periodic table that sets forth the relationship of all the elements, based then on atomic weights, which defined bedrock physical reality as so many ordered series. And the problematic nature of the ordered series, in all its arbitrary glory, is a key to understanding Kafka's epistemological doubts.

In 1932, after the final organization of the periodic table, the French epistemologist Gaston Bachelard evaluated chemistry's triumph in the reduction of physical phenomena to an ordered series. He did so with an enthusiasm that captures the sense of victory that early-twentieth-century science felt in claiming to finalize our understanding of the organization of what were then often considered to be the basic elements of nature. According to the rationalist Bachelard, the mathematical organization of the periodic table showed that mathematics was the hidden law constitutive of the "science of order" which the scientist could reveal in the universe.[5] Specifically with regard to the triumphs of organic chemistry, Bachelard claimed, with a curious Kafkan turn of phrase, that each chemical substance "is the isolated sign of some general law" (66). Given the mathematical organization of the elemental series, discoveries of new substances "prove the existence of a law by their very existence" [On a affaire dans cette partie de l'épistémologie chimique à des substances qui prouvent une loi par leur seule existence] (68). My point here is not, of course, that Kafka had to immerse himself in organic chemistry to describe a metamorphosis that proves, or not, some law of the series; it is rather that triumphant scientific epistemology conceived the law as the organizing principle of a series whose existence need merely be described in order to prove the existence of the law governing the series. And if early-twentieth-century scientists encountered problems in ordering elements in terms of their mass, this merely showed that the investigators of order were somehow defective. As Bachelard describes the situation chemists faced in 1900, it was not the law that is aberrant, it is rather the knowledge that we have of the law that is aberrant.[6] Kafka's questers for the law would not demur.

Two overlapping questions press forward when one reads Kafka with one eye on 1901, the year he entered the university, and one eye on the supposedly postmodern era Kafka helped usher in after World War II. On the one hand, Kafka's work abounds in motifs presenting analogies with the search for the law conceived as the order of the series that allows one to entertain the belief that there is order in the world—even if our knowledge of that "necessary" order is aberrant or if measurement of that series is an infinite task. On the other hand, his work is full of skeptical parodies of the quest for knowledge accompanied by a respectful despair about whether there even is an order of the series that can be revealed in any meaningful sense. Moreover, as suggested earlier, because something can be ordered as a quantitative series does not necessarily imply that that order can be expressed by human language—for Kafka's concept of the law demands that it be meaningful in human terms, which is to

5. Bachelard, *Le Pluralisme cohérent de la chimie moderne*, 9. Hereafter cited parenthetically in the text.

6. Bachelard is drawing heavily upon Kahlenberg's teacher, Ostwald, for this commentary. It should also be noted that many confusions and inaccuracies in observation were largely cleared up once Moseley put the periodic table on a different footing by using atomic number, instead of atomic mass, to order the elements.

say, mediated by language. If Kafka's work is full of measurement, full of distances expanded and contracted in potentially quantitative terms, full of inferences about some necessary series that should explain itself, it is because Kafka is an epistemologist for whom quantification is a necessary, but not necessarily sufficient, condition for knowledge of the law—in all the confused and conflated senses of that alluring term. Quantification describes a relation; it is not a revelation. Echoes of Mach's thought also seem to reverberate in Kafka's demonstrations that measurement is simply an arbitrary operation of a mind that could pursue an indefinite number of metric possibilities. But, for Kafka's searchers, the indefinite number of possible relations does not add up to knowledge of a law, at least a law that can satisfy the human need for some substantial reality—substantial because it is grounded in the law. Young Musil would have understood this all too well.

Before pursuing a more detailed reading of Kafka's relation to science, I must concede that Kafka's works offer a springboard to the most varied of interpretations, and rightly so, since Kafka's stories, parables, and novels usually take the form of an open self-referential allegory. One need not study a logician like Gödel to understand that any self-referential system is never closed, but can always generate further axioms, and paradoxes, about itself. For example, if all is described or prescribed by the law, what is the law that prescribes the law—and prescribes that law, ad infinitum? To get around self-reference—which is not a likely event in Kafka—Kafka's allegories demand that the reader look beyond the often bizarre and frequently comic manifest content of the fictions and ask what kind of symbolizing process can endow the fiction with meaning. In other words, the reader must ask if the allegory might point at something other than the allegorical procedure itself. By obliging the reader to ask what can be known through the text, Kafka's texts oblige the reader to ask if literature might have some epistemic function, such as revelation of the law, though the regressive nature of self-reference usually means that the reader finds merely the revelation of the search for revelation.

This type of representation was once the function of those literary forms called sacred texts, myth, or, simply, The Book, containing all laws, descriptive and prescriptive. Kafka's texts concede that today the revelation of the law is rather much a function of science. In modern terms, then, Kafka's question is, Can literature, or writing, offer some access to an invariant regularity that can be called a law? In Kafka's work, traditional and modern senses of the law simultaneously are maintained, and the questions his texts ask often seem to oscillate between myth and science, as well as between jurisprudence and chemistry. This questioning places Kafka's readers, like many of his characters, in a situation in which they wonder how, or if, they can know that they know anything at all in the very opaque world in which all laws, in every sense of the term, are darkly encoded, to use Feynman's term. Kafka's readers, like his characters, find themselves embarked on a quest in which they are obliged to wonder if they can discover some hidden pattern that rules over the incongruous manifest phenomena that constitute the world. But because of the self-referentiality attendant upon this questioning, Kafka's epistemic quest frequently runs the risk of following an itinerary of infinite regress as reader and quester alike wonder if they know that they know—with the attendant risk that the law forever recedes, across an infinite distance as it were, as questioning proliferates.[7]

The search for the law becomes all the more complicated in that the quest for discovery is usually not directly presented, but rather is signified itself by allegorical indirection. For example, in *The Trial,* the protagonist, Josef K., arrested for unknown reasons, spends the entire novel looking for the unknown law that would describe his case. It appears that all he finds out is that the law can remain hidden, but nonetheless condemn him. So finally the reader is puzzled by a law that apparently has condemned K. for no reason, and whose existence remains in doubt. A series composed of the novel's one dubious trial and one certain execution offers only flimsy evidence that the law's existence is more than mere hypothesis. The situation in which Josef K. finds himself is, however, mirrored by another narrative within the narrative. Toward the end of the novel Josef K. enters a church and listens to a priest who narrates the parable "Before the Law," a tale of a man who waits a lifetime to gain admittance to the law, only to learn after years of fruitless waiting that not only would the gate never be opened, but that he had been waiting at a gate that was only meant for him. After the narration of the parable, Josef K. and the priest argue about its possible meanings.

In discussing interpretations of the parable, Josef K. and the priest do not directly address the meaning of the novel in which Josef K. finds himself, though it appears that the priest initially intends for the parable to disclose something about Josef K., his trial, and the law presiding over it. The reader hungry for meaning must, like Joseph K., witness the proliferation of interpretations of

7. These comments are greatly expanded upon in my *Franz Kafka: A Study of the Short Fiction.*

the parable within the novel that the priest offers, almost as if the priest's function were to frustrate the reader's own attempt at finding access to the law. Finally, the possible meanings of the parable in the text stand in direct analogy to the possible meanings that readers can find for the novel itself in its portrayal of the difficulty of access to the law.

Kafka's strategy of self-mirroring narratives obliges the reader to try out as many interpretive hypotheses as possible in order to find some law that will fit the manifest narrated experience and limit the meaning to one that the reader can clearly "know." Once the reader accepts the hypothesis that there is a law describing the manifest experience—and this is only a hypothesis, after all—the reader becomes a researcher looking for the law that is hidden in the world of the text. However, the allegory that questions our possibility of interpreting it also makes it most difficult to hit upon any final certainty. The possibility of an indefinite, if not infinite, genesis of allegorical meaning entails the impossibility of closure. And the law remains elusive, a hypothetical principle that should, but apparently may not, lie behind the series of events the character confronts.

With this example of the self-mirroring parable, it is clear that modern scientific epistemology looms large in Kafka's work, for the underdetermination of possible hypotheses seems to work hyperbolically in the text. Phenomena are wildly unconstrained in the number of models one can apply to them. Moreover, the literary staging of the narrative, with character and reader as searchers, duplicates the situation of a scientist looking at the flux of experience. Or, if one prefers, the reader doubles the character who doubles the scientist-searcher, with other doubles multiplying in the fictions themselves. Kafka often pushes to a parodistic limit the epistemic situation described by modern epistemologists from Mach and Poincaré through Popper and Quine: an indefinite number of hypotheses or models may (or may not) work to explain phenomena. If "reality" is underdetermined, where can certainty exist in this proliferating process of unfolding hypotheses—except in the paradoxical certainty of uncertainty?

Kafka's short fictions dramatize even more concisely the epistemological quest for the law that is central to novels like *The Castle* and *The Trial,* novels that define for many readers what one means by modernist fiction, while, for others, they represent the origins of postmodernity and its skepticism about knowledge in literature. I want, therefore, to deal now with several of Kafka's short fictions because they are extraordinary thought experiments about the relation between language and the discovery of knowledge of the law, and then, with these experiments in mind, return to *The Trial* and especially *The Castle*. Many of Kafka's short fictions ask quite pointedly if language can reveal a law that explains the often absurd series of events that one observes in the world of the text, and sometimes in the putatively real world as well. These short fictions play with the modern epistemological axiom that any exemplar should be capable of revealing the law of the series of which it is an example. This is an important axiom in science itself, for, without it, there can be no principle of falsification—the principle that allows one negative example to disprove any theory or law of the series. It is a working principle that every element in a system must confirm the hypothetical law that governs the system, for if there are exceptions, there can be no falsification and, hence, no confirmation. With great intuition about epistemology—with insight comparable to the views of philosophers of science like Popper and Quine—Kafka implicitly posits this axiom in order to play with its ambiguities, for he shows well before Quine that if a single particular seems to give the lie to one's hypothesis, one can always adjust the data to continue to confirm the hypothesis. Or, more pungently, Kafka's work shows the absurd tenacity of the very hypothesis that there even is a hypothesis capable of explaining the incongruous data that proliferate in the world.

Given the axiom that every exemplar should be capable of confirming the existence of its law, the searcher for the law can randomly begin research anywhere. Let us begin Kafka's investigations of the law in the various tales that Kafka himself published in the collection *A Country Doctor* in 1919. (These, along with the collection of stories *A Hunger Artist,* and the stories "The Judgment," "The Metamorphosis," and "In the Penal Colony," are the main works that he actually saw into print.) I admit I am not entirely following Kafka's principle of random revelation, since I have a motivation: the tales in *A Country Doctor* allow one to measure how Kafka had moved along in his investigations of the law after he turned from chemistry to jurisprudence—with all due caution about the idea of measuring things in Kafka. The law is present from the beginning of this collection since the first story, "The New Advocate," centers on a specialist in the law who is none other than Bucephalus, the horse of Alexander the Great. Kafka delineates a historical "character" who seems to exist now, in the present moment of enunciation, as in a sense does every character whom we call upon, in our present moment of need to know the past, for an illustration of the laws of history. The text implies, with uncertain irony, that, in their "world-historical meaning," historical characters perform as exemplars of the law, and for this reason people seek a meaning in Bucephalus.

But, says the narrator, that meaning is ambiguous. Once that meaning was to point with a sword toward regions to be conquered, toward the untraversable distances that expand infinitely toward an India that is farther away today than before. Today, Bucephalus can no longer traverse the great distances he once covered with great speed. The distance is too immense to be measured now. But, for knowledge to exist, science says that meaning must be defined and pinned down by measurement. Thus the search for historical law seems to founder on the impossible quantitative understanding of the distance separating the seeker from the object of knowledge, in space or in time.

The impossibility of the measuring, necessary to know the law, seems spelled out in this story by the impossible distances both in time and space that separate Bucephalus from a time past in which he once could entertain the possibility of completing a journey—Alexander apparently did make it to India. A successful journey is one marked by closure, which would again mean, in theory at least, it could be measured. In the face of the impossibility of completing mensuration, the narrator concludes that only books—language encoding a dusty promise—are left to today's moderns. The narrator suggests that, in turning to ancient writings, Bucephalus, now a lawyer, offers a lesson for those seeking the law of history: "So perhaps it is really best to do as Bucephalus has done and absorb oneself in law books. In the quiet lamplight, his flanks unhampered by the thighs of a rider, free and far from the clamor of battle, he reads and turns the pages of our ancient tomes."[8] It seems inevitable that it is a lawyer who thinks the law might be found in ancient books, once he has abandoned the voyage that science makes, which is always an active journey to measure the law in the present moment—for what could mensuration as a preterit act mean?

Kafka's irony about the law, here and elsewhere, frequently turns on metaphors tying science to travel in space and time. Without the present journey, the movement forward toward closure, there is no quest, and thus no encounter with a possible law. Recourse to books, as Bucephalus knows, is to content oneself with the texts that speak of what the law *was,* perhaps, but not necessarily of what it is. Sedentary Bucephalus points up with negative irony that, without the journey, epistemic revelation always lies, alluringly to be sure, on the distant horizon. In fine, Kafka's imagined voyages in space and time point toward

8. Kafka, *The Complete Stories,* ed. Nahum Glatzer, 415. All quotations of stories are from this edition and are hereafter cited parenthetically in the text.

possible discovery, and the measure of that travel might describe the law to be discovered; thus every journey, taken or not taken, is a key to these allegories about the evasive nature of the law. The journey represents the necessary movement toward knowledge; and, if it were completed, then a voyage would also be necessary for the communication of that knowledge. But first the journey must proceed along an itinerary in space and time that is measurable if it is to come to an end. There is no knowledge without closure, the trip must have a goal, and, with this, the itinerary must lead to a return. Wittgenstein pointed up much the same thing when, in his later philosophy, he insisted that all explanations come to an end. They must come to end and, if they don't, knowledge becomes a Kafkan journey toward the infinite wherein the law recedes forever from view.

Not only space, but also time can destroy the itinerary that the quester must make, a point illustrated in the story in *A Country Doctor* called "An Old Manuscript." All narrated acts in the manuscript seem to take place in the present, as nomads rage senselessly and destroy the narrator's city even while he writes about their barbarous acts. Yet readers also realize that they know of these barbarians only from a self-naming old sheet of manuscript that tells what the nomads did once in an indefinite past. The absurd presence of the nomadic invaders exists only through the presence of language, enunciated in the present tense. The reader wonders, moreover, if there is some mysterious law that would explain the meaning of this horrible series of events of which the manuscript offers individual exemplars. If so, that law exists in the past, but laws should seemingly exist in the present tense. The narrative situation obliges one to ask if one can find some commensurate measure relating the present narration and the absent past that continues to exist, absurdly, in language. This near-paradox suggests that no law ever exists except as an inference from what no longer exists—the past. And since the past is infinitely absent, though present in language as meaningless and savage destruction, this text does not bode well for epistemic quests.

In the second, eponymous story of *A Country Doctor,* Kafka offers one of his many versions of a scientist, here the country doctor, who must negotiate, again in the present, the infinite spaces that expand at the story's end and prevent his returning home, which is to say, to his point of departure for the trip that took him to a patient's house. This dilemma occurs after space has first been condensed, since at the story's beginning, after receiving a call for help, the doctor could cover ten miles in a second, though this speed takes him away from his helpless serving girl at home who is being ravished by a groom the doctor discovers in a pigsty. In spite of this unexpected discovery, the doctor is propelled to a patient whose main desire is to die of a worm-infested wound. Attending this patient, whose wound demands a scientific explanation, the doctor finds that the people in the patient's village expect the modern scientist to replace the priest with his doctor's "omnipotence." However, all the hapless doctor can do is escape from the patient's house by leaping through a window—only then to find that the space he must cross to return home has expanded into infinite snowy wastes he will never traverse. Space expands beyond any possible measurement as the doctor flees from the singular case of festering disease for which he was expected to find an explanation, a cause, a law. The individual case here reveals itself to be merely a blip on the infinite expansion of the ways and byways that expand into time and into space.

With this geometric expansion of space, Kafka brings the paradoxical logic of the Pascalian cosmos into daily life, allowing the infinite to show its perverse free play in sabotaging measurement. At the end the doctor seems trapped in Zeno's logical paradox, a paradox designed to show the impossibility of using measurement for knowledge when one confronts the possible infinite contained within geometric expansion and contraction. For each step in measurement demands that one complete a first step that points back regressively to a first step, ad infinitum. This infinite regress in space is analogous to the comic regress that Kafka dramatizes in other allegories about allegories that lead us to wonder how we can know that we know that we know, ad infinitum. Pascal's evil infinity lies lurking in both cases to sabotage every attempt at closure.

All is not motion, and contrasting with the possibility of infinite forward motion toward the law is the quintessential Kafka allegory dramatizing immobility, such as the previously mentioned parable narrated in *The Trial,* "Before the Law," in which the supplicant is not allowed to go through his appointed gate to encounter the law. Published separately in *A Country Doctor,* the parable stands out as an allegory in immobility. Coming to the law, the seeker finds his forward progress stopped by the gatekeeper, who warns him not to attempt to go forward, since he is only the first of many gatekeepers, each guarding another gate offering, and forbidding, access to the law. "Before the Law" illustrates thus a variant on how allegory allegorizes itself. Taken in itself, the tale is the allegory of a reader's relation to a text, for the quester's desire to know the law is analogous to the reader's desire to know the meaning of the parable. Or, to allegorize that allegory, the parable presents the problematic quest motivating every trip seeking the law that governs the meaning one might find for the trip. Every text—like a unique event—illustrates some higher law whose existence is inferred simply because the text exists. This situation exemplifies the axiom of the meaning of the individual exemplar. But here the protocol for meaning runs afoul of the explicit textual message: the seeker can wait for all eternity for the knowledge that is meant for him, but his years of waiting and study will never advance beyond counting the fleas on the gatekeeper's coat. He could of course attempt to force the gate, but the gatekeeper warns the quester: "From hall to hall there is one doorkeeper after another, each more powerful than the last. The third doorkeeper is already so terrible that even I cannot bear to look at him" (3). And beyond? Could one ever quantify the number of doorkeepers? The threatened expansion of space, of the infinite distances and infinite obstacles to be encountered on the journey, produce infinite stasis in the seeker: he is immobilized before the door, trapped again in the dilemma of Zeno's Achilles—"immobile à grands pas" as Valéry put it in "Le Cimetière marin," or "motionlessly striding forward," to translate what infinite space does to Kafka's seeker of knowledge.

So time, too, follows its infinite path until, by default, the present moment inevitably acquires its negative meaning as the moment of failure. The present is thus the moment of the revelation of the fall. The fall is an ongoing event in Kafka, the ongoing moment at which today becomes infinitely remote from yesterday—the "once upon a time" that Kafka's narrators frequently evoke as *damals*—the time when the law was perhaps still visible, if distantly visible, to those who looked for it. This remembrance of a vision of the law lives on in decaying manuscripts and worm-eaten tomes, as well as in that uncertain collective memory called myth. Myth has its role in Kafka as in most modernist fictions. For example, the shadowy remembrance of the mythic historical presence, or absence, of the law is central to "In the Penal Colony," a parable that Kafka had published during his lifetime. In it, the present moment of scientific enlightenment is explicitly contrasted with a mythic past, lying on the horizon of modern history, when a contemporary European explorer visits a prison colony situated somewhere remote from modern civilization. He is interested to find that there has been preserved in the colony an execution machine that once functioned by literally writing the law on the body of the condemned. Witnessing an execution on the machine, he finds little evidence of any revelation of the law that the machine supposedly "once produced." All the scientific observer sees is the horribly mangled body that the machine makes of its self-immolating guardian who, for the observer's edification, murders himself by supposedly inscribing the law on his body, "Be Just." The explorer sees no revelation of the law; rather, all he observes is a parodistic convulsion.

Revelation or not, the myth exists nonetheless; it pervades the belief of the last guardian, even if, under the explorer's scientific gaze, the execution machine comes apart like an assemblage of cogs and gears invented for a silent movie farce. The explorer remains excluded from the myth, for he lives today, separated from the realm in which the law and myth seem to exist intertwined like a promise that history cannot deliver. But the myth also opens onto the future, and the explorer's discovery that the island's former commander has promised to return offers a bizarre suggestion that a prophet might return with future revelations. This might seem to be a parody of Christianity, though it is probably more appropriate to interpret the commander's promise as an aspect of any messianic myth promising a future revelation of the law. The old commander's grave is under a table in a tea house, put there because the priest refused him burial in the graveyard. With his usual uncanny insight into politics and the law, Kafka seems to suggest that if myths live on, it is often as parodies of themselves, even after the power of modernity tries to repress them—yet who is to say when myths will not return as movements whose hold on the imagination is not to be underestimated? In any case, in the moment of perpetual fall, in the present moment of modernity, myth can only hold sway through its absence.

"In the Penal Colony" is like many of Kafka's tales that point up that origins pose special problems for the seeker of the law. Myth proposes one type of origins, both for judicial and scientific law. For the modern scientific mind, however, myth is not necessary, or, as the explorer shows, it is not possible. For this mind, the simple fact of the present existence of anything demands axiomatically a law to relate it to the past. For the modern mind one such law would be, for example, the principle of evolution. It should be embodied in any ape-become-human, as Kafka humorously interprets it. So in the "Report to the Academy" of *A Country Doctor,* Kafka describes such a former ape, having now become a scientist, who says that he finds his origins increasingly closed to him as he persists in his present project of being a human being. The origins of the species become infinitely remote with the passage of time as the ape acquires the habits of a scientific thinker. Even the origins that one should find in oneself are alienated from the seeker, since science itself is fissured by time, split between Kafka's favored pair, *heute* and *damals,* the present that is always becoming infinitely remote from the once upon a time when things may (or may not) have been more transparent. And so the law of apedom recedes, taking on the very appearance of the myth that the once-upon-a-time ape's scientific mind wants to avoid.

As the reader finds in "A Visit to a Mine," another tale in *A Country Doctor,* the polarity between today's science and yesterday's law constantly undermines what one thought one once knew even when vestiges of yesterday are found in the fallen present. "Today" is the first word of this story describing a series of engineers descending into a mine's underground tunnels in order to measure it. They engage in mysterious mensuration to build new tunnels that will, one suspects, proliferate like the possible meanings of a Kafkan fiction. The series of engineers can itself be measured: there are ten of them (perhaps significantly one less than the number of "Eleven Sons"). The observer-narrator, a worker in the mine, can measure the measurers, but this produces little knowledge about the knowledge that the engineers seek, for the law of the series is hardly evident:

> A ninth man pushes a kind of perambulator in front of him with the surveying instruments. (. . .) He is probably the youngest, perhaps he doesn't even understand the apparatus yet, but he keeps his eye on the instruments all the time, which brings him often into danger of running his vehicle into the wall.
>
> But there is another engineer walking alongside who prevents that from happening. Obviously he understands the apparatus thoroughly and seems to be really the man in charge of it. (406)

But the narrator can only guess at what it all means. He finally prefers to turn his attention to the porter who accompanies the engineers: a porter with a fine uniform with gilt buttons, not unlike Gregor's transformed father in "The Metamorphosis." Like some representative of time gone by, this porter struts with arrogance, demanding respect for his decorated presence and for his status, recalling the historical respect that consecrated ceremonial forms once demanded. The narrator notes that the porter is also an unsolved riddle for the workers to respect. The contrast of enigmatic engineers and pointless porter underscores the polarity of today and yesterday, though with no clear ordering of that polarity. Today's science is an enigmatic process, a series commanded by unknown purposes, whereas yesterday's riddles live on as rather comic presences for which one has scarcely a better explanation. Little wonder that the workers in this tale decide not to resume work that day.

Other stories Kafka published himself pursue these themes in multifarious parodies. "The Judgment" brings the father's law to bear upon the son, whereas "The Metamorphosis" is a comic challenge to find the law of the deviant series of which Gregor Samsa, transformed into an insect, is a most curious, singular manifestation. "A Hunger Artist" shows the seeker for true sustenance as an artist in privation, which is to say, the brother in suffering of every quester for the law. These tales are justifiably well known. To pursue further Kafka's encounter with science, however, I suggest that the reader turn from these stories to discover Kafka's epistemological doubts about discovery in the less known, post-humously published tales and parables grouped together in the *Nachlass*. Kafka's parodistical probing of science is perhaps even more concisely and pointedly expressed in some of these thought experiments than in the famous stories, or in the novels, like *The Castle,* whose land surveyor never gets to measure anything, or *The Trial,* with its search for the law that governs the series of encounters that seem as arbitrary as the obscure accusation that condemns the novel's hero. The shorter texts Kafka left unpublished are often explicitly and brilliantly enacted epistemic allegories about the stories' own functioning. As such they are thought experiments that put into question the possibility that a narrative might retrieve some knowledge about the law generating it and then carry that knowledge over the distance that any message must travel if it is to be received as a revelation of knowledge. One might say that Kafka discovered the entropy of information before it was mathematically formulated by informa-tion theory. Perhaps this accounts in part for Kafka's failure to publish them: these brilliant experiments succeed in proving that they cannot communicate anything—and for this paradoxical proof we may well compare Kafka with Gödel.

For example, in a short text like "The Bridge" (1917), the communicative allegory is physically staged, as it were, since the narrator himself, describing his body as being stretched out like a bridge over a chasm, is logically and literally the path any message must take to get to its destination. Interpreted from the perspective of information theory, the narrator is the physical contact or channel that the coded message must traverse to get from sender to receiver. Much of Kafka's short fiction is, at the most literal level, simply a description of how knowledge, carried by travelers or messengers, might, but doesn't, get over the space leading from point A to point B. In a variant on Kafka's favored destruction of information by the infinite dilation of space, a message-traveler in "The Bridge" finds that space opens up vertically, for when he steps on the narrator, he causes the narrator to fall into the depths. Information theory has few ways to measure such transactions—except to state that, according to entropy, the least probable event encodes the greatest amount of information. Kafka's allegories do indeed illustrate that proposition by showing the improbable ways information has for going astray, which is rich in paradoxical information.

In his parables Kafka usually traffics in negative information theory, a theory informed in part by Pascal's sense of the contradictions of the infinite as well as Zeno's analogous paradoxes about the impossibility of traversing space and time. Distances cannot be measured, for they are too great to ever be negotiated by messages, like those spaces investigated by the narrator in "The Great Wall of China" or the distances from the borders to a fictional town in "The Refusal." In the latter story the narrator's town is too far from the nation's capital for messages to arrive, and thus dynasties can go under without the community's receiving the information. What does manage to cross spaces and get to the city are petitions to the courts—all of which are regularly rejected. This procedure generates constant traffic, uninterrupted coming and going, as people come to the court seeking their encounter with the law postulated to exist behind the series of events. The series exists, as one clearly sees, but without the law's ever appearing. The constant rejection of the petitions assures, however, that the appeal to the law, in its absence, will continue. The hypothesis that there is a law generates the unending quest for the law. Or, again in terms of information theory, the failure of information flow generates ever more flow in the circle of ever-negative feedback. In "The Refusal" Kafka has combined a description of our belief that knowledge of the law must be available—because we are constantly refused it—and a portrayal of our quest for knowledge that must continue—because it constantly fails.

In the parable "Advocates," forward motion suffices to generate the infinite spaces to be filled by that motion. Kafka's science of negative information demonstrates that this forward motion can be a movement generated by language itself. Central to these doubts about language's capacity to offer knowledge is Kafka's playfully ironic demonstration of language's capacity to keep up an infinite play with metaphorical transference. Language allows everything to be compared with everything. For example, in "Advocates," the narrator climbs up unending steps, in search of the law, steps which are, among other things, a metaphor for a possible transcendence. And, conversely, the transcendence that all desire is a metaphor for steps. Running in search of advocates, those allusive representatives of the law, the narrator advises the reader:

> If you have started out on a walk, continue it whatever happens; you can only gain, you run no risk, in the end you may fall over a precipice per-haps, but had you turned back after the first steps and run downstairs you would not have fallen at once—and not perhaps, but for certain. So if you find nothing in the corridors open the doors, if you find nothing behind these doors there are more floors, and if you find nothing up there, don't worry, just leap up another flight of stairs. As long as you don't stop climb-ing, the stairs won't end, under your climbing feet they will go on growing upwards. (451)

This text illustrates why it is questionable to affirm Kafka's belief in the rational-ity of language itself, a point to which I will return presently. The parable "Ad-vocates" is an allegory anticipating the reader's desire for a closure leading to the constitution of meaning that rationality demands. But Kafka's metaphors then refuse closure; they offer an unending allegory of that desire for knowl-edge of the law explaining the series of steps that lead away on an endless trip. The metaphors point to the infinite expansion that one can find in them, lead-ing ever upward toward an encounter with more and more metaphors. It is as if Pascal's view of the infinite and hence contradictory nature of space could also apply to the space of language. Microspace is infinitely divisible, and macro-space offers no stopping points of reference. Comparably, in the space of lan-guage, words never stop referring to words, metaphors creating more meta-phors, and the genesis of meaning is without end.

In brief, in Kafka's fiction messages circulate unceasingly as a movement that describes, among all other things, the existence of the text itself. The texts propose metaphors for their own communication that goes, or does not go, to some problematic destination. There is nothing extraordinary about this play of metaphor undermining knowledge. It is part of "A Common Confusion," to cite the title of a text in which ordinary, daily transactions founder upon the impossible negotiation of the space-time complex that every traveler, like every message, must cross for ordinary business purposes.

Kafka's exploration of metaphorical exchanges results in increasingly ran-dom branchings and crossings. These exchanges result in thought experiments about the creation of what a scientist or logician after Gödel might call comic undecidables. Such is the creature described in "A Crossbreed," a being that challenges the scientist to find a law describing the series of crossings that might have produced it. The creature seems to be half-cat, half-lamb. If not a genetic hybrid, it is perhaps a random crossbreed produced by the combinatory powers of language. In any case its existence causes the "strangest questions" to be asked (426). Such a creature naturally elicits a desire for knowledge, for its existence is a challenge to the rules of science and language alike. Like a Kafkan text, the crossbreed sometimes even seems to be expressing something, such as a great desire to be done with it all, since no explanation can seemingly have a final purchase upon it. Kafka's short texts comically distrust their own random crossings produced by chance couplings of language. However, by pointing out these chance encounters, products of series that should embody some law, Kafka wistfully offers an homage to a dreamed-of rationality in language that would bring explanations to a justified end. And one recalls again that in his late philosophy Wittgenstein asserted that, for language to function, explanations have to end somewhere. Kafka would undoubtedly have agreed with Wittgenstein, but then only to suggest that this is a cause for despair.

In this vein Kafka seems to want to suspend the potentially infinite random branchings that the free play of metaphor produces almost automatically. After all, the existence of law should eliminate the aleatory by explaining the random series as the product of a hidden principle. So with their belief in the law, some texts of the *Nachlass* declare that the random should be unthinkable and that the undecidable ought to be eliminated. This refusal of the random is another epistemological axiom that some of Kafka's narrators endorse while they fruitlessly try to find the law explaining the chance series that proliferate in these works. Moreover, the narrators of these fictions are often quite conscious of undertaking epistemic research into causes and effects. These short tales of the *Nachlass* offer an introduction to what one can call Kafka's science: the unending quest for the laws, or the Law, that might order the texts' disparate events and lay bare a periodic table classifying the elements of our absurd lives. Usually caught up in the very randomness they seek to abolish, these fictions and parables look nonetheless for ways to certainty that would eliminate the random production of meaning produced by, among other things, untamed metaphors. Working within the legacy of Flaubert and Mallarmé, these texts by Kafka propose that the elimination of the aleatory is the task of art. It is an impossible task, and Kafka's often comic thought experiments point to the fact that learning to live with chance, with the stochastic processes that science seems to find throughout nature, has been the great epistemological challenge to the development of the physical sciences since the end of the nineteenth century. Not all have been happy with this challenge, neither Einstein nor Kafka, for example.

Kafka's sense of paradox was only sharpened by the certainties of uncertainty, as one sees in "The Village Schoolmaster," also translated as "The Giant Mole." Science in this short story takes the form of investigation into the existence of a giant mole, a digger of burrows and labyrinths, and, as such, a potential generator of metaphorical ways and allegorical spaces. In this tale, unlike in the story called "The Burrow," Kafka does not focus on that underground travel called burrowing, but rather on people's efforts to make sense of the mobile beast itself, another hybrid creature who appears to be a contingent product of language's arbitrary combinatory powers. The authorities have ignored the giant beast, so that the only learned person around to investigate its existence is an old village schoolmaster. His task is to "write the sole account in black and white of the incident, and though he was an excellent man in his own profession, neither his abilities nor his equipment made it possible for him to produce an exhaustive description that could be used as a foundation by others, far less, therefore, an actual explanation of the occurrence" (168–69). Like every discoverer of something truly new, the old schoolmaster is inadequately equipped to grasp and formulate what his discovery is about: a giant mole disturbs both taxonomy and language usage. In a sense the school teacher stands in a relation to his discovery analogous to that of every language user who must attempt, while forever lacking adequate means, to describe the inventions that language can generate in its metaphorical crossings, allowing oxymorons to come to life. Giant moles infest our linguistic landscape in many guises. At times they may even exist outside of language. If so, one must nonetheless find the language adequate to describing this discovery.

The tale's narrator sets out to aid the old schoolmaster in his difficult task of researching and then communicating his results. The narrator attempts to communicate something about the old man's communication, but his metacommunication fares no better than the first instance of communication. The narrator sends his report to the city, but, obeying the negative law of communicative entropy, the report naturally goes astray. He sends a second report, but journalists assume that his second report is only a repetition of the first, and, in their common confusion, they dismiss it as a ridiculous redundancy. And if another report were sent, as the narrator explains, it would make little difference. Official science would take that report and make it disappear into the sum total of knowledge; or, as the narrator explains to the schoolmaster, the law of the series actually only serves to obscure the individual instance of knowledge:

> Your discovery, of course, would be carried further, for it is not so trifling that, once having achieved recognition, it could be forgotten again. But you would not hear much more about it, and what you heard you would scarcely understand. Every new discovery is assumed at once into the sum total of knowledge, and with that ceases in a sense to be discovery; it dissolves into the whole and disappears, and one must have a trained scientific eye even to recognize it after that. For it is related to fundamental axioms of whose existence we don't even know, and in the debates of science it is raised on these axioms into the very clouds. How can we expect to understand such things? Often as we listen to some learned discourse we may be under the impression that it is about your discovery, when it is about something quite different, and the next time, when we think it is about something else, and not about your discovery at all, it may turn out to be about that and that alone. (180)

Conjoining the various meanings of the law, the narrator suggests that science in the broadest sense is an enterprise that uses the laws of the random series to construct harmonious wholes that make the random disappear by making the individual event disappear. Moreover, so considered, the whole of science exists as that space of metacommentary that stops all self-reflexive questions and regress by absorbing all our isolated, random, and arbitrary phenomena into a great metaphysical whole. The narrator suggests that the edifice of knowledge, taken as a whole, will be of little solace to anyone desiring to find a law for the particular series that an individual confronts. The closure of meaning is achieved for a totality, but not for any of the specific giant moles that language and experience serve up so often.

The object of investigation can also be an investigator, and Kafka reverses the poles of investigator and investigated when he allows the presumably mole narrator of "The Burrow" to take charge of eliminating uncertainty. This metaphorical scientist fitfully entertains the idea of investigating a mysterious noise that he hears in his underground labyrinth. To discover what it is, he knows that he should devote himself to research, dig more tunnels, traverse a space, and perhaps decode a noise that might be more than a mere random sound. Such a "reasonable plan" for research, though never undertaken, does point up again with the greatest clarity that constructions of scientific notions about causality are in complicity with a metaphor, one rarely absent in a Kafkan allegory, identifying the path, or the way, with epistemological insight. This metaphor draws together, by association, notions of travel and space, of distances traversed, as well as points marking trajectories on the path that is then defined as a causal chain. Finding causality means establishing a pathway from point A to point B. From the perspective of the underground narrator of "The Burrow," knowledge and science are equated with the path he could dig in order to arrive at a goal, presumably the source of the noise. With this tunnel he might arrive at the law of the series of disturbances that have entered the burrow. Yet the burrowing seeker of knowledge believes but little in his own plan, comes finally no longer to understand it, and, in any case, prefers to spend his time imagining random hypotheses about the noise. His fear of encountering the law of the series degenerates and gives rise to an entropic disorder in which the random is not only the most probable, but even the preferred order of events.

The burrowing narrator's fear of causal pathways also points up that, literally and figuratively, metaphors can impinge upon one's existence. However, in self-mirroring parables such as "On Parables," it is not always clear whether it is in the parable or in the extratextual world of literal language that one can say that one has won or lost with the parable. The allegorical and the literal merge in the identities fostered by metaphor. This merging engenders problems of knowledge, for metaphor's complications for knowledge spring from the quester's incapacity to sort out science and metaphor. Perhaps the most wistfully comic example of this incapacity is found in "Investigations of a Dog." In this story it is postulated that, if all are (like) dogs, then in this dog's life all should behave in accord with the law of dogs. But laws do not always hold true, for it appears in "Investigations of a Dog" that the (linguistic) law of metaphor can be superseded by other laws, or so one can infer through scientific investigation. One can infer the suspension of the law of language from events that appear to violate the law. For instance, the law of dogdom that is described in this tale does not hold unitary sway, for some dogs begin to sing. This event provides the story's narrator with matter for research, since these beasts have violated both the prescriptive and descriptive law of their (metaphorical) dog existence. This violation leads to, among other things, a crisis about language use that the narrator had when he was young and first faced dogged uncertainty:

> Perhaps they were not dogs at all? But how should they not be dogs? Could I not actually hear on listening more closely the subdued cries with which they encouraged each other, drew each other's attention to difficulties, warned each other against errors; could I not see the last and youngest dog, to whom most of those cries were addressed, often stealing a glance at me as if he would have dearly wished to reply, but refrained because it was not allowed? But why should it not be allowed, why should the very thing which our laws unconditionally command not be allowed in this one case? I became indignant at the thought and almost forgot the music. Those dogs were violating the law. Great magicians they might be, but the law was valid for them too, I knew that quite well though I was a child. (283)

Not only do they sing, but these dogs walk upright on their hind legs. What is one to make of a singing dog-metaphor that walks and therefore violates the semantic and biological laws of its own (metaphorical) being?

The violation of these apparent laws generates the demand for more science, since the basic axiom of knowledge demands that there be a law that explains this series like any other—it demands a law of the deviant to explain singing dogs that walk upright. The story claims, however, that all knowledge, the totality of all questions and all answers, is contained in the dog. Perhaps this claim can be acknowledged if one recognizes that the dog is the total system, not unlike the self-enclosed world of language, in which every metaphor, including all those generated by "dogs," can lead and connect to every other metaphor, through the passages provided by the infinite expansive possibilities of transfer and comparison. In other words, the totality of what can be said and, hence, known can be related to dogs and dogdom by mere metaphorical transfer. It is not at all clear that this is a satisfactory state of epistemic affairs.

In any case the need for science leads the story's canine investigator to more research. These dogs sing. In Kafka's work, song is often associated with food. Music is, as for Gregor Samsa in "The Metamorphosis," a form of sustenance, which is another metaphor for knowledge. So the metaphor of music leads to an inquiry into the nature of food and knowledge, which, in turn, as the narrator knows well, will go astray in other metaphors:

I understand my fellow dogs, am flesh of their flesh, of their miserable, ever-renewed, ever desirous flesh. But it is not merely flesh and blood that we have in common, but knowledge also, and not only knowledge, but the key to it as well. I do not possess that key except in common with all the others; I cannot grasp it without their help. The hardest bones, containing the richest marrow, can be conquered only by a united crunching of all the teeth of all dogs. That of course is only a figure of speech and exaggerated; if all teeth were but ready they would not need even to bite, the bones would crack themselves and the marrow would be freely accessible to the feeblest of dogs. (291)

The narrator finds metaphor merging with knowledge, though in this case it is metaphor about knowledge. He finds himself comparing shared knowledge to sustenance—to bones with the marrow that Rabelais compared, in another famous metaphor, with the metaphorical substance of gnosis. It is noteworthy that the dog narrator, fearing confusion, first denies value to his metaphor, but only to go on to elaborate it. One does not easily escape figural language, if at all, however much the narrator wishes to find a "marrow that ... is not food" (291). Finally, Kafka seems to propose that, in the curse of dogdom, all we can bear is the random and the arbitrary, for a vision of true necessity would, in its purity, annihilate us. This is not an infrequent theme in Kafka. Therefore, science is tolerated only so long as it remains a mythic provider of metaphorical sustenance, such as those laws that we know to be arbitrary, but which give us provisional succor in our need for knowledge that we could not abide.

Among Kafka's last works, "Investigations of a Dog" is a key story for understanding his doubt about the possibility of finding ways leading to a law that would abolish the random. It proposes the most condensed demonstration of Kafka's negative epistemology, and the circularity characterizing the quest for the law of the random series that constitutes our doggy existences. There is no closure to this circular quest—another shape that the infinite takes—because the random always generates new (metaphorical) possibilities of inquiry. Moreover, the pages in which the dog-scientist laments the fall of his people is also a prolegomena to a science of history or, alternatively, a history of science. The polarity between yesterday and today tears knowledge asunder, for who can speak of knowledge today when it was yesterday that the "true Word" was on the tip of every tongue? Yet, the canine narrator claims, and no modern thinker would disagree with him, that knowledge is increasing at an increasing rate among the dogs. But it would also appear that this acceleration is only an

accelerating form of the fall away from the Word—or the law that we supposedly knew once upon a time. History is thus another pathway, along an ever
expanding distance, leading from a crossroads where dogs and humanity separated company with the Word, or the Law, or true knowledge. History is,
metaphorically, another form of travel, travel into the random that no longer
submits to the law, or as the narrator laments, it is a voyage into true dogdom:

> When our first fathers strayed they had doubtless scarcely any notion that
> their aberration was to be an endless one, they could still literally see the
> crossroads, it seemed an easy matter to turn back whenever they pleased,
> and if they hesitated to turn back it was merely because they wanted to en-
> joy a dog's life for a little while longer; it was not yet a genuine dog's life,
> and already it seemed intoxicatingly beautiful to them, so what must it
> become in a little while, a very little while, and so they strayed farther.
> (300)

With this marvelous parable Kafka encapsulates in one tale the myth of the fall
and the Enlightenment myth of eternal progress. He conflates belief in unending progress with belief in humanity's infinite fall, both of which one knows
must exist—since, if the law does not reveal itself in the present, by logical
necessity it must do so in the future, or have done so in the past.

With this view of history in mind, I return to the question of whether Kafka
believed that rationality is vouchsafed by the very form of language and that
knowledge of the law might be communicated—even if the law itself remains
forever elusive. Arnold Heidsieck has proposed that Kafka's approach to
knowledge is not completely negative. Recognizing that Kafka hardly rejected
the natural sciences, as did much of the European avant-garde, Heidsieck finds
a form of rationality in Kafka; to wit, Kafka implicitly appeals to language:
"Although he explores the uncertainty of objective knowledge and the paradoxical outcomes of norms, he always appeals to our linguistically shaped inter-
subjective rationality. Thus, he affirms social institutions, science, law, and
literate culture as conditions for the possibility of shareable knowledge, non-
paradoxical norms, and individualism."[9] This is an attractive argument, reminiscent of Habermas's defense of language as the basis for political democracy on
the basis of shared communication. However, it is one that must be approached
with a sense of the dialectical paradox that informs Kafka's self-referential

9. Heidsieck, *The Intellectual Contexts of Kafka's Fiction: Philosophy, Law, Religion,* 1.

texts parodying their own being. And from this viewpoint I am not sure that one can be so optimistic about Kafka's view of language as Heidsieck is. From a logical point of view, self-reference always threatens the belief in the epistemic power of language, for, quite simply, self-reference generates contradiction.

This question of the reliability of language is an old issue for science and philosophy. The belief that language is constitutive of rationality is a variant on the Greek belief in logos. According to Greek thought from the pre-Socratics through Plato, logos participates in the disclosure of being, manifesting itself in forms as varied as reason, proportion, and mathematical relations. For Christians after Plato, logos was interpreted as the divine reason that created the world in accord with its knowledge of possibility. As the Bible famously says, in the beginning there was logos. From the perspective of rational metaphysics, logos should be the pure, unambiguous language of science as well as the transparent law. But, as Kafka's logician dogs know well, after the Fall language has become infected with metaphors that turn in self-reference upon themselves and create all the paradoxes of self-reference and unending comparison. (Luther knew well that ambiguity is a sign of original sin.) And in metaphor and self-reference lie the paradoxes that even modern logicians cannot exorcise. Moreover, language then seemingly infects being, calling into existence soaring dogs, *Lufthünde,* whose very existence violates our notions about air and dogs. But once they are granted metaphorical existence, as the narrator says, soaring dogs enter our language and become part of our picture of the world. So language does indeed form at least part of the structure of the world, a very curious world in which the language user finds unicorns, infinite space, beliefs declaring that human beings ought to be just, propositions about the unknown law, and, thanks to Kafka, soaring dogs. All these things exist somehow in a world disclosed through language. Or, in other words, in Kafka's hands, language is just as capable of designating its own inadequacy as it is of affirming, by hopeful implication, the structure of rationality, the presence of logos, and the tenacious hypothesis that the law exists. However, it is not clear that dog researchers can ever get beyond mere hypothesis in a world of infinite complication. Kafka's researcher—be it a dog, mole, or ape-human—is condemned to live with the uncertainties that surround all hypotheses.

In the light of these thoughts, it is fruitful to consider again Gödel's theorem, or, more precisely, theorems published in 1931, several years after Kafka's death. Gödel's demonstration that no formal system can be completely proved in terms of its own axioms casts light upon Kafka, for it shows an important commonality of interest shared by literature and modern science and logic. According to Gödel, there is always at least one formula in a formal system that is not provable, which implies that the consistency of a formal system cannot be proved from within the system. The reason for this impossibility is that self-reference is involved in such proof, and self-reference always allows infinite regress. So there are always statements in a system that cannot be proved, even though the statements may be true. They can only be proved by statements in another system, or, as Gödel put it in a companion paper: "The undecidable propositions constructed for the proof of Theorem 1 become decidable by the adjunction of higher types and the corresponding axioms; however, in the higher systems we can construct other undecidable propositions by the same procedure, and so forth."[10] This produces a very strange situation in which we can know that a proposition is true, but can prove it only by creating another, higher system that can be proved only by creating another system. Mathematician John Kasti interprets this to mean, in commentary on theorems and formal proof, that "the statement can actually be seen to be true by jumping outside the logical system and viewing the statement from a metalinguistic perspective."[11] Kasti takes this situation to mean that mathematical propositions can be likened to semantic propositions found in a metasystem containing statements that cannot be decided from within that system; and, I add, thereby demanding a meta-metalinguistic perspective.

I return to Gödel because the implications of Kafka's work are in many ways analogous to the implications of Gödel's theorems. Gödel's work put an end to the belief that formal systems could exist in complete autonomy with no reference to anything aleatory in the world. For logicians like Bertrand Russell and poets like Mallarmé, this is a distressful situation: "Un jeu de dès n'abolira jamais le hasard," as the poet put it, to say that chance may never be abolished, even before Russell attempted to ground all formal systems with his program for reducing mathematics to logic. Literary theorists, often quite excited by the idea of undecidable propositions, should note that, for most mathematicians, Gödel's theorem is not problematic. Norbert Wiener, to cite a famous example, notes that he was relieved to no longer have to be a follower of Russell's program to turn all of mathematics into a series of formal logical propositions. Wiener, the inventor of cybernetics, recalled that, for him, "logic and learning

10. S. G. Shanker, ed., *Gödel's Theorem in Focus,* 225.
11. Kasti, "Formally Speaking."

and all mental activity have always been incomprehensible as a complete and closed picture and have been understandable only as a process by which man puts himself *en rapport* with his environment."[12] Wiener would have perhaps agreed with Kasti's affirmation that Gödel's theorem suggests that there is an "irreducible semantic component to mathematics." Conversely, the literary scholar may feel justified in finding that there are logical or perhaps even mathematical implications in Kafka's play with self-referential systems.

Kafka dramatizes implications analogous to those found in Gödel's theorem by showing that the proof of the law can never be encapsulated in an autonomous system in which logos would ground itself on the model of a formal system. The grounds for the autonomous system should be, as logicians and theologians once believed, some ultimate self-evident axiom. A metaphysician would also like this axiom to be some ultimate Law of Being. In their self-reference, Kafka's texts demonstrate the impossibility that the law might be revealed as the foundation of all that is, or, more prosaically, anything that is. Proof of the law, in every sense, is always lacking, and there is no Book of Revelation, alas, that is not subject to interpretation. The necessity of interpretation itself demonstrates that a metasystem is always needed for every lower level of meaning. Some elusive laws may be tentatively proved in Kafka, though never with certainty, indeed rarely with conviction. But Kafka's narrative always contains statements that cannot be demonstrated in terms of the narrative system that contains them. This situation imposes the necessity of interpretation, which demands that one set up a metanarrative system, which in turn demands another system to demonstrate the first, ad infinitum. So that, interestingly, as Wiener put it, one is thrown back upon the world, on the rapport that one has with a world in which many mysterious things may happen.

The analogies to be drawn between Gödel's theorems and Kafka's work are actually quite straightforward. A few considerations of *The Castle* and *The Trial* can complete this discussion, if the preceding commentary on Kafka's shorter fictions has not already convincingly illustrated how much Kafka is part of the modernist climate that critically examined the belief in the autonomy of epistemic discourse. For example, *The Castle* is centered on a potential hero, the enigmatic K., who supposedly can mark off the boundaries of systems and measure them. Quite pointedly, he is a *Landvermesser,* a surveyor supposedly skilled in using mathematics to close off open domains. Submitting open

12. Wiener, *I Am a Mathematician,* 324.

spaces to systemic description is his trade. It is also remarkable that Kafka's would-be scientist-hero in *The Castle* recalls Schopenhauer's description of the modern scientist, and I suspect that K.'s scientific vocation is an, admittedly oblique, illustration of Schopenhauer's critique of science. According to Schopenhauer, the scientist is a quester who never really gets into things in themselves to discover their true nature. In his critique of post-Kantian science— one that anticipates Musil's critique of Mach—Schopenhauer declares that scientific "laws which merely combine objects, ideas, among themselves" are not really knowledge and that the scientist who deals with names and images is "like a man who goes around a castle seeking in vain for an entrance, and sometimes sketching the facades."[13] As if in answer to Schopenhauer, to show why one doesn't get into the castle, Kafka adds a gatekeeper to protect the castle entrance in the parable "Before the Law." And in elaborating this portrayal of knowledge's failure, in portraying the Castle itself in the novel *The Castle*, Kafka makes a potential scientist of his hero, K., the surveyor. K. also wants to get within the law, to get inside the Castle, whose facades promise, enigmatically, a place in which one presumably knows the rules and constraints governing life, or the laws that are somehow responsible for K.'s being there. If K. is to practice his science, he must first know the laws that rule over his existence and which have called, or have not called, him to this encounter with the Castle. As every reader may readily recall, K. finds no access to the Castle, at best only tentative interpretations of interpretations as to why he might have been called there, of what might be conducive to possible contacts with the Castle, and of what might be the meaning of the few indirect contacts that he does have as he moves about the village in a series of random and rather improbable encounters.

His only almost affirmative encounter with the law occurs when K. is charged explicitly with ignoring the law, *das Gesetz,* late in the course of this uncompleted novel. K. spends the night in the halls of the *Herrenhof,* the inn for officials, after his rapidly acquired fiancée Frieda has left him to go back to the inn to live with his helper. K. himself is summoned to the inn for an interrogation. Stumbling with fatigue, he disturbs the early morning distribution of the files that takes place according to some enigmatic routine that he watches in sleepy bewilderment. He observes a series of phenomena that seem to obey

13. My attention was called to this passage in Schopenhauer by Thomas Mann's essay, stressing the ongoing importance of Schopenhauer for modernist epistemology, in *Thomas Mann Presents the Living Thought of Schopenhauer,* 38.

certain regularities and which seem to be subordinate to some larger systemic meaning. In effect K. has, according to the innkeeper in a later conversation, witnessed what nobody is allowed to witness, which is to say, what one might suppose to be the functioning of the law. K. learns from the angry innkeeper that not even the innkeeper himself is allowed to witness this event in his own establishment: only an outlaw could dare such an intolerable intervention, or as Kafka's narrator says, in indirect quotation of the innkeeper, "Well, yes, it must be a person like K., someone who rode roughshod over everything, both over the law and over the most ordinary human consideration."[14] In spite of this charge, the bewildered K. knows well that he has not learned in the least what the law is. He is told only that he has set himself above it. At most, in typical Kafkan fashion, the innkeeper's angry charge might allow the tentative affirmation of the proposition, "The law exists."

To prove this statement more is needed than the accusation that K. has put himself above the law—even if this indeed appears to be the case. Since meaning, in Gödel's sense, is isomorphic, proof of the undecidable statement about the law's existence demands what the logician calls an isomorphic operation: the statement must be mapped from one narrative system onto another system in which it can be demonstrated. In fact, even before K. witnesses the incomprehensible distribution of the files, Kafka has already begun such a proof of the statement that the law exists. The proof takes the form of a secondary narration that, as a double of the tale of K.'s situation, might allow the mapping of statements in K.'s narrative onto the secondary narrative. The main metanarrative in this regard is the tale that Olga tells K. when she narrates the story of her family's disgrace and decline after her sister Amalia refused to answer the summons of Sortini, one of the powerful officials who come from the Castle to the village where K. finds himself. Her tale is a masterful description of a fall from grace, and it has many political ramifications for life in a bureaucratic despotism. It also stands in an isomorphic relation to the main narrative in which K. finds himself looking for a summons from the law.

In this sense Olga's tale can be likened to an attempt to formalize a system of proof, since it stands in relation to the main narration as the main narration stands to the quest for knowledge. Notably, it is a failed demonstration, for no

---

14. Kafka, *The Castle*, trans. Willa and Edwin Muir, 369–70. Hereafter cited parenthetically in the text. In the original: "Nun, es muss ein Mensch wie K. sein, Einer, der sich über alles, über das Gesetz sowie über die allergewöhnlichste menschliche Rücksichtnahme... hinweggesetzt..." (*Das Schloss*, 236).

direct proof of anything emerges from Olga's tale. After her sister Amalia refuses to heed an obscene missive summoning her to come to the inn, the family loses its connections and its wealth, the father must give up his diploma (from the fire department), they lose friends as well as their house, and finally the father begins to spend all his time looking for a bureaucrat to whom he may confess his guilt. He must "prove his guilt" so that he can be forgiven— but "proof" of guilt would entail finding the law that he has violated (275). As *The Trial* demonstrates in an analogous manner, the unknown law can apparently condemn with all the force of a known law, a situation to be appreciated from both the scientific and the bureaucratic viewpoint. The law may not be revealed, but that has nothing to do with its effects. From a formal point of view, the law must be proved to exist in order to prove its effects. This demand produces logically a Catch-22, which is pointed up when, in describing how her father endures their "punishment," Olga asks for what her father might be forgiven. Since he can't prove his guilt, he can't prove that he should be forgiven. At most, she says, he was pointlessly bothering the officials, but precisely that was unforgivable ("Was könnte ihm verziehen werden? Höchstens, das er jetzt zwecklos die Ämter belästige, aber gerade dieses sei unverzeihlich").[15]

Olga's brother Barnabas takes the job of messenger so that he can get into the Castle and find the messenger who brought his sister the summons. Barnabas is a messenger, which may suggest to those who are mapping the tale onto a theological framework that the brother has a role like that of an angel. His mediation, or lack thereof, in effect connects Olga's tale with K.'s story, for the brother receives his first commission, after two years of waiting, when he is finally entrusted with letters for K. This connection proposes a mapping from K.'s tale to another metanarrative that doubles K.'s tale. It should prove something about K.'s fruitless attempts to know something about what goes on inside the Castle. The mapping is a tenuous one, even if in formal terms the metanarrative perspective is clear. If anything, the metalinguistic perspective simply proves again that one cannot have access to the law, which one knows is true, intuitively, from the first level of narration. But this is precisely the case with many formal systems. We intuitively learn, through rote memorization, that $2+2=4$ without formal number theory; we intuitively learn, with K., that the obscurity surrounding the law is not dispelled by further and regressive proofs that the way to the law is obscure. However, the textual dynamics invites

15. Kafka, *Das Schloss*, 179.

endless mappings in a quest for proof, which demands more mapping and more interrogation of the overlapping proofs, as much negative as positive in their effects: does an official's refusal of a message prove more about the operations of the law than his accepting a message? Does the father's decline prove more than K.'s own sense of failure? The mappings are endless, the proofs obscure, the regressions infinite. The surveyor could continue endless mapping, in all senses of the term, until his death.

As Kafka's friend Max Brod observed in his *Nachwort* to the original edition of *The Castle, The Trial* and *The Castle* are closely related: "Essentially it is the case that the hero in *The Trial* is persecuted by invisible, secret officials who charge him before a court, whereas in *The Castle* he is rejected by the same judicial appeal [*Instanz*]."[16] Viewing the law first as a matter of justice and bureaucracy, Brod then made a quite religious allegorical interpretation of both Joseph K. and K.'s quest. This is quite proper, for, as the atheist physicist Stephen Hawking likes to say, the knowledge of ultimate laws would be knowledge of the mind of God.

The ultimate laws remain a mystery, and in *The Trial* Joseph K. is no more successful than K. in discovering what might be on God's mind. Kafka's condemned hero wanders throughout the novel, looking for help and vainly attempting to find out what exactly is the law that he has violated. The priest offers him a metanarrative in the parable "Before the Law," but the commentaries on the commentaries generated by it only offer another proof that Kafka is as adept at generating infinite regress as Gödel. For a third perspective on this parable, one can view it as another isomorphic operation, standing in relation to the first narration, doubling it as an attempt to prove statements in the first narration, to wit, that Joseph K. has not been deceived in his quest for the law. Like Olga's tale of punishment, the parable "Before the Law," through the isomorphism it entertains with the main narrative about Joseph K., should illuminate the entire narrative, or so thinks the priest who tells it to Joseph K. in the darkened church. The endless interpretations to which the parable is subject, and interpretations of the interpretations, are so many obscure mappings projected from one narrative to another in an endless play of proliferating metanarratives, each failing to prove something about a lower-level system.

At the end of *The Trial* Joseph K. is taken out and killed like a dog, a not indifferent image in Kafka's world of dog questers. By contrast, there is no end

16. Ibid., 302.

to K.'s narrative in *The Castle,* though Max Brod said that Kafka intended to have K. die of exhaustion at the projected end of the novel—this accompanied by the Castle's allowing him to stay on in the village even though K.'s legal claim thereto was not valid. Ironic grace? In any case this capricious suspension of the law would not have overcome the basic entropic spiral entailed by the quest for the law. Neither novel is complete, and both suggest by their proliferating narratives an entropic spiral downward; as energy is lost, chaos grows, and all hope of proof goes aground. Or, from a strictly logical perspective, the narrative's downward spiral will never be arrested by any foundational proof that might ground the narrative as a system. There is no proof, simply truth or fragmented propositions that seem true, that one knows as profoundly as one knows that one wants proof, that proof that Gödel showed could never be finally obtained from within the system itself. Gödel was not quite Kafka's contemporary, for he received his Ph.D. in Vienna the year Kafka died prematurely of tuberculosis and was buried in that part of the Hapsburg Empire that had become Czechoslovakia. However, for all practical purposes they shared the same cultural space. Moreover, with no little irony one can note that the half-mad Gödel died prematurely as a practicing hunger artist. I leave it to the reader to contemplate the fact that an imaginative and a real hunger artist were among the most influential minds for understanding the possibilities of writing the laws of discourse.

In conclusion, and in anticipation of a later discussion of postmodernity, I want to stress that if Kafka is probably one of the two or three most influential writers of the twentieth century, it is because he experimented with the limits of language in ways that no writer has surpassed. Perhaps with regard to this understanding of limits one must again compare Kafka's work with Wittgenstein's later philosophical thought in the *Philosophical Investigations.* Both Kafka and Wittgenstein probe in multiple parables and thought experiments the view that language, in molding a *Weltbild* or our vision of the world, imposes upon us the rationality and the forms of knowledge that our cultural matrix has encoded as true. One side of what has come to be called the postmodern mind has been formed by the way that Wittgenstein and Kafka reinforce each other. Their work explores the dialectic between the belief that language is the founder of rationality and the suspicion that language merely allegorizes its own rationality in circular loopings that alienate the language user from a substantive world; or, alternatively, others believe that their work challenges the belief that there might be any invariant world at all beyond the one created by language.

Such suspicions are not necessarily part of Kafka's worldview, though arguably they derive directly from interpretations of Kafka and Wittgenstein. It is also clear that postmodern suspicions often derive from the early Wittgenstein's positivistic conclusion in the *Tractatus* that silence may be a superior knowledge to propositions found in the world, a viewpoint that finds support in Kafka's many parables about the fallen nature of language. However, as Kafka would surely have pointed out in a parable about postmodern silence, Wittgenstein's aphorism that one should be silent about that which one cannot speak has generated infinite reams of interpretation and commentary. Kafka would not have been surprised.

Chapter Five

James Joyce and the Laws of Everything

In *Ulysses* James Joyce pairs the Celtic Greek with the Irish Jew in associating Stephen Dedalus and Leopold Bloom. He classifies his two characters according to their relation to the law conceived as both aesthetic order and epistemic rules, since Dedalus has the artistic, Bloom the scientific temperament. However, in the union of opposites that dialectics allows, it is hard to say that the contrary might not also be true. Stephen seeks knowledge of the order of things in the broadest sense, and his epistemic quest is dialectically mirrored in Bloom's aesthetic musings about his knowledge of the quotidian. And so in his association of characters Joyce shows himself to be a dialectician of the law and its multifaceted presence in daily life. Once one has grasped the principle according to which the law can appear simultaneously in Joyce in all its dialectical opposites, one is ready to read *Ulysses,* and then *Finnegans Wake,* Joyce's panlogistic celebration in which everything can be known by identifying everything with everything else. In *Ulysses* Joyce implies that one could know infinitely much about the trivia of a single day in Dublin; and in *Finnegans Wake* that one day, ever recurrent, can encompass everything, in the infinite play of connections through logos.

The joyous celebration of knowledge means that parody is Joyce's natural rhetorical mode. This parody is highly ambivalent. Parody is often affirmative, but Joyce indulges in such parodistic exuberance that one finally wonders if the knowledge of everything really has much importance. In celebrating all knowledge Joyce abolishes the hierarchies of knowledge that Kafka implicitly respects, if only because hierarchy is part of the demonstration that we are infinitely distant from the highest ranking knowledge, the law encoded in logos. In Joyce, everything can be the object of knowledge, and there is no more reason, it seems, to grant greater importance to the principle of the conservation of energy than, say, to the somewhat shabby contents of Bloom's memory—though Bloom's memory may well call forth the principle of the conservation of energy, and that principle may in turn explain some aspects of his memory. Significantly, parody is also a favored rhetorical mode in Kafka, characterizing the unending quest for the law, so that the final result of Joyce's hyperbolic celebration is the communication of much the same feeling of uncertainty expressed by Kafka's unending search for the law. When the mind has infinite knowledge at its disposition, as is the case in *Ulysses* and *Finnegans Wake,* the world dissolves in the multitudinous hypotheses that make everything at once clear and at the same time subject to unending investigation. Uncertainty then appears to be as much the result of knowing everything as knowing nothing. Joyce seems to take great pleasure in celebrating the hyperplenum that shows itself to be a void, a void not unlike that springing from Pascal's infinite complexity.

By uncertainty I do not mean in this context the formal principle of quantum mechanics that says, with a fair amount of certainty, that if one knows the position of a particle, one cannot at the same time know its momentum. Heisenberg's uncertainty principle has been used to explain Joyce's epistemology, and I will return to Heisenberg when discussing *Finnegans Wake.* However, Joyce did not know anything about Heisenberg or quantum theory when he was writing *Ulysses.* In fact, quantum mechanics didn't yet exist when he was writing *Ulysses,* and Joyce probably knew little at that time about Einstein and relativity. It is dubious that Joyce knew much of anything about the new physics until after publishing *Ulysses,* when he began documenting himself on everything in order to write *Finnegans Wake.* He had probably worked through Russell's *Introduction to Mathematical Philosophy,* among other things, to document himself for *Ulysses,* and he already knew a great deal of received science. But, as knowledgeable critics like Alan David Perlis and Alan J. Friedman have correctly argued, the universe of *Ulysses* is classical and Newtonian, and, I add, as in much of modernist fiction, Pascalian.[1]

Finnegans Wake is another matter, and one can plausibly argue that Joyce thought his panlogism in the *Wake* could accommodate the uncertainty principle as well as any other scientific principle the new physics invented while he was writing his novel. By the time Joyce was writing the *Wake,* versions of the new physics had begun to enter popular as well as philosophical and literary

1. Perlis, "The 'Ithaca' Chapter of Joyce's *Ulysses,*" and Friedman, "*Ulysses* and Modern Science," both in Bernard Benstock, ed., *The Seventh Joyce.* Friedman points out that Bloom confronts through the science of 1904, "a vast universe without teleological nature or moral center" (202), whereas Perlis speaks of a "Newtonian nightmare" in *Ulysses* (196).

consciousness. Einstein's theories of relativity were the subject of the mass media, for the fact that clocks can slow down and twins age at different rates was ready-made fare for the media and the show business of the twenties. And as that decade unfolded, the work of Bohr, Heisenberg, Born, and others was also immediately the object of well-informed philosophical interpretation — but, I stress, this occurred after *Ulysses* was published in 1922.

That Joyce documented himself on the new theories in physics does not mean that he radically broke with his own beliefs about fiction. Thomas Jackson Rice, in his excellent *Joyce, Chaos, and Complexity,* comes down very hard on those who fail to see that Joyce started out as a realist who never gave up on the belief that there was something like a realm of "reality" to which it was his task, through logos, to come ever closer:

> Joyce remained a realist throughout his career.... Joyce clearly moves away from the conventions of literary "realism" as early as his second work of fiction, his autobiographical novel *A Portrait of the Artist as a Young Man.* In doing so, however, he adopts the position of a scientific "realist," sometime pejoratively called a "naive realist" (a label he can share with Einstein) by continuing to accept the existence of a concrete, aboriginal real that exists independently of the subjective individual's act of observation. For Joyce... reality exists "without you" (3.27) in both senses of that phrase as a paradigm of a possibly unstatable rule.[2]

In a sense then, there is a metaphysical realm for Joyce—the real whose description Rice offers in paraphrasing Samuel Beckett, to whom he owes the insight that "to Joyce reality was a paradigm, an illustration of a possibly unstatable rule."[3] For Joyce, as for Musil, "reality" was, if not a metaphysical belief, then a normative ideal, defying the writer, as it were, to find the literary means that could at least approach it, even though the underdetermined nature of the real means that nothing will ever adequately encompass it, much less exhaust it. And even the skeptical critic can see that laws are so many illustrations, unending demonstrations, of facets of the metaphysical realm to which logos gives access. So laws permeate *Ulysses,* laws as constant revelations of some possible order of things, especially the laws of the body as set out by physiology, medicine, and biology as well as the cosmic laws, ruling over that infinite space

2. Rice, *Joyce, Chaos, and Complexity,* 7–8.
3. Ibid., 1. Lacanians pursuing their master's interest in Joyce may find a resonance here with Lacan's definition of the real.

that Pascal found so threatening. It must be said that *Ulysses* has at times the feel of a medical textbook written by a parodistic Jansenist.

The very notion of paradigm and a hidden rule, to recall Richard Feynman's ideas in *The Character of Physical Law,* entails that the seeker of knowledge decode phenomena, and this necessity in turn imposes a search for a code. Referring to this quest for a "possibly unstatable rule," Beckett describes in effect another way of understanding the commonality of modernists like Kafka and Joyce, united in their difference. Joyce's symbolic transcription of all the laws in *Ulysses* and *Finnegans Wake* has much the same effect as Kafka's demonstration that we never encounter, with certainty, any law, because when one confronts Joyce's surfeit, his panlogism and its explosive representation of all the codes, one can never be certain which law might be *the* law—the hidden rule underlying it all. Joyce's text can encode everything, everything can be celebrated, although the cataloging of every detail of Dublin, or the history of humanity, results in no more certainty than, in Kafka's novel, the surveyor's listening to buzzing messages on a telephone that may be connected to the Castle.

Perhaps it is not so immediately evident that Joyce's protagonists are questers in the sense that Kafka's are. Parodistic celebration can mislead. But it is arguable that, beginning at least with the Stephen Dedalus who, in *The Portrait of the Artist,* must fly from Ireland in search of the "reality" that eludes him there, Joyce marks out his literary itinerary as a quest. *Ulysses* continues this quest, with its evocation of Ulysses' travels, though the narrated experience of a day in Dublin is derisively prosaic, and hence parodistic, when compared with the Homeric quest to find a way home. The mythic quest doubles the novel's narration as the ironic structure that Joyce uses to integrate the disparate knowledge one can have of modern life, of its legends and histories, its miscellaneous brawls and drunken revels, as well as its laws and gnostic underpinnings. Joyce uses myth to endow modern life with an epistemic structure, albeit an ironic and parodistic one. Nonetheless, Joyce imposes an ironic unity, in the midst of the dingy heterogeneity, on modern culture. This unity is created by the reprise of the myth of Ulysses, the myth of the man driven by the desire for knowledge and for the desire to find his home in the universe, the cosmos in its full sense. Thus, in *Sulle orme di Ulisse,* literary scholar Pietro Boitro argues that Ulysses illustrates the central myth that brings poetry to science, and science to poetry, throughout the history of Western literature, from Homer to Dante, and beyond, through the creators of Anglo-American modernism: Eliot, Pound, and

Joyce.[4] In Joyce, Homer's narrative is transformed into an existential myth, centered on ordinary fallen humanity like Leopold Bloom, the wandering Jew upon whose life is centered the quest to know what one can know about one day, one culture, one humanity—all this encapsulated in the power of logos.

This use of the myth of Ulysses is one basis for parody, though not all is parody in Joyce's *Ulysses*. Much that is parody can also function as straightforward narration or description, celebration or gnosis, before converting itself, as the reader takes a critical look, into a parody of itself. Logos contains dialectically all its own possibilities, including self-parody of its own purport. Analogous to Kafka's play with self-referential analogy, which leads the reader into the labyrinth of infinite regress, Joyce's narrative strategies in *Ulysses* impose a constant double reading in which all can be known and, at the same time, all can be parodied. In this play of double vision Joyce certainly undermines certainty. However, unlike Kafka's rhetoric, with its use of self-reflexive allegorical images, the surface of Joyce's narration, even in its most extravagant mimickery of historically marked styles or hyperbolic use of narrative formulas, is deadpan. Little is inscribed in Joyce's rhetoric that directly obliges the reader to find self-reflexive synecdoches or other indices that would allegorize the narration as a narration indulging in self-referentiality—except the parody that perforce refers to its own performance in referring to other texts. As the novel unfolds, the reader is increasingly swamped by hyperbolic verbal play. In despair the reader may decide that the only way to continue reading is to interpret this play as a parody of its own intentions. This can be very funny, as when Bloom is put on trial in Nighttown for his many crimes, or when, in the "Ithaca" section, the narrator describes with scientific precision Bloom and Stephen's pissing together. But initially the hyperbole can also be disconcerting: when one must decipher the history of English prose styles, the parody may seem suspended as the reader struggles to master the evolution of the English language as illustrated by master parodistic savant James Joyce—but only momentarily.

In brief, *Ulysses* demands that we read modernity by reading myth, the primordial myth of epistemic quest and of a return to origins. In so doing it reduces all to a plot that centers on twenty-four hours of the putative real—in Dublin, in Ireland, in the history of the West—while allowing a hyperbolic linguistic performance that often wildly exceeds any realistic limit. It proposes that one can know everything that can be known there, and that one recognize one has

4. Boitro, *Sulle orme di Ulisse,* 18.

done little for knowing all that, except to have explored a possible reality with exhaustive gusto.

From the viewpoint of the epistemic quest, *Ulysses* culminates in a reading of the world in the "Ithaca" section, the penultimate chapter in the novel, in which Leopold, at home under night skies, seems to have regained the cosmos. He also seems reconciled with Stephen, mythic Telemachus, now the surrogate for the son whom Bloom has lost to death. The form of this chapter's narration, a series of questions duly followed by answers, is on one level a parody of the catechism, or perhaps of a school primer once used by Irish children; and, by extrapolation from these forms of "knowledge," a parody of the shape that scientific curiosity takes when it asks questions about everything. Joyce's panlogism excludes nothing, and both of these interpretations are useful, especially since school and church are always at work in shaping the modern scientific consciousness that would ignore its Greek and Jewish origins, or so Joyce implies. As a scientific catechism, the chapter's form alludes to the church and to positivism, a dual reference that Nietzsche would have seen as confirming his view of the Christian origins of the scientific will to truth. As a parodistic demonstration of the will to truth, the "Ithaca" chapter shows that the scientific mind knows no limits. The desire to know something about everything elicits questions that are followed by tentative answers that can only be followed up by more questions, indefinitely, and by implication ad infinitum. There is no end to the quest. The belief in "reality" as a hidden structure can apparently generate an infinite number of questions with an equal number of answers. Kafka's science comes immediately to mind when one recognizes that the "unstatable rule," as Beckett calls it, elicits an infinite number of statements striving to pin it down. However, the subject matter of knowledge can be as arbitrary as the objects about which one can be curious—the character of water or the nature of a home without Plumtree's Potted Meat. This is parody as well as metaphysics. It is a representation of the epistemic quest in a universe of underdetermination. Anything can be an object of investigation, for there is no ontologically privileged realm for modern science, and knowledge about anything leads to a demand for knowledge about everything else. As in Mach's world of infinite relations, of infinite possible models to be described, there is no final answer to questions, only the dream of the hidden paradigm.

Astute critics have found the "Ithaca" chapter hilarious, while others, equally as informed, have found it depressing. I confess to both reactions according to the critical perspective selected for reading the chapter. It is true that the chapter responds well to virtually any interpretive framework one proposes, so long as the framework brings out the way that the chapter mimics the human desire to know. And one can be comically amused and cosmically depressed in equal proportions by this staging of the quest for knowledge under the Pascalian skies of the infinite cosmos. On a starry night, Odysseus and Telemachus recognize that they seek knowledge in the framework of the Pascalian universe in which the description of the eternal silence of infinite space is also an answer to some of their questions. For example, to Stephen is attributed the following answer to a question as to whether he suffers from the dejection that Bloom suffers in contemplating cosmic emptiness: "He affirmed his significance as a conscious rational animal proceeding syllogistically from the known to the unknown and a conscious rational reagent between a micro and a macrocosm ineluctably constructed upon the incertitude of the void."[5] Confronting the same void, bumbling Bloom suffers in part because of his utopian desire for social amelioration. He also looks at the skies and reacts much like a fellow Pascalian astronomer in making the inevitable comparison of himself with the cosmos. He must take note that the so-called fixed stars are "in reality evermoving wanderers from immeasurably remote eons to infinitely remote futures in comparison with which the years, threescore and ten, of allotted human life formed a parenthesis of infinitesimal brevity" (17.1053–55).

Not especially parodistic, nor inaccurate, in themselves, these lines stress the cosmic consciousness of ordinary humanity in the person of Leopold Bloom, who knows and accepts what three centuries of cosmology since Galileo and Pascal had taught about the universe. Joyce pointedly intensifies this awareness when he gives Bloom, in the next lines, an anguish-filled mathematical consciousness induced by Bloom's consciousness of the potentially infinite expansion of every mathematical series. Bloom may not soon win a Field prize, but his consciousness is inflected by the history of mathematics. Pascal's ghost hovers over his discovery that mathematical infinity seems a menace to any attempt to arrive at knowledge, since the infinite inhabits every meditation upon the world, be it on geological eons or on the

> myriad minute entomological organic existences concealed in the cavities
> of the earth, beneath removable stones, in hives and mounds, of microbes,

5. Joyce, *Ulysses,* ed. Hans Walter Gabler, 17.1012–15. Hereafter cited parenthetically in the text.

germs, bacteria, bacilli, spermatozoa: of the incalculable trillions of billions of millions of imperceptible molecules contained by cohesion of molecular affinity in a single pinhead: of the universe of human serum constellated with red and white bodies, themselves universes of void space constellated with other bodies, each, in continuity, its universe of divisible component bodies of which each was again divisible in divisions of redivisible component bodies, dividents and divisors ever diminishing without actual division till, if the process were carried far enough, nought nowhere was never reached. (17.1059–69)

To evoke the belief in the "anxiety of influence" formulated by another Bloom—the Harold Bloom who has written admirably upon the Joycean Bloom—one may think that Joyce is engaging in rivalry with Pascal's rhetoric of negation. Facing Pascal's two infinities in which "nought nowhere was never reached," the Joycean quester finally decides that knowledge is a utopia, "there being no known method from the known to the unknown" (17.1140–41). In contrast with Pascal, Joyce allows that there may be an "esthetic value to the spectacle," of which Bloom, the scientist, is convinced by the "reiterated examples of poets in the delirium of the frenzy" that they show when contemplating the cosmic spectacle (17.1146–48).

Do Stephen and Bloom opt for poetry or science—or poetry in science, science that can never triumph over the paradoxes of its own infinities? This question could be added to their list, as indeed could nearly any other question in the demonstration of the possible infinite expansion linking questions and answers. *Finnegans Wake* brings some control to what is implicit at the end of *Ulysses,* that questions can go on forever, for Finn's history wraps its story up in a circle, joining the end to the beginning. In *Finnegans Wake* Joyce's tale of everything is infinite in duration, but limited by its circularity. Was Joyce inspired by one of Friedmann's models of the cosmos, which makes of the universe a bounded surface? The Russian cosmologist Friedmann will probably not replace Vico as recommended reading for understanding Joyce's figural thinking, but the overlap is interesting, since the paradoxes of Pascalian infinite space can be avoided by the kind of circular model Friedmann proposed (though it seems that the jury is still out as to whether or not we inhabit a universe whose cosmic configuration bounds infinity). In any case the epistemic quest ends in *Ulysses* with this Pascalian vision, in homage to the mathematics of despair, and with this end calls attention to the fact that Joyce's use of dialectics is also a renewal, in homage through parody, of the Pascalian debate of reason with itself through dialectics.

Pascalian dialectics also allows the reader to make some sense of a problem that has bothered some critics: the errors in the novel. Critics have pointed out errors in Joyce's calculations, for example, in his parody of using mathematical reasoning, and in his use of concepts. I suspect that Joyce intentionally, and perversely, put in some of the errors to keep his future critics busy—as he knew he would. Other errors may be due to indifference, since Joyce is not writing a textbook, but a novel in which the effects of discourse are the issue, not exact calculation or precise facts. In other words, the proliferations of what can be known, the hyperbolic overflow of knowledge, is the object of representation, not exact calculations. There are also undoubtedly some intentional errors present as part of a dialectic sense that error is part of knowledge, that truth cannot be grasped without untruth, and that every affirmation can carry with it its negation. Joyce's grasp of the science of 1904, the fateful year of *Ulysses'* day in Dublin, is solid: he knows far too much for the errors not to be largely intentional. In his representation of the workings of the Pascalian play of the proliferation of the infinite, for example, there is no reason to speak of inaccuracy. Joyce has accurately captured and transposed to Bloom's star-illuminated consciousness the consciousness that Pascal bequeathed us in anguish and longing. But, from the right perspective, it is comic in Joyce.

Political readings of the "Ithaca" chapter offer another approach to the question of Joyce's errors. For example, Andrew Gibson argues that Joyce shows his mastery of science in the chapter while not hesitating to fill "Ithaca" with errors and nonsense. Gibson sees this strategy as motivated by Joyce's desire to show that an Irishman can learn science and to satirize at the same time the Irish Revivalist movement that was alarmed by scientific materialism. While satirizing the Irish, Joyce was also motivated by an equally strong desire to give science back to the English establishment in a "twisted, perverted, distorted form":

> Joyce "masters science," in a sense, as one of the stranger's preserves, and then deliberately goes beyond or "overcomes" it, interrogating it and displacing its emphases. He does so, in large measure, by introducing into scientific discourse precisely those qualities that Englishmen and Anglo-Irishmen from Haldane to Plunkett were saying the Irish needed to be rid of: fancy, inconsequence, random thinking, whimsy, the darkness of soul

beyond enlightenment. It is hardly surprising that the chapter ends with the image of a dark sun or total eclipse.[6]

In other words, from this postcolonial perspective, Joyce is working from within the imperial science of the English colonizer, from a position of knowledge, to show himself superior to it in his rejection of English cultural imperialism. Yet knowledge detaches itself from its English origins, filling consciousness with an inevitability that not even the British conqueror could foresee: knowledge can permeate even an Irishman, the ignorant Paddy created by English imperialism to justify that imperialism, since he may learn the laws of science well enough to use them, or so Joyce insinuates. No power can keep laws out of consciousness. This argument is attractive in the way that it stresses the dialectical side of Joyce's attraction to science: he is drawn to it for its being a master discourse — or a discourse that must be undone for its complicity with history — as well as a discourse that molds consciousness through science's own power.

If, with Kafka, Joyce is the most influential novelist in the twentieth century — and I think that this is the case — it is in part because he showed how the representation of consciousness in the novel could accommodate itself to the representation of anything else. Nearly every modernist after Joyce, from Woolf through Faulkner and beyond, took a lesson in rhetoric by studying the way that Joyce uses Bloom as a vehicle for an ironic portrayal of science's permeation of daily life; or, more generally, a lesson about the effect of laws on daily consciousness. Bloom, the Everyman of modern life, knows a great deal, gathered here and there, but the knowledge he has garnered never seems to function to any special purpose. In contrast to Kafka, for whom the law is forever hovering beyond our reach, in Joyce laws are always quite near, immediately at hand, bouncing around in consciousness as it were, but often offering little more than filler for consciousness or, at best, a disparate source of aesthetic meditation.

For example, from the outset Bloom is an observer of nature, specifically that nature closest at hand in the form of his cat. It is clear that his knowledge of ethology is based on close observation, for he studies attentively puss and her relationship to mice, while wondering what animal consciousness might be,

6. Gibson, "An Aberration of the Light of Reason: Science and Cultural Politics in 'Ithaca,'" in Andrew Gibson, ed., Joyce's "Ithaca," 165.

how he appears to her, and why she is afraid of chickens (to which pussens answers, "Mrkrgnao!") (4.25–30). Zoology is not Bloom's only scientific interest, as the reader notes slightly later when Bloom walks in the streets, meditating on whatever happens to impinge upon his consciousness. Physics is also useful as a guide to understanding daily phenomena:

> Where was the chap I saw in that picture somewhere? Ah yes, in the dead sea floating on his back, reading a book with a parasol open. Couldn't sink if you tried: so thick with salt. Because of the weight of the water, no the weight of the body in the water is equal to the weight of the what? Or is it the volume is equal to the weight? It's a law something like that. Vance in High school cracking his fingerjoints, teaching. The college curriculum, Cracking curriculum. What is weight really when you say weight? Thirty-two feet per second per second. Law of falling bodies: per second per second. They all fall to the ground. The earth. It's the force of gravity of the earth is the weight. (5.38–46)

What has science done here to consciousness? Clearly, it has somehow transformed consciousness or endowed it with structures, shaky as they may be, that in Bloom generate the recurrent attempt to fit laws to observations and to experience. Whimsically, but recurrently, he wants to make of science something that fits the world of daily life, or vice versa, and thus make sense of what is going on in the confused midst of countless phenomena.

There is a misfit here between curriculum and consciousness, or a comic disproportion, and this disproportion is an important part of Joyce's comedy, culminating, in "Ithaca," in a parody showing modern life in its comic cosmic fallenness. The disproportion characterizes Bloom at many moments in the twenty-four hours that make up the novel. In a bar in which anti-Semitism is about to explode like an angry Cyclops, Bloom shows that he incarnates faith in science, in all its uselessness, with his belief that science can explain everything, such as why hanged men's "tools" will be "standing up in their faces like a poker" (12.461). Panlogism and science coincide in this faith that knowledge, expounded in the bar filled with barbarians, may triumph in the explanation of everything. A character named Joe claims the "tool" reflects the effect of passion, to which Bloom naively retorts in the murderous anti-Semitic context, "That can be explained by science":

> The distinguished scientist Herr Professor Luitpold Blumenduft tendered medical evidence to the effect that the instantaneous fracture of the cervi-

cal vertebrae and consequent scission of the spinal chord would, according to the best approved tradition of medical science, be calculated to inevitably produce in the human subject a violent ganglionic stimulus of the nerve centres of the genital apparatus, thereby causing the elastic pores of the *corpora cavernosa* to rapidly dilate in such a way as to instantaneously facilitate the flow of blood to that part of the human anatomy known as the penis or male organ resulting in the phenomenon which has been denominated by the faculty a morbid upwards and outwards philoprogenitive erection *in articulo mortis per diminutionem capitis.* (12.468–79)

Bloom's faith in the law is doubly useless, for the Jew-hating citizens only consider him to be "putting on swank with his lardy face" (12.501). Joyce's parody of medical thought and the way that it inflates consciousness shows the comic incongruity of a mind committed to the maximum understanding of the most useless detail, in the most inappropriate surrounding.

Perhaps Bloom's faith in science, manifested in the bar, is not so comically out of place as his lecturing on the stars while male friends delighted at the sight of the curvaceous breasts that Molly Bloom offered them as they all traveled together—while in fact Lenehan seems to be caressing her. Joyce makes a pointed rhetorical shift to show Bloom from Lenehan's lascivious viewpoint:

> Bloom was pointing out all the stars and the comets in the heavens to Chris Callinan and the jarvey: the great bear and Hercules and the dragon, and the whole jingbang lot. But, by God, I was lost, so to speak, in the milky way. He knows them all, faith. At last she spotted a weeny weeshy one miles away. *And whatstar is that, Poldy?* says she. By God, she had Bloom cornered. *That one, is it?* says Chris Callinan, *sure that's only what you might call a pinprick.* By God, he wasn't far wide of the mark. (10.567–74)

Knowledge is impressive, but futile, in the comically fallen world where scientists—unlike mythic Ulysses—are cuckolded, at least verbally with Shakespearean puns, when not literally in their marital bed, like everyone else. Joyce's comic sense often seems to combine Shakespeare's word play with the love of the incongruities of science, first found in Rabelais, the Renaissance doctor whose lusty love of learning presents many parallels with Joyce.[7]

7. It is more than a little instructive to compare Joyce with Rabelais, even if Joyce disclaimed, probably falsely, knowledge of Rabelais. See Claude Jacquet, *Joyce et Rabelais,* for example, for Joyce's use of Rabelais's vocabulary in *Finnegans Wake.*

Joyce is attracted to the science of medicine, though with little interest in the small succor medicine may bring to a world in the grip of the laws of sickness and death. As with Rabelais, medical science is most interesting as a comic compendium of human frailties. It is not surprising that a doctor, though perhaps ultimately as futile as any other scientist, has a privileged role in Joyce. In *Ulysses,* this scientist is Buck Mulligan, the medical student and Renaissance man par excellence who is contrasted with Stephen. Contrastive foils are flexible in *Ulysses.* If Bloom, the Everyman savant, embodies science in contrast to the poetry embodied in Stephen the poet, it must be said that Stephen, too, possesses wide learning, knows his science, and, in Hamletesque melancholia, presses forward toward knowledge. But he does so without the exuberance that characterizes him at the end of *The Portrait of the Artist.*

The exuberance about the quest for knowledge is reserved in *Ulysses* for Buck Mulligan. Moreover, if one wanted to press the point that Joyce inscribes two cultures in *Ulysses*—mainly in order to undo this schematic opposition— then one should consider that Stephen the poet is confronted by a rather more powerful scientist than Bloom in Mulligan, the Rabelaisian medical student who shares quarters with Stephen. Mulligan is a representative of science, in the form of medicine, the science of the cyclical laws of birth and death. In Mulligan Joyce embodies much the same spirit of parody that Rabelais unleashed in the service of science.[8]

Mulligan has several roles. *Ulysses'* first chapter stages from the outset a joust between science and literature when "Stately, plump Buck Mulligan" enters the novel to confront his friend Dedalus with his "absurd Greek name" (1.1, 34). Mulligan's language is full of the scientific terminology one might expect from a medical scientist who wants to Hellenize the Irish, and also worries about the performance of his white corpuscles. Like the would-be scientific schemer Bloom, Mulligan also has traits of the poet. If all oppositions in Joyce mirror each other in exchange and displacement, perhaps it is accurate to say that Mulligan the scientist is also a poet who is also a scientist. For example, Mulligan combines an interest in literature and science when he invents for Stephen a mathematical literary criticism in order to astound a tradition-bound English Oxonian. Thus Mulligan claims that Stephen "proves by algebra that Hamlet's grandson is Shakespeare's grandfather and that he himself is the ghost of his own father" (1.555–56). Mulligan's satire obliterates the two cultures "by

8. See M. M. Bakhtin, *Rabelais and His World.*

algebra" well before Joyce takes the reader through "Nighttown" to "Ithaca," with these later chapters' rhetorical strategies for parodistically staging science.

The lines of demarcation between art and science are already blurred in the opening chapter's contrast between the intransigent poet Stephen, who would not honor his religious mother's desire for prayer as she died, and the medical positivist Mulligan, who believes only in the functioning of cerebral lobes. At the outset of the novel, however, a-religious Stephen is angry because Mulligan can look upon the death of Stephen's mother as simply one more case of "tripes in the dissectingroom," or of cerebral lobes not functioning (1.206–8). In contrast with his own positivist attitude, Mulligan reproves Stephen for refusing to pray at his mother's bedside. Mulligan may be a medical positivist for whom life is ultimately reduced to senseless laws condemning us to physiological degradation, but he is also endowed with empathy.

Later in Nighttown, Mulligan shows what a Rabelaisian scientist he is when he reinvents medical logos. In these scenes parody sublimates humanity's many dysfunctions in momentary comic triumph, as exemplified in Mulligan's celebration of medicine's capacity for discoveries, most notably when he is charged with proving scientifically that the notorious Dr. Bloom, charged with crimes of perversion, is most innocent:

> Dr Bloom is bisexually abnormal. He has recently escaped from Dr Eustace's private asylum for demented gentlemen. Born out of bedlock hereditary epilepsy is present, the consequence of unbridled lust. Traces of elephantiasis have been discovered among his ascendants. There are marked symptoms of chronic exhibitionism. Ambidexterity is also present. He is prematurely bald from self-abuse, perversely idealistic in consequence, a reformed rake, and has metal teeth. . . . I have made a pervaginal examination and, after application of the acid test to 5427 anal, axillary, pectoral and pubic hairs, I declare him to be *virgo intacta* (15.1774–86).

Mulligan draws with ease upon a plethora of medical laws of recent vintage: the language of clinical medicine, psychiatry, and psychoanalysis, not to mention a medical ethics concocted with these discourses. This is language that parodies itself by the hyperbolic evocation of laws to explain everything—which in turn parodies the common faith among even the most skeptical that science, especially medical science, should be able to explain all, especially every toothache and pain in the back, not to mention dispositions to necrophilia. However, there is a strongly ambivalent dimension to this parody. It rejuvenates the discourse it inflates, but this inflation also ironically undermines science when applied with the hyperbolic dialectical logic Mulligan uses to show that logos can encode everything. The reader recognizing the expressionist side to this scene may retort that it owes as much to Faust's Walpurgis Night as to Panurge's disquisitions, not to mention the wacky science found in Flaubert's homage to Goethe in *The Temptation of Saint-Anthony*. And that is true, too.

Bloom is shown by science to be at once the greatest ruler and the greatest pervert of our time. He is thus the Everyman in which humanity's ordinary, daily deviance explodes as a form of life-affirming power, especially when it is set against those dark laws of medical science that condemn us, in Joyce as in Proust, to the daily deaths that kill one and all in relentless confirmation of the power of the law. Yet, if the laws of medical science are finally predicated upon the laws of death, then it appears that only parody has the power to effect resurrection. This is of course true in *Finnegans Wake*, but also in *Ulysses*. A central event in *Ulysses* is the funeral that Bloom attends, which sets the stage for the parody in Nighttown that allows dead Patty Dignam to live, like Finnegan, again (15.1210). Taking place after the funeral, the Nighttown episode is set in Joyce's Netherworld, that region that Bakhtin described in medieval culture wherein the power of parody resurrects all that the power of logos, in the guise of the laws of society, had repressed. In this sense Joyce, like Rabelais, affirms that a major function of literature is to oppose the rigidities of knowledge that science and convention bring to life, and even to death. Destruction and rejuvenation are two sides of the same dialectical coin, in Joyce as in Rabelais.

Joyce's display of what happens when the laws of nature become the stuff of consciousness is, one can see, hardly limited to the penultimate "Ithaca" chapter. It is found to various degrees throughout *Ulysses*. For example, in chapter fourteen the "display of discursiveness" (14.954) in the National Maternity Hospital revels in its review of science, squarely centered on medicine, physiology, biology, and the history of these disciplines. In this regard the doctors and medical students, with their friends at the hospital including Stephen and Bloom, resemble actors on the unfolding historical stage of scientific knowledge. The enacted display of science is prodigious. The topics they cover range from the "consideration of the causes of sterility" (14.668), brought up by Mulligan, to general meditations on Darwin and adaptation. These rambling discussions call up many biological and medical problems, each mirrored through the rhetorical prism of shifting consciousness, distributed "among tempers so divergent" (14.955), including Bloom, now a knighted Sir Leopold, "who had ever loved the art of physic as might a layman" (14.256). An adept of "perverted transcendentalism," Stephen is singled out for resisting "accepted scientific methods" (14.1225–26), a characterization that sets him apart again as much for his rigidity as for his poetic inclinations. The others present are squarely men of science who debate such notions as whether, in accord with Empedocles of Trinacria, the right ovary is responsible for the birth of males, or, as believed such embryologists as Culpepper, Spallanzani, Blumenbach, Lusk, Hertwig, Leopold, and Valenti, a mixture of both is at work (14.1235–36). Joyce reproduces literally the marvelous heterogeneity of theories and ideas recorded by the history of science, which results in an incongruous demonstration that no scientific law is ever lost, no absurd model or ludicrous explanation ever disappears, so long as language can reproduce it.

The laws reigning over birthing and dying are multiple and yet ultimately mysterious in their meaning, so that, in an appropriate hospital setting, the scholars can muse forever upon mortality and natality. Medical student Lynch launches forth in a discussion that illuminates what Beckett meant by the suggestion that "reality" is, for Joyce, finally an unknown paradigm:

> An ingenious suggestion is that thrown out by Mr V. Lynch (Bacc. Arith.) that both natality and mortality, as well as all other phenomena of evolution, tidal movements, lunar phases, blood temperatures, diseases in general, everything, in fine, in nature's vast workshop from the extinction of some remote sun to the blossoming of one of the countless flowers which beautify our public parks is subject to a law of numeration as yet unascertained. Still the plain straightforward question why a child of normally healthy parents and seemingly a healthy child and properly looked after succumbs unaccountably in early childhood (though other children of the same marriage do not) must certainly, in the poet's words, give us pause. Nature, we may rest assured, has her own good and cogent reasons for whatever she does and in all probability such deaths are due to some law of anticipation by which organisms in which morbous germs have taken up their residence (modern science has conclusively shown that only the plasmic substance can be said to be immortal) tend to disappear at an increasingly earlier stage of development, an arrangement which, though productive of pain to some of our feelings (notably the maternal), is nevertheless, some of us think, in the long run beneficial to the race in general in securing hereby the survival of the fittest. (14.1268–85)

The hypothetical unknown law may be suggested by the most recent theories—here, for example, Darwinian theory with its global vision of life. But this is just one exemplar of one law, and in this context a rather drunken one. Drunk or not, Lynch offers the hypothesis that there might be a great unity of science proposing the total "law of enumeration" by which all will be known. This is a rather grandiose view postulating an "end of theory," though in the context it also mocks our thirst for a law granting solace in a universe in which knowledge can never justify a child's suffering. Lynch's beliefs founder on the idea that what benefits the species may demand a mother's anguish. The net effect is not unlike what one encounters in Dostoyevsky's *The Brothers Karamazov,* in Ivan Karamazov's refusal to accept the torture of children, or later, in Camus's *The Plague,* in Doctor Rieux's revolt against the senselessness of a child's death. No law, however god-sanctioned, could justify an infant's suffering, not even the influential biologist August Weismann's sanguine views about the germ line's immortality that Lynch cites in speaking of the eternity of the "plasmic substance."

Facing the mystery of death, Lynch puts forth ideas in a way that shows their powerlessness, and in this inebriated celebration of science, the law recedes to become one more indifferent bit of data, part of rhetoric or consciousness or, perhaps more precisely, the rhetoric of consciousness. The law is reduced to another phenomenal feature of the world in which the self, as Bloom shows, must negotiate funerals, frying pans and toilet paper (or substitutes thereof), and ultimate theories. In this regard Joyce's world bears much resemblance to Pascal's in that the proliferation of laws, like the potential extension of the infinite in Pascal's cosmos, destroys all certainties by the simple fact that the proliferation will never come to an end. There is no stopping place, no final destination for meanings. Joyce comes to terms with this potentially infinite extension by parodistically replicating it.

In résumé, *Ulysses* embodies science as a fact of consciousness, and, as such, it is as arbitrary and as heterogeneous as all other perceptions that organize the mind or, alternatively, that the mind struggles to organize. Scientific laws, like religious ideas or political beliefs, are part of the stuff of consciousness, deriving from all manner of sources, whether written, such as through curricula and magazines, or oral, such as in drunken jousting and late-night conversation. Framed within consciousness science of all provenance is present throughout the novel, exemplified variously by the medical science studied by everyone from Mulligan to the local chemist, the high-school physics that Bloom cannot remember, and finally the multiple sciences that Joyce quotes in the catechism enacted in "Ithaca." In this penultimate chapter science is the center of narration, if "narration" is the proper term for the catechistic series of questions and responses that make up Joyce's version of Telemachus and Odysseus's encounter when they plot to slay the suitors (of which Molly, Penelope's analogue, apparently has only one at the moment). The near-concluding position of the "Ithaca" chapter, with its final presentation of Bloom and of Stephen, together, argues for the idea that Joyce puts science in a stressed position in *Ulysses:* by placing it in the foreground, Joyce underscores the role science plays in informing consciousness. However, Stephen and Bloom's recourse to science and its description of the world under the nocturnal Pascalian skies is of little succor to these characters seeking a home, their Ithaca, in the fragmented cosmos of 1904.

Infinite Repetition: *Finnegans Wake*s

The world of *Ulysses* is not the world of *Finnegans Wake.* The later novel embodies, in an even more radical way, the principle of panlogism that Joyce used in *Ulysses,* because the world of *Finnegans Wake* is literally dominated by a dialectic of contraries. As even the most casual reader of *Finnegans Wake* notes in delight or dismay, Joyce embodies this dialectic in the very language he uses. Constantly melding words taken from different languages, Joyce creates words capable of meaning one thing, its opposite, and often several other things in addition. The world becomes pun. With this created language Joyce proposes a science that purports to know, through a vast synecdoche, the total history of the world. Thus history-science is represented in *Finnegans Wake* as nothing less than the totality of what is and was and will be again. Since this totality includes perforce the book *Finnegans Wake,* every event in the novel also refers to the novel itself, which means that the novel is finally one long pun on itself. Nearly everything in the book obeys what one can call the axiom of self-reference, or the axiom that, if the book is about the totality of what is, it is about itself. Punning his way through the history of science, as well as chiasmatically the science of history, since both may be taken to offer knowledge of the totality of what is, Joyce perforce alludes to an undetermined number of sciences in this grandiose vision that makes Hegel's absolute spirit seem rather limited in its pretensions to grasp everything. To be sure Joyce's history oscillates around an Irish pub, whereas Hegel's culminated in Prussian law. But for this reason, too, one might argue that Hegel's linear history is impoverished in comparison with Joyce's view of cyclical recurrence, with the infinite wakes that, well washed in whisky, will recur forever.

When it suited his purposes Joyce also took notice of ongoing contemporary history, for example, the fact that physics was being transformed by relativity theory and quantum mechanics. My argument now is that these two domains in physics offer different ways of getting into *Finnegans Wake*. Turning first to relativity theory, then to quantum mechanics, I want to make some interpretive comments about what Joyce found in contemporary physics and, with these comments, offer a way of reading this history obeying a universal law of historical cycles. Relativity theory, in fact, suggests a very fruitful way to view the cycles the *Wake* narrates. The law of eternal return can look very much like a description of relativistic temporality, and since, in the underdetermined universe of Mach, Poincaré, and Finnegan, every law is one of the many laws that can describe the same thing or, alternatively, everything, it is also the case that no law excludes another.

To make the transition from the almost "readerly" world of *Ulysses* to *Finnegans Wake*, it is relevant to note that what is common to both is that the law is displayed, and often hyperbolically celebrated, within the framework of a universal myth. In *Finnegans Wake* it is no longer the myth of Ulysses, a myth characterizing the universal desire for knowledge. *Finnegans Wake* is informed by the universal law of all becoming, which underwrites the dreams of resurrection that explode periodically to mark each new cycle upon the pages of this tale of "here comes everybody," HCE and his family, or of you and me, in other dialectical incarnations. Therefore, it seems reasonable to say that all laws mentioned or illustrated in *Finnegans Wake* are so many undetermined variants of laws that are subordinate to the general law of cyclical return, or laws that illustrate return and fall in their own way. A theory of cycles functions thus much like *The Odyssey* does for *Ulysses:* it provides a mythical scaffolding on which Joyce could peg a narrative of cycles and recurrences, examples and counter-examples, laws and counter-laws, such as what he saw in time and space, or, to anticipate, relativity against quantum theory. Underlying all this is undoubtedly a tautological side: all laws are in some sense laws of what is, and whatever is, is described by law, so that the existence of the law of what is is a tautological necessity. This is suggested by Beckett's formulation that, for Joyce, the law was unstatable; at most one can simply say that it is. With that tautology Joyce is again not far from Kafka, who reasons from phenomena back to the law that must exist because the phenomena exist. With this tautology, Joyce could narrate the universe illustrating all the laws one can imagine.

At least since Beckett's essay "Dante . . . Bruno, Vico . . . Joyce," published under Joyce's aegis in 1929, ten years before Joyce finished *Finnegans Wake,* an initiated public has known that one model for this law of cycles was furnished by the Italian Enlightenment philosopher Vico, whose theory of history described historical becoming as a series of cycles. It is not the only one, however. Beckett concedes that another model for cyclical return comes from the Renaissance in heretic Giordano Bruno's theory of infinite worlds and infinite becomings.[9] Beckett would have it that Vico's exposition of the circular progression of society was new, though the germ of it was contained in Bruno's treatment of contraries in his vision of the infinite worlds making up the universe. One can point out that Greek political theory also had theories in which cycles dominate in the historical transformation of society, but perhaps it is more illuminating to suggest a parallel closer to Joyce in noting that he seems to have been attentive to that modernist inheritor of the Greeks, Nietzsche, who was obsessed by historical becoming. Nietzsche, the theorist of science as a form of the will to power, was also another theorist of eternal return. Although Nietzsche is mentioned in *Finnegans Wake,* Joyce scholars rarely consider Nietzsche's hypothesis that the nature of actual infinity means that, logically, everything must recur an infinite number of times. For Nietzsche this proposition then entails that the supreme form of saying yes to life is affirmatively to accept this eternal return and to desire an infinite repetition of the life one has just led, no matter how dreary it may have been. This is Nietzsche's answer to what he called Pascal's philosophical suicide, in Pascal's saying no to life and wagering for Christianity. Intentionally or not, Joyce invented in *Finnegans Wake* a literary form that embodies Nietzsche's vision of eternal return; and there is hardly a work in world literature in which the eternal return is more affirmatively presented than in *Finnegans Wake*—even if the opposite can also be affirmed.

With regard to scientists in these cycles, Joyce seems to put them at certain nodal points where history begins again. Scientists such as Planck, Poincaré, and Einstein are thus joined to evoke the knowledge of time's elusive ways. Einstein is mentioned several times, especially with regard to the fall of Newton, brought about by the advent of relativity theory and its displacement of

9. Beckett, "Dante . . . Bruno, Vico . . . Joyce," in *Our Exagmination Round His Factification for Incamination of Work in Progress,* 5.

Newtonian thought. This event is marked several times by the fall of the apple on Newton's head, which combines dialectically the advent of classical physics, in Newton's famous discovery, and the "fall" of the apple-physics—classical physics being replaced by relativity physics. Apparently, as I write, direct references to neither Bohr nor Heisenberg, the two most important scientists in the early development of quantum mechanics, have yet been discovered in *Finnegans Wake*. No negative statement of this sort is ever conclusive about the text, since an allusion may be waiting deciphering and discovery.[10] This possibility seems all the more likely in the case of scientists associated with quantum physics, since, as we will see, quantum theory is explicitly named by none other than the right-wing Professor Jones, noted spatialist.

In fine, the laws of science are present in the *Wake* as possible illustrations of the postulated law decreeing the rise and fall of everything and everyone. In this regard science, like myth, plays a role in offering a structure to universal experience. In fact, one may wonder if, from the perspective of total history and its cyclical repetition, the distinction between science and myth is very meaningful. One follows the other in the infinite repetition of the forms of human knowledge.

Finnegans Wake unfolds in a way consonant with what an imaginative reading of relativity theory might entail for literary representation. To be sure, relativity is not a recipe for reading a work that must be read word by word for a semantic play that relentlessly narrates the tale of its own becoming and dissolution. But in a study of modernism's relation to science, there is hardly a more interesting case of how a seminal writer represented innovations in science—the discovery of new laws as it were—to create a myth of the law itself. If both relativity theory and quantum mechanics are alluded to in *Finnegans Wake*, it is essential to understand, as Joyce clearly did, that relativity theory cannot be equated with quantum mechanics. They cannot be conflated historically or conceptually. Moreover, Joyce grasped the opposition that exists between them. Recall that, historically, relativity theory was developed by Einstein as a theory of macro-phenomena and had little to do with the quantum descriptions of the behavior of subatomic particles, which gave rise to Heisenberg's uncertainty principle.

10. For a list of recognized characters, see Adaline Glasheen, *Third Census of "Finnegans Wake": An Index of Characters and Their Roles,* supplemented by Roland McHugh, *Annotations to "Finnegans Wake,"* rev. ed. More undoubtedly remain to be found.

It is also important to recall in this regard that Heisenberg's uncertainty principle has little to do with uncertainty as I have used the term up to this point. In speaking of certainty and uncertainty in Proust, Musil, Kafka, and *Ulysses,* I am speaking of uncertainty as an epistemic condition that is ascribed sometimes to conditions of knowledge, and sometimes to a psychological state. Uncertainty in this sense can be looked upon as an epistemic insufficiency, or as a lack of knowledge, whereas Heisenberg's uncertainty principle implies that, at the level of microphenomena, uncertainty may be an ontological state underlying the formal impossibility of simultaneously describing the momentum and position of a particle like an electron or a photon. This was the position of Heisenberg and Bohr, though some of their writings also suggest that quantum uncertainty is a result of the mathematical formalisms used in quantum measurement and cannot be ascribed to nature. In no case do they describe uncertainty as the kind of epistemic deficiency that tortures modernists like Musil and Kafka, or Stephen and Bloom. The formalisms of quantum mechanics work in fact with near certainty. However, in anticipation of antagonisms in *Finnegans Wake,* one should also recall that not all scientists agreed with Heisenberg and Bohr. Along with physicists like de Broglie, Schrödinger, and later David Bohm, Einstein thought that, with the uncertainty principle, science had not yet found the proper description of subatomic particles which would eliminate uncertainty and reestablish the reign of causality at every level of physical description. In other words, Einstein stood opposed to the philosophical interpretation of quantum mechanics that introduced indeterminacy into the heart of the atom. And at this writing relativity theory has still not been reconciled with quantum mechanics, for no uncertainty of the sort described by Heisenberg is built into the relativistic physics that describes macrophenomena. However, there is little inclination to reject the basic interpretation of Bohr and Heisenberg; on the contrary. But the opposition remains.

Relativity involves time and space. Spatial relativity is an old issue in science. It is already present in Joyce's favored Giordano Bruno, not to mention in Galileo and Newton. Bruno's hypothesis concerning an infinite number of worlds in infinite space entails necessarily the loss of any privileged spatial framework. This loss of an absolute spatial framework was recognized in anguish by Pascal. It underlies the angst about the destruction worked by the mathematical infinite which, from Pascal through Musil, Kafka, and Joyce, is a dominant motif in the development of modern consciousness. Joyce was certainly sensitive to this relativistic aspect of Bruno's thought. But the relativity of time does not accompany spatial relativity in Bruno, Newton, or Pascal, and Joyce clearly understood this aspect of relativity theory. He understood it, not only because Einstein had become a media figure, but because, as Joyce was finishing *Ulysses* and beginning *Finnegans Wake,* relativity theory was being explained by a host of eminent philosophers, such as Schlick, Russell, Carnap, Cassirer, Whitehead, and Reichenbach—not to mention Einstein himself, in his own, very persuasive expositions written for a general public. It was clear in these writings, offering various degrees of technical interpretation, that the worldview based on classical mechanics had undergone a profound transformation. Rejecting classical common sense, relativity asked normal people to visualize, as Lorentz and Fitzgerald had already hypothesized before Einstein, that objects moving in a straight line contract in the direction of their movement as they approach the speed of light. It proposed against intuition that light has an absolute and uniform speed, regardless of the speed of the object emitting the light. It even suggested the remote possibility of time travel.

From the axiom of the absolute speed of light, Einstein deduced logically that the relativity of time must necessarily be the case. For if the speed of light is constant regardless of the motion of the source, then measurements of space and time must therefore vary between frames of reference in order to maintain the absolute value for the speed of light. Simultaneity can have meaning only relative to a given inertial framework. This means that what one observer perceives as coming after an event, someone else, located in a different framework, can perceive as coming before the same event. In short, with the development of relativity theory, Vico's classical theory of the cyclical nature of history could, certainly from Joyce's perspective, be viewed as coinciding with the developments of modern epistemology. The new recycled the old, since, depending on the temporal frame work, the old could be viewed as coming after the new. One could hardly say whether Finnegan dies before he is born or afterward; both events could even take place "seemaultaneously."[11] With Einstein's special theory of 1905, therefore, one of the basic axioms of epistemological realism seemed shaken, since there is no longer any absolute temporal metric by which the real can be defined. Einstein was aware of the philosophical implications of his work, and it is important to see what Joyce could have taken from, say,

11. Joyce, *Finnegans Wake,* 161. Hereafter cited parenthetically in the text.

Einstein's popular book *Relativity,* first published in 1916, in which he describes how time and space act together, as conceived by classical mechanics, to function as a carrier of events.[12] Space and time function as the "inertial system" that allows the law of inertia to lay claim to validity (144). This is because the role played by space and time allowed the classical physicist to think of "physical reality" as existing independently of the subject's experience of that reality. Or, in Einstein's words, physical reality "was conceived as consisting, at least in principle, of space and time on one hand, and of permanently existing material points, moving with respect to space and time, on the other" (144). In dismissing the ether, Einstein dismissed the privileged inertial system that classical physics postulated as permeating the universe. With this dismissal, in a most Joycean statement, Einstein stressed that the notion of simultaneity could no longer be independent of the inertial system one selected. Einstein said quite simply that the basis for the "now" of classical temporality had lost "for the spatially extended world its objective meaning" (149). *Finnegans Wake* seems described by, if not contained in, this statement.

Yet, realism is not destroyed by this loss. Einstein, like Joyce, is a realist in any important epistemological sense. The axiom about the invariance of the speed of light postulates a universal law, and this law means that the capacity for the transmission of information is guaranteed as an invariant feature of the world. Light can be defined as information, and it is in this important sense that nothing can exceed the speed of light. Moreover, Einstein firmly believed, as he argued on many occasions, that the universe was subject to causal processes that could be described as deterministic. As historian of science Max Jammer aptly suggests, and, as we shall see, Joyce also implies in *Finnegans Wake,* Einstein was our modern Spinoza.[13] In Spinoza's ontology, temporality is a question of perspective on the infinite unfolding of the manifold aspects of substance. This can apply to Einstein. If applied to Joyce, it would seem that the unfolding of universal substance according to absolute necessity, with its infinite accidents and temporal perspectives, is another apt way of describing *Finnegans Wake.*

Contextual arguments aside, the evidence in *Finnegans Wake* also affirms that Joyce was very aware of the new theories science was elaborating in the early twentieth century. Against critics who believe Joyce knew no more about

12. Einstein, *Relativity: Special and General Theory,* trans. Robert W. Lawson, 143. Hereafter cited parenthetically in the text.

13. Jammer, *The Conceptual Development of Quantum Mechanics,* 286.

science than they do, Jean-Michel Rebaté documents, in *Joyce upon the Void,* that Joyce began, in fact, updating himself on contemporary science in 1918 when he was preparing to write the "Ithaca" chapter for *Ulysses.* He used sources that acquainted him with Poincaré and the theses of *La Science et l'hypothèse;* and later, after Eddington's verification in 1919 of the deflection of light by gravity, Joyce continued reading various sources, including, in 1926, Bertrand Russell's *The ABC of Relativity.*[14] Rebaté finds that Joyce transposed a paragraph of Russell's work in the following lines of *Finnegans Wake:*

> Because, Soferim Bebel, if it goes to that, (and dormerwindow gossip will cry it from the housetops no surelier than the writing on the wall will hue it to the mod of men that mote in the main street) every person, place and thing in the chaosmos of Alle anyway connected with the gobblydumped turkery was moving and changing every part of the time: the travelling inkhorn (possibly pot), the hare and turtle pen and paper, the continually more and less intermisunderstanding minds of the anticollaborators, the as time went on it will variously inflected, differently pronounced, otherwise spelled, changeably meaning vocable scriptsigns. (118)

This passage is, when read in light of the axiom of self-reference, a self-description of *Finnegans Wake,* but it also alludes in Joycean paraphrase to Russell's description of electrons, considered the smallest elements of reality at the time, here used to describe the letter that a chicken digs out of a garbage dump.

Indeed, a letter in a garbage dump—logos after the Fall—is a central parodistic self-reflexive image of *Finnegans Wake,* and the passage can be read as a brief lesson about writing and the dialectics of Joycean science as he interrelates the law and the language of the revelation of the law, found after the fall of logos into a garbage dump. Bebel, suffering Babel, is the source of our logos and hence our fall, which, dialectically, means our resurrection. *Finnegans Wake* presents itself as a "chaosmos" of all and everything interconnected, in the infinite divisions which the hare and turtle suggest for their role in Zeno's paradoxes. One paradox states that if space can be infinitely divided, then motion does not exist, and time also stands still if it can be infinitely divided. But everything moves nonetheless, to paraphrase Galileo in his discomfort. And so this letter is the unfolding tale of our chaos and our cosmic home, dialectically disordered and ordered, subject to the law of return and the law of

14. Rebaté, *Joyce upon the Void,* 1–10.

unknown distributions and entropic intermisunderstandings for which the void is perhaps the ultimate image. The law is made manifest, even if the law seems self-contradictory in the multiple manifestations of how it can be written.

This dialectical demonstration of science in the *Wake* hasn't quite gotten a reader to relativity, even if it is teasingly suggestive that the moving bird, looking for the letter, "was moving and changing every part of the time." Nor does the simple fact of numerous allusions in *Finnegans Wake* to scientific laws as well as to Einstein, Newton, and Poincaré mean that Joyce has used science in any interesting way. An allusion means little in itself. But, as I suggested, relativity is a scientific theory that coincides with Joyce's own desire to write a version of history that demolishes the linear history from which Stephen-Telemachus wants to awake in *Ulysses*. The same desire that drew Joyce to Vico and Bruno undoubtedly drew him to consider relativity theory—the desire to create a history illustrating a law of cyclical return. One can ask if *Finnegans Wake* would have been significantly different if Einstein had never published his 1905 paper. The question is really rather pointless, however, for once absolute time had "fallen," then it was inevitable that Joyce should incorporate this fall into his tale alluding to the fall of everything, from Adam to Newton's apple. What exactly this implies is not immediately clear, however, and the vast critical literature on Joyce is not too helpful in this regard.

Several critics have claimed that Joyce used relativity theory, by which they mean that relativity theory is in some sense embodied in the novel. For example, in his influential study *Structure and Motif in Finnegans Wake* Clive Hart says that Joyce had Einstein and Minkowski "at his back" in writing *Finnegans Wake,* and he claims that Joyce "was trying to build up a faithful verbal analogue" to the new world of physics.[15] However, Hart then interprets this claim to mean vaguely that one can view the world of *Finnegans Wake* from any framework. This is of course true of everything in the universe, and hence says little about how the principle of relativity might find an analogue in the novel itself. In a dissertation richly documenting allusions to science in Joyce, *The Joyce of Science,* Andrez Duszenko enthusiastically claims that *Finnegans Wake* shares complementarity with quantum physics just as it shares spatiotemporal unity with relativity theory.[16] What sharing spatiotemporal unity might mean isn't too clear, but Duszenko finds Joyce using relativity theory in the fact that, in

15. Hart, *Structure and Motif in "Finnegans Wake,"* 65.
16. Duszenko, *The Joyce of Science,* 111 and 136.

the central fable of the Ondt and the Gracehoper, space and time are pro-
nounced to be one, since each can only develop in opposition to the other. In
this fable the opposition of space and time is clear, but this opposition isn't necessarily relativity, it is more like dialectics, and the opposition of Shem and
Shaun, of time and space (and of Joyce and his critic Wyndham Lewis) is in
most contexts a dialectical opposition born of Joyce's panlogism—or what Harry
Levin felicitously called an "aggressive reconciliation of the antitheses of the
schoolmen."[17] However, I will return to this point presently to develop further
Duszenko's fertile suggestions.

In fact, after surveying much of the criticism on Joyce and science, one may
be tempted to agree with Grace Eckley that the central parable about space and
time in *Finnegans Wake* is about the failure of science; or at least it queries if
whatever science cannot explain might not be better turned into art. That is the
way in which, in her very informative *Children's Lore in "Finnegans Wake,"*
Eckley interprets the following line about the Gracehoper, "hoppy on akkant
of his joyicity":[18] "For if sciencium (what's what) can mute us nought, 'a thought,
abought the Great Sommboddy within the Omniboss, perhops an artsaccord
(hoot's hoot) might sing ums tumtim abutt the Little Newbuddies that ring his
panch" (415). So sings the Gracehoper, or Shem the penman, Joyce's proponent
of time and defender of Bergson and Einstein (and Joyce), in his argument
with the defender of space, the ant-Ondt, and whose lyric complaint ends by
asking his opponent:

> Your genius its worldwide, your spacest sublime!
> But, Holy Saltmartin, why can't you beat time? (419)

Science, or what's what, must make room for a bit of hooting from Shem's
point of view; but, I think, this is not the total viewpoint of the novel itself, it is
only one dialectical viewpoint within the flow of universal experience about
which the novel narrates, after all, everything and its opposite.

If one takes the viewpoint of the Omniboss and looks at those things that, in
cyclic display, "ring his panch," one may find that there is an important analogy between the overall structure of *Finnegans Wake* and Einstein's portrayal of
how different observers view events as being earlier or later, according to their
system of reference. The necessary relativity of temporal perception, as described

---

17. Levin, *James Joyce,* 102.
18. Eckley, *Children's Lore in "Finnegans Wake,"* 22.

by Einstein, suggests a way of understanding how one can situate events in time in *Finnegans Wake*. If every nuclear event can be likened to an independent inertial framework or system of reference, events can be situated relative to different temporal frameworks such that no event in the novel can be said to occur in any absolute sense before or after any other. And were one to find the proper framework, one could even say that all events take place simultaneously. It is strongly suggested in the *Wake* that such a framework must exist. Of course, one must also agree that there are events in *Finnegans Wake:* that there is a minimal level of narration involving probable nuclear events constituting its universal history, such as Finn's fall, HCE's mysterious crime, or arguments between Shem and Shaun. And, one must allow that there is another level of events to which the narration alludes, drawn from the public chronology that is usually called "history." These events include England's occupation of Ireland, the Crimean War, Newton's possibly receiving an apple on the head, or the distasteful events constituting the existence of the historical Wyndham Lewis. The fact that there are "real" events emerging from the flow of phenomena justifies the claim that *Finnegans Wake* is realist in the sense that it has a referential dimension. Or, if one prefers, Joyce affirms therewith his belief in an ontological realm that does not depend upon perception for its existence. So stated, Joyce's realism coincides with Einstein's realism: the invariant real is postulated to exist by necessity, however much trouble we have perceiving it. Postulating that the invariant exists, subject to yet-to-be-discovered laws over which the seeker has no control, the questing mind must seek the invariant by looking for it from a chosen inertial framework having no absolute coordinates. From this viewpoint, then, *Finnegans Wake* is a playful demonstration of the manifestation of law, a hypothetical law, of the return of every event, subject to the principle of relativity, in that nothing can be privileged over anything else for localizing space or time. Time and space exist in function of the event that sets out the temporal framework for space-time. Every event in the novel exists in itself. The game rule is then that the reader must situate the event with regard to some inertial framework within the novel and then see if the event can be perceived in relation to any other event. Since the novel itself varies its frameworks, the game involves the reader in a constant tussle to pin down time and space so that "before" and "after" have any meaning—while recognizing they are relative.

Dialectics born of the infinite and relativity theory coincide from the novel's beginning, though "beginning" here means little more than the novel's having an arbitrary first page. The novel begins with its conclusion, "riverrun, past Eve and Adam's, from swerve of shore to bend of bay, brings us by a commodius vicus of recirculation back to Howth Castle and Environs." The beginning is contained in the conclusion, or vice versa, depending on your frame of reference. The law of cyclic return—borrowed from Vico or Bruno or Nietzsche or innumerable myths—is the "vicus" or way leading through all events. This way is the principle of repetition, a putative law underlying all these events to come that have already been and that can hardly be differentiated from each other. This law of infinite repetition means that at any moment, any event in the novel, once identified, can be said to have occurred before or after any other event in the novel. The river flows, but any imposition of identity, in space or time, is somebody's act of intellection, localized by the framework of that person's inertial system. And so the wake awaits one and all, infinitely recurring before and after and at the same time as all the other wakes that one can chose to privilege as a frame of reference. Once the reader has picked out a wake framework, all deaths are the same, and all obey the same laws, for, as Einstein also postulated in 1905, the laws are always the same, no matter what the framework. It was Joyce's genius to show that the sameness involves a repetition that is fundamentally comic—the infinite is a great comic machine for iteration, as Bergson might have said. Described by relativity, the infinite generates humanity's existential comedy—or tragedy, if you prefer the dialectical opposite—that describes the structure of the void.

This use of relativity, or dialectics for that matter, is not paradoxical. It is the systematic use of self-reflexivity in *Finnegans Wake* that fosters paradox. For example, like the identifiable event of Ana-*cum*-chicken finding the letter in the litter, many events in the novel can be taken as synecdoches representing the work itself, which means that nearly every isolated event can be taken to symbolize its own repetition and a representation of the whole. This is consonant with the repetition of the various laws of the wake—for the law itself entails the repetition of the same, the reprise of invariant recurrences. By indulging in constant self-referentiality, Joyce ensured, with perhaps malicious irony, that an indefinite number of contradictory interpretations lie ahead for all the revelers at the wake. As every logician knows, not to mention readers of Kafka's parables, one need only ponder the truth of the statement that declares that the statement itself is not true, to find oneself embarked on a journey through unending contradiction. But the relativistic framework I have suggested for reading *Finnegans Wake* is not paradoxical. As David A. White argues, in his thoughtful *The Grand Continuum: Reflections on Joyce and Metaphysics,* the *Wake*'s structure is a continuous present with a cyclical configuration of history that forms a "consistent metaphysical whole."[19] To which I add that, if this consistent metaphysical whole respects relativity theory, then it also allows every event to be viewed as existing in the present—though from another inertial framework it will be past or even future—and this is not a paradox, but merely a consequence of the varying temporal frameworks recurring in the novel. Or in Joycese, in which time is also the *Zeit* of German science: "But abide Zeit's sumonserving, rise afterfall" (78). One can rise after all others or before, or after one's own fall before the others, as you like.

Joyce's enchantment with relativity theory seems to have led him to oppose it to quantum theory, partly out of a love of the symmetry opposing time and space, but partly, I think, because he intuited the opposition of Einstein and Heisenberg, or because he saw the conflict between relativity theory and quantum mechanics. The debate or opposition surfaces, for example, when Joyce deals in the novel with his hostile critic, Wyndham Lewis, an anti-time proponent of space culture. This occurs in the aforementioned fable of the Ondt and the Gracehoper and in the earlier (or later) scene in which Joyce's Professor Jones also represents, among others, the protofascist Lewis, distinguished for his hostility toward the "time" culture of which Bergson, Einstein, and Joyce are representatives. Accordingly, Bitchson, Winestain, and *recherché* Proust are among those criticized when the professor lectures on the misunderstandings of time and space (149). The professor appears in a chapter recalling the "Ithaca" chapter of *Ulysses* in that it consists of a series of twelve questions and answers. The eleventh question was apparently written in 1927, as a direct response to Lewis's *Time and Western Man,* but it also appears to make allusions to the very recent development of quantum mechanics.[20] In the eleventh question Professor Jones, also an embodiment of Shaun, emerges to give a lecture on the dime-cash problem, by which Joyce conflates economics and the time-space problem of physics—since time is cash—though cashdime also sounds like a parody of space-time.

The professor, "so eminent a spacialist," wants to confute "impulsivism" and hence, in his use of Einstein's terminology, seems to oppose relativity (149) He wants to do a "postvortex piece infustigation of a determinised case of

19. White, *The Grand Continuum: Reflections on Joyce and Metaphysics,* 48.
20. See E. L. Epstein, Chapter Four of Michael H. Begnal and Fritz Senn, eds., *A Conceptual Guide to "Finnegans Wake,"* 65.

chronic spinosis" (150). In this "infustigation" Joyce sets up an opposition between, on the one hand, Lewis, his doctrine of vorticism, and the rejection of relativity that characterized conservative, not to say fascist, thought; and, on the other hand, the thought that from Spinoza and "chronic spinosis" through Einstein could deal with the determinisms of chronos or time—a thought not coincidentally associated with Jewish thinkers with whom Joyce identified. From the outset of Jones's long and self-undermining lecture, the professor shows grand pretensions. For example, he claims, "Talis is a word often abused by many passims (I am working out a quantum theory about it for it is really most tantumising state of affairs)" (149). What that "quantum theory" might be is hard to say, though it is difficult to avoid the thought that Joyce is making a direct allusion to Bohr, Heisenberg, and other scientists who were working on particle physics: thinkers who abuse "talis" or claim to know qualities are found "passim" in every part. And if we can speculate that Joyce sensed the opposition between relativity theory and quantum theory, then it makes even more sense that his quantum theorist Professor Jones opposes space to time.

The professor is besieged by time culture. Therefore, Jones resorts to his fable about The Mookse and the Gripes for listeners whom he treats as "muddlecrass pupils." These include the Bruno figure, Bruno Nowlan, who, in a Joycean image of self-directed comedy, has his tongue in his inkpot. Jones's fable proves little, though it does underscore the opposition of his space culture and relativity theory. It begins with a line that, in paraphrasing the first line of Joyce's *Portrait of an Artist,* apparently puts Einstein at the beginning of time: "Eins with a space and a wearywide space it wast ere wohned [German, "lived"] a Mookse" (152). The parable also results in little, except that each figure, representing time and space, collapses and is unable to respond to the erotic call of Nivoletta, the woman-river who embodies space moving through time. So the professor renews his attack with a proclamation of scientific diffidence that might sound more like a cautious James Joyce than a hostile Lewis (or perhaps, typically, Joyce ironically agrees with his hostile critic and merges with his opposite):

> My heeders will recoil with a great leisure how at the outbreak before
> trespassing on the space question where even michelangelines have fooled
> to dread I proved to mindself as to your sotisfiction how his abject all
> through (the *quickquid* of Professor Ciondolone's too frequently hypothe-
> cated *Bettlermensch*) is nothing so much more than a mere cashdime how-
> ever genteel he may want ours, if we please (I am speaking to us in the sec-

ond person), for to this graded intellecktuals dimes *is* cash and the cash system (you must not be allowed to forget that this is all contained, I mean the system, in the dogmarks of origen on spurios) means that I cannot now have or nothave a piece of cheeps in your pocket at the same time and with the same manner as you can now nothalf or half the cheek apiece I've in mind unless Burrus and Caseous have not or not have seemaultaneously sysentangled themselves, selldear to soldthere, once in the dairy days of buy and buy. (160–61)

I read this passage as a direct parody of quantum theory and the uncertainty principle, especially the last lines' description to "have and nothave." Jones seems to say that quantum mechanics and economics, like any other system, can be incorporated in foolish fiction—"sotisfiction," like a medieval farce or *sotie*— but no transactions can take place in any system unless one can disentangle those simultaneously entangled particles that, in a macrosystem, we would call characters, universal pairs like Burrus and Caseous, milk and cheese, Shem and Shaun, or all the particles in a system of exchange that can be characterized as book, myth, history, Shakespearean play, or the selling of dairy products. The professor may be against relativity—he seems to want to believe in the absolute nature of time—for the simultaneity of epistemic relations is a quantum fact for him. Yet, disentangling particles in the system only gives you half of what you want to have: "I cannot now have and nothave a piece of cheeps in your pocket at the same time and with the same manner as you can now nothalf or half the cheek apeice I've in mind." Heisenberg might not have recognized his ideas about mass and momentum here, but in Joycese it sounds like a version of the uncertainty relation expressed by a pretentious critic for whom space is all, but who, in confusing micro- and macroscopic domains, expresses his theory in a self-parody that undermines itself even as it outlines the uncertainty principle.

These probable references to quantum theory should give warrant to make an analogy between Joyce's experiment in the *Wake* and quantum theory. Analogies are of use if they point up, for instance, a common approach to representation reflecting common axioms of the cultural matrix shared by writer and scientist. For example, there is an analogy to be drawn between the classical realism of, say, Flaubert and the coordinate system of classical physics that describes macrophenomena simultaneously in terms of position and velocity. Clearly in *Finnegans Wake* Joyce has rejected the coordinates that Flaubert uses in his realist works, and it is tempting to argue that quantum mechanics suggests the new Joycean way of describing characters and events in a narrative. Consider characters: one can situate Madame Bovary in terms of her location and her trajectory with total clarity at any given moment in Flaubert's novel. The reader can picture her running through her French village toward the pharmacy in which she then finds the poison to put an end to her amorous deceptions and financial problems. Space and velocity, with its temporal dimension, are explicitly and implicitly represented, and these parameters determine in a sense the character's unique identity, or, more precisely, the unique point at which one can fix the traits that give her an identity: in a public space fixed at a moment in absolute universal chronology. Moreover, determinacy reigns in this world where causality is never questioned. Can one apply indeterminacy to *Finnegans Wake*? Or uncertainty in Heisenberg's sense? Both of these notions seem plausible. Specifically with regard to uncertainty, when discussing HCE, Shem, or Shaun, does the greater the probability of one measurement, say location, entail a lesser probability of the second, say direction including its temporal vector? Or does the greater certainty about identity entail a lesser degree of knowledge about event? Intuitively, something like this seems to be the case, though I admit that I am obliged to leave the precise demonstration to someone who can figure out how to formalize such relations in *Finnegans Wake*.

Let us leave the uncertainty principle and take a different tack for the role of the quantum theory that Professor Jones claims to be working on. Joyce was writing the first book of *Finnegans Wake* at the moment when the most important papers in quantum mechanics were being produced, and Jones's speech shows that he might have been an ideal interlocutor for Bohr. In support of this assuredly debatable point, I suggest that another aspect of quantum theory finds more parallels in Joyce than the uncertainty principle that Jones outlines in his garbled way. This is Bohr's principle of complementarity, which, I will argue, is explicitly mentioned in the *Wake*. Some scientists hold that the most epistemologically interesting aspect of quantum theory is its description of the complementarity that allows particles at the subatomic level to be represented either as waves or as particles. The French physicist de Broglie put forward a wave description of the electron in 1924, and the Austrian Erwin Schrödinger began publishing papers on wave mechanics in 1926. This work was joined with Heisenberg's matrix mechanics to set out a virtually complete version of quantum mechanics late in that year. Because wave mechanics allows an even more accurate probabilistic description of particle behavior, it solved many of the problems involved in Bohr's model of the atom. So Bohr, considering the epistemological conundrum created by the existence of the wave-particle, theorized that no single model can be used for explaining subatomic phenomena. Sometimes it is more advantageous to describe microscopic phenomena as a wave, sometimes as a particle. Bohr's work has highly suggestive epistemological implications for anyone meditating on the difficulties of knowing the law in Joyce—or simply trying to sort out when a character is Shem and when he is Shaun. For every reader must wonder what to make of the fact that a given character is sometimes one, or the other, or perhaps both, and at times somebody else.

With Joyce's characters in mind, one can meditate on the following description of complementarity that Bohr presented in 1927 at the International Congress of Physics. In his paper Bohr made the following conclusions about the new principle:

> On the one hand, the definition of the state of a physical system, as ordinarily understood, claims the elimination of all external disturbances. But in that case, according to the quantum postulate any observation will be impossible, and, above all, the concepts of space and time lose their immediate sense. On the other hand, if in order to make observation possible we permit certain interactions with suitable agencies of measurement, not belonging to the system, an unambiguous definition of the state of the system is naturally no longer possible, and there could be no question of causality in the ordinary sense of the word. The very nature of the quantum theory thus forces us to regard the space-time coordination and the claim of causality, the union of which characterizes the classical theories, as complementary but exclusive features of the description, symbolizing the idealization of observation and definition respectively.[21]

In prose that seems to anticipate *Finnegans Wake*, Bohr construed causality as a feature of observation that is disallowed by the temporal nexus necessary for establishing identity. (Mach's positivism hovers in the background here, with its rejection of anything but what is perceived in the moment of epistemic appropriation.) Moreover, identity is dissolved by this conclusion, for particles no longer have any individual identity. Identity depends upon the coordinates of space-time. In effect, what has come to be called the Copenhagen interpretation of quantum mechanics means that like particles are indistinguishable. For, again according to historian Max Jammer, particles "may lose their identity,

21. Quoted in Jammer, *Conceptual Development,* 351.

a conclusion which follows from the uncertainty relations or, more precisely, from the impossibility of keeping track of the individual particles in the case of interactions of like particles."[22]

Did Joyce reflect upon the theory of complementarity? In spite of a reference to complementarity, allusions in the text are difficult to interpret. Clearly, Joyce had some idea about what was going on in Copenhagen and Göttingen, though it would also be misguided to claim that he found a recipe for writing fiction in the scientific work being done there. We need some other way to describe the fact that, if we reflect for a moment on Bohr's description of complementarity and its implications, we find that the denial of the possibility of individuation describes with remarkable accuracy our experience of reading *Finnegans Wake*.

Perhaps the notion of "homology" is better in this context to describe a relation, not necessarily of influence, but of structural analogy between literature and science. We encounter the characters in the *Wake*'s space-time in such a way that it requires our intervention to give them either probabilistic location or to find a probabilistic causal sequence. In any case it is the reader's intervention that produces these moments of narrative clarity or "idealizations," to use Bohr's term—something Shaun typically seems to deny and affirm with vehemence: "Where do you get that wash? This representation does not accord with my experience. They were watching the watched watching. Veechers all" (509). The possibility of differentiation is often suspended in that any character can take on the identity of other characters—though sexual difference seems to be respected. So that, as we readers watch the watched watching, at best we can speak of clusters of identities that we sort out by fixing upon a most probable identity in any context in which we find a characteristic event. The reader often identifies one character only by excluding the identity of the others. But this is often a temporary reading, since one can reread a passage and, if useful, attribute another identity to a putative character. With regard to the homology between physics and fiction, then, it is tempting to say that Shem and Shaun are the wave-particle duality of literature. And of course this is frightfully overdetermined by the fact that Joyce's play of dialectics also means that anything can be identified with its opposite when apposite.

Moreover, the scientifically minded Joycean will probably be tempted by the idea that Bohr's making space-time complementary with causality could describe

22. Jammer, *Conceptual Development*, 344.

Joyce's textual play, at least to the extent that causality seems to be a notion that one can apply only with great difficulty to relations in the text: reading is the process of asking what causes what where. The complementarity of space-time and causality can be restated for Joyce as the difficulty of stating the what and the where or when of any character and event. For example, Ana Livia is, to say the least, not Emma Bovary, and most of the time, with regard to her or any other character, "we nowhere she lives" (10). The "where" and "when" requiring space-time are constantly problematic, whereas the "what" implied by causality is at the heart of the great self-referential question in the *Wake*, since the answer to the question as to why there was, is, and will be the fall animates the entire novel. The novel wants to explain "What then agentlike brought about that tragoady thundersday this municipal sin business?" about which a narrator enjoins us: "Stay us wherefore in our search for tighteousness, O Sustainer, what time we rise and when we take up to toothmick and before we lump down upown our leatherbed and in the night and at the fading of the stars!" (5). So the search for the law of causality is inscribed in this universal history at the outset, which is to say everywhere, and at every moment someone is asking about the cause of Finn's coming again, and fall, of Finn and all. Hypotheses in this regard are not lacking, but the search for causality often goes astray as readers watching characters watching events are obliged to try to situate in space-time what might be going on. This "complementarity" of causality with the loss of individuation in space-time largely replicates the situation described by Bohr, at least as I understand it.

In practical terms I admit that my argument suggests more a heuristic device for reading than a program for interpretation. And I do not want to lose sight of the equally important idea that Joyce intentionally inscribes laws in his work to show that the law is merely one element among many that make up universal consciousness and history. Placing the search for the law in the foreground, Joyce highlights the inquiry that would find causal relationships describing the fall, but this inquiry often seems to founder upon the principle of the indeterminacy of identity of whomever it was who fell or is going to fall. So it is plausible to argue that complementarity—along with every other law and belief—is at work in his depiction of universal history. Thus one reads parenthetically in the Fourth Book's cyclical return or *ricorso:* "for beingtime monkblinkers timeblinged complementarily murkblankered in their neutrolysis between the possible viriditude of the sager and the probable eruberuption of the saint" (612). Here Joyce surely is alluding to Bohr's principle when his narrator claims that such opposite states as those represented by science and religion, sage and saint, can complement each other in the knowledge of the world. Dialectics and quantum mechanics offer principles that Joyce bends to fit his needs.

In fine, in *Finnegans Wake* characters meld into each other, and the episodes identifying these characters also dissolve into each other, so that the reader is engaged in constant application of a version of the complementarity principle to identify one character and event to the exclusion of others. This is a probabilistic enterprise, close in spirit to Heisenberg's interpretation of quantum reality. Or, more generally, reading Joyce demands the acceptance of reading as a kind of stochastic process. In this Joyce demands acceptance of a principle that breaks with classical determinism and with the epistemology of the nineteenth century when, before Mach, most of the scientific, not to mention literary, community still largely thought that the principle of causality was the basic principle for knowledge and that chance processes were to be relegated to the realm of the absurd. In this very general sense *Finnegans Wake* reflects the extraordinary epistemological changes that had occurred in roughly two generations, from Poincaré's work on the three body problem through the development of quantum mechanics.

I have waited for this concluding moment to comment on the very widely held view that Joyce undertook the imitation of dream in *Finnegans Wake*. If the novel is a dream—and this is a useful metaphor—then my discussion shows that it is one organized by the law of eternal return and presenting characters who act much like the particles described by quantum mechanics. It is a dream enacting universal history, or in which history is dream, and in which characters appear as recurrent clusters of images or names, popping into view with no antecedent cause, and transforming themselves before one can clearly identify them. It would thus be a dream with a narrative framework whose level of abstraction can be likened to the kind of system that a scientist can describe from complementary viewpoints. And, if one finds the dream metaphor useful, it would be a dream of all the laws that one can ever know, but in which, the laws notwithstanding, true knowledge seems hovering forever beyond our grasp. From this perspective Joyce shows that we use the law, in dream—this dream we call history or our life—to shore up the ground upon which uncertain fluctuation polarized by a postulated law is the essence of being. With this uncertainty even about uncertainty, Joyce places his readers in a position from which they can survey universal history, represented in the book through so many synechdoches, in *Finnegans Wake,* as one great system that they can explore forever, with constant laughter, without ever being certain they have found the final law. The existence of some final paradigm may be implied by the many lesser laws, subject to the law of eternal return, that emerge in history, from Bruno, Galileo, and Newton's laws to Darwin and Einstein's discoveries, and most recently quantum theory.

The proliferating surfeit of laws in Joyce, in Bloom's consciousness, or in the universal mind that some readers find dreaming *Finnegans Wake* lead finally to the same interrogative void as the forever receding absence of the law in Kafka. By contrast with Kafka, Joyce is, to be sure, an ebullient celebrator of knowledge, of all knowledge, which is to say, that the knowledge of any and every thing can be a cause for singing. This constant celebration points up a dialectical contrast with Kafka: logos in Kafka only promises a knowledge that remains forever elusive, distant, uncertain. However dialectically opposed the two writers may be, the final result is a paradoxical affirmation of uncertainty.

If Joyce and Kafka are probably the most influential of the modernists, one reason is that they obliged the next generation of writers to encounter science in literature critically at a time when many moderns were angry with science for not offering the ultimate unknown law that they had been seeking ever since modernity discredited the belief in the revelations of logos. Literature, no more than science, cannot rescue us from our fall into history. Perhaps one might mark the fall with the apple's fall on Newton's head—apples seem to be a favored fallen fruit—or perhaps with humanity's descent from animals, after Darwin introduced the randomness of temporal change into that aspect of universal history know as biology. The time-hostile Professor Jones finds, in reference to the time-bound Darwin, that the system is contained "in the dogmarks of origen on spurios," which I gloss to imply that dogma about origins makes us all bastards of the animal world (161).

Accepting literature as a fallen sacerdotal function, Kafka and Joyce confront the modern demand that science function as a surrogate to satisfy the thirst for that logos that might once have offered knowledge of the hidden law, but which science no more than literature can now reveal. Recall Kafka's country doctor or his dog scientists. At best, Joyce's professor implies, literature can show us dogmarks—perhaps non-spurious *Spuren* or traces—that give us some hope of approaching the law as it recedes. Joyce and Kafka ask what invariant relation lies behind flying dogs or dogmarks, what are the laws that Kafka shows receding in Gödelian infinite regress, and which Joyce shows in such self-annulling profusion that he may ultimately seem even more skeptical than Kafka. Kafka and Joyce's comic encounters with science parody even their own skepticism and despair while doubting that science can ever offer access to the law that our culture once believed it possessed, perhaps before it had so many laws. But there is also a salutary, even emancipatory, side to this play, for another part of their extraordinary influence was, and is, to teach writers and readers to encounter science in ludic terms, and thus to reconcile writers and readers with science and literature as discourses that, one no more than the other, will never finally chase mystery from the universe. Finally, Joyce and Kafka are the defrocked priests of logos who made of literary epistemology a form of play. Playing with the law, inventing the laws that govern alternative universes, and celebrating the ludic joys of seeking knowledge are also part of what Kafka and Joyce brought to fiction. Their work points to the future of fictions as diverse as those of Queneau and Borges, Faulkner and Beckett, Nabokov and Robbe-Grillet, Woolf and Saurraute, Pynchon and Calvino, to name some of the writers for whom science has interfaced with literature in recognition that knowledge can be considered a ludic invention allowing readers to play at knowing a world. After Joyce, this world is a fragmented world for which there is no totalizing encyclopedia, as demonstrated by the very encyclopedia Joyce created for the (f)all of history.

Chapter Six

Modernist Thought Experiments after Joyce

Modernists wanted to know the world, or at least great expanses of the world, at the same time they interrogated the possibilities for knowledge. Rejecting the limits imposed on fiction by a preceding generation of realists, modernist fiction was predicated on the assumption that nothing is excluded from literature. This openness remains part of what is meant by a literary text in today's economy of discourses. The novel especially seems open to all the heterogeneity the world offers, including disputes about what the world is. This openness does not mean that literary genres no longer exist, nor that there are no limits to what representation may plausibly undertake. But as Joyce demonstrated in using all the genres history offered, literary conventions are often used only to provide a springboard for inquiry when the writer asks what one can know and represent in a fiction. Parody frequently accompanies this attitude. Joyce again is the precursor, determining the development of fiction at least through the work of American fabulators like Gass, Coover, Sukenick, and John Barth, who once argued that literature's self-conscious relation to its past could only take the form of parody and pastiche. This is undoubtedly not true, but Barth's attitude was typical of many postmodern writers.

The reader educated in, or at least attuned to, classical or conventional realist aesthetics may react in dismay to the potential for hubris that the modernist viewpoint implies, especially the idea that there are no limits to what the novel may encompass. I admit to great sympathy for the classical mind that demands clear boundaries between types of discourse; and I understand that this mind may justly remonstrate the modernist. It may be salutary to point out, by way of counterexample, that scientific discourses are scientific, not to mention successful, precisely because they set limits upon themselves. Since the scientific revolution, such self-limitation is one of the things expected from scientific discourse. In reaction to these limitations, post-Joycean writers like Borges, Queneau, or

Calvino point out in sometimes rueful irony that the separation of literature and science has not always been the case. By their own example these writers recall notable cases of literature used for scientific discourse, such as the Epicurean philosopher Lucretius and his atomistic cosmology in the epic *De natura rerum,* or, sixteen centuries later, Francastor, with his poem of 1530 on the new disease *Syphilis sive morbus Gallicus.* Rare are poems of late on the nature of atoms or syphilis, though as recently as the nineteenth century, major scientists from Davy to Maxwell wrote competent lyrics to celebrate their science.[1] But when the polymath Raymond Queneau wrote an epic poem on the evolution of the solar system, it could only take the form of a comic odyssey.

There is today an asymmetry between science and literature. Literary writers need feel no obligation to respect the kinds of limits scientific discourse demands for self-definition, unless, of course, they want to write fiction that can be called realist. Then there are indeed limits. I propose that these limits are analogous to those once imposed by the classical notion of literary genre. I note this similarity for the light it sheds upon a recurrent conflict in evaluation of literary texts, especially modernist texts that do not respect the limits demanded by realism. I suggest that it is the very notion of epistemic limits which largely defines the conventional realist notion of verisimilitude, a notion that, for many readers, retains its value as a fundamental criterion for the epistemic value of literature. The notion of realism functions, then, as a definition of genre, a genre that limits itself by respecting knowledge of the real. What does that mean? This is usually understood, implicitly, as the real as it is codified within the limits of a rationalist scientific understanding of what is possible and plausible. The conflict between proponents of modernism and conventional realism should be explicitly recognized as a genre question that is also an epistemic question.

Many conservative readers and critics dislike the fact that modernists and their later experimental followers place epistemological inquiry in the foreground of their fictions, which results in the questioning of what is usually taken to be real. Proper realism in a novel, these readers feel, means keeping these things in the background, since they believe that the illusion of the direct appropriation of "reality" can only be obtained when scientific laws are respected, but not named. In the properly realist text, gravity always functions, and pathogenic bacteria make one sick, but relativistic play should not be self-consciously

1. Good examples of these poems are found in J. A. V. Chapple, *Science and Literature in the Nineteenth Century.*

evoked to question the epistemic framework within which time moves along a regular one-way arrow and energy is neatly conserved. In this way conventional realism, discreetly veiling its adherence to a thousand scientific assumptions about what is the case, assures that fiction pays allegiance to the real. Anything that deviates from this realism, when not part of a clearly received genre like fantasy or satire, is usually relegated to the catch-all category of "experimental."

The conservative idea is correct in pointing out that much nonrealist fiction often enacts an experiment. These texts perform an experiment in that they lay bare and imaginatively test assumptions, often having the form of scientific axioms, that underlie the construction of the metaphysical notion which deems that there is a "reality" that, when accurately represented, bestows upon a narration the appellation of "realist." Moreover, literary conservatives can (or could) buttress their argument by pointing out that most contemporary narratologists ultimately agree with them: the dominant trend in narrative theory has been to accept the idea that all narration turns upon the articulation of discourse and story. Story, defined as the realist concatenation of events in time, is contrasted to discourse, or the way a narration is told or enunciated, which need not respect linear unfolding. Sometimes called the fabula, the story is almost always defined in terms of metaphysical realism, since the story extracted from discourse is a linear succession of events respecting the one-way arrow of time. Each event is linked to subsequent events such that they unfold sequentially in a Newtonian time frame set in a world of absolute space usually capacious enough to encompass Dickens and fairy tales. Behind a fiction's most contorted distortions of time and space, narratologists contrive to ferret out a conventional linear tale. This interpretive activity usually means that time is conceived as an absolute framework by which are measured all deviations in the narrative discourse in which the story is embodied. The structuralist idea that every narration embodies a story, or fabula, is testimony to the way literary theory borrows categories from scientific understanding—in this case from the Newtonian physics of the seventeenth century.

I hardly want here to challenge the hold that metaphysical realism has upon some of the most demanding theoretical minds of our time. The distinction of story and discourse is extremely useful. But it does seem necessary, if one is to understand much fiction written since 1900, to come to a better understanding of why experimental fiction may not conform to the realism that narratologists posit as underlying any narration. The very notion of experiment implies that some writers have experimented, for example, to see what happens if fiction is not grounded in absolute temporality—writers, after Joyce, like Borges, Woolf, and Faulkner. Agreeing with conservative critics, I want to make the point here that, since Joyce and Kafka, the notion of experiment is accurate to describe the way some fiction tests science, and may challenge notions grounded in scientific beliefs about the real by experimenting with their implications. In other words, the notion of experiment describes what has been at stake in much modernist and postmodern fiction. Disagreeing with conservative defenders of traditional realism, however, I would contend that much, if not most, interesting American and European fiction in the past century has been consistently experimental. This contention may not be true about the twenty-first century.

Considering fictions as experiments offers a means of understanding much of what has happened in the passage from modernist writing to what has come to be called postmodern fiction. My point in making this claim is not to add to the existing welter of definitions and claims about postmodernity. Rather, I want to make some observations that, in perhaps limiting the claims of postmoderns, point out that many of the important fictions after Joyce show a common commitment to experimentation—experimentation understood as an imaginative exploration of epistemic concerns. These fictions share many of the concerns that characterize science, even when they contain a sharp critique of science. These epistemic interests are found, moreover, in both modernists and postmodernists. To make this argument, I want now to show that three undeniably important modernists can illustrate the broad scope of later modernist experimentation that continued well after World War II. I do not intend to make definitive critical statements about these writers, but to make rather an argument about the historical continuity of modernist thought experiments. The historical continuity of modernism should emerge from a discussion of three writers who all were indebted to *Ulysses,* to wit, Woolf, Faulkner, and Borges. If any new insight about these writers also emerges from the following discussion, perhaps it is because this historical context, emphasizing the scientific nature of thought experiments, has rarely been used in critical discussions.

From this perspective the notion of experimental fiction links modernism to postmodernism. By experimental fiction, I mean literary works that embody thought experiments. If both fiction writers and scientists can be said to undertake thought experiments, it is because the following proposition can be applied to both scientists and writers: a thought experiment is an experiment worked out in the imagination, usually by supposing the truth of a given model or theory and then imagining the consequences of the application of that model or theory. Scientists usually imagine conditions on which they have some, but not much, empirical purchase, which is to say, conditions in which it is difficult to make an application of a model or theory. The goal of a thought experiment is to work out the implications, in the imagination, of the model that interests the scientist. Those implications are deduced in the imagination as the scientist tries to take into account interlinking axioms about what will be the case if such and such happens. The thought experiment can be limited by the verified and verifiable real, or one may assume that what has been taken to be proven real, or true, is actually false and then work out the consequences by proposing alternative explanations. Suppose, for example, the sun weren't the center of the universe, what then? Or that the speed of light is an absolute that is independent of the velocity of its source? What conclusions follow from that thought experiment? (Relativity theory, for one thing.)

Experimental fiction often presupposes conventional realism by using it as the expected backdrop against which an experiment is enacted. But this is not always the case since, as with Faulkner and Borges, the imagined model may abrogate basic received axioms about what constitutes the real by proposing different axioms. This is not unlike what Einstein, in his thought experiments about time, did to the Newtonian framework for defining reality. After Joyce and Kafka, thought experiments may propose models abrogating basic received postulates about the real, or they may change isolated parameters to see what is the effect on what is usually accepted as the real. Thus considered, experimental fiction may differ little from a scientific procedure, since a scientific thought experiment is also a procedure relying upon the power of the imagination to foresee consequences. In literature or science, then, a thought experiment is the logical, but imaginary, working out of conclusions from axioms or variables that are hypothetically accepted in order to see what implications they have.

In a certain sense, one might argue that Cervantes undertook the first modern thought experiments by positing demonstrably false axioms in the dolorous knight's mind and then imagining the consequences of a world in which objective facts could be defined with some clarity. Historians of science would probably retort, however, that Galileo undertook the first modern thought experiments. Galileo accepted axioms about motion and imagined what they entailed for inertia, for which it is difficult to do direct observation or experimentation. Galileo imagined in fact an ideal world in which there is no friction in order to see the implications of his model for gravity. In a quite literal sense, then, Galileo's imagined "fictions" or experiments became the basis for modern science. They led to Newton's imagining the force of gravity in its infinite simultaneous working—arguably the most universal experimental fiction of all time. Before Newton, Galileo's experiment was, to paraphrase philosopher Roy A. Sorensen in his study of thought experiments, a procedure for answering or raising a question about the relationship between variables by varying one or more of them, and tracking, in a fiction, the response. Sorensen maintains that there is then no qualitative differences between philosophical and scientific thought experiments, which suggests the conclusion that he does not draw: the thought experiment will be alluring for any creative mind wanting to participate in the adventure of knowing through speculation.[2] From Galileo through Einstein and beyond, thought experiments have often been key procedures in the elaboration of scientific theories, offering potential validation for them while permitting evaluation of their philosophical implications. In a parallel manner, the literary mind has, increasingly from the Renaissance to the present, also sought procedures for questioning the relations among variables and working out possible consequences—often to the detriment of such bastions of realism as common sense, logic, or tradition.

In a historical investigation of the nature of thought experiments, the influential historian Thomas Kuhn proposed another view of the role of thought experiments in intellectual history. According to Kuhn, a thought experiment produces not so much a new understanding of nature as a comprehension of the scientist's conceptual apparatus.[3] Kuhn suggested that the thought experiment often carries with it a self-referential dimension bearing on the nature of how one works out the consequences of thought in the imagination. Einstein's reflections on the relativistic nature of scientific observation come immediately to mind as an illustration of the self-reflexive thought experiment that imagines the limits of what the knower can know. First postulating the absolute nature of the speed of light, Einstein's experiment then shows, in images, that a consequence of this axiom is that two observers may have different time frameworks. This conclusion, worked out in the imagination, then serves as the basis for postulating the relativity of all observation according to the special theory

2. Sorensen, *Thought Experiments,* 186, 198.
3. Kuhn, "A Function for Thought Experiments," in *The Essential Tension: Studies in Scientific Tradition and Change.*

of relativity. Applied to literature, Kuhn's ideas illuminate the self-reflexive dimension in Proust, Musil, and Kafka, not to mention many later experimental texts that examine the conditions of possibility for knowledge in a fiction.

Kuhn and Sorensen's discussions of thought experiments in science can make sense of the idea that literature is often experimental. The literary experiment, like the scientific version, works out what may be deduced by postulating axioms or changing variables; and in so doing, fiction often self-reflexively examines the apparatus of knowledge itself, or the mind in its workings. But note that not all modernists were happy with the idea that fiction, when it explores the world, resembles an experimental procedure. Musil, for example, was tormented by his thirst for knowledge grounded in something beyond fictions imagined by the knowing mind, which suggests another reason why he felt antagonism toward Mach. Mach was probably the first scientist who, in his role as epistemologist, consciously emphasized the importance of the thought experiment. Mach believed that the mind, as the sole locus of those relations called knowledge, is obliged to examine, in its own private laboratory as it were, those constitutive beliefs with which the mind orders sensations. This ordering gives rise to those relations that the mind then perceives to constitute knowledge. As the locus of knowledge, according to Mach, the mind is always a place of experimentation. Musil disliked the implications of such ideas, even as he experimented with the multiple possible ways of working out the plot of *The Man without Qualities*. Quite literally, Musil's novel proliferated and floundered like a never-ending experiment in which he imagined the implications of one conclusion and then another.

A contemporary philosopher like Sorensen is also critical of Mach for not having made any systematic distinction between thought experiments and related mental phenomena such as fantasy or storytelling.[4] This is a strange criticism, since it is fantasy that unites science and literature in experiments, with a notable example provided by contemporary cosmologists and their marvelous fantasies of infinite universes and interconnecting worm holes, all this, to be sure, worked out with mathematical rigor in the imagination. I think some scientists and writers would agree with Mach in blurring the distinction between scientific thought experiments and fiction. If some works of fiction can be called thought experiments—and not simply metaphorically—it is because some

4. Sorensen, *Thought Experiments,* 68.

writers see their minds to be something like private laboratories wherein relationships and variables taken from the world can be imaginatively changed, and the putative outcomes of these transformations predicted in the imagination. These outcomes are then depicted experimentally in the fiction that ensues. Perhaps not all experimental writers self-consciously conceive of their work as thought experiments, but many do: Borges, Queneau, Sarraute, Robbe-Grillet, and Calvino are cases in point. The dividing line between self-consciousness and intuitive experimentation may not always be clear, but that is a secondary issue. What is clear is that the modern belief that epistemic invention is first elaborated by the imagination has empowered writers. The historical successes of imaginative thought experiments from Galileo to Einstein have encouraged writers to feel that they, too, can be experimentalists in a quest for knowledge.

The histories of science and of literature show that the fantasy tale is often a first step toward experimental resolution of theoretical problems. It is not within my purview to write here a history of the combined efforts of literature and science to open epistemic spaces. (It would take another book to prove or disprove that Cyrano anticipated space travel, or that Poe empowered Friedmann to think of an expanding universe without empirical evidence.) I will simply observe that, after the Renaissance, after Galileo and Descartes's experimental fictions, Diderot may have been the first writer to feel a clear sense of kinship with the scientist, to be followed notably by Goethe and then Balzac. In the late nineteenth century Zola proclaimed in *Le Roman expérimental* that writers would soon share the research agenda of the scientist, this with an optimism that seems naive today. But shortly thereafter—let us say after Joyce and *Ulysses*—there was hardly a writer of serious fiction who did not feel obliged to account for his or her work in relation to its experimentation, or lack thereof. Within this modernist context, to undertake conventional realism became a self-conscious refusal of experimentation.

The notion of literary experiment enlarges our understanding of modernist dialectics, both in its affirming, but also in its contesting, science. In this light, modernist dialectics also includes much of what is called postmodern. The postmodern mind is usually taken to be antiscientific in its relativism and in its skepticism about the foundations of knowledge, but the questioning of science and the grounds for knowledge, especially through fictional thought experiments, was an essential part of the modernist project. Contemporary suspicions about the foundations of knowledge in literary texts are largely a development of modernist epistemology. The demise of objective certainty is recorded centrally in modernists like Proust and Musil, and the exploration of the epistemological void is at the heart of both Joyce and Kafka. An argument can also be made that postmodernity is the result of a loss of belief in symbolism and the transcendence that symbolism can bring about. But even in this regard nearly all that we find in postmodernity is already present in the major modernists, since a deep suspicion about the possibility of symbolic revelation is dramatized in Kafka's hermeneutic play, Joyce's skepticism, and, subsequently, in Beckett's comedies about the fall of logos.

After Joyce, Proust, and Kafka, and largely because of their example, experimentation became an important trait of the most important modernists and, I think, many postmodernists. To support this argument, let us now turn to fictions by the three authors who can admirably serve to illustrate the scope of later modernist experimentation: the quintessentially English Virginia Woolf, lost at times in madness; William Faulkner, living a self-imposed exile in his own mythic South; and Jorge Luis Borges, a cosmopolitan finding refuge in English literature while creating a mythic Argentina. In their experimental works these three modernists pursued the ongoing dialectic with science begun by Proust and Joyce and set out models for experimentation that influenced writers for the rest of the century. (I note that, historically, because of the vagaries of publishing histories caused by the Nazis and World War II, Musil and Kafka really only began to exercise wide influence after World War II, which is to say, they are in a sense our postmodern contemporaries.)

Fictions by Woolf, Faulkner, and Borges delineate the major epistemic domains in which later fiction staged its thought experiments, at times affirming, at other times contesting, science. These domains are varied. A minimal list would include experimental cognitive play exploring the interface of consciousness and knowledge, or, as Woolf depicts this domain, the play of knowledge as it inflects and informs consciousness. Equally as important, especially in Faulkner, is the quest for knowledge, through fiction, of the contours of history. (History remains today a central focal point for fiction—in spite of what some critics, confusing theory with literary practice, see as a supposed postmodern lack of concern with history.) Under Faulkner's influence, experimental models for knowing history have proliferated in many national literatures. Another major domain, sometimes taken as a defining trait of postmodernity, is the demonstration of the ludic nature of knowledge. Especially in Borges, fiction takes the form of self-reflexive experiments that flaunt the rules of the game. These fictions often ironically demonstrate their own futility as self-contained forms of play. They also point up the near mathematical nature of fictions that self-consciously display the axioms generating them. With these experiments Borges aims at demonstrating the aporia of scientific theory or, more generally, the paradoxes of any self-referential epistemic project.

Woolf's Experiments with Consciousness

An essential fact of Virginia Woolf's literary biography is that she read Proust and Joyce at crucial moments. Interestingly, Woolf's Hogarth Press did not want to publish *Ulysses,* but Woolf read parts of it in 1919, three years before it was finally published. In her literary thought experiments drawing upon Joyce, Woolf created works that record the penetration of daily life by scientific knowledge. With less irony than Joyce, and without parody, Woolf speculates on the ways in which science permeates daily consciousness, and she seeks to show that knowledge affects sensibility as it orders the characters' perception of the world. Woolf portrays the world of ordinary, though well-educated people, such as Mrs. Dalloway, Mrs. Ramsay, or the friends in the overtly experimental *The Waves* (1931). With a few exceptions, such as young Jacob Flanders of *Jacob's Room* (1922) or Mr. Ramsay of *To the Lighthouse* (1927), most of Woolf's characters are not intellectuals, but through their education and background, they have absorbed science as part of the milieu in which they live. They ponder the meaning, for their own lives, of the cosmos described by science, showing the extent to which science determines what ordinary middle-class characters believe about their place in the world, and consequently, what meaning their life has in that cosmos.

Woolf's novels are modernist in their epistemic ambivalence. Her fictions often entertain scientific propositions about the world, but they also embody a narrating consciousness skeptical about those propositions. Woolf generally accepts Proust's epistemic separation of science and literature. Her narrators and characters contemplate science, and the reader sees the effect of scientific law in the world of impressions registered by the characters' consciousness. In this regard there is often a dichotomy between the knowing self and the objective world, and each is subject to different types of knowledge. Woolf's work is, at times, weighted in favor of one side or the other, but one finds that almost always a wistful desire for transcendence of the objective world of laws permeates her work, a transcendence affirmed by indirect when not by direct expression of desire. Pascal's anguish is never far from the yearnings felt by her characters and narrators.

Characterized by a desire for transcendence, Woolf's novelistic worlds are nonetheless resolutely Darwinian, unflinching in their recognition of the animal nature of a humanity dominated by physiology and aware of its paleontological past. Her novels are, therefore, permeated by a consciousness of the constraints that science—especially biology and physics—imposes upon what her characters recognize as knowledge. Relevantly, her characters often know a great deal of science, even a character without intellectual pursuits, such as the heroine of *Mrs. Dalloway.* The reader learns, for example, that Mrs. Dalloway's favorite writers, when she was young, were the scientists Huxley and Tyndall—the agnostic Darwinian and the materialist physicist whose discovery of wave scattering explained why the sky is blue. In her first appearance in an earlier novel, *The Voyage Out* (1915), young Mrs. Dalloway also keeps a volume of Pascal by her bed. The Pascalian cosmology, as well as his dialectic between reason and heart, are, in this early novel, on Mrs. Dalloway's mind as she sets sail upon the waves—those waves later emblematic of the nature that science masters by finding in it patterns and laws. The first Mrs. Dalloway looks beyond the material waves described by physics and contrasts the Pascalian desires of the heart with the claims of reason as defined by the scientists. This contrast is also true of the later *Mrs. Dalloway,* in which Woolf's characters agree that the brain doesn't matter much when compared to the heart—or so Mrs. Dalloway's friend, Sally Seton, explicitly affirms at the conclusion of *Mrs. Dalloway* in paraphrasing the Pascalian notion that the heart has reasons that reason does not know. In fine, sensitive to the reasoning desires of the heart, Woolf speculates how one might possibly realize these desires in a world subject to the laws elaborated by Cambridge physicists for whom waves are invariant patterns described by equations.

Whether narrated by a superior consciousness, or indirectly from the point of view of one of the characters in the fiction, the world of Woolf's novels is often centered upon the aging body of characters who, like Mrs. Dalloway or Mrs. Ramsey, know intuitively, and sometimes self-reflexively, that they are subject to the physiological limits of a biological destiny described by modern science. The heart strains to go beyond these limits, and, as it does so, Woolf's narrating consciousness may speculate about a knowledge of something that cannot be named. This speculation may take the shape of a thought experiment. For example, in Woolf's posthumously published novel, *Between the Acts*

(1941), the narrating consciousness wants to posit things, beyond the laws of optics, which "escape registration," as the narrator says in describing the clouds and the sky:

> Here came the sun—an illimitable rapture of joy, embracing every flower, every leaf. Then in compassion it withdrew, covering its face, as if it forebore to look on human suffering. There was a fecklessness, a lack of symmetry and order in the clouds, as they thinned and thickened. Was it their own law, or no law, they obeyed? . . . Beyond that was blue, pure blue, black blue; blue that had never filtered down; that had escaped registration.[5]

Woolf's literary epistemology is dualist, and it underlies the rupture in this passage seemingly testing the idea that there is experience which eludes the law—say, the law that Tyndall had described for the scattering of light which makes the sky blue. In this passage the narrator sounds out the edges of the invariant constraints imposed by law, looking for the place where consciousness might encounter a freedom from the law, a freedom that nothing in science recognizes. In this hypothesized freedom is contained a thought experiment that attempts to work out what might be inferred or discovered if consciousness were able to escape from the law.

Woolf often alternates her narrating center of consciousness, allowing different voices to describe their quest for something beyond scientific objectivity. This technique is used to offer a phenomenology of daily life that undoubtedly finds antecedent in *Ulysses*. Where Woolf goes beyond Joyce in experimentally opening up a narrative domain is in her representation of madness. Woolf, forever on the edge of sanity herself, gives due recognition in works like *Mrs. Dalloway* to the Pascalian heart's power to construct, in the shadows of its desire, its own inferno; and in this novel's depiction of insanity Woolf confronts science with a mad consciousness that challenges science in its foundations.

Madness in Woolf, as in many later novelists, is a privileged mode of consciousness for testing science. In *Mrs. Dalloway,* Woolf asks straightforwardly, How can science account for madness? Writers like Diderot, Hoffmann, and even Musil had asked this question in satire and irony, which is to say, from a viewpoint largely exterior to insanity; but I know of no other novelist before Woolf who asks this question from within madness, unless it be Dostoyevsky's

---

5. Virginia Woolf, *Between the Acts,* 21. My attention was drawn to this passage by Gillian Beer, *Virginia Woolf: The Common Ground,* 12.

underground ironist. Without irony, Woolf asks how science can manage a disease consisting in the destruction of the relations that consciousness maintains with the world. Woolf knew that there is no reliable biological marker for sanity or insanity. The insanity to which she periodically fell victim revealed to Woolf, I believe, nothing less than a periodic destruction of science's objective purchase on the world. In *Mrs. Dalloway* science is tested in the experimental portrayal of the shattered consciousness of Septimus, a former soldier who, having survived the suicidal battles of the Great War, now views death without feeling. Having returned to peacetime London, he must attempt to make connections with the world, those connections often symbolized in Woolf by the waves that visibly and invisibly link all to all. Septimus's dilemma is that his shattered consciousness makes too many connections; he overinterprets every sign. In effect, he falls victim to a paranoia over which science has no mastery. Septimus is treated by two doctors, one a general practitioner, the other a knighted psychiatrist, who actually drive Septimus farther into the realm of insane representations. In their arrogance, the doctors illustrate graphically the failure of science to come to grips with the workings of consciousness. The doctors' refusal, or incapacity, to empathize with Septimus's disordered consciousness results finally in his throwing himself out a window. He believes that his only recourse is to use up his remaining freedom — if that is the right term for his final flight from the torment he feels at the doctors' hands.

Woolf's portrayal of madness and its unbearable trauma is an existential thought experiment undoubtedly having roots in her own attempts to resist suicide. The results of this experiment in the novel may seem to predict her own demise. However, the interest we take in this experimental probing of a mental state beyond reason is more than biographical — though the biographical interest is great. In portraying the outcome of living in a state of psychic hyperconnections, Woolf undertook an experiment that challenges the diagnostic rationality found in psychiatric manuals. In this, her novel links up with literary works wanting to experiment with representation lying beyond the limits of rationality, works that posit madness as initial conditions and then work out their implications. There is a historical lineage of works experimenting with the power and limits of rationality, beginning with Descartes's imagining that his perceptions are insane, continuing, as suggested above, in Diderot's portrayal of the madman in *Rameau's Nephew* and in Hoffmann's tales experimenting with insane characters, and culminating before the twentieth century in Dostoyevsky's exaltation of insanity articulated in the defense of the individual in *Notes from the Underground*. Musil's portrayal of a madman, with Ulrich's meditation there, continues this tradition. But it is after Virginia Woolf's depiction of madness from within that this lineage proliferates in multiple experiments, such as the feminist depictions of women's madness after the sixties and seventies, and in the often jubilant representation of paranoia, the dominant form of insanity found in many, usually masculine, postmodern texts. There is little doubt that a dominant source of modernist ambiguity about science is, after Woolf, the challenge with which madness confronts the belief that the mind, the all-too fragile human mind, may offer secure foundations for knowledge—especially knowledge of the mind that seeks that knowledge.

For many writers, a significant side of medicine is its hubris in claiming to master consciousness and mind as well as the body. The madman's perceptions are as "real" as any others in Woolf's novel, but science has nothing to say about them. In a sense, then, Woolf is making a claim for the epistemic power of literature against science: literary phenomenology can get some concrete purchase on deranged impressions about which science can speak with only the most general diagnostic abstractions. Like Musil, Woolf is unsettling in the portrayal of madness. If science can exert no mastery over consciousness—in an era admittedly before pyschotropic agents—then her thought experiment appears to confirm the autonomy of madness and its freedom vis-à-vis the constraints of reason. The experiment is disturbing, moreover, in that Mrs. Dalloway's joy and Septimus's madness have the same ontological weight when taken as forms of consciousness. (About which a cynical biological reductionist might observe that all contents of consciousness are arbitrary accidents—which undoubtedly was one of Woolf's fears.) Septimus's madness is his own, untouched in its autonomy by the classifying names of clinical syndromes that a doctor attaches to it. With prescience, moreover, in this contrast between madness and medical attempts at mastery Woolf delineates the drama that divides psychiatric therapy into two camps, one composed of those who deal with a clinical entity, and the other made up of those who are phenomenologists of a tortured soul. Perhaps needless to say, modernists, especially poets like Robert Lowell or Sylvia Plath, have been drawn to the latter camp in greater numbers, often in a struggle to deal with their own insanity.

Recognizing the power of science, Woolf shows that scientific laws dealing with nature are omnipresent in educated consciousness. There is, therefore, little innocent vision in her work, however much her narrators and characters yearn to entertain such a vision, transcending the constraints of law and scientific objectivity. One such exceptional moment of transcendence may be the painter's vision concluding *To the Lighthouse*. But science can also shape vision in affirmative ways, for the law can take other shapes than that of constraint. In Woolf's novelistic phenomenology, laws can actually glimmer in consciousness at times like objects of desire, not least of all for the certainty they appear to offer about the world's appearances. The near erotic attraction that the law can exert in its imbrication with consciousness is another unique feature of Woolf's novelist worlds. *Mrs. Dalloway* can serve as example for the experimental interface of amorphous desires and the sharp presence of scientific law. In the novel this interface is present in the delineation of Mrs. Dalloway's "waves" of consciousness, to use the metaphor with which Woolf experiments to represent interiority. It is a metaphor for consciousness informed notably by Maxwell and the laws of field theory about wave propagation as well as by classical acoustics and optics. In this central metaphor the desire for connections and the implications of field theory seem to mesh, proposing a way to describe consciousness with the image of the waves to which field theory grants the power to penetrate everything, in accord with the equations that are one of the glories of nineteenth-century physics.

The narrator uses science, therefore, in an experiment to find ways of describing perception. The narrator describes Mrs. Dalloway's experience by evoking the laws of matter and by comparing her consciousness with the waves that can communicate beyond their point of origin. Narrative consciousness coincides with the character's perception when the narrator makes connections between consciousness and scientific thought as, for example, when Mrs. Dalloway reflects upon her world, on her beloved London and on her once beloved friend Peter, and finally on the ebb and flow of waves that tie all together:

> ... did it matter that she must inevitably cease completely; all this must go on without her; did she resent it; or did it not become consoling to believe that death ended absolutely? but that somehow in the streets of London, on the ebb and flow of things, here, there, she survived, Peter survived, lived in each other, she being part, she was positive, of the trees at home; of the house there, ugly, rambling all to bits and pieces as it was ...[6]

The narrator in effect proposes the hypothesis that a law of connections is immanent to consciousness. This idea implies that the world perceived by consciousness

---

6. Woolf, *Mrs. Dalloway,* 11. Hereafter cited parenthetically in the text.

is composed of relationships that the narrator can describe by likening them to, and perhaps actually perceiving them as, waves, like the "the ebb and flow of things" here, or as a "mist" that unites her to all beings. The waves are undoubtedly a recurrent motif because they offer an experimental image of the rhythms of the natural world, such as the light that, propagated from being to being, ties the world together. In other words, if the image of waves offers access to an understanding of a fundamental state of being, Woolf asks, what does this imply for our being in the world? One answer is that the image of waves describes the movement of consciousness, parallel to the scientific description of propagation that manifests the presence of a law in the world. In Woolf's work waves are at once the links of desire and a reflection of scientific law.

Consciousness and its contents are unified in this image suggesting a poetic equivalent of the field of field theory, or, considered as a thought experiment, the experimental positing of the axiom that consciousness can be likened to such a field. In this field all things communicate; they are drawn together, much as when Mrs. Dalloway draws her needle to collect folds of silk together:

> So on a summer's day waves collect, overbalance, and fall; and the whole world seems to be saying "that is all" more and more ponderously, until even the heart in the body which lies in the sun on the beach says too, that is all. Fear no more, says the heart. Fear no more says the heart, committing its burden to some sea, which sighs collectively for all sorrows, and renews, begins, collects, lets fall. (44–45)

The image of the speaking heart, redolent again of Pascal's knowing heart, presents a parallel to Musil's mystical temptation: the temptation of the modernist mind that, having worked through science and its laws, is drawn, experimentally as it were, to a mystical position that may seem to be the result of a materialist mysticism. I say experimentally, since, if one applies science's materialist axioms and finds they do not account for perception, then, as Musil or Woolf might have said, a mystical hypothesis may be a better axiom for accounting for what one perceives. Comparably, in *La Prisonnière* Proust's narrator also makes an explicit contrast between a mystical and a materialist hypothesis in an attempt to account for the power of art: one or the other seems necessary to account for the effects of art that the narrator finds at work in his perception of real works of art, including the one that he wants to create. Because Proust's narrator reaches no conclusion, the reader must weigh each hypothesis on its own merits.

Woolf's narrator—and, intuitively, Mrs. Dalloway herself—speculates about her perception of the unity of all things, suggested by the immaterial and material linkages of the waves. This unity would seemingly characterize a realm that the rational mind may not fathom, perhaps a mystical domain. The scientific mind at work in Woolf's narrators usually hesitates to accept mystical revelation. In Woolf's work, the modernist belief in revelation actually needs to be seconded by science, the same science that systematically puts revelations in doubt. In fine, Woolf's texts trace out with unparalleled finesse how desire gives rise to a dialectical struggle between belief and anguish, in the most subtle modernist update of the Pascalian tug-of-war between heart and mind. In *Mrs. Dalloway* the image of the waves seems reassuring, as if field theory and perhaps even particle physics were on the side of the heart—as long as the heart can connect in sanity with the material world.

The recurrent image of waves, the ebb and flow that describe at once the swells of the ocean and the waves of light that produce the sky described by Tyndall and which were theorized by Maxwell, returns in Woolf's threnody about friends and lovers, *The Waves*. Most critics find this novel to be her most intentionally experimental work, or as Gillian Beer puts it in an introduction to the novel, "Woolf's hints and touches in her diary from 1925 on towards the work that became *The Waves* makes it clear that this was to be experimental work, work that would fundamentally challenge the bounds of fiction."[7] In the novel the oceanic waves are positioned exterior to the characters' consciousness. The moving waves of water, reflecting the waves of light of the revolving sun, constitute the framework that encloses the novel's voices that speak of their lives in a world in which science is a source of enigma. Woolf's experiment in this work is to combine the naturalism of these framing sections, describing nature manifested in the sun's rays and the sea's waves, in alternation with the monologues describing life trajectories; and then to bring together these two realms in a final act of nonreconciliation of human life and pure nature in which the natural waves of matter seemingly dominate. In counterpoint to *Mrs. Dalloway* then, *The Waves* portrays a nonmystical phenomenology of the life trajectories of its six characters, who recite individual narratives of their days and ways, culminating in Bernard's final monologue.

At the novel's end, an aging Bernard wonders what has been the significance

7. Beer, introduction to *The Waves,* by Virginia Woolf, xv. Hereafter this edition of *The Waves* is cited parenthetically in the text.

of his and his comrades' life. He experiences a kind of materialist epiphany, informed explicitly by his awareness of science—if "epiphany" is the proper expression for the final narrative movement in which Bernard first follows the "falling wave" (240) down into doubt and loss of self before "the wave rises" (247). In his downward trajectory, in his confrontation with his body's aging, Bernard is seized by doubt about the solidity of the world. His doubt is largely provoked by the new physics of relativity and atomic theory, as was described in numerous popular works by physicists like Eddington and Jeans. The physicist's description of worlds unseen, of galaxies and electrons, undermines the solidity of the world of immediate perception. Bernard experiences a typical crisis about perception that the new physics brought to the modernists. In a thought experiment performed for himself, Bernard tries to imagine how the unseen world of particles whirling about him can give rise to the fixity of the phenomenal world that he actually perceives before him (240). In a moment of self-seizure after his dizzying doubts about matter, Bernard imagines within himself a being attached to the earth, "the old brute" that paleontology has decreed to be his forebear. He experiences himself as an animal tied to the solid ground of the here and now, but this solidity is vouchsafed by another thought experiment: the present configuration of his body is the product of what he imagines to be the work of the time of eons past, sublimated into the present animal. This is an image of temporal sublimation evoking the way the Darwinian Ernst Haeckel found phylogeny in every ontogeny. The application of this biological theory to his own body, living in the present moment, is a thought experiment whose results give Bernard reassurance about the solidity of his being. The ironic epistemologist can note that biology trumps physics in this experiment, which points to the many debates to come about the relation of the two sciences, especially to the debate about whether biology can be reduced to physics: evanescent particles may be kept in their invisible place if their paradoxical laws cannot suffice to explain the emergence of hairy biological beings.

Scientific awareness, informing Bernard's consciousness, is part of an ascetic process by which Bernard tries to accept the inevitability of his nature, and thus nature itself, in the rising wave that directs him to cast away the "veil of being" (245) and to address himself directly to nature. In an attempt to limit the purchase science can have on his aging body, Bernard evokes Schopenhauerian metaphysics. Beyond Schopenhauer's veil of being would lie a metaphysical reality escaping the determinations of both physics and biology. Entertaining Schopenhauer's metaphysical doubts about science may allow Bernard to accept nature, but that does not really mean that he is reconciled with it. Bernard's final words rage with the desire to remain undefeated by the biological destiny that he finally accepts and rejects at the same time: "Against you I will fling myself, unvanquished and unyielding, O Death!" (248). In the finale to *The Waves,* biological and physical rhythms continue: the sun sinks, a thrush goes quiet, and, in the one-line conclusion that brings the framing sections and the novel to an end, the waves break upon the shore. This final image of waves is open in its meaning, for it seems to suggest the inevitable processes of nature and the rhythms that bind all together, but these waves are set in a night that promises no great illumination. And the image of going under in the night is one that Woolf understood well as an image of the madness of existence itself. Her experiment seems to eventuate in proof that modernist consciousness is divided against itself, going under and unvanquished in the Pascalian night.

Faulkner's Relativity

The humanist knows that knowledge always entails knowledge of death. At the end of *The Waves* the reader, humanist or not, may muse that the Bible offers in its first book that same bitter knowledge about knowledge, before biology theorized death or Schopenhauer saw life as part of the veil of Maya. It is true that biblical myth is rarely present in Woolf's works, for which recent physics and biology are more regular references. The Bible is, however, omnipresent in the work of the American celebrator of the unvanquished, William Faulkner, a modernist who clearly draws upon the bitter knowledge that the Bible places at the origins of consciousness. Indeed, the Bible may seem of greater import for understanding the unvanquished southerner's novels than biology or physics. Eddington and Jeans, the English physicists who explained relativity and nuclear theory for Woolf's generation, are not usually listed among the thinkers given as influences upon Faulkner. True, Darwin, Freud, and Bergson figure on that list, and that should alert Faulkner's reader to an important dimension to his work: one should not underestimate the extent to which Faulkner was open to all the currents of modernity, including modern physics. For example, Daniel J. Singal has convincingly shown that Faulkner set out self-consciously to transcend his provincial setting to become a modernist.[8]

---

8. Singal, *William Faulkner: The Making of a Modernist.*

Faulkner's genius was to use the Greek and Hebrew traditions in elaborating a modernist worldview that understood not only modern biology, but, I will argue, the transformations brought about by modern physics. This is suggested first by allusions throughout Faulkner's work to scientific theories and laws. Once one begins to read his work with a scientific eye, it becomes clear that Faulkner's best work is more than merely consonant with the modern scientific worldview; it is informed by science. Of course, his use of science does not preclude his recourse to mythic narratives. Joyce gave the most convincing example that tradition can be used in the most experimental work. In fact, for Faulkner and many other writers, one of Joyce's lessons was that tradition must be interpreted, if it is to be known at all, through new experimental forms of fiction.

Unlike characters found in Joyce, not to mention those in Musil and Woolf, the southerners in Faulkner's work usually have little knowledge of science. His characters' consciousness rarely coincides with the knowledge and perception of the narrating consciousness. Even in novels using first-person narration like *As I Lay Dying* (1929) or *The Sound and the Fury* (1930), an implied author or narrative intelligence ranges far beyond the monologues spoken by Faulkner's illiterate and retarded characters. In a sense that is obvious. But perhaps it is less obvious that scientific understanding in Faulkner's later major novels, such as *Light in August* (1932) or *Absalom, Absalom!* (1936), is the basis for experimentation. For example, *Absalom, Absalom!* offers a thought experiment undertaken by a narrative intelligence that narrates relativistically with multiple perspectives on temporality.

Before pursuing this point, I concede that Faulkner's use of physics is perhaps less obvious than his biological naturalism, often giving expression to macabre grotesqueries. Faulkner's biological naturalism can be compared to what one finds in Joyce and Woolf insofar as these writers, in rueful or macabre terms, accept that human beings are animals endowed with a thirst for transcendence, but who are circumscribed finally by hapless bodies. Faulkner joins Joyce and Woolf in finding that the human animal, abandoned in a Pascalian cosmos, takes many shapes—such as the decaying body of Woolf's successful "hostess" Mrs. Dalloway, the Bloomian body of dubious tumefactions in Joyce's *Ulysses,* or the mother's decaying corpse smelling like a fish in the ambulatory funeral of Faulkner's *As I Lay Dying.*

Faulkner's black humor deriving from biology is of less interest, however, for an understanding of Faulkner's unparalleled influence on world literature than is his dealing with temporality. Faulkner is the patron saint of modern literary efforts to understand history through fiction. This is primarily because Faulkner created an epistemic novel in which the truth of propositions about history is relative to the framework of the questing narrative voice. Faulkner's experiments in representing history are part of the way in which Faulkner represents time, and, in his most experimental works, this involves working out speculations deriving from the implications of modern physics. Faulkner understood that, when time can be perceived by multiple observers, a relativistic situation is created. This relativistic situation allows Faulkner to dramatize the search for knowledge of the past with a use of multiple temporal perspectives that is unabashedly experimental in shape.

Experimental, too, is the way that knowledge about the past is derived from hypotheses that are tested against the work's present fictional world. This world is that of the American south, polarized between a nearly mythical past and the fallen present of degraded modernity. Faulkner's genius is to juxtapose these worlds in such a way that history emerges as the truth of the concrete particular that can also appear to be the illustration of a world of timeless myth. In setting forth hypotheses about the historical framework that encapsulates the narrative voice, Faulkner experiments to see if the referential context can give plausible knowledge of the past. This experimentation is dramatized in characters who strain to find a temporal relationship that can make sense of the history engulfing them. In this sense the narrating intelligence, using the characters or directly offering his own speculation, develops, in thought experiments, inferences proposing truths capable of explaining the present fallen moment.

In this quest for the truth of the past that pervades the present, the formulation of imaginative hypotheses in Faulkner's fiction resembles the imaginative formulation of results in scientific thought experiments. Once perceived, this analogy may seem obvious, though few critics have looked for precise analogies between scientific thought and Faulkner's work. A noteworthy exception is Steven T. Ryan's study of *The Sound and the Fury, As I Lay Dying, Light in August,* and *Absalom, Absalom!*.[9] He compares Faulkner's hypothetical procedures in these novels to the work of the physicist who, in interpreting the subatomic world, is restricted to complementary perspectives. Knowledge of

9. Ryan, "Faulkner and Quantum Mechanics." Other useful essays on science include Francine Ringold, "The Metaphysics of Yoknapatawpha County: 'Airy Space and Scope for Your Delirium,'" and Mick Gidley, "Another Psychologist, a Physiologist, and William Faulkner."

some facts about particles excludes knowledge of others, and Ryan argues that complementarity illustrates the limits of knowledge characterizing Faulkner's observers. His argument implies that the sense of epistemological limits in modern fiction can be compared to the limits of description discovered in the elaboration of quantum theory. Heisenberg himself had concluded that the modern observer finds the world categorized by, when not fragmented into, epistemological realms that are defined by their limits. These comparisons with complementarity are highly suggestive, in that they highlight the epistemological limits felt by modernists in both literature and science.

The sense of epistemological limits does not necessarily predispose a writer to experimentation, however. Faulkner's experimentation in representing time is undoubtedly informed by a sense of the limits of the individual seeking knowledge, and it is better illuminated by a comparison with relativity theory. This analogy can function heuristically for several of Faulkner's works in which temporality is shaped by reference to a relativistic framework, which means that the same events may seem to be situated at different times. This relativist situation is found notably in *Absalom, Absalom!,* a novel whose biblical title is redolent of the multiple sources that offer the knowledge that one is damned by history. Faulkner's reference to the Bible suggests mythic images, but these images are read within a, or rather several, frameworks in which linear temporality is no longer the unquestioned order for historical knowledge. I note, in prelude to a commentary on this novel, that Faulkner need not have read Einstein to come to the viewpoint that there is no absolute temporal framework, though it seems very unlikely that he did not have some fairly sharp impressions about what Einstein's theories meant. Faulkner was also influenced by Conrad, who made knowledge a function of the framing narrative hypothesis. Conrad suggests different ways of envisaging the relativity of knowledge to an observer's framework. Probably equally as important was Faulkner's reading of Proust, since Faulkner's relativizing is analogous to what Proust did with one narrative voice re-creating time past: the work's temporality is perceived relative to a privileged narrative framework that organizes all temporal perspectives. But Faulkner goes beyond Proust in this regard. In a work like *Absalom, Absalom!* there are at least four narrators—critics disagree as to how many narrators there may be. And as every reader of Einstein knows, once there are two potential observers in two different temporal frameworks, relativistic considerations show that there is no absolute temporality to which they can make appeal. With his multiple narrators in *Absalom, Absalom!* Faulkner makes the act of narration into a relativistic revel.

It is important not to conflate relativism and relativity. Faulkner is not a relativist in the usual postmodern sense. Faulkner's work presents a world in which truth is posited, in some sense, as existing. It exists independently of the individual mind, even if every observer exists as an independent framework when it comes to situating this truth. This view is consonant with relativity, not with relativism. In this sense Faulkner was no more of a relativist than Joyce or Einstein. If Faulkner dramatizes in *Absalom, Absalom!* that the truth about what happens in time is not easy to ascertain, it is because the most that one can often know is a hypothesis deriving from an imaginative thought experiment. There is a probabilistic dimension to all knowledge, and that is simply the best that the narrating voice can do. Thought experiments offer no easy certainty, probably no certainty at all. Yet it seems clear that Faulkner believed that, if truth is to be found, knowledge of it exists in function of the imaginative framework that allows that truth to be thought out or deduced as an imagined possibility. The framework, however, is relativistic, in the sense that situating knowledge in time is relative to an observer-narrator's temporal framework. With more than one narrator in more than one framework, it is problematic to know what came before what, or what occurred at the same time, when simultaneity has only a relativistic meaning. Einstein's famous example of observers on and off a train poses similar problems: what happens first for one observer happens subsequently for the other.

To begin a discussion of *Absalom! Absalom!* and its complicated relativistic temporal structure, let us detour a bit and consider a later text in which Faulkner makes a clear, if ironic, illustration of the relativity of past and present. In the description of the jail that serves as the prologue to Act Three of *Requiem for a Nun* (1951), Faulkner dislocates the temporal order in a demonstration that the past can be narrated as a present, or the present can precede the past, according to the shifting narrative framework. There is much black humor implicit in his description of a jail as the embodiment of temporality; and I suspect that Faulkner had Proust in mind for this near parody, specifically the way that Proust, in making a church the center of his fictional village of Combray, posits time as the church's fourth dimension. Yoknapatawpha County is not the center of paradise lost, however, and Faulkner characteristically situates a ramshackle jail at the center of his world. Around and through this building, time can be described relativistically. The jail's age depends on the framework for observation, which can change without rupture, as Faulkner demonstrates in what is one of the most complex sentences in literature, both for its temporal complications, as well as its length. The narrative, "The Jail (Nor Even Yet Quite Relinquish—)," begins thus:

> So, although in a sense the jail was both older and less old than the courthouse, in actuality, in time, in observation and memory, it was older even than the town itself. Because there was no town until there was a courthouse, and no courthouse until (like some unsentient unweaned creature torn violently from the dug of its dam) the floorless lean-to rabbit-hutch housing the iron chest was reft from the log flank of the jail and transmogrified into a by-neo-Greek-out-Georgian-England edifice set in the center of what in time would be the town Square (as a result of which, the town itself had moved one block south—or rather, no town then and yet, the courthouse itself the catalyst . . .

In Malcolm Cowley's famous *The Portable Faulkner,* the book that most critics credit with bringing Faulkner critical recognition in the United States, the sentence continues for another thirty-eight pages.[10] In this sentence, simultaneity, past, present, and future are all narrative possibilities. The narrative voice moves seamlessly, changing its position vis-à-vis the jail, so that in effect it changes temporal frameworks by acting as if it were a series of potential observers situated in different frameworks. Like Einstein's observer on a train perceiving light from one source before perceiving light from another source—though the light beams are seen simultaneously by an observer outside the train— Faulkner's potential observers perceive before and after, earlier and later, according to their possible positioning with regard to the jail, whose existence seems at once to be simultaneous with all events in the town, but also preceding them or coming after them, according to the observational framework.

What is comically explicit in "The Jail" is already at work in the procedures Faulkner uses in earlier novels. In works like *The Sound and the Fury, Light in August,* and most notably *Absalom, Absalom!,* the narrating voices experience a temporality that is relative to the narrative framework they inhabit. Faulkner's relativizing is not always easy to follow. To obviate difficulties, or perhaps to

10. Cowley, *The Portable Faulkner,* 665.

compound them, Faulkner obligingly appended a chronology and a map to
Absalom, Absalom!; or, as a critic like Peter Brooks has observed, Faulkner gave
back to the reader "the traditional schemata for the ordering of time and experience from which *Absalom, Absalom!* markedly departs."[11] Rather mischievously
inventing a linear chronology and a spatializing map for his novel, Faulkner
endowed *Absalom, Absalom!* in effect with fictional Newtonian coordinates
of absolute time and space. In other words, to oblige his readers, and perhaps
especially his publisher, he located the narrative world in time and space by
means of coordinates codified by classical physics. His appended chronology
purports to translate the dislocated, relativistic description of events in the novel
with a classical linear interpretation—this with a sense of humor about perceiving space, since according to the map's legend, it represents territory belonging
to one William Faulkner.

Faulkner's guide to absolute space and time is amusing, but perhaps of dubious help. Nonetheless, critics have been troubled by the question, Does the
guide work? Finding that it does not, some have even tried to improve upon
Faulkner's chronology. The lure of linearity appears to be an absolute, if time is
not.[12] But perhaps it is best to recognize that, entertaining multiple hypotheses
with multiple narrators, Faulkner dissolves linearity in *Absalom, Absalom!* and,
with this, the epistemic certainty that Proust's narrator found in his own subjectivity. In Faulkner's novel each narrator proposes a hypothetical construction
of a world, in a thought experiment or experiments, contrasted and conjoined at
times with those of other voices. For example, in addition to the four principal
voices of *Absalom, Absalom!,* several other narrators appear to be contained
within the major narrative voices, and these other voices also join in the attempt
to narrate the history of Thomas Sutpen's plans, the story of the rise and fall of a
plantation owner whose design for grandeur founders upon incest and the fear
of miscegenation. Voices telling Sutpen's tale fuse, overlap, and interrogate each
other as each speaker seeks to reveal the particular "truth" of what the legendary
Sutpen did and what he wanted, a truth that would then be a synecdoche for
the history of the American South, and perhaps of Western civilization itself.

11. Brooks, "Incredulous Narration: *Absalom, Absalom!*" in Harold Bloom, ed., *William
Faulkner's "Absalom, Absalom!"* 105.
12. Dirk Kuyk, in his *Sutpen's Design,* has redone Faulkner's chronology, for Kuyk
believes that Faulkner's appended chronology often fails to match the facts in the novel
itself (45).

Part of our difficulty in deciphering Faulkner is that narrative events are characterized as only probably or possibly true within the fictional framework. They are possibly true even though it is also clearly the case that each narrative voice is engaging in a long thought experiment as it describes events by conjecturing or imagining what has happened. Imaginative conjecture is a necessary part of a thought experiment, and it perforce must take place from the viewpoint of a character or narrator desiring knowledge—since all knowledge is relative to the framework from which it is perceived. This type of imaginative conjecture happens in *Absalom, Absalom!* when, for example, Quentin begins to relate the events that have happened to Sutpen. Quentin's voice is then joined by the voice of his roommate Shreve, and together they begin to tell the tale of Sutpen's attempt to found a dynasty that comes to an end in the conflagration that burns Sutpen's house and, with it, his son, Henry. In this perspectival imagining there are statements that are true within the context of the fiction: for example, Sutpen's house burns with Henry in it. Or, the conflagration apparently occurs years after Henry killed his half-brother, Charles Bon. Each statement is a narrative truth, in the sense that it is also true that these truths are contained within the act of narration itself. But each truth exists in a framework relative to an observer. From the perspective of one framework it is logical to accept that the past determines the present act of narration that is imagining the past. This determination of the present by the past, in one imagined narration, is the basis for standard historical knowledge based on linear causality. But Faulkner superimposes on this framework a different perspective, set within a different framework. Then the narrative act is perceived as a future event reaching back to enter the past in order to know it from within the same framework. Hence a nonlinear simultaneity: existing in the past, the future ordered by Newtonian linearity can be perceived to precede the present, depending on the frame of reference, and it can also precede the past.

Let us read literally the following passage in which Faulkner depicts his narrators Shreve and Quentin as they seek to know, for example, the events that led up to Henry killing his mulatto half-brother, Charles Bon, who wanted to marry Henry's sibling, his half-sister, Judith. In their room at Harvard, Shreve and Quentin imagine Henry and Bon together in their regiment during the Civil War: "They were both in Carolina and the time was forty-six years ago, and it was not even four [narrators] but compounded still further, since now both of them were Henry Sutpen and both of them were Bon, compounded each of both, yet either neither, smelling the very smoke which had blown and faded away."[13] After this passage Faulkner puts his narration into italics, emphasizing that in another framework the past is perceived as the future, or perhaps the future as created by the past narration. This framework offers a truth illustrating the destiny of the South, floundering upon its fear of miscegenation, and, given the uncertainty of blood lines, incest:

> —*You are my brother.*
> —*No I'm not. I'm the nigger that's going to sleep with your sister. Unless you stop me, Henry.* (357–58)

The explosive narrative truth here is set within several frameworks so that the event can be taken as a past with regard to Quentin's present narrative framework, a present with regard to the time of the war and the collapse of the South, and even as a future once the narrators are ensconced in the past observing destiny as a form of truth. Greek tragedy and Einstein are at one here. As Joyce also knew, the circularity of mythical temporality is consonant with the continuous relativity of past, present, and future.

This use of relativity in the narration of history—often coinciding with a mythic vision of history—has found important elaboration in writers as diverse as French Nobel laureate Claude Simon and American Nobel laureate Toni Morrison. However, the world of Latin American fiction, in its extraordinary diversity, probably offers the greatest number of examples of the ways Faulknerian literary epistemology has engendered approaches to history. Suffice it to say here that for many Latin American writers the relativity of narrative frameworks permits a vision portraying that the future often comes first in what we know of the past. The future can literally come before the past if one shifts the observational framework. And so what appears as fantasy, or magical realism, in Latin American fiction, often drawing upon indigenous myths, is also consonant with the scientific imagination. A history of the continuities relating Faulkner, the modernist vision of science, and Latin American writing can draw upon a most varied array of novelists: Sabáta, Cortázar, Asturias, Capentier, Fuentes, García Márquez, Vargos Llosa—to name a few who use the novel for epistemic exploration, which is to say, who believe that fiction is an essential means of knowing history.[14] These writers are at home with the implications

13. Faulkner, *Absalom, Absalom!* 351. Hereafter cited parenthetically in the text.
14. See Lois Parkinson Zamora, *The Usable Past: The Imagination of History in Recent Fiction of the Americas.*

of the modern relativistic cosmology and the fantastic conjectures that it allows about the universe, or universes, that we may inhabit.

Borges and the Trials of Logic

These writers are also tributary to the third writer I consider among the most important, after Proust, Joyce, and Kafka, for developing the experimental possibilities of an interface between science and literature: the Argentine poet, essayist, and short story writer Jorge Luis Borges. In a series of collections of short stories, such as *Ficciones* (1944), *El Aleph* (1949), or *El libro de arena* (1975, *The Book of Sand*), Borges shows himself to be perhaps the most sophisticated writer of fictions conceived as ludic thought experiments among the moderns—which can be taken here as modernist or postmodernist as one likes. Borges's cosmopolitan background, as in the case of Conrad or Nabokov, makes it seem almost irrelevant to assign him a nationality, though his demonstrations of the contradictions of systemic thought and the power of dreams often unfold in Buenos Aires and are written in a language that has established a model for literary Spanish. Borges's cosmopolitan openness is an essential aspect of modernism, and one is not surprised to learn that the Borges who wrote poetry in English translated a passage from *Ulysses* in 1926 and was also an early translator of Kafka, about whom he also wrote one of the most important and wittiest essays in the critical canon.[15] Kafka is, as Borges wrote, the precursor whom Borges was destined to create for himself.

In works by Woolf and Faulkner, the interface of science and the world is often embodied in and shaped by the narrative consciousness trying to make sense of the world. By contrast, Borges's narrators often examine, with ironic distance, epistemic models in which a narrative experiment turns on events narrated with an almost mathematical sense of logical entailment. In this regard some of Borges's fictions are often pure thought experiments that, were it not for the skeptical and often fantastical irony permeating them, might scarcely be differentiated from the modeling usually associated with a purely scientific thought experiment. Theoretical cosmologists have perhaps not looked askance upon Borges in their verbal descriptions of their models. One can hardly avoid

15. For Joyce, see Jean Franco, *An Introduction to Spanish-American Literature,* 300; for Kafka, see Beatriz Sarlo, *Jorge Luis Borges: A Writer on the Edge,* 70.

thinking of the Borgesian resonances found in the string theorists' concept of the "multiverse," in which "the supposition that our entire universe is but one instance of an infinity of continually created universes…"—to cite almost at random a recent description from the journal *Nature*.[16]

Mathematical cosmologists can experimentally imagine an infinity of infinite universes. Drawing upon quantum mechanics they have hit upon one of Borges's working axioms, to wit, that books themselves contain infinite numbers of universes of post-Einsteinian spacetime. A string theorist can thus feel at home in "The Garden of Forking Paths," in which the narrator of the book within the book, Ts'ui Pên, "different from Newton and Schopenhauer…did not believe in a uniform, absolute time. He believed in infinite series of times, in a vertiginous and expanding network of parallel, convergent, and divergent times."[17] Like one of the mathematical combinatory systems of contemporary cosmology, Ts'ui Pên's garden is described as a book, and the book in turn as a labyrinth, since the structure of any narration in a book is a framework implying at any moment the infinite number of alternative possibilities it might contain. Like modern cosmology, then, Borges's fiction does not hesitate to postulate that an infinite number of alternative events coexist, as in so many multiple universes or so many infinite sets. Every narrative is only one possible universe whose existence entails staggering ontological possibilities. Moreover, as Borges repeatedly suggests with sly irony, every narrative is contained within a book that may well be contained within another book, and this within another, ad infinitum, in the logical unfolding of possible multiple universes, some parallel, but others encompassing, in their infinite proliferation.

Every book, or fiction, is nonetheless a unique universe offering a hypothetical ordering of events. The ironic Gnostic whom Borges sometimes uses as a narrator finds this situation abominable, for every representation augments the number of worlds. In his disgust for being's increase, the Gnostic finds that mirrors are sources of horror, as are encyclopedias, since, like all agents of representation, they augment in detail the infinite proliferation of being. Borges illustrates the consequences of this idea in *Ficciones,* in the story "Tlön, Uqbar, Orbis Tertius." This fiction dramatizes the proposition that a well-wrought encyclopedia might replace all other systems of knowledge, and hence all other imagined universes, through the power that the encyclopedia has to confer

16. W. A. Zajc, "The Pull of Weird Horizons."
17. Borges, "El jardín de senderos que se bifurcan," in *Ficciones,* 116. Hereafter cited parenthetically in the text.

order on that metaphysical dream called "reality." The imagined encyclopedia describing a unique fictional cosmos, contrived by men desirous of greater order than can be found in their usual seedy universe, begins to supplant all other representations. The new encyclopedia and its orderings impose themselves as "reality." If coherence is a fundamental criterion for accepting that a proposition is knowledge, then it is logical that an imaginary order may well be deemed superior to the universe known through fragmented sciences—as the narrator of "Tlön, Uqbar, Orbis Tertius" observes in looking at recent history. He notes that the imaginary universes promoted as knowledge by fascism and dialectical materialism had been deemed superior, and hence as real or true, by considerable populations of the globe. Borges's thought experiments aim in irony at the epistemological urge that fosters the ten thousand different beliefs that humanity has considered to be knowledge, at the same time as he satirizes the undying thirst for the transcendence once granted by absolute knowledge.

The Borgesian narrator thirsting for coherence confronts in dismay the heterogeneity of knowledge. Heterogeneity may be mastered by the arbitrary orders of the encyclopedia, or perhaps by the system created by the library, or even by the stochastic play of the lottery—to allude to the subject matter of three of Borges' *ficciones* and their representations of representation. But every means for achieving order must confront the fact that every diverse source of knowledge in the world enters with equal plausibility into any representation—encyclopedia, book, or dream—which seeks to mirror the world and what is in the world. The world includes, moreover, all the claims to know the world, and claims about those claims, ad infinitum. Borges points up with bemused irony that Pascal's bad infinity hovers over every text that claims to represent the world—and this by logical definition, for what criteria allow a supposedly mimetic text to exclude anything? Everything and its opposite exists, and so dialectics is generated by the infinite proliferation implied by any text that claims to represent the world. A true representation would demand every thing and its mirror image, or every proposition and its opposite—not to mention mirror images of mirror images.

Borges does not offer dialectics in an attempt to find a solution to contradiction as Pascal did. Rather, in Borges, dialectics is the scandalously inevitable result of any attempt at knowledge and representation. This result is found, for example, in the experiment undertaken in the story "The Library of Babel" in *Ficciones*. Borges begins the tale by accepting the axiom that, if the initial variables of the universe can be described as an infinite play of relations, then one may conclude that the universe is, among all other things, also a representation of those relations, to wit, a library and all the representations it contains. The universe is logically the collection, or set, of all the texts that would represent and explain it, including all the texts that one can imagine to explain all the texts that explain all the texts that explain all the texts, etc. Infinite regress, the logician's horror, is the natural condition of knowledge generated by the infinite, quite simply because by definition the infinite maintains an infinite number of possible relations with everything else. And these relations would be total knowledge. Negotiating the two poles of assertion and counter-assertion, or the claims of knowledge and the contradictions that these claims engender, Borges's experimental imagination spins out this kind of fiction in a demonstration that there is an endless series of models that represent the universe—and that an infinite series of contradictions compose "reality."

Borges's tales can encompass the dialectical opposite of the arbitrary ordering that systems and models impose to create an order called a world. The opposite of the universal model is the world of infinite nominalism in which knowledge would be knowledge of every particular that can be perceived, such as in "Funes el memorioso" (most recently translated as "Funes the Memorius"). Pascal's foundering on the infinitely small takes a new twist in Borges's exploration of the fragmentation of the world brought about by empiricism. Accepting the nominalist axiom that all knowledge derives from knowledge of a concrete particular, the narrator of this story works out the implications of this epistemological axiom by imagining a mind capacious enough to stock all these particulars—he imagines neither God, nor a computer, but Funes, a lad with a photographic memory and a postmodern dislike of Platonism. The result is a nightmare, for all Funes can know is ever increasing amounts of details about details. Funes rejects the idea that every bird and leaf on a tree might be known with a proper name, for this individual naming is also too general and betrays the fact that "Funes not only remembered every leaf of every tree, of every mountain, but also each of the times he had seen it or imagined it."[18] Refusing the impoverishment that science and language bring to the world, Funes cannot sleep. Sleep itself takes him away from the riches of his knowledge of concrete particulars: it interferes with the bedridden boy's repetition of memories of memories, and with the imagination's imagining the memories of more memories of memories. Perhaps needless to say, Funes dies young.

18. Borges, *Collected Fictions,* trans. Andrew Hurley.

Attempting to order the riches of individual representations, hypothetical laws abound in Borges's tales, for order demands invariant axioms. Hence Borges looks for laws that might preside over the chaos of his fictions. These laws often resemble fantastic but logical axioms that are tested by the experience that Borges narrates to see, usually in irony, if they are confirmed, or not, by the ensuing thought experiment. Laws of representation are ironically confirmed in "Tlön, Uqbar, Orbis Tertius" as in "The Library of Babel," while "The Garden of Forking Paths" works out the law of implication. An ironic reversal of these ironic confirmations is found in "La lotería en Babilonia" (The Babylon lottery). In this tale the initial axiom is the lack of law: all is subject to chance. A community of believers, having discovered that "the lottery is the principle part of reality," (67) therefore decide to collaborate with chance by submitting all events in life to stochastic determinations. For example, death is decided by lottery drawings. Then the inhabitants realize that not just the final outcome, but every step in the process leading to that event should be logically decided by chance: "Was it not derisive that chance should dictate someone's death and that the circumstances of this death—the reservation of time, making publicity, the hour and the century—were not also subject to chance?" (73). Therefore, the Babylonians attempt to make each step in the process a matter of random determination, which entails that each step leading to each step should be a chance decision. Inevitably, they encounter the classic Stoic paradoxes: the division of any process becomes subject to infinite regress when divided mathematically without a procedure for stopping the division. Thus, no decision can ever be final, for every decision can bifurcate into an infinite number of preceding decisions leading to the event ("Ninguna decisión es final, todas se ramifican en otras," 74). In despair, finally, the scribes of Babylon are reduced to celebrating mistakes and errors, or inventing fictions, in order to correct the random by celebrating its truest manifestations. The arbitrary lie is especially effective in this regard: the narrator slyly suggests in fact that the tale the reader is reading is an example of such a lie, thereby converting the entire tale, dialectically, into a self-denying paradox. As a celebrator of stochastic processes, Borges renews the classical paradoxes of logic to demonstrate the ultimate vanity of any epistemic quest in a world ruled by utter chance.

Borges's texts are at once affirmations of the whims of gnosis and demonstrations of the inevitable contradictions that destroy all epistemic dreams. A reader familiar with the history of the philosophy of mathematics and logic suspects that Borges's fictional worlds were created to torment with mockery the logician who knows that, within every axiomatic system that has ever been created, there lurks a contradiction that posterity will surely find. Borges is an ironic successor of Cantor, Frege, Hilbert, Russell, and Gödel, ironic in that he celebrates the destruction of the systems that the mathematical logicians have tried to shore up against the contradictions that every attempt at totally consistent thought seems to generate. (To simplify the history of logic, I recall that Frege was undone when Russell found a contradiction in Frege's work on the foundations of mathematics, and that in their turn Russell and Hilbert were undone in their attempts to systematize the foundations of mathematics by Gödel.) This celebration of the failures of science is true not only in the explicit contradictions of stories like "The Library of Babel," but also in the intertextual relations among the stories. Consider "The Circular Ruins," in which a dreamer discovers that he is dreamed by another dreamer. If dream is a form of representation, then it is logical that it can be contained in other representations. So perhaps the reader is not surprised to learn that the narrator of "An Examination of the Work of Herbert Quain" admits that he had stolen the earlier story, "The Circular Ruins," from the work of the fictional author Herbert Quain. The ontology of fiction and "reality" is ironically undone when a "real" fiction can be plausibly taken from a fictional fiction, while the endless nature of borrowings also mimics infinite regress. Wherein lies the grounds for the axiomatic finality that logic and mathematics once sought?

In later stories Borges underscores that the mathematician Cantor's search for ordinals for the transfinite numbers of infinite sets was a useless game, since the universe itself, by definition an infinite set, admits of all orders and so, as the reader finds in the later tale "El libro de arena," that the "Book of Sand" is paginated chaotically, with different series for even and odd pages: "Perhaps to make one understand that the terms of an infinite series allow any order of numbers" [Acaso para dar a entender que los términos de una serie infinita admiten cualquier número].[19] The infinite can thus be augmented by chaos, in the random patterns found in everything, especially in a true library catalog that—horrible to contemplate—would contain an infinite number of false orderings of knowledge as well as any true ones.

All that fosters the illusion of order is a target for Borges's experiments. Consider in this regard the alphabet, the basis for writing and hence for infinite illusions, or, more precisely, for the permutations that allow the genesis of

19. Borges, *El Libro de Arena,* 97.

descriptions of an infinite number of relations. Borges chooses the letter aleph, the beginning of the Hebrew alphabet and hence of writing, as the representative sign of the infinite. The aleph is the symbol of the totality of knowledge and also of the fiction that would be a useless addition to that knowledge, since fiction is a representation of an infinite series that purports to duplicate the infinite number of things. In homage to the Kabbalah's use of this letter, and to Cantor's use of it to symbolize an infinite set, "The Aleph" is a story in which mysticism and Cantor's set theory intersect. The story envisages what might happen if one attempted to view the physical infinite. When viewed in this tale, the aleph acts as a prism opening onto an infinite set. Found in a Kafkaesque basement, it offers a view that nobody apparently can abide, except by apparently going insane and then by trying to write a poem that will encompass the universe. At least this is what has happened to the basement's owner; he wants to encompass the proliferating infinite. Borges's narrator in "The Aleph" decries the aleph, suggesting that it would be better to find solace, from the dream and horror of total science, in forgetting. Another analogy with Kafka's tales suggests itself. Were the law to reveal itself in all its logical rigor and perhaps infinite contradictions, Borges, after his precursor Kafka, suggests that the law could not be tolerated. Oblivion is clearly to be preferred to the glory conferred by science, for oblivion is perhaps the only concept that can oppose the infinite as a true negation. One may imagine that for both Kafka and Borges, God's great dilemma is that He cannot forget the infinite contradictions He contains.

In résumé, then, the random and the infinite are key concepts upon which Borges builds his system-destroying systems. Borges's thought experiments sometimes imagine the representation of the infinite, thus embodying the axioms of early modern cosmology and its founding belief that the physical infinite somehow inhabits our cosmic home. For Borges, as for Pascal, the attribution of the infinite to the cosmos means that our cosmos is founded upon a contradictory notion. But for Borges, the infinite also characterizes the heterogeneity of knowledge: every object can be the source of infinite gnosis since everything can entertain a relation with everything. Modern epistemology is called to account in this regard. Mach and Poincaré's doctrine that knowledge is always knowledge of relationships is carried in Borges's fictions to the limit — to use metaphorically that notion from calculus that usually serves to tame the infinite. Going to the limit, everything would unendingly offer knowledge of everything. This is a proposition that finally undermines itself by its own hyperbole, as well as the infinite regress inevitably found therein. Finally, it is only in the negative triumph of ironic lucidity that Borges recognizes that the human mind may rise above the splendid futility of its attempts at mastery of the universe through knowledge. But the futility is splendid, and Borges is as much a celebrator of the ludic joys of useless knowledge in all its forms as he is the disabused surveyor of the history of science and philosophy, these forms of what he calls fantastic literature.

After Proust, Joyce, and Kafka, the examples of Woolf, Borges, and Faulkner clearly continue to inform fiction and its techniques today. This is not to say that much experimental fiction continues to be written, for mere rhetorical technique is hardly sufficient for the execution of an experiment. Moreover, interesting experimental fiction has nearly always encountered science directly, in critique and emulation, and it is hard to say that fiction today is as interested in that encounter as modernism was. This is troubling, for we clearly are living at a moment of portentous accomplishments in science. The very nature of human existence may well be changed by what is occurring today, especially in biology and medicine. The question is, then, whether literature at the current moment is attempting to come to grips with this challenge, be it a threat or a promise. Whatever the answer to that vexing question, the great modernists discussed here undoubtedly remain the grounds for understanding how literature can use as well as criticize science. Modernists wanted to know the world, or at least great expanses of the world, at the same time that they interrogated the possibilities for knowledge. Rejecting the limits imposed on fiction by preceding generations of realists, modernist fiction was predicated on the assumption that nothing is excluded from literature. It is not clear that this is still the case. With critical distance and a clear sense of what the great modernists accomplished, let us now examine some more recent experiments, since Faulkner, Woolf, and Borges, to see if we can make some sense of what some recent fiction has done.

Chapter Seven

Conclusion
Science and Postmodernity

I propose to entice, and perhaps challenge, my English-language reader with a few comments illustrating briefly some disagreements about recent American and English fiction. For purposes of comparison, I will also consider a few Latin American works, and finally several Austrian writers who well illustrate a few propositions about postmodernism. I do not take it to be axiomatic that something called postmodern fiction exists, though the frequent use of the notion does oblige one to ask, If it does exist, what is it? For an answer one usually turns to some academic work such as *The Oxford Guide to Contemporary Writing* (1996). In this guide's essay on American literature, for instance, the reader discovers that contemporary American literature begins with Truman Capote's *In Cold Blood* (1965). Oxford's guide for the perplexed holds that since the 1960s American fiction has been interested essentially in the study of criminal mentality.[1] The reader may wonder if this thesis implies that all contemporary American fiction derives from Dostoyevsky's *Crime and Punishment,* or perhaps from Edgar Allen Poe. In any case this guide's essay on American literature implies, by notable omission, that American fiction is not interested in philosophy or science, unless it be criminology. The skeptical reader may doubt that Capote's presumably postmodern sensationalism is of great interest, even if his creation of a tale that might have been serialized in some tabloid journal once led hasty critics to proclaim the end of the separation of fact and fiction in the novel. The seasoned reader may also comment to him- or herself that Capote's substitution of imagined fact for fiction has little to do

---

1. Wendy Lesser, "United States," in John Sturrock, ed., *Oxford Guide to Contemporary Writing,* 407.

with knowledge: facts can be as bereft of epistemic interest as the most arbitrary fantasy. As readers of Jules Verne, H. G. Wells, or Philip K. Dick know, fantasy can, on the other hand, have great epistemic interest.

It is noteworthy that the Oxford guide has little to say about what once was called the avant-garde in fiction. The guide manifests no interest in experimental writing, but its promotion of popular culture does point to a general postmodern trend. The postmodern academy has willfully worked to bring about the demise of modernism and its values by promoting various aspects of pop culture. This trend is clear in the way the Oxford guide discards in effect American fiction written by writers such as Barth, Hawkes, Sorrentino, Heller, Kesey, Brautigan, Pynchon, Vonnegut, Coover, Gass, Barthelme, Roth, Sukenick, Federman, and others, who are scarcely or not mentioned at all. In brief, Oxford omits most of the writers who have been writing in the wake of Joyce, Kafka, and Beckett. The guide's promotion of popular culture reflects the contradictory ways the postmodern academic practioners of pop study their subject. On the one hand, they put it forward as a model, celebrating the joys and universal meaning found in advertising, TV, movies, cartoons, and comic books; on the other hand, they deplore popular culture's destructive workings upon cultural values that might oppose mindless consumerism, sexism, and unbridled capitalist destruction of culture and environment. Clearly, one meaning of postmodernity is a confused, simultaneous celebration and denunciation of the savage brutality of much pop culture. This is not the last contradiction we shall see in this conclusion about postmodernity.

If after perusing the Oxford guide, the reader still trusts Oxbridge editions to offer insights into American literature, she or he may turn to the weightier *Cambridge History of American Literature* (1999). In the third tome of this history, the list of experimental American writers is categorized as the male canon of postmodern writing. In her introduction to "Postmodern Fictions, 1960–1990," Wendy Steiner states that interest in experimental fiction, often concerned with formal innovations, has dwindled since the sixties, to be replaced, in works by women and minorities, with "sociological" or thematic, rather than formal, experimentation.[2] Experimentation is thus taken to mean that women and minorities have enlarged fiction so that it now includes interest in their lives. The reader may respectfully disagree, however, that this desirable

2. Steiner, "Postmodern Fictions, 1960–1990," in Sacvan Bercovitch, ed., *Cambridge History of American Literature,* 3:441.

widening of the scope of fiction is experimentation in any meaningful sense, unless one simply equates experimentation with subject matter or themes, which hardly seems adequate.

In making the case that recent American fiction offers more varied types of representations than it did in, say, 1970, Steiner is perhaps using "experimental" in some metaphorical sense. If critics find this metaphor useful, then I hardly want to quibble about it, except to point out that it does obscure the fact that experimental thinking, not unlike that done in science, has been done in fiction. In the most general sense, fiction about women or minority groups has opened up a new epistemic dimension of fiction insofar as it offers insight into lives that may not have been well represented before, but this has little to do with science, experimentation, or the epistemological challenges science offers. On the contrary, a heavy climate of suspicion with regard to science has emerged in some of this fiction. This suspicion is paralleled by the way some postmodern literary scholars endorse the idea that American feminist and ethnic fictions reveal the shallowness of science's claims to universality. This charge has been repeated in many variants. The historical grounds for some of these often acerbic attacks are clear, such as the history of science's collaboration with racism, or science's exclusion of women. However, these historical grounds do not justify today the wide-ranging rejection of science characteristic of much *postmodernity*. On the contrary, modern science has also been a source of the knowledge of history and biology that has validated the claims of minority groups—and of a majority group like women—to press forward in affirmation of their rights and their identity. However, by and large, postmodern theory has excluded inquiry into the liberating role that science has played: science has been considered a suspect activity.

Anglo-American fiction since 1945 is, I suggest, much richer in epistemic play and thought experiments than the compilers of the Oxford and Cambridge guides would have one believe. This is seen in the writings of the many novelists who take Joyce or Faulkner as a model in seeking ways to construct knowledge of history, including ethnic history; or in the works of those who follow Kafka, Borges, and, later, Beckett in experimenting to see if fiction can have an epistemic purpose—writers who, in their best works, get beyond the now worn topos of fiction's self-contained nature and the aporia generated by self-reference. These two types of fiction, the historical and the epistemological, offer a rough but useful typology pointing up, on the one hand, that, in the wake of Joyce and Faulkner, writers like Morrison, DeLillo, and Doctorow have tried to bring us knowledge of how the dead determine the present, as Doctorow put it on a radio interview on BBC 1 (May 2000); and that, on the other hand, in the wake of Beckett, Borges, and Kafka, writers like Gass, Vonnegut, Pynchon, and other experimentalists have confronted science for its epistemological challenge. Having made the observation that there is ongoing concern with epistemic issues in American fiction, I must nonetheless concede that postwar American writers have not encountered science as directly as European modernists and postmodernists such as Queneau, Robbe-Grillet, Sarraute, or Calvino.

It can also be argued that English writers, compared with their confreres across the channel, have taken less direct interest in using science for launching literary experiments. Writers like Golding, Lessing, and Swift draw at times upon science, though few writers in the homeland of Virginia Woolf and C. P. Snow have attempted to embody science in fiction with the anguished intensity that characterized Woolf or, on the continent, the ludic spirit found in Queneau or Calvino. Even the very notion of experimentation is routinely subject to misinterpretation in Newton's homeland. For instance, in the Routledge introduction to *British Culture* (1999) it is claimed that English women writers began experimental writing in the eighties: A. S. Byatt, Angela Carter, Zoe Fairbairns, Marina Warner, and Sara Maitland are cited as examples. It seems hard to believe that, in the country of Jane Austen, the Brontë sisters, and Virginia Woolf, simply writing about women can be conceived as experimental. What "experimental" apparently means here is a trend that, by British standards, represents a departure from conventional realism, often involving use of fantasy, myth, or even fairy tales.[3] "Experimental" appears to mean something like "non-realist," if not simply "fantasy." Many of these English women are fine writers, especially the marvelous A. S. Byatt, but it is difficult to see that their "experimental" texts have much to do with epistemic or formal experimentation.

This quirky use of "experimental" probably reflects a distrust of modernism permeating English literary culture. This distrust surfaces, for example, when a novelist who might be thought to be sympathetic to modernism, such as the talented Peter Ackroyd, unwittingly caricatures it when he writes, "Modernism is that movement in which created form began to interrogate itself, and to move toward an impossible union with itself in self-identity."[4] Using a very

---

3. Alistair Davis and Alan Sinfield, eds., *British Culture of the Postwar: An Introduction to Literature and Society, 1945–1999,* 46.
4. Ackroyd, *Notes for a New Culture: An Essay on Modernism,* 145.

British reading of Derrida, Ackroyd turns modernism into a metaphysical quest motivated by the desire to imitate an ontologically self-sufficient deity. This reductive description of modernist writing, focusing on the yearning of some modernists for transcendence, is not unusual among postmodern academic critics who denigrate modernism, perhaps in order to mark off their own identity. However, it does little justice to the epistemological complexity of the literary search for knowledge found in Proust, Musil, or Joyce, not to mention Woolf, Faulkner, or Borges. To do justice to English postmodernity, however, it must be pointed out that Virginia Woolf has now become an advertising icon. But, as every history of modern art points out, "pop" was an English invention, after all.

Pop immediately suggests parody, and a frequent generalization about much postmodern American literature, since at least John Barth, is that it is essentially parodic. It is true that much American postmodern fiction parodies quests for knowledge in fiction. Drawing directly upon Kafka and Borges, this parody is often a response to the idea that any self-contained text must end up a contradictory failure locked in a hermeneutic hall of mirrors. In reaction to this failure to get beyond the self-contained text, the next step in much American postmodern fiction is to emulate madness. This emulation is often a response to a vision of self as a self-enclosed construct, often lost in some system that it cannot understand, but which threatens it with messages that it cannot decipher. The self relates to the system with hysterical delusions, fantastic revolt, or paranoia. By and large masculine in origins, and this in noted contrast with continental feminist writings using insanity, American postmodern madness is often an aggressive response to the system—scientific or technological—that would account for it. Names like Heller, Kesey, and Roth immediately come to mind in this regard, though the most cited master of paranoia is Thomas Pynchon. His example is inevitably adduced when discussions of literature and science focus on the postmodern American scene, for his fiction is considered emblematic in its portrayal of science as part of a technological culture flying out of control. In *The Crying of Lot 49* (1966) Pynchon showed himself the master satirist of, or in, paranoia when his Oedipa Maas goes on a quest to find out if a communication conspiracy exists, or not, in the middle of the military-industrial complex in California. And with *Gravity's Rainbow* (1973), Pynchon became a cult figure for his experiments depicting science in which he mixes visions of demented entropy centered on shifting paranoid consciousness while describing an ever almost-present apocalypse. Pynchon is undoubtedly the writer who has defined the way many readers expect literature to confront the mad system of a technological society born of scientific dreams of control. For this reason Pynchon, not Capote, is considered by many to be the most important American writer after World War II.

Pynchon's fiction is symptomatic of a disenchantment with science promoted by American writers far less knowledgeable about science than Pynchon. By contrast, such disenchantment is not the case in Latin American or French fiction, and it is instructive to compare Pynchon's paranoid vision of science, and the society engendered by science and technology, with the viewpoint of a Latin American. Science in the New World can receive quite different treatments. For example, in probably the most widely read work by a Latin American writer, *Cien años de soledad* (1967, *One Hundred Years of Solitude*), García Márquez plays with the magical enchantments of science. In the novel the origins of the city of Macondo are bound up with knowledge, and its characters are concerned with questions of science, for one must have knowledge to overcome that solitude known as history. This point invites a comparison of García Márquez's reading of history as erasure with Pynchon's vision of history conceived as the apocalypse that science is always about to unleash.

García Márquez does not see knowledge or science at the origins of destruction wrought by history. Knowledge is at the origins of civilization, at least as represented by the founding of the city of Macondo. In Macondo magic and science are not fully sorted out, but the figure of Melquíades, the roving gypsy, suggests that the origins of science lie in the wanderings of shaman-like figures whose quasi-sacred function is the dissemination of knowledge. Moreover, the patriarch of Macondo, José Arcadio Buendía, is an epistemic quester. He is at once reminiscent of Balzac's seeker for the absolute in *La Recherche de l'absolu* and a positivist for whom the only proof of God's existence will be his image on a daguerreotype. The presentation of a magus and a scientist as the founders of the civic order of Macondo points out, admittedly with great ironic reserve, that knowledge lies at the heart of civilization. By contrast with Pynchon, there is no paranoia here, no fear of knowledge. It is the abuse of power, not knowledge, that creates the nightmares of Macondo. Science can know everything, or as the novel puts it concisely, "todo se sabe"—everything is known. But the fact that everything can be known is of little import in a world dominated by brute power. In fine, Pynchon's mad conspiracies, produced perhaps by some hostile combination of science and power, or perhaps simply by demented forces out of control, is foreign to Macondo's world, in which knowledge is integrated, albeit helplessly, into the complexities of civilization and its relentless demise.

One Hundred Years of Solitude provides a remarkable example of epistemic experimentation testing an understanding of history. Knowledge in Macondo is situated in a series of relativistic frameworks. To no avail, alas, the past is known in the future, and the future can be known in the past. Or, viewed from another framework, the novel unfolds with a linearity punctuated by the future. This linearity unfolds in cycles, with the past and the future chasing each other in eternal repetition. However, the wheel of time is running down, for García Márquez and his magi know, with Einstein, that thermodynamics operates in every framework. Entropy characterizes all histories and is the limit of knowledge. For instance, the magician, Pilar Ternera, has knowledge of what the future holds for other characters, though what she knows will be causally determined by entropic loss: "There was no mystery in the heart of a member of the Buendía family that was impenetrable to her, because a century of cards and experience had taught her that the story/history [historia] of the family was a mechanism of irreparable repetitions, a turning wheel that would have continued turning for all eternity, were it not for the progressive and irremediable wearing down of the axle."[5] Her revelation of the future is situated before the incestuous rape through which the penultimate Aureliano engenders the final Buendía, finally born with the pig's tale that has been foreseen from the beginning. Einsteinian temporal relativity and tragic knowledge are conjoined when Aureliano discovers that his future destiny has been known in some past framework, the past found in the shaman scientist's texts: upon looking at them, "then he knew that in the parchment texts of Melquíades was written his destiny" (493).

The future, in the past, is written in parchments in Sanskrit. Destiny is encoded as the Borgesian encyclopedia of all that exists. To the infinite number of events to be known correspond the infinite number of frameworks from which they can be known: the total encyclopedia. This encyclopedia contrasts with the arbitrary nature of the representation of things in time. There are conventional times and conventional orders, but there can also be the sequences

5. Gabriel García Marquéz, *Cien años de soledad,* 471. Hereafter cited parenthetically in the text.

in time when all is known, or the simultaneity of all things can be seen from the framework granted by absolute knowledge, or from the encyclopedic shaman's viewpoint: "Melquíades had not arranged facts according to the conventional time of men, but rather had concentrated in a century daily events so that all coexisted in an instant" (494). This instant could be taken to be the instant of simultaneity held within the novel itself, within the simultaneous totality of its pages of representation, which grant readers the possibility to hold a century in their hand as an immense encyclopedia in which past, present, and future are instantaneously contained in one framework, though the reader must choose to view them unfolding in the order selected for reading.

The reader enters *One Hundred Years of Solitude* as into an encyclopedia proposing knowledge of a forgotten world that is nonetheless a historical world. The useless fullness of this knowledge contrasts vividly with the way that *Gravity's Rainbow* predicts the destruction of all knowledge when, at the novel's end, a V-2 rocket—the emblematic creation of advanced scientific culture—descends toward the cinema in which the readers have been watching the novel and its display of scientific prowess called World War II. However, Pynchon's scientific knowledge is madness created by science, whereas in Macondo science tries to work against the erasure by oblivion that has been, or will be, the fate of the inhabitants of Macondo, that great synecdoche of Latin American and, indeed, world history that García Márquez created in a novel that wants to remember the future. In fine, both Pynchon and García Márquez write epistemic works concerned with what science can achieve in the historical world. Both novels are pessimistic in the extreme—in this regard they can both be considered disabused demonstrations of the impossibility of modernist revelation—but they grant quite different roles to science in the unfolding of historical catastrophes. The Latin American writer finds an alliance with science in the attempt to shore up the world against its inevitable fall at the hands of obscure forces of historical degradation, while the North American finds complicity between science and the forces, perceived in paranoia, that rage out of control.

The paranoia and distrust of science often reigning north of the Rio Grande contrasts strikingly with the ludic sense of knowledge as a game, which one finds in many French, Italian, and Latin American writers. It is difficult to think of any North American writer comparable, for example, to Julio Cortázar, a compatriot of Borges who preferred to live in Queneau and Robbe-Grillet's Paris. Cortázar's works often resemble epistemic games in which the rules of the game are placed in the foreground, stressing the equal arbitrariness of the rules for science, literature, and knowledge. (I take this to be one of the most felicitous developments of modernism that postmodern writers have made.) In some of his short stories, moreover, a sense of the conventional limits of knowledge is violated by terrible and comic transgressions that are among the most successful and fantastic thought experiments in modern fiction. These experiments are matched by his novels that play with the combinatory possibilities of fiction, ironically revealing the stochastic processes that science finds at work throughout nature. Stochastic ordering can resemble play, as all children know and as the reader should experience in following Cortázar's plan for permutations of events in *Rayuela* (1963, *Hopscotch*), a novel that proposes alternative reading orders for its chapters. If *Hopscotch* is read as a conventionally printed book, it proposes a linear order, mimicking a causal relationship. If read according to an alternative order given by instructions in the text, the novel presents patterns representing a simultaneity of action, or so says a critic like Jean Franco.[6] If one has some doubts about the possibility of actually experiencing simultaneity—as opposed to recognizing it as a logical possibility—then one might prefer to say that in *Hopscotch* Cortázar creates a sense of the openness of unfolding experience that precedes any explanation which pins a causal model on the experience. From this belief that everything is underdetermined emerges an existentialism looking upon every determination as a ludic choice; in short, all is play. And so, playfully proposing a way to translate indeterminacy into a literary procedure, Cortázar finally tells his readers to read the chapters in any order they please. With this final game rule, he pays ironic homage to the principle of the aleatory ordering of events and processes that science uses in many theoretical modelings.

In his play with indeterminacy Cortázar uses scientific models, with no disenchantment, to enlarge the compass of literary epistemology. Pursued with the unflappable logic of a Borges, Cortázar's experimentation often leads to comic disjunctures worthy of Kafka, among the most unsettling in postmodern literature, as for example in the stories in *Fin del juego* (1956, some of which are found in *"The End of the Game" and Other Stories*). A thought experiment undertaken in the story "Axolotl" plays, for instance, with the epistemological requirements of natural history. In "Axolotl" an observer ends up embodied in the object of his observation, a salamander kept in a tank in a natural history

6. Franco, *An Introduction to Spanish-American Literature,* 327.

museum. The plausibility of the story—and it has an unsettling plausibility—is due to the way the thought experiment respects the basic conventions of science by literally embodying them. If, with Mach and other positivists, the writer begins with the axiom that the observer's mind is the locus for those relations called knowledge, then what is more logical than an experiment in which the observer should find himself identified with the observed—and thus replace the observed in the tank that has been the locus for observation? Knowledge is a mental phenomenon that positivists placed in the mind, wherein, experimentally, may live galaxies and nematodes in ludic coexistence, as Cortázar demonstrates with the deadpan objectivity of a scientist who finds himself to be the ultimate locus of knowledge and thus comes to live underwater in a tank. Rigorous positivism leads to the fantastic.

Return to Vienna

Latin American fictions do not suggest reasons for the development of the suspicion toward science that seems to be a general part of the postmodern climate in German-speaking regions as well as in the Anglo-Saxon lands. To explore this aspect of postmodernity and to develop an argument about the ongoing influence of positivism in contemporary literature, I want to conclude by looking at several Austrian writers who bring us back to where I began this study: Musil and Mach's Vienna. Austrian writers are aware that they are the inheritors of a cultural tradition in which science has been at the center of all inquiry, but it is also a tradition in which science has been historically tainted by ideological corruption. These writers cannot forget the horrible fact that many scientists, in Austria as well as in Germany, collaborated with National Socialism after it imposed its research agendas on scientific institutes and universities. The Nazi debacle meant that progressive writers in both Germany and Austria, after World War II, confronted the task of explaining to themselves how an advanced culture, distinguished in art, philosophy, and science, could collapse into barbarism. They were well aware, moreover, that scientists voluntarily participated in criminal collaboration with the regime by, for example, carrying out for it immoral experimentation on human subjects. These writers were also critically aware that, after the war, the reemergence of liberal values coincided with a desire to forget the recent past. A few writers—hardly a majority—wanted to resist the outbreak of cultural amnesia.

Immediately after the war, at that "zero hour" when every aspect of German culture had to be put in question, it was mainly a few German writers, and not scientists, who felt morally compelled to deal with history and with ideology. A major example in Germany was the *Gruppe 47*, an association to which belonged future Nobel laureates Günter Grass and Heinrich Böll, major German writers like Uwe Johnson and Siegfried Lenz, well-known Austrian women writers like Ilse Aichinger and Ingeborg Bachmann, as well as many other lesser writers who have been little read outside of Germany and Austria.[7] These German-language writers by and large refrained from directly confronting science, per-haps because they felt deceived by it, for writers in Germany faced a scientific establishment that did not want to recognize its complicity with barbarism. (It is striking that, as I write, it is still a matter of debate as to what was Heisen-berg's role in the German war effort, or, with regard to research institutes, what exactly was the support they gave to the Nazis.)[8] The dismal fact that many scientists, doctors, and professors actively worked to achieve Nazi goals probably explains why writers in Germany have generally refrained from cele-bratory fictions drawing upon science, such as one finds in Queneau, Borges, Cortázar, or Calvino. Disenchantment with science was widespread in Germany once the Enlightenment ideal associating freedom, knowledge, and progress seemed to have been tarnished beyond hope.

The most succinct description of postwar German fiction is that for several decades it has oscillated between the poles of social realism, with a muted com-mitment to political praxis, and the desire to withdraw from politics and to explore an inner self, in novels expressing the "neue Innerlichkeit" or the "new subjectivity." In the nineties, however, the success of a work like Bernard Schlink's *Der Vorleser* (1995, *The Reader*), with its depiction of an ordinary Ger-man woman's work in the concentration camps, was undoubtedly a sign that the new generation of Germans could directly confront the Nazi past—as was Grass's willingness to reverse the question of guilt and to portray innocent Germans as victims of the war in his controversial novel *Im Krebsgang* (2002, *Crabwalk*).

Progressive Austrian novelists, on the other hand, live in a society that has been even less willing than German society to face its history—and this to the present moment. In contrast with their German counterparts, a number of

7. See the *Almanach der Gruppe 47, 1947–1962*, edited by founder Hans Werner Richter.
8. For a recent overview of research institutes and Nazis, see Marco Finetti, "Fertile Ground for Politics."

Austrian writers have, however, chosen to deal with the epistemic possibilities of literature through a direct, critical confrontation with science. In this regard Austrians have contributed to the postmodern suspicion of science by looking upon it as a force for repression or by casting it in the role of an ideological enemy. In other words the disenchantment with science in Germany that resulted in its neglect by writers has led some Austrian writers to engage in a critique of science. In large measure, one can attribute the literary critique of science in Austria to writers who want to confront the Austrian failure to come to grips with its past. In fact, as Donald G. Daviau has pointed out, many Austrians felt that they did not need to wrestle with the problem of historical guilt, as has been the case in the Federal Republic, since Austrians were absolved by the Allied governments for any responsibility of the war.[9] This type of thinking leads to the kind of dubious rationalization of modern Austrian history undertaken when a scholar like Hans Wolfschütz claims that it is actually because of the Nazi annexation that Austrians learned to appreciate republican values and, hence, did not need to confront the "tabula rasa" that German writers such as those in *Gruppe 47* faced.[10] Confronting a general lack of intellectual honesty and ethical will, progressive Austrian literary intellectuals have seemingly made a critique of science into a springboard for a critique of Austrian culture. Theirs is a postmodernity with the greatest ethical ambitions. These ambitions have been responsible, for example, for the establishment of publishing collectives in the cities of Graz and Salzburg, which have given writers the possibility to document the oppression of minorities, including gypsies, and to examine the ongoing political dangers created by a climate in which racism and xenophobic nationalism flourish.[11]

I want to stress the fact that Austrian writers have had to deal with a society in which members of the educated classes could pretend that they had been forced to be barbarians. The widespread myth of Austrian innocence has fostered an atmosphere in which, in response, a critique of ideology appears to be a necessity. Because Austria is a country where science has traditionally played

9. Daviau, ed., *Major Figures of Contemporary Austrian Literature,* 4.

10. Wolfschütz, "The Emergence and Development of the Second Republic," in Alan Best and Hans Wolfschütz, eds., *Modern Austrian Writing: Literature and Society after 1945,* 5.

11. An example of this work can be found in the book *Sichten und Vernichten: Von der Kontinuität der Gewalt,* a collection of essays documenting the camps and the oppression of minorities published by the Grazer Autorenversammlung and the Salzburger Autorengruppe (1994).

a central role in all cultural questions, the critique of ideology has inevitably led to the conclusion that science must be questioned, particularly the scientists' belief in the beneficent neutrality of cultural institutions dedicated to knowledge. However, the critique that aims at the cultural matrix in which the critique itself is embedded runs the risk of becoming an activity that turns back against itself. The suicidal dangers of this kind of dialectic are clear, in Austria, when the intellectual foundations for the critique itself risk being subverted.

This dialectic threatening intellectual suicide arises in the historical context in which originated the very idea that one could undertake a critique of language, philosophy, and science as interrelating domains. It was in this "liberal Empire," which Musil satirized for its own oxymoronic existence, that began a fundamental critique of modernity in the work of the same thinkers who played a major role in founding modernity: Boltzmann, Mach, Musil, Freud, Carnap, Kafka, Rilke, Kraus, Mauthner, Schrödinger, Schlick, and the many others who lived in and around a cultural space whose center was Wittgenstein's Vienna.[12] They developed a modernity that, in suspicion of unfounded epistemic claims, promoted a fundamental self-critique of representation, which is to say, in various ways a critique of the languages of science, philosophy, and literature. If Austrian writers have subsequently been active in the quintessentially postmodern attempt to remove science from the position of epistemic arbitrator, it is in part because they inherited this position from a tradition that includes Mach, Mauthner, and Musil. It is this tradition of critique that was renewed in the postwar's suspicion about science's complicity with various forms of repression, and it is this tradition, at times intensified to the point of self-destruction, that exemplifies what many mean by postmodern.

Austrian Postmodernism

Few North American writers today have received an advanced education in science. By contrast, the attack on science in Austrian literature has often been undertaken by writers who have been educated as scientists. In fact, it is a salient fact that many Austrian writers, from modernists like Musil

---

12. See in this regard Allan Janik and Stephen Toulmin, *Wittgenstein's Vienna*, 254; see also Carl E. Schorske, *Fin de Siècle Vienna: Politics and Culture.*

and Canetti to contemporaries like Gerhard Roth and Helmuth Eisendle, have also been educated as scientists and doctors. Thus I turn first to Helmuth Eisendle, because in his fictions he is explicitly concerned with science as representation. Educated in psychology and biology, living science from within, Eisendle is emblematic of postmodern writers who have turned to literature explicitly to contest the science enshrined in official culture. Recalling the psychologist at work in Musil, Eisendle writes fiction that embodies the double bind involved in trying to critique a science that offers knowledge of the mind that would critique it. Moreover, Eisendle's work shows that these dilemmas are permeated by positivism's legacy, especially his works written in the seventies like *Jenseits der Vernunft oder Gespräche uber den menschlichen Verstand* [1976, Beyond reason or conversations about human understanding] and *Exil oder Der braune salon* [1977, Exile or the brown salon]. In these novels Eisendle has made inquiry into the mind, informed by despair about science, the means of exploring the paradoxical double bind of a self-critique.

To make this critique Eisendle accepts the postmodern axiom that the self is dependent upon language for its existence. Whether taken from Wittgenstein, Mach, Heidegger, or the French structuralists, this axiom about language has been a keystone idea for the postmodern critique of a belief in the autonomy of self. It is also an axiom whose roots are found as much in Viennese positivism as anywhere else, especially in positivism's critique of the metaphysical illusions fostered by the abuse of language. The postmodern view that language has the power to constitute the self is accompanied by a comparable distrust of the deceptions that language may work—among which that metaphysical construct, the self, would be a prime example. This distrust of language entails an attitude of suspicion toward representation, since postmoderns usually believe all representation needs language for semantic mediation. Whence the axiom: no language, no meaning. The suspicion of language demands strategies, using language nonetheless, for making all means of representation problematic, since the first task of the critique is to show up the deceptive nature of language involved in the critique itself.

In Eisendle's two novels of the seventies, one such strategy is embodied in his creation of characters who, like Musil's Ulrich, are fictional epistemologists. In the novel *Jenseits der Vernunft,* the characters play at being "guests of reality." They are guests of a realm in which it appears that science and its language have the power to create reality—reality being a metaphysical construct that the characters comment on with all the distance of visiting observers who believe that language is foisting the construct upon them. The narrative is playfully interrogative and ironic, reminiscent of the type of experiment found in Diderot's dialogues probing Enlightenment science and rationality. Or with Wittgenstein in mind, one might say that the characters play at ironic alienation from the language they use. This is a postmodern language game, a ludic activity whose rule is to distrust the rule of the game. The ludic nature of this fictional language game is also portrayed in the billiards played by the epistemologists in Eisendle's novel "Exile or the Brown Salon." This novel is perhaps the epitome of the ludic novel of language games in which epistemic beliefs are demonstrated to be semantic constructs. The novel presents a mechanical Marxist, a mystical savant, and an enthusiast of the scientific method who shoot ideas at each other as they take turns at the billiard table. The result is an experimental demonstration of the implicit axiom that ideas and theories are like billiard balls: they move in response to the pressure applied, they fasten to reality but rarely, and they serve as much to fill up the void as to offer purchase on anything other than themselves. In this novel playing at exile from language, Eisendle is a ludic successor to Diderot, Queneau, and Borges.

To get a sense of the changes that have taken place in the landscape of fiction in the recent past, one can pass over the twenty years since Eisendle published "Exile or the Brown Salon" in 1977 and turn to a novel he published in the nineties, *Der Egoist* (1996). In this novel Eisendle's narrator now bears only a very distant resemblance to Musil's psychologist in *Man without Qualities*. Eisendle's narrator still wants to study feeling, but two decades have apparently convinced Eisendle that the power of language to create a world is little short of omnipotent—and that any language has this capacity, not only the constructs of philosophy or science, and especially the language of pop culture. Disenchantment with science on Eisendle's part means that the difference between his early novels and this later one is the difference between Diderot and Warhol. Eisendle's focusing on pop culture is typical of much fiction and academic theory in the late twentieth century, and not just in America. In Austrian as well as North American fictions, pop culture and theory have joined hands in a strange marriage of opposites, giving rise, on the one hand, to the type of specialist theorist who, in Don DeLillo's novel *White Noise,* reads nothing but the texts written on cereal boxes; and, on the other hand, an intellectual novelist like Eisendle who quotes gangster fiction in a critique of contemporary ideology. One is not sure where parody begins or ends.

Theory invests the world of pop, or vice versa, when in Eisendle's novel *Der Egoist* the narrator hypothesizes that feeling cannot be detached from the associations that call forth feeling. For an experimental investigation, the application of theory obliges the use of all manner of preexisting modes of pop representation with which feeling is associated. The narrative experiment results in a disparate collage in which Eisendle narrates a love story, of sorts, by inserting such things as long quotations from a gangster novel that his protagonist, the inquisitive egoist, is reading. Literal quotations in *Der Egoist* of a presumably fictional text of pop culture eliminates the type of ludic irony that Eisendle used in his earlier experiments, with their self-questioning dimension. Nonetheless, the hyperbole and incongruities that characterize the narration imply a self-conscious dimension, what one might call deadpan postmodern irony. This hyperbole offers no intellectual irony, no self-reflexive questioning, but simply points out in parody the incongruous existence of the dominance of pop. It seems reasonable to interpret Eisendle's shift in rhetorical mode to signify a certain despair about contemporary culture—but that is not certain.

The rise of pop in fiction has a history. Direct reflections of popular culture are found throughout Joyce's *Ulysses,* often comically embodied in Bloom's consciousness, and parts of it resemble a parodistic catalog of the quotidian. Musil satirizes pop culture when, for example, Ulrich meditates, with ironic revulsion, upon the determinations of feeling already exerted by mass culture in 1913: a boxer or a racehorse are objects to be emulated and, as such, are pop determinants of values and attitudes. American modernists like Dos Passos offer examples in their collages, and, in the next generation of Americans, writers like Barth and Barthelme use pop modes with explicit irony and satire, which is to say, the rhetoric used by the work's implied author dominates the icons and myths of popular culture. By contrast, recent pop representation, as in Eisendle's *Der Egoist,* functions much like the play with pop icons found in artists like Lichtenstein or Warhol. Even if the reader supposes that there is some ironic distance vis-à-vis the pop representations imitated in the novel, that irony finally pays homage to the power of pop. Perhaps this is a lesson that the current generation has taken from Roland Barthes's *Mythologies,* with its demonstration of the power of pop myth to recuperate all meanings.

In any case Eisendle's novel pointedly shows that the triumph of pop follows, experimentally as it were, from the postmodern axiom that feelings are determined by representations: if all we have are pop representations, then the logical implication is that all we have are pop feelings. The writer is obliged accordingly to record what pop culture imposes upon (pop) consciousness. In this experiment, narration resembles a theoretical tautology. What makes *Der Egoist* an interesting novel is the skepticism that the narrative intelligence manages to exhibit about the very psychological science whose consequences he works out. For, in accepting that there are no autonomous modes of representation, Eisendle's narrator also accepts that there are no foundations to knowledge. This typical postmodern skepticism about the foundations of knowledge blocks the narrator, since he has no choice but to use arbitrarily accepted codes and axioms as surrogates for the "true" knowledge that science once promised. The arbitrary reigns supreme, then, as Eisendle skips about, changing narrative modes, which include, in addition to a gangster novel, a collage of meditations about the novel in the making and a campy dialogue between the heart and the head. These contrasting modes, joining Pascal and Wittgenstein, logically follow from the belief that all models are arbitrary. With no grounds for making claims to knowledge, the narrating self must consider that even its own status is at best quasi-mythical, for it exists simply because language functions. Its status is not unlike that of the self Mach postulated, with greater tranquility, as a fiction necessary for observing relationships in the world. However, Eisendle, jettisoning the epistemological necessity for the self, finds the self at best to be a postulate allowing one to decipher gangster tales.

Postmoderns like Eisendle take a belief in the power of language to be axiomatic; they believe that language invests the world with qualities that could not exist without language. Let us look further at this belief. Logically and empirically, it is self-evident that in many senses there are things in the world that have not always existed and that language changed when these things came into historical existence. Among these are not only portentous things such as law, money, or love, but also, more trivially, Potter's tinned meat, toilet paper or newspaper substitutes theretofore, and cereal boxes. (Chaucer had none of the latter in his vocabulary, though all of the former.) However, this insight about the historical becoming of language is often the grounds for an illusory historicism, especially when the relation of language and world is taken to offer a statement of cause and effect. Quite simply, it is not at all clear, obvious, or proved in any sense that language confers existence on anything. If expressed as a causal statement to the effect that language is the cause of the existence of something, this postmodern belief in the ontological power of language is certainly dubious. One might even suspect that it is an updating of the biblical metaphysics about the power of logos.

Alogically postmodern in this regard, Eisendle's theoretical doubts about everything do not entail doubting the idea that language has ontological power. Language plays a causal role in *Der Egoist* when the egoist falls in love, since love exists only because the concept "love" exists and thereby allows, or obliges, him to construct his feelings. The pop narrator becomes on occasion a postmodern theorist:

> In what's spoken and what's written a secret imperative determines perception in the other. Certainly a selective perception. And out of this selection of things we produce reality [stellen wir die, ja, die Wirklichkeit her]. That is the case with someone who narrates something, or has written something out, or represents something. And the closer is the identification with what is said, or written, or reproduced, the more real it is, and the more we believe in it or at least in its meaning. Only what has meaning is reality [Nur das Bedeutende ist die Wirklichkeit.].[13]

What is remarkable here, as in much contemporary fiction reflecting theory, is that the writer contesting knowledge accepts a theoretical point of view. Perception is described in terms of a law of selective codes, and this seems to be underwritten by a kind of Hegelian belief in the "rationality" of the real, since meaning is the guarantor of the real. Yet this quasi-scientific viewpoint is then turned around, in despair or paranoia, to deny validity to science, since the apparently arbitrary nature of the encoding operation is taken to mean that all truth is arbitrary. Finally, in parodying the autonomous "code" of gangster fiction, *Der Egoist* shows it to be absurd while having all the force of an absolute, admitting no self-reflexive doubt. Pop reigns supreme while science cuts its own throat.

In all this deadpan, Eisendle is, like Joyce and Kafka, a notable epistemic parodist. I note in this regard that at the same time he wrote his seventies novel "Exile," he also produced, in 1978, a photo-novel, *Daimon und Veranda oder Gespräche eines Mädchens vor dem Tode,* a "conversation of a maiden before death" whose images parody pop narration by using photographs of Charcot's female hysterics from the nineteenth century. One century's science becomes the next century's joke. Twenty years later Eisendle's love of parody remains apparent in *Abendsport. Zweimal: Minutentexte* (1998), a small volume of "minute texts" that offer a dictionary of some basic pop concepts and popular clichés, which is

---

13. Eisendle, *Der Egoist,* 121. Hereafter cited parenthetically in the text.

to say, essentially a lexicon of stupidity, or a codification of the antiknowledge that has fascinated moderns ever since Flaubert began an exploration of it in his dictionary of received ideas.

Distrusting science, embracing the tyranny of pop, Eisendle is emblematic of many writers who came to maturity in the latter part of the twentieth century. Austrian writers may be contrasted with their American counterparts in that, distrusting science, they have also been educated to rely upon it. They are crucially aware that they have not been able to resolve the dilemmas brought about by their difficult belief that all forms of representation are autonomous and thus should be in some sense justified by their coherence. However, the belief in the autonomous status of discourse seems difficult to reconcile with the postmodern belief that these forms are arbitrary creations lacking foundations— a scandal Musil pointed out long ago. This has become an essential problem for postmodernity. On the one hand, postmodern belief proposes that, as Eisendle's narrator declares, people live in a "reality" that in some sense is created by concepts. Consciousness is tributary to ideas or language—a belief often buttressed, for example, by Thomas Kuhn's idea that each era's scientists live in a different world from their forebears because they experience it through different paradigms. On the other hand, if no concepts or representations are grounded in anything other than their own gratuitous autonomy, then it seems plausible to believe that one can change "reality" as rapidly as a psychotic inventing a new world every few days, or a child playing with a comic book and dreaming of his or, more rarely, her Batmobile. Indeed, viewed from this perspective, postmodern life does appear to be a series of comic book inventions viewed on a universal television screen—and then the ideas of a postmodern theorist like Jean Baudrillard, as illustrated by a novelist like Eisendle, almost make sense, for it would appear that media, madness, and social reality are conjoined. I say "almost," for probably most of us do not have a psychotic identity, nor do we inhabit the world of postmodern theory.

It is often suggested that many of us inhabit the universe dreamed of by positivism. This may also be questionable, but Austrian fiction demonstrates, as I suggested earlier, something that is usually overlooked in discussions of postmodernity, namely, that postmodern axioms about representation are either analogous to, or derivative from, early-twentieth-century positivism. The positivist self is a hypothetical vantage point for seeing the relations obtaining between representations, which means that the positivist self is a malleable construct having existence only in representation. The positivist self is thus presupposed by the self deconstructed by postmodern theory when it declares, following Heidegger, Derrida, or Foucault, that the self is something like a point in a linguistic space. The rationalist humanist is obliged then to ask what one should make of this reduction of self first undertaken by positivism and then by the postmodern theory that usually is hostile to positivism? If in fact the postmodern rejection of the humanist self depends upon the axioms that positivism propagated as part of the modern scientific worldview, then we see a curious complicity between two modes of thought usually considered antagonistic. Perhaps one may conclude that postmoderns are ignorant of their own genealogy, to use a Nietzschean notion they favor; or that at the very least they maintain an ambivalent relation with the positivism that they take to be the hallmark of scientific thought. But, given this complicity, the skeptic of postmodern relativism can deduce that postmodern theory is largely a negative mirror image of positivism. The self is a metaphysical illusion, once constructed by language, now by media images.

Though an illusion, the postmodern self, as portrayed in much fiction, is inundated by data that it cannot control. This situation throws light on another dominant theme of fiction since World War II: the fear of losing control of a self that exists only as a function of the sense data pouring in upon it from an exterior world. The prevalence of this fear is seen in much postwar fiction trading in paranoia. The implosion of sense data forces the self to try to make sense of things by relating everything to everything—but nothing can make sense of the plethora of relations generated by the perceptual flow of bombarding sense data. Meaning is everywhere, and hence nowhere. Well-known Austrians like Peter Handke or Thomas Bernhard, or Americans like Thomas Pynchon and many of the American metafiction writers, provide examples of fictions based on this model of floating insanity. Another Austrian writer deserving an international audience, Gerhard Roth, has also written texts illustrating the science, or antiscience, of literature experimenting with the madness within. Roth's early work portrays with deadpan irony the self in a world in which insanity is an almost normal condition when the illusive self loses its moorings. Madness then appears to be the normal abnormal state.

Science is almost always involved in any depiction of madness. Even during the era of antipsychiatry and its utopian celebration of madness, any description of madness had to be predicated upon a scientific model. Neither Foucault nor Deleuze, nor Cooper nor Laing, could undo the fact that, if there is to be a distinction between madness and nonmadness, there must be criteria taken from the side of nonmadness; there must be minimally a theoretical standard for madness to exist, which contradicts any claim that all is madness. If all is madness, then nothing is. Experimental writing in madness must perforce be accompanied by an implicit diagnostic understanding that recognizes some criteria for madness—which, in the wake of Virginia Woolf, points up a problematic side of many postmodern attempts to use madness. A literary experiment in madness is obliged to contain signs that point beyond madness, which differentiates it from a really insane discourse. Truly insane literary texts do not often carry within them any metadiscourse commenting on their madness, as one sees, for example, in the poems written by schizophrenics in Leo Navratil's very influential anthology of insane poetry, *Schizophrenie und Sprache: Zur Psychologie der Dichtung*—to mention a book and a psychiatrist whom Gerhard Roth knows well.[14]

Contradictory attitudes toward science and madness are found in the ambivalence that characterizes the early work of Roth, who had been a medical student before becoming a full-time writer. In texts in the seventies, Roth wrote several fictions that seek experimentally to test the rationality found in the scientific epistemology that takes madness in charge. His texts question whether this rationality is grounded in something beyond the coherence of its own discourse. To this end Roth uses madness to frame the experimental model of a counter-discourse to science. Madness is an outcome when the literal application of scientific thought results, in effect, in unreason engendered by reason itself. With the lessons of positivism in mind, Roth undertakes a phenomenology of the truncated consciousness that results if one literally applies scientific theory to describe the mind. Playing with the phenomenal inside and the diagnostic outside of mad discourse, then, Roth derives madness from science's own axioms in, for example, fictions such as *Die autobiographie des albert einsteins* (1972, *The autobiography of albert einstein*) or *Der Wille zur Krankheit* [1973, The will to sickness]. In effect, these narrative texts challenge the scientific reduction of the self to a recorder of relations that positivists are wont to call laws. These texts lay down their challenge with zany representations of experience reduced to fragments, for fragments are the result of recordings of consciousness when it looks at itself as if it were the object of scientific observation.

---

14. Gerhard Roth had himself photographed with Navratil for a picture in Roth's book on Vienna, *Eine Reise in das Innere von Wien.*

The autobiography of albert einstein, marvelously translated by Malcolm Green, is an especially successful thought experiment working out the consequences of a positivist reduction. Einstein's "autobiography" is a series of fragmented descriptions with which Roth shows that the literal enactment of a positivist description of the self's interface with sensation replicates an insane state. It is not immediately clear that this insanity is necessarily a bad thing, for Roth is absolutely deadpan in this portrayal of madness from within. This contrasts notably with Woolf's portrayal of the misery of the insanity upon which medicine has no purchase. Moreover, at no point in the *autobiography* does Roth overtly contest the power of science to operate on consciousness. He even includes a disclaimer about rejecting scientific research, though he doubts that science can reduce human *Befindlichkeit* to a category system.[15] (*Befindlichkeit* is an erudite term, co-opted by Heidegger, to mean one's affective state of being in the world.) Rather, in offering a flat description of a protagonist who looks at his own mind functioning according to positivist epistemology, Roth dramatizes an incommensurable gap between theory and the mind to be explained by that theory. There is of course a perverse homage to science in that Roth's insane narrator writes an "autobiography" of himself as the world's most famous scientist. However, the protagonist and sometimes narrator called Einstein also claims to be Dostoyevsky—that famous engineer who gave up science for literature. The double reference points up that Roth has created in his Einstein something analogous to an insane scientist who, from his underground cellar—which is to say, buried in his own brain—writes mad notes for the scientific culture to which he belongs in his demented fashion. He is not unlike Dostoyevsky's narrator in *Notes from the Underground* who proclaims his potential madness as a victory of freedom over scientific determinism.

Roth's narrator begins his "autobiography" of Einstein where a developmental biologist would begin, with a description of the embryonic development of the scientist's brain, starting with the moment of insemination and following it through gestation, so that at four weeks of uterine age the hero has the following shape: "his neck was not yet present. the ectoderm at the sides of the head bulged forward as a result of the optic vessels. in front of the eye region lay the nasal fossa, visible behind it were the four pharyngeal arches" (9). The

---

15. Gerhard Roth, *The autobiography of albert einstein,* trans. Malcolm Green, 61. Hereafter cited parenthetically in the text.

"autobiography" willfully confuses realms of discourse, for a description of embryological development is not, I suppose, what we usually ask of a life history, not even of a scientist, though from the viewpoint of developmental psychology as well as physiology, this stage is certainly an essential part of a life history. The deliberate confusion of literary and scientific discourse prefaces the narrator's literal acceptance of the proposition that mind is to be identified with the organ called the brain. This is a materialist proposition that weighs upon the narrator for the rest of the autobiography, because it obliges him to imagine what is happening to his brain cells as he goes about gathering sensations. (A comparable literalization of the materialist proposition about mind is found in Roth's "The Will to Sickness," in which the protagonist is depicted as a chemical machine.) Reiterated confusion of realms of discourse can be a form of insanity, and the identification of embryology with biography is one of the funnier forms of madness found in postwar fiction. The comic intent is also, undoubtedly, to challenge neurology's reduction of mind to brain. Roth's disclaimer about research notwithstanding, his scientific narrator's insane observations cast doubt upon finding any knowledge simply through exact replication of data.

Exact observation founders on a world overflowing with sensations, and any attempt at observation is submerged in a hyperbolic overflow of perceptions. However, like a properly positivist scientist, the narrator claims to bring about a synthetic reality in his head. Synthesis in this case appears to mean the amalgamation of the most disparate perceptions that the world offers. The result is a jumble, or a disjunction of perceptions symptomatic of madness. This disjunction may also be symptomatic of the postmodern condition, for the self that lives out its autobiography in these pages resembles an observer who is, to use poststructuralist terminology, ruefully decentered. Data inundate him: "while my ego resembles an insect twitching back and forth in empty space, whose motion the eye vainly tries to take in, at the same time walking sticks shoes taxi cabs people houses trees etc. wander, no *flow,* through my cerebrum ..." (43). Like Mach's ideal positivist, einstein's ego has no visual space of its own; it exists by grasping data and attempting to relate them, and so, in this pursuit, the narrator spends his time "injecting" himself with reality, with the flow of garbage and dying birds that makes up a world in which the sometime first-person narrator can transform detritus into knowledge. In this vein einstein, not surprisingly, also gives lectures on all that can be known, such as "isthmuses, pornographic photographs and arithmetic" (79).

The listing of things in consciousness takes the form of a listing of words, and language is, of course, another obligatory subject. Roth is well aware that, according to some theorists of physiology, evolutionary biology, and linguistics, language is a "natural" function like any other organic function, evolutionary in origin, and genetically determined in its acquisition. This viewpoint, consonant with Piaget and Chomsky, is not necessarily a postmodern viewpoint, and Roth's einstein is not necessarily, on the surface at least, a postmodern. Rather like a positivist neurologist, einstein finds language localized on his brain: "for days on end i walked through clouds of word vapour, or rather i transpired, or masturbated, sentences. word eczemas broke out all over my inflamed cerebral membranes" (53). Working out implications of a positivist physiology, the narrator describes words as so many secretions—sweat, ejaculate, or perhaps pus—subject to pathologies like the products of any other physiological function. This satire turns on what one might call physiological introspection: the scientist becomes an observer of his own brain, watching it generate the very sentences that describe it watching itself. It is as if a neurologist were sticking probes in his brain to localize the region in which the brain tells itself to stick probes into the region. Roth's novel focuses, with telling satire, on the double bind of the mind critiquing the mind knowing mind—though the demented loop produced here is rather more from within science itself, and less by the binds created by structuralist theories of language.

Roth's einstein undergoes a series of stages in the development in his perceptions. First he is a voyeur walking the streets—the voyeur being another parodistic image of the scientist as observer. But the novel's narrator also believes that he is being observed, the reverse side of the epistemological coin, in which the universal observation characterizing science becomes, in inversion, universal paranoia. And in the main section of the novel einstein makes a promenade through the cerebrum, in which the identification of brain and mind means that his walk is a stroll through a shower of sense data that the world pours down upon the brain. Finally, a medical certificate says that the narrator died of a nosebleed. With this, the autobiographical fiction delivers up an entire life lived out as a consistent demonstration of scientific theory, from embryo to corpse, the latter state being the inevitable end of an organism subject to a complete scientific study, if not the usual end of an autobiography.

Roth's subversive ploy is to make madness the center of science, while knowing full well that one must use science to know madness. In its parody of epistemic fiction, the work thus experimentally effects a most vicious and, at times, comic circle. One might be tempted to call this circle the postmodern turn, if, like Roth, one were not aware that the reduction of epistemic fiction to a discourse in madness has a relatively long history, inaugurated for modernity by Swift in his portrayal of the insanity involved in Cartesian physics and philosophy, and going through Pynchon and Vonnegut. Roth's experiment is related to Swiftian parody, drawing upon the topos of the madness of knowledge. This topos presides over the strategies found in later writers who have used madness in thought experiments to test the dominance of rationality over irrationality, especially the works by Diderot and Hoffmann. Virginia Woolf offers a modernist development of this motif. Joyce's development of pop parody may have provided Roth with his rhetorical tools for constructing consciousness full of everything.

However, the most important antecedent for Roth's confrontation of science and literature is the thought experiment Dostoyevsky proposes in *Notes from the Underground*. In his thought experiment, Dostoyevsky's narrator accepts the possibility of applying scientific thought to all domains, including himself; but then he predicts, with a patina of logical necessity, that, for every prediction of his behavior made by scientific law, he will do something different from what the law forecasts. And if this negative prediction about predictions is not enough to demonstrate that the mind that wants to reduce itself to an expression of law is caught in contradiction, Dostoyevsky's narrator then taunts his rationalist reader with a prediction that cannot be tabulated by any formalism: "If you say that all this, the chaos and the darkness and cursing, could also be reduced to tables, so that the mere possibility of taking it into account beforehand would put a stop to it, and reason would still hold sway—in that case men would deliberately go mad, so as not to possess reason, and thus still get their own way!"[16] Dostoyevsky's thought experiment, affirming human power freely to create chaos in a nondeterministic sense, is an important precursor to the postmodern fiction that challenges science to a logical duel.

Kafka's work reshapes this experiment in many parables to test the capacity of knowledge to rise to knowledge of its impossibility. Then variants on the strategy of pitting madness against science, against the restraints of reason symbolized by medical psychology, are found with increasing frequency, after Virginia Woolf, throughout European and American literature: in the North American Sylvia Plath's early short fictions as well as her poems, in the Austrian

16. Dostoyevsky, *Notes from the Underground/The Double*, 38.

Thomas Bernhard's narrations of medically induced paranoia, in the textual experiments in madness by French feminists like Emma Santos and Jeanne Hyvrard, or, more generally, in avant-garde attempts, after surrealism, to invent new forms of transrational consciousness through new forms of narrative logic. And it culminates in contemporary Austrian works such as those by Eisendle and Roth.

For its satirical elaboration of the duel between science and madness Roth's *autobiography of albert einstein* has a stellar place in recent literary experimentation. Roth's narrator seems to go deliberately mad, not by defying the law's power to predict, but by becoming literally the hyper-determinist imagined as the enemy in Dostoyevsky's thought experiment. Roth's critique is emblematic of texts—postmodern, if one likes—that turn the tables on the type of psychiatry Woolf portrayed in *Mrs. Dalloway,* psychiatry that gives the insane no voice. By giving voice to insanity, Roth's mad narrator implies in *the autobiography* that science should be reduced to silence. Whatever one may think of this satire of scientific reductionism, it is clear that the portrayal of madness in fiction obliges the rationalist mind to hesitate in a facile affirmation of its mastery of the world, and to contemplate the limits that circumscribe the mind in its attempt to grasp its own nature. The double bind may not be the universal description of madness that its promoters once claimed, but it certainly describes the drama of mind found in much fiction in the second part of the twentieth century.

Since the seventies Roth has changed his goals for his writing. Reflecting a general trend found in both European and American literature, he has turned away from experimental fiction. He now prefers to address directly the problem of Austrian silence about its past with a series of works called *Die Archive des Schweigens (The Archives of Silence/Silencing),* a series motivated by an explicit desire to challenge Austrian complacency through a recall of the Nazi past. This desire animates a work like *Die Geschichte der Dunkelheit: ein Bericht* (1991, *The Story of Darkness: A Report*). *The Story of Darkness* is a biographical report, put together by Roth, in which an aging Austrian Jew tells of life in Vienna under the Nazis. Roth solicited a narration and then edited it, as he said in an interview, to give the impression that the reader is encountering a series of snapshots in an imaginary photo album.[17] This work can be called a

---

17. Interview in Uwe Wittstock, ed., *Gerhard Roth: Materialien zu 'Die Archive des Schweigens,'* 93.

documentary novel taking the form of an autobiography in which a victim of history speaks directly about his life in the totalitarian state that drove him into exile. Roth's concern with history is political in the broadest sense. By assuming the primacy of the political, Roth may appear to have discarded the epistemological concerns he had as an experimental novelist. However, perhaps one should see in this turn to history a reverse side of the positivist coin: it manifests a belief that the direct empirical documentation of history is the only way to construct knowledge of the past. This work could be construed as an oblique affirmation of the Austrian scientific tradition. Moreover, the turn to history does not contradict the experiment with madness of the *autobiographie*. Rather it enlarges upon it with an investigation of the madness of the Nazi use and abuse of power. Madness inhabits many quarters.

Experimental fiction probably began to wane when the critique that it enacted became a conditioned response. Thomas Anz makes this observation specifically about the development of Roth's work by asserting that by the early nineties, the "critique of communication and a unmasking of the wiles of language" had become a moribund convention.[18] Anz maintains that in Austrian writing in general, and in Roth's in particular, the subversion of representation had become a received code. Experimental testing of axioms of knowledge was often interpreted as subversion, though this may not have always been the goal of the experiment. In any case, when subversion became a convention, writers faced a situation in which, as information theory would describe it, there is ease of communication because the code is well known and because the messages encoded do not depart from what is expected. When the code includes large redundancies, and when the message sent with it departs little from what is expected, little information is transmitted. Information exists in inverse proportion to expectation. In other words, repetition of the same experiment, achieving the same results, may have pedagogical value, but little else. Many French and American avant-garde "texts," metafictions, and fabulations of the sixties and seventies well illustrate this repetition of the same. Experimentation became in effect a codified genre, demonstrating the relation of inverse proportion between ease of comprehension and transmission of information. This continues to be a postmodern dilemma. Many representations of pop fall into the category of communication that predictably does not deviate from the

18. Anz, "Kommunikationskritik und Sprachentlarvung," in Wittstock, ed., *Gerhard Roth,* 228.

norm—that is the essence of pop—but this is also the case today of much of what now passes in the academy for postmodern critique. The codes are mastered, the communication is ritualized, and information is often minimal.

The pop collage and the paranoid text are not the only types of postmodern fiction to emerge after the relative demise of experimental modernism having epistemic ambitions. More numerous probably are the many postmodern minimalist fictions abounding in many national literatures. For example, in Germany and Austria, expressions like "new realism" and "new subjectivity" have been used to characterize fictions that turn their back on modernist ambitions. Whatever the realism of these texts, it is also true that madness often hovers on the edges of the deviate consciousness found in the anomie characterizing the "new subjectivity." This willfully minimalist German-language fiction offers, like many of its American counterparts, in fact a truncated realism that takes the description of elementary states of consciousness to be its primary goal. This reduced realism involves a shrinking of the scope of fiction, which is reduced to a hesitant narrative consciousness suspicious of the language that it must nonetheless speak. In its most radical form this fiction eventuates in the borderline madness of consciousness without mooring, characterized by a schizoid split between the center of narration and the language it is obliged to use. This fiction often embodies a double bind taking the form of using language to distrust the (distrustful) language the narrator must use. This is less a question of theory—though theory may lurk in the background—than a disbelief in anything other than immediate experience. Positivists and mystics are frequently united in this regard.

Examples of this truncated realism, at once positivist in range and near mystical in implication, are found in several novels by Peter Handke, probably the best-known Austrian novelist of the postwar period. Handke uses deadpan realism in portraying the consciousness of contemporary protagonists who learn to live with their sensations while they wonder, in laconic states bordering on anomie, if language has deformed what little they have experienced. Language seems incapable, for many of Handke's characters, of reaching the world. This short-circuiting of reference is the experience, for example, of Handke's semi-sane soccer player in *Die Angst des Tormanns beim Elfmeter* (1970, *The Goalie's Anxiety at the Penalty Kick*). The player's perceptions float in a consciousness alienated from the self-sustaining play of the meanings encoded in language, and so the player flounders as his consciousness is split between raw perception and the web of meanings that language foists upon him. Facing borderline paranoia, he fears becoming lost in language. In a quiet, but savage reaction, he commits a murder, seemingly to perpetrate an act that connects the self with the world.

This kind of paranoia is generated by a reduction of consciousness; it springs, unknowingly perhaps, from a truncation that is respectful of the limits imposed by positivism upon knowledge. The portrayal of limited consciousness consistently characterizes Handke's works, from the *Der kurze Brief zum langen Abschied* (1972, *Short Letter, Long Farewell*) to, nearly three decades later, *In einer dunklen Nacht ging ich aus meinem stillen Haus* (1997, *On a Dark Night I Left My Silent House*). In the novel written in the early seventies, Handke describes the travels of a hero making a trip across America. Pursued by his wife, he journeys in the hope of escaping to that realm of myth promised by the Far West of film-maker John Ford. Evasion appears motivated by a promise of something unsayable, by something ineffable dreamed of in silence, but which should reveal itself at the end of the journey. The distrust of language is, of course, a common postmodern topos. In Handke's case, this distrust points up the direct relationship of many postmoderns with the Romantics who, two centuries before them, made the ineffable into the goal of literature. The dream of revelation, moreover, relates Handke's work to those modernists whom he dislikes. Handke's distrust of language goes beyond theory, for it is coupled with a passionate rejection of all modernist predecessors and the ease with which they used language. His overt rejection of modernism first surfaced in a notorious attack he made on the *Gruppe 47* in the sixties and has been repeated in various ways since, such as this vituperation published in 1982 and anthologized since then:

> When writing, remain always within the image. If you allow yourself to be carried away by words, it is quite natural that these will crumble in your mouth like a decaying mushroom (unless you are a slothful, pedantic, or word-trap-setting modern text-maker who, chatter-boxing, permutating, splitting hairs, is setting about on a second, even more monstrous Ulysses or Man without Qualities); as soon as you see the danger (it stands by every sentence), turn back to the image (to the essential model) and write (in an image); "Get out of language!" Only so will literature begin anew.[19]

19. Handke, *Die Geschichte des Bleistifts,* 94; reprinted in *Die Tage gingen wirklich ins Land,* 67.

"Heraus aus der Sprache!" With this cry to "get out of language," Handke rejects language in the name of some presupposed superiority of images, of pure mimesis, but mimesis of something that can't be named. There is a dialectical cliché in this rejection of words, since it endorses the postmodern belief that there is no meaning without language, in order to then decry meaning. Handke's ill-tempered remarks about Joyce and Musil add another dimension to his rather old-fashioned preference of images to words: like many a postmodern, Handke is unhappy about coming, in a post-position, after the accomplishments of modernity. Perhaps his ire is due to the anxiety of influence, or perhaps it is also due to the fact that modernist experimentation seems to have closed off his options. In either case Handke's tantrums point out a central postmodern problem of living with what the American postmodern Donald Barthelme called "the dead father"—to use the suggestive title of his parodic novel about writers today.

In conclusion, I underscore that, in contrast to his polemics, Handke's novels illustrate that much recent fiction is content to live with the times, simply recording, either lyrically or with irony, the interface of consciousness and what is minimally perceived to be the real. This perception rarely opens upon the world problematized by the science confronting the narrators created by Musil, Proust, Woolf, and Faulkner. Many epistemological views have undoubtedly come together to foster the truncated realism of much European and Anglo-American fiction written in the late twentieth century, but it is hard to avoid the conclusion that the Vienna of Mach, Freud, and Wittgenstein continues to live in contemporary thought and fiction, in its fantasies about reading the absent self as a text as well as its dream of mastering the language that it radically distrusts. Musil would find many of his fears realized upon seeing that Mach and the Viennese pop culture he disliked have been conjoined in what one can call late postmodernity, or perhaps simply the frivolous debacle of contemporary culture. Musil would certainly have ironized about the way that, in minimalist or truncated realism, positivism continues to work an influence in fiction. He undoubtedly would have found choice matter for satire in the fact that this influence reflects the ongoing dominance of an impoverished "scientism" at a time when interest in science has greatly waned among writers. It does seem perversely ironic that the positivist suspicion of language and metaphysics has probably entailed a loss of interest in science among writers, at the same time positivism has, unknowingly perhaps, shaped much fiction in the late twentieth century. But it seems nearly certain that the ultimate result of the positivist suspicion of language and metaphysics has been the reduction of fiction's scope in ways that respect the limits imposed on knowledge by positivism—if one allows that some form of positivism is at work whenever, in suspicion of language and metaphysics, the epistemological axioms underlying a fiction decree that truth is located only in the description of relations derived immediately from the realm of the senses. Minimalist realism thus presents us with a paradoxical situation in which it is begrudgingly believed that science decides the truth of representations, even if, according to the postmodern critique of science, there is no place wherein well-grounded truth is to be found. These are some of the contradictory beliefs that have underwritten the postmodernity whose end may be in sight.

Bibliography

Ackroyd, Peter. *Notes for a New Culture: An Essay on Modernism.* London: Vision Press, 1976.

Albertsen, Elisabeth. *Ratio und "Mystique" im Werk Robert Musils.* Munich: Nymphenburger Verlag, 1968.

Arnold, Matthew. *Discourses in America.* London: Macmillan, 1894.

Bachelard, Gaston. *Le Pluralisme cohérent de la chimie moderne.* Paris: J. Vrin, 1973.

Bakhtin, M. M. *Rabelais and His World.* Trans. Hélène Iswolsky. Cambridge: MIT, 1968.

Beer, Gillian. *Virginia Woolf: The Common Ground.* Ann Arbor: The University of Michigan Press, 1996.

Begnal, Michael H., and Fritz Senn, eds. *A Conceptual Guide to "Finnegans Wake."* College Park: The Penn State University Press, 1974.

Benstock, Bernard, ed. *The Seventh Joyce.* Bloomington: Indiana University Press, 1982.

Bercovitch, Sacvan, ed. *Cambridge History of American Literature.* Vol. 3. Cambridge: Cambridge University Press, 1999.

Best, Alan, and Hans Wolfschütz, eds. *Modern Austrian Writing: Literature and Society after 1945.* London: Oswald Wolff, 1980.

Bloom, Harold, ed. *William Faulkner's "Absalom, Absalom!"* New York: Chelsea House, 1987.

Boitro, Pietro. *Sulle orme di Ulisse.* Bologna: il Mulino, 1999.

Borges, Jorge Luis. *El Libro de Arena.* Mexico City: Alianza Editorial, 1984.

———. *Collected Fictions.* Trans. Andrew Hurley. New York: Penguin, 1998.

———. "El jardín de senderos que se bifurcan." In *Ficciones.* Madrid: El Libro de Bolsillo, 1996.

Bouveresse, Jacques. *L'Homme probable.* Paris: Editions de l'éclat, 1993.

Boyers, Robert. *F. R. Leavis.* Columbia and London: University of Missouri Press, 1978.

Bradbury, Malcolm, and James McFarlane, eds. *Modernism, 1890–1930.* Atlantic Highlands, N.J.: Humanities Press, 1976.

Brock, William. *The Norton History of Chemistry.* New York: Norton, 1993.

Burtt, Edwin A. *Metaphysical Foundations of Modern Physical Science.* London: Kegan Paul, Trench, Trubner, 1925.

Chapple, J. A. V. *Science and Literature in the Nineteenth Century.* London: Macmillan, 1986.

Cordle, David. *Postmodern Postures: Literature, Science, and the Two Cultures Debate.* Aldershot, U.K., and Brookfield, U.S.A: Ashgate, 1999.

Crombie, A. C. *The History of Science from Augustine to Galileo.* Vol. 1. New York: Dover, 1995.

Coughlan, G. D., and J. E. Dodd. *The Ideas of Particle Physics: An Introduction for Scientists.* 2d ed. Cambridge: Cambridge University Press, 1991.

Cowley, Malcolm. *The Portable Faulkner.* New York: Viking Press, 1967.

Daviau, Donald G., ed. *Major Figures of Contemporary Austrian Literature.* New York: Peter Lang, 1987.

David, Marc. "Weighing the Universe." *Nature* 410, no. 6825 (March 8, 2001): 153.

Davis, Alistair, and Alan Sinfield, eds. *British Culture of the Postwar: An Introduction to Literature and Society, 1945–1999.* London: Routledge, 1999.

Descartes, René. *Le Monde, ou Traité de la lumière.* Trans. Michael Sean. Mahoney, N.Y.: Abaris Books, 1979.

Dostoyevsky, Fyodor. *Notes from the Underground/The Double.* Trans. Jessie Coulson. London: Penguin Classics, 1972.

Dreyfus, Hubert. *What Computers Can't Do: The Limits of Artificial Reason.* New York: Harper and Row, 1972.

———. *What Computers Can't Do: The Limits of Artificial Intelligence.* New York: Harper and Row, 1979.

Duszenko, Andrez. *The Joyce of Science.* DAI, Southern Illinois, 1989.

Eckley, Grace. *Children's Lore in "Finnegans Wake."* Syracuse: Syracuse University Press, 1985.

Eddington, Arthur Stanley. *Space, Time, and Gravitation.* Cambridge: Cambridge University Press, 1920.

Einstein, Albert. *Relativity: Special and General Theory.* Trans. Robert W. Lawson. New York: Bonanza Books, 1961.

Eisendle, Helmut. *Abendsport. Zweimal: Minutentexte*. Innsbruck: Haymon, 1998.

————. *Daimon und Veranda oder Gespräche eines Mädchens vor dem Tode*. Erlangen: Renner, 1978.

————. *Der Egoist*. Innsbruck: Haymon,1996.

————. *Exil oder Der braune Salon. Ein Unterhaltungsroman*. Salzburg: Residenz Verlag, 1977.

————. *Jenseits der Vernunft oder Gespräche über den menschlichen Vertstand*. Salzburg: Residenz Verlag, 1976.

Encyclopedia of Philosophy. Vol. 6. Ed. Paul Edwards. New York: Macmillan, 1972.

Encyclopedia of Physics. 2d ed. Ed. Rita G. Lerner and George L. Trigg. New York: VCH Publishers, 1991.

Faulkner, William. *Absalom, Absalom!* New York: Vintage, 1972.

Feynman, Richard. *The Character of Physical Law*. London: Penguin, 1992.

————. *QED: The Strange Theory of Light and Matter*. Princeton: Princeton University Press, 1985.

Finetti, Marco. "Fertile Ground for Politics." *Nature* 420, no. 6915 (December 5, 2002): 464–65.

Franco, Jean. *An Introduction to Spanish-American Literature*. Cambridge: Cambridge University Press, 1969.

Gamow, George. *Thirty Years that Shook Physics: The Story of Quantum Mechanics*. New York: Anchor Books, 1966.

García Marquéz, Gabriel. *Cien años de soledad*. Barcelona: Plaza and Jamés, 1999.

Gardner, Martin. *Relativity Simply Explained*. Mineola, N.Y.: Dover, 1997. Reprint of *The Relativity Explosion*. New York: Vintage, 1976.

Gibson, Andrew, ed. *Joyce's "Ithaca."* Amsterdam: Rodopi, 1996 [European Joyce Studies 6].

Gidley, Mick. "Another Psychologist, a Physiologist, and William Faulkner." *Ariel* 2, No. 4 (1971): 78–86.

Glasheen, Adaline. *Third Census of "Finnegans Wake": An Index of Characters and Their Roles*. Berkeley: University of California Press, 1977.

Greene, Brian. *The Elegant Universe*. London: Vintage, 2000.

Handke, Peter. *Die Angst des Tormanns bein Elfmeter*. Frankfurt: Suhrkamp, 1970.

————. *Einer dunklen Nacht ging ich aus meinem stillen Haus*. Frankfurt: Suhrkamp, 1997.

————. *Die Geschichte des Bleistifts*. Salzburg and Vienna: Residenz Verlag, 1982.

————. *Der kurze Brief zum langen Abschied.* Frankfurt: Suhrkamp, 1972.

————. *Die Tage gingen wirklich ins Land.* Stuttgart: Reclam, 1995.

Hart, Clive. *Structure and Motif in "Finnegans Wake."* London: Faber and Faber, 1962.

Hawking, Stephen. *The Cambridge Lectures.* New York: Dove Books, 1996.

Heidsieck, Arnold. *The Intellectual Contexts of Kafka's Fiction: Philosophy, Law, Religion.* Columbia, S.C.: Camden House, 1994.

Heisenberg, Werner. *Deutsche und judische Physik,* ed. by Helmut Rechenberg. Munich: Piper Verlag, 1992.

————. *Ordnung der Wirklichkeit.* Munich: Piper Verlag, 1989.

————. *Physics and Philosophy: The Revolution in Modern Science.* New York: Harper and Row, 1958. Torchback edition, 1962.

————. *Schritte über Grenzen.* 2d ed. Munich: Piper Verlag, 1973.

Henderson, Linda. *The Fourth Dimension and Non-Euclidean Geometry in Modern Art.* Princeton: Princeton University Press, 1983.

Heydebrand, Renate von, ed. *Robert Musil.* Darmstadt: Wissenschaftliche Buchgesellschaft, 1982.

Hickman, Hannah. *Robert Musil and the Culture of Vienna.* La Salle, Ill.: Open Court Publishing Co., 1984.

Hu, Wayne. "Ringing in the New Cosmology." *Nature* 404, no. 6781 (April 27, 2000): 939–40.

Huxley, Thomas. *Collected Essays,* Vol. 2. London: Macmillan, 1893.

————. *Lay Sermons, Essays, and Reviews.* New York: Appleton, 1880.

Jaccottet, Philippe. *Eléments d'un songe.* Lausanne: l'Age d'homme, 1961.

Jacquet, Claude. *Joyce et Rabelais.* Paris: Didier, 1972.

Jammer, Max. *The Conceptual Development of Quantum Mechanics.* New York: McGraw-Hill, 1966.

————. *Concepts of Space: The History of Theories of Space in Physics.* 3d ed. New York: Dover, 1993.

Janik, Allan, and Stephen Toulmin. *Wittgenstein's Vienna.* New York: Simon and Schuster, 1973.

Joyce, James. *Finnegans Wake.* New York: Penguin Books, 1959.

————. *Ulysses.* Ed. Hans Walter Gabler. New York: Vintage Books, 1986.

Kafka, Franz. *The Castle.* Trans. Willa and Edwin Muir. New York: Schocken Books, 1974.

————. *The Complete Stories.* Ed. Nahum Glatzer. New York: Schocken Books, 1976.

————. *Das Schloss.* Ed. Max Brod. Frankfurt: Fischer, 1964.

Kahlenberg, Louis. *Outlines of Chemistry.* New York: The Macmillan Company, 1916.

Kasti, John. "Formally Speaking." *Nature* 411, no. 6837 (May 31, 2001): 527.

Kline, Morris. *Mathematics: The Loss of Certainty.* Oxford: Oxford University Press, 1980.

————. *Mathematics for the Nonmathematician.* New York: Dover, 1985.

Koyré, A. *From the Closed World to the Infinite Universe.* Baltimore: Johns Hopkins Press, 1957.

Kuhn, Thomas. *Black-body Theory and the Quantum Discontinuity, 1894–1912.* Oxford: Oxford University Press, 1978.

————. *The Essential Tension: Studies in Scientific Tradition and Change.* Chicago: University of Chicago Press, 1977.

Kuyk, Dirk. *Sutpen's Design.* Charlottesville: University of Virginia Press, 1990.

Lattre, Alain de. *La Doctrine de la réalité chez Proust.* Paris: J. Corti, 1978.

Lavine, Shaughan. *Understanding the Infinite.* Cambridge: Harvard University Press, 1994.

Leavis, F. R. *Two Cultures? The Significance of C. P. Snow.* London: Chatto and Windus, 1962.

Levin, Harry. *James Joyce.* London: Faber, 1944.

Loeffel, Hans. *Blaise Pascal.* Basel: Birkhäuser, 1987 [Vita Mathematica, Tome II].

Luckhurst, Nicola. *Science and Structure in Proust's "A la recherche."* Oxford: Oxford University Press, 2001.

Lyell, Charles. *Principles of Geology.* Ed. James A. Secord. London: Penguin, 1997.

Mach, Ernst. *Erkenntnis und Irrtum.* 2d ed. Leipzig: Verlag Johann Ambrosius Barth, 1906.

Mann, Thomas. *Thomas Mann Presents the Living Thought of Schopenhauer.* London: Cassell, 1939.

Mavrides, Stamatia. *La Relativité.* Paris: Presses Universitaires de France, 1988.

McGraw-Hill Encyclopedia of Physics. 2d ed. Ed. Sybil P. Parker. New York: McGraw Hill, 1993.

McHugh, Roland. *Annotations to "Finnegans Wake."* Rev. ed. Baltimore: Johns Hopkins University Press, 1991.

Mesnard, Jean, et al., eds. *Méthodes chez Pascal,* Actes du Colloque tenu à Clermont-Ferrand, 10–13 juin 1976. Paris: Presses Universitaires de France, 1979.

Müller-Schwefe, Gerhard, and Konrad Tuzinski, eds. *Literatur-Kultur-Gesell-schaft in England und Amerika: Aspeckte und Forschungsbeiträge. Friedrich Schubel zum 60. Geburtstag.* Frankfurt: Diesterweg, 1966.

Musil, Robert. *Beitrag zur Beurteilung der Lehren Machs.* Hamburg: Rowohlt, 1980.

———. *Diaries, 1899–1941.* Ed. Mark Mirsky. Trans. Philip Payne. New York: Basic Books, 1998.

———. *Gesammelte Werke.* Ed. Adolf Frisé. Hamburg: Rowohlt, 1978.

———. *On Mach's Theories.* Intro. G. H. von Wright. Trans. Kevin Mulligan. Munich, Vienna: Philosophia Verlag, 1980.

———. *The Man without Qualities.* Ed. Burton Pike. Trans. Sophie Wilkins. New York: Alfred A. Knopf, 1995.

———. *Precision and Soul: Essays and Addresses.* Ed. and Trans. Burton Pike and David S. Luft. Chicago: University of Chicago Press, 1990.

———. *Robert Musil: Selected Writings.* Ed. Burton Pike. Trans. Eithne Wilkins and Ernst Kaiser. New York: Continuum, 1986.

———. *Sämtliche Erzählungen.* Hamburg: Rowohlt, 1968.

———. *Tagebücher.* Vols. 1 and 2. Ed. Adolf Frisé. Hamburg: Rowohlt, 1976.

———. *Tagebücher.* Rev. ed. Vols. 1 and 2. Ed. Adolf Frisé. Hamburg: Rowohlt, 1983.

Navratil, Leo. *Schizophrenie und Sprache: Zur Psychologie der Dichtung.* Munich: DTV, 1966.

Norris, Christopher. *Quantum Theory and the Flight from Realism: Philosophical Responses to Quantum Mechanics.* London: Routledge, 2000.

Nye, Mary Jo. *From Chemical Philosophy to Theoretical Chemistry: Dynamics of Matter and Dynamics of Disciplines, 1800–1950.* Berkeley: University of California Press, 1993.

Our Exagmination Round His Factification for Incamination of Work in Progress. [James Joyce/Finnegans Wake Symposium.] Northfolk, Conn: New Directions, 1962.

Pääbo, Svante. "The Human Genome and Our View of Ourselves." *Science* 291 (February 16, 2001): 1220.

Pascal, Blaise. *Les Pensées.* Trans. W. F. Trotter. Intro. T. S. Eliot. London: J. M. Dent, Everyman's Library, 1940.

Penrose, Roger. *The Emperor's New Mind: Concerning Computers, Minds, and the Laws of Physics.* New York: Oxford University Press, 1989.

———. *The Large, the Small, and the Human Mind.* Cambridge: Cambridge University Press, 1997.

Peters, Frederick G. *Robert Musil, Master of the Hovering Life*. New York: Columbia University Press, 1978.

Pike, Burton. *Robert Musil: An Introduction to His Work*. Ithaca, N.Y.: Cornell University Press, 1961.

Poincaré, Henri. *The Foundations of Science*. Trans. George Bruce Halsted. New York: The Science Press,1913.

———. *La Science et l'hypothèse*. Rueil-Malmaison: Editions de la Bohème, 1992.

———. *The Value of Science*. Trans. George Bruce Halsted. New York: The Science Press, 1907.

Proust. Marcel. *A la recherche du temps perdu*. Ed. Pierre Clarac and André Ferré. Paris: Editions de la Pléiade, 1954.

———. *Correspondance*. Vol. 3. Ed. Philip Kolb. Paris: Plon, 1973.

———. *Du côté de chez Swann*. Ed. Serguei Botcharov. Moscow: Editions du Progrès, 1976.

———. *Remembrance of Things Past*. Vols. 1 and 2. Trans. C. K. Scott Montcrieff. New York: Random House, 1934.

Rae, Alastair. *Quantum Mechanics: Illusion or Reality?* Cambridge: Cambridge University Press, 1994.

Rebaté, Jean-Michel. *Joyce upon the Void*. London: Macmillan, 1991.

Rice, Thomas Jackson. *Joyce, Chaos, and Complexity*. Urbana: University of Illinois Press, 1997.

Richter, Hans Werner, ed. *Almanach der Gruppe 47, 1947–1962*. Hamburg: Rowohlt, 1962.

Rinderler, Wolfgang. *Introduction to Special Relativity*. 2d ed. Oxford: Oxford University Press, 1991.

Ringold, Francine. "The Metaphysics of Yoknapatawpha County: 'Airy Space and Scope for Your Delirium.'" *Hartford Studies in Literature* 8 (1975–1976): 223–40.

Ronan, Colin A. *A Natural History of the Universe*. New York: Macmillan, 1991.

Roth, Gerhard. *Die autobiographie des albert einsteins*. Frankfurt: Suhrkamp, 1972.

———. *The autobiography of albert einstein,* trans. Malcolm Green. London: Atlas Press, 1992.

———. *Eine Reise in das Innere von Wien*. Frankfurt: Fischer, 1991.

———. *Der Wille zur Krankheit*. Frankfurt, Suhrkampf, 1973.

Runes, Dagobert D., ed. *Classics in Logic*. New York: Philosophical Library, 1962.

Ryan, Steven T. "Faulkner and Quantum Mechanics." *Western Humanities Review* 33 (1979): 329–39.

Sarlo, Beatriz. *Jorge Luis Borges: A Writer on the Edge*. London: Verso, 1993.

Schorske, Carl E. *Fin de Siècle Vienna: Politics and Culture*. New York: Knopf, 1979.

Seife, Charles. "Eternal-Universe Idea Comes Full Circle." *Science* 296 (April 26, 2002): 639.

Shanker, S. G., ed. *Gödel's Theorem in Focus*. London: Routledge, 1988.

Sichten und Vernichten: Von der Kontinuität der Gewalt. Vienna: Verlag für Gesellschaftskritik, 1994.

Singal, Daniel J. *William Faulkner: The Making of a Modernist*. Chapel Hill: University of North Carolina Press, 1997.

Smith, Peter D. *Metaphor and Materiality: German Literature and the World-View of Science, 1780–1955*. Oxford: European Humanities Research Centre, Legenda [Studies in Comparative Literature 4], 2000.

Snow, C. P. *The Two Cultures: And a Second Look*. Cambridge: Cambridge University Press, 1964.

Sorensen, Roy A. *Thought Experiments*. New York: Oxford University Press, 1992.

Sturrock, John, ed. *Oxford Guide to Contemporary Writing*. Oxford: Oxford University Press, 1996.

Thiher, Allen. *Fiction Rivals Science: The French Novel from Balzac to Proust*. Columbia: University of Missouri Press, 2001.

———. *Franz Kafka: A Study of the Short Fiction*. Boston: G. K. Hall, 1990.

Toulmin, Stephen Edelston. *Cosmopolis: The Hidden Agenda of Modernity*. New York: Free Press, 1990.

———. *The Return to Cosmology: Postmodern Science and the Theology of Nature*. Berkeley: University of California Press, 1982.

Trilling, Lionel. *Beyond Culture*. New York: Oxford University Press, 1980.

———. *The Portable Matthew Arnold*. New York: Viking, 1949.

Valéry, Paul. *Oeuvres*. Vol. 1. Ed. Jean Hytier. Paris: Editions de la Pléiade, 1957.

Wagner, Pierre, ed. *Les philosophes et la science*. Paris: Gallimard, folio inédit, 2002.

Wald, Robert M. *General Relativity*. Chicago: University of Chicago Press, 1984.

———. *Space, Time, and Gravity*. Chicago: University of Chicago Press, 1977.

Wallace, Richard R. *Paradox Lost: Images of the Quantum*. New York: Springer, 1996.

White, David A. *The Grand Continuum: Reflections on Joyce and Metaphysics.* Pittsburgh: University of Pittsburgh Press, 1983.

Wiener, Norbert. *I Am a Mathematician.* Cambridge: MIT Press, 1970.

Wigner, Eugene Paul. *The Collected Words of Eugene Paul Wigner.* Vol. 6. Berlin: Springer, 1995.

Wittstock, Uwe, ed. *Gerhard Roth: Materialien zu 'Die Archive des Schweigens'.* Frankfurt: Fischer, 1992.

Wolf, Fred Alan. *Taking the Quantum Leap: The New Physics for Nonscientists.* San Francisco: Harper and Row, 1981.

Woolf, Virginia. *Between the Acts.* Intro. Frank Kermode. Oxford: Oxford World's Classics, 1998.

———. *Mrs. Dalloway.* London: Penguin Popular Classics, 1996.

———. *The Waves.* Intro. Gillian Beer. Oxford: Oxford World's Classics, 1998.

Zajc, W. A. "The Pull of Weird Horizons." *Nature* 299, no. 5603 (January 3, 2003): 47–48.

Zamora, Lois Parkinson. *The Usable Past: The Imagination of History in Recent Fiction of the Americas.* Cambridge: Cambridge University Press, 1997.

Index